NATIVE LANGUAGE AND FOREIGN
LANGUAGE ACQUISITION

ANNALS OF THE NEW YORK ACADEMY OF SCIENCES

Volume 379

NATIVE LANGUAGE AND FOREIGN LANGUAGE ACQUISITION

Edited by Harris Winitz

The New York Academy of Sciences
New York, New York
1981

Library of Congress Cataloging in Publication Data

Main entry under title:

Native language and foreign language acquisition

(Annals of the New York Academy of Sciences; v. 379)

Papers presented at a conference held Jan. 15–16, 1981, sponsored by the New York Academy of Sciences and the University of Missouri—Kansas City.
Includes bibliographies and index.
1. Language acquisition—Congresses. 2. Language and languages—Study and teaching—Congresses. I. Winitz, Harris, 1933– . II. New York Academy of Sciences. III. University of Missouri—Kansas City. IV. Series.
Q11.N5 vol. 379 [P118]   500s [401'.9]   81–22295

ISBN 0–89766–147–8   AACR2
ISBN 0–89766–148–6 (pbk.)

PCP
Printed in the United States of America
ISBN 0–89766–147–8 (Cloth)
0–89766–148–6 (Paper)

Dedicated to the memory of
JUDITH OLMSTED GARY

ANNALS OF THE NEW YORK ACADEMY OF SCIENCES

VOLUME 379

December 30, 1981

NATIVE LANGUAGE AND FOREIGN LANGUAGE ACQUISITION *

Editor and Conference Organizer

HARRIS WINITZ

———◆———

CONTENTS

* This volume is the result of a conference entitled Native Language and Foreign Language Acquisition, held on January 15–16, 1981, by The New York Academy of Sciences and cosponsored by The University of Missouri–Kansas City.

Financial assistance was received from:

• THE UNIVERSITY OF MISSOURI–KANSAS CITY

PREFACE

Harris Winitz

Department of Psychology
University of Missouri–Kansas City
Kansas City, Missouri 64110

With the encouragement of my colleagues and with the gracious cooperation and support of the New York Academy of Sciences and the University
of Missouri–Kansas City, we are now prepared to engage in serious discussion of the relationship between native-language acquisition and foreign-
language acquisition. In recent years the pace of research in second-
language learning has markedly accelerated, motivated, in part, by an
interest in the dynamic properties of second-language acquisition and, in
general, by a desire to learn more about universals of language acquisition.

Testing instructional methodologies has been an ever-pressing concern
for language teachers, perhaps for as long as language teaching has been a
profession. Only recently have these investigations been placed within
the perspective of a growing body of theoretical and empirical research in
child language acquisition. This research on second-language acquisition
has stimulated the question, What are the similarities and differences
between first-language learning and second-language learning? This question is sometimes dismissed as unworkable because it is too generally
stated. First, it seems not to consider the age of the second-language
learner. Second, it seems unreasonable to equate adults and children in
the affective domain. Third, it has been stated that the quality of language
input is so vastly different for the young child in contrast to the older child
and adult that no reasonable similarities can be drawn. Fourth, comparisons between first- and second-language acquisition are often regarded
as empty because of their fundamentally different relationship to cognitive
development. Fifth, the biological differences across age levels must be
addressed. Sixth, the learning of the first language must surely be taken into
account. Finally, the relationship between articulation and phonology is
obviously different for the first- and the second-language learner, and needs
to be considered.

Nonetheless there are certain fundamental similarities in acquisition
between first language (L1) and second language (L2) that cannot be
dismissed out of hand. Recent research has generally supported the position of universal processing strategies in the acquisition of L1 and L2.
These general principles of acquisition should be taken into account when
differences between L1 and L2 are considered.

The general questions for this conference are: (1) What are the similarities and differences between L1 and L2 acquisition? (2) How can these
relationships be assessed? (3) Can each separate area of inquiry introduce
methodological procedures and suggest areas of study that are of benefit

to the other? and (4) What are the implications of these areas of study for the development of procedures that can be used to teach foreign languages or that can benefit children who fail to learn their native language?

This conference brings together colleagues active in L1 and/or L2 research. The papers that are to be presented and the discussion they will provoke may provide a beginning in cooperative understanding between these two areas of study.

ISSUES OF MAJOR CONCERN IN FOREIGN-LANGUAGE LEARNING AND FOREIGN-LANGUAGE ACQUISITION

James E. Alatis and Barbara De Marco

School of Languages and Linguistics
Georgetown University
Washington, D.C. 20057

This discussion of current issues of major concern in foreign-language learning and foreign-language acquisition takes the point of view of language educators both in exploring the implications of the results of first- and second-language acquisition studies for programs of instruction in a second or foreign language, and in suggesting possible directions for future psycholinguistic research.

The review of the research is restricted to recent studies in Canada and the United States that bear most directly on the issues proposed for discussion. The issues are grouped under two general headings: (1) the question of bilingual-education programs and (2) the general problem of foreign-language instruction. The latter is an issue of long-standing importance, and one recently reevaluated by the President's Commission on Foreign Language and International Studies; the former is at once an old and a new issue, and one recently focused upon by the hearings on the Department of Education's proposed regulations describing the responsibilities of United States public schools to serve students whose primary language is not English, the so-called Lau guidelines.

To put it simply, one might say that there are two major issues to contend with: (1) How do we teach English to speakers of other languages? and (2) How do we teach foreign languages to native English speakers? The first issue could be subdivided further, again in very general terms, into (a) adult learners at the university level, whose purposes in learning English are primarily instrumental, and (b) other learners, children and adults, whose purposes in learning English are primarily integrative. For the purposes of this paper, however, attention will be directed primarily to that segment of the population whose needs are addressed by the Department of Education regulations, that is, school-aged children of limited or no English proficiency.

The 1979 report of the President's Commission on Foreign Language and International Studies offers a suitable starting point for discussion of the two issues. The commission's report, a "critique of U.S. capability," decried "Americans' incompetence in foreign languages" [1] and offered a series of recommendations designed to correct this fault.

The report revealed little new to members of the language-education profession; in fact, many professionals were disappointed that the report said so little about foreign-language studies vis-à-vis international studies in

0077-8923/81/0379-0001 $01.75/2 © 1981, NYAS

general. However, the report did contain one recommendation that is of particular interest because it underscores the interrelatedness of the two major issues under discussion at present.

The report suggests that gaps in the nation's foreign-language expertise might be filled by drawing on the vast, untapped national resources of native speakers of foreign languages. In other words, we should capitalize on our assets. This rather crass materialistic figure of speech is employed here quite deliberately, for the key word is *assets*.

If we were to follow the commission's recommendation, the result would be an interesting role reversal: those very people who, according to the social and economic measures of mainstream American society, are considered to be the "have-nots" would, by this language exchange, be the very ones who have something valuable to offer that same society. As we can see so well from the response to the Department of Education's proposed regulations, we have a long way to go before this point of view is commonly accepted. At present, the foreign-language speaker is not considered an asset to the community or to the nation, but rather a liability, and bilingual-education programs generally are perceived to be corrective or remedial measures.

Thus, although on the surface the recommendation of the commission seems quite reasonable, and the prospects for exchange and mutual benefit quite heartening, there seems to be little cause for optimism.

In the first place, the general tenor of the country is far from encouraging. In addition to the popular reactions against the Department of Education's proposed regulations, there were clues to the popular mood to be found in the adverse publicity due to circumstances surrounding the entry of immigrants, most particularly the Cuban refugees, and in the recent flare-up of the long-standing issue of undocumented aliens; and, perhaps the most telling, there was the obvious clue to be picked up from the results of the recent elections.

Furthermore, it is not only in the sphere of recent political events that one can hear the cautionary note being sounded. One need only review recent literature from the field of psycholinguistics to hear warnings of the risks entailed in planning language exchanges of the kind recommended by the commission.

Tucker, reviewing the implications of the Canadian immersion programs for bilingual-education programs in the United States, noted that one of the important elements was voluntary participation and parental and community support.[2] By and large, these two elements are missing from programs in the United States.

Lambert has worked on defining motivations for foreign-language learning and has differentiated between "instrumental" and "integrative" motivations for language learning.[3] The primary objective of bilingual-education programs has been the integration of minority-language populations into the mainstream of American society. Again, we can look at psycholinguistic research better to understand the effects of that integration on the individual. To begin with, we have noted already that any efforts to redirect the thrust of bilingual-education programs to become, as the literature has termed them, "additive" rather than "subtractive" have met with less than popular support. Further, to suggest that the mainstream English speaker has as much (or more) to gain as the minority-language speaker is an equally unwelcome suggestion. Last year, at the 1980 Georgetown University Round Table on Current Issues in Bilingual Education, we did have a panel that chose as its title "The Monolingual Child is Underprivileged." However, we are only too aware that this expression does not concur with popular attitudes.

For the mainstream English speaker, government attempts to legislate bilingual-education programs are viewed as threatening. One major argument revolves around the age-old question of states' rights. State and local authorities fear federal interference in what, traditionally, has been their preserve.

Another popular argument, subtly pervasive in American mainstream society, is based on the threat that many perceive in official recognition, and even encouragement, of linguistic diversity within our borders. Many fear that recognition of foreign languages is a recognition of foreign ways. Many fear the encouragement of such diversity, claiming that it will create separatist movements. Giving other languages the go-ahead is the prelude to a general breakdown of society.

These theories may sound somewhat extreme, but, as psycholinguistic research has documented,[4] we know well how distorted perceptions about foreigners and foreign ways can be.

In fact, there is a slight touch of irony to be noted in the results of research on the effects of bilingualism on the individual. In a sense, they may be interpreted as confirmation of popular fears, for it seems to be very true that a major factor in successful language learning is identification with the target-language population. According to Schumann's acculturation model, the degree to which a learner acculturates to the target-language group will control the degree to which he acquires the second language.[5]

Identification with the target-language group carries its own set of problems. We can see that, on the one hand, minority-language (and minority-culture) individuals will be torn between maintaining home ways and adopting new mores. By the same token, mainstream English speakers will be pressed to readjust their social and cultural preconceptions.

Lambert also discussed this aspect with reference to Canadian and American immersion programs.[6] He noted that in these programs, more attention was given to the dominant group—as he describes it, "the segment that is most secure in its ethnic and linguistic identity, but the one that is most in need of knowledge about and sensitivity towards other ethnic and linguistic groups." [6]

Lambert describes the ideal situation:

To the extent that mainstream children are sensitized to and educated in another language and culture, the better the chances are of developing a fairer, more equitable society. The better too are the chances of improving the self-views of ethnolinguistic minority children . . . when they realize that mainstream children are making sincere gestures to learn about them, their ways of life, and their language.[6]

We see, then, that psycholinguists already had explored the implications of an exchange program such as that put forth by the president's commission. Furthermore, they already have explored the implications of identification with the target-language group. Studies that investigated the effect of bilingualism on the individual have reported mixed outcomes (see, for example, Reference 7). Some individuals orient themselves toward the target-language group at the expense—even to the exclusion—of their native-language group. Others do just the opposite. Still others try to avoid the issue entirely. Once additional variables—peer pressure and community support, for instance—are included, there is constructed an intricate setting in which to investigate effects of language learning and the factors that contribute to its success.

Whatever the strategy and whatever the outcome, however, we do recognize the importance of identification with the target-language group. Further, we know that identification with a second language group will be heavily influenced by the social status of members of that group.[5]

If we apply these findings of psycholinguistic studies to the situation in the United States, we find ourselves in a vicious circle. As long as minority or immigrant or refugee languages are accorded low status, that is, as long as they are considered a feature that necessitates remedial or compensatory measures, minority languages and cultures will not be a valued part of American society. At the same time, until these languages and cultures are valued by the mainstream society, members of that society will have relatively little interest or incentive to learn those languages, since the social status of the target-language group is lower than that of the American mainstream. As long as the mainstream society dissociates itself from the minority cultures and, further, considers integral features of those cultures only as something that needs correction (or something that is a threat to the dominant society), the minority group always will be the recipient and never the contributor.

The federal government has tried to address this social crisis, just as it has tried to remedy similar discrepancies in the social structure. However, we know very well that the question of whether the federal government is the appropriate body or has the appropriate means to correct the situation is hotly disputed. The president's commission may issue as many reports as it can write, and the Department of Education may issue as many regulations as it can devise, but whether either body will effect a change in attitudes toward foreign-language learning generally or toward minority languages in particular is a matter for debate.

Again, we here may adduce testimony of the psycholinguists. Taylor, discussing the relationship between second-language learning and ethnic identity, states that according to social psychological theory, the attitudes of the dominant group should be changed, and this should lead to a greater motivation to learn the language of the other group.[8] He draws the following conclusion:

> According to this view, legislating a language policy with a view to promoting bilingualism will yield little or no effective results.[8]

D'Angeljan issues a similar warning. Following upon her argument that language, as a form of behavior, should be acquired as the result of communicative interaction between the learner and a well-disposed native speaker, she further suggests that

> if there is sufficient reason for a society to officially promote second language teaching on a widespread basis, there should be equally sound reasons for promoting and sustaining intercultural contacts at the individual level. There is something alarming in the growth of the second language educational establishment in contemporary North American society. It suggests we are placing on the shoulders of educators a responsibility which should be shared to a much greater extent by society in general.[9]

It may seem unfair to end the review of the first issue on this cautionary note, but it is the very existence of the ambiguity toward bilingual education programs that creates the interest for further psycholinguistic research.

Turning, then, to the second issue, what conclusions may be drawn from a brief review of psycholinguistic studies of foreign-language learning? More to the point, how can these studies help explain why foreign-language programs in the United States have met with widespread failure? Although the government-sponsored program Foreign Languages in the Elementary Schools (FLES) does not account for all foreign-language learning programs, nonetheless, a critique of this program may be of assistance in evaluating the more general lack of success. Cohen suggested three faults of the FLES program:

1. Materials were sequenced without consideration of "natural" second-language acquisition processes;
2. Production of the language was stressed before students had time to hear and comprehend the language;
3. Language exercises focused directly upon patterns and not upon the informal communication by which patterns are learned.[10]

We can easily recognize the stamp of psycholinguistic research on first- and second-language acquisition in these criticisms. Additional research is important to future attempts to construct foreign-language programs in the schools, programs that, incidentally, are another recommendation of the President's Commission on Foreign Language and International Studies.

We also may thank studies on child language acquisition for focusing our attention on the need to take language learning *out* of the classroom. As d'Angeljan suggests, we need to exploit potential for informal language acquisition within the community.[9] At the same time, those of us with vested interests in classroom language learning will be working to introduce real communicative situations *into* the classroom, knowing that classroom structures must allow for the hypothesis testing necessary to the learner's acquisition of the rules that govern language.

Psycholinguistics has been rich in descriptions of language development in children and adults. Consequently, we are better prepared to judge how and when skills are best taught. We understand that language learning cannot be reduced to measures of aptitude and intelligence, but rather must consider affective factors—attitudes, motivation, identification with teachers and perceptions of speakers and their social roles, and personality traits.

In conclusion, this brief review may nonetheless suggest important directions for further research.

With reference to the first issue, it hardly is prophetic to suggest that we may witness continuing controversy over the merits of bilingual education, with the burden of proof being placed on its proponents. Therefore, we need to continue testing hypotheses upon which bilingual-education programs are built: Is language learned best through instruction in the subject matter?* Does an integrative motivation facilitate second-language learning more than does an instrumental motivation? [12] What are the harmful and beneficial effects of bilingual education? What are the results of the immersion programs (e.g., Culver City) in the United States?

These are among the questions that cannot be answered without careful, systematic, and long-term evaluations of existing programs (cf. also Reference 13).

We still are riding the crest of the bilingual-education wave. Whether the wave takes us safely to shore or leaves us in mid-sea may depend very much on how convincing the results of these studies are.

With reference to the wider context of foreign-language studies, at present there is a general feeling among language-education professionals that we have some reason to expect a renewed interest in foreign-language learning.[14] Therefore, it is most important that we find ways of sparking any glimmerings of interest into a fire of enthusiasm. Language educators long have relied on theories of psychology to develop classroom strategies. The recent flood of the so-called nonconventional language-teaching methodologies—from the "silent way" to the Dartmouth method—is but the latest illustration of that reliance.

More specifically, the evidence from studies of language acquisition that the need to communicate is of fundamental importance to the learner has had far-reaching consequences for classroom methodology and curriculum design. One of the most important consequences, and one relating to the recommendations of the president's commission referred to at the outset, is

---

* For an evaluation of this and other underlying presuppositions in bilingual education programs, see Reference 11.

the attempt by language educators to introduce learners into the language community and to bring the language community into the classroom.

On a more theoretical level, debates over the nature of language—habit formation vs. cognitive code—no doubt will engender at least a few more studies and research papers, and will continue to rely on arguments from psycholinguistics.

All of these issues are of interest and importance. However, the one issue that should merit the best efforts of future psycholinguistic research is the key issue of attitudes. As mentioned above, many psycholinguistic studies have established the importance of this affective factor. Many psycholinguists have written that changing attitudes is the *sine qua non* of successful language programs, especially of successful bilingual-education programs.

We should take these research findings one step further and explore any avenues that might open ways of changing attitudes. If attitudes cannot be changed, the research referred to here seems to suggest that methods to increase or improve language instruction can only lead to failure.

The point is strengthened by some recent remarks by G. Richard Tucker, who stated his belief that one of the greatest challenges facing language educators in North America is that of providing effective second-language teaching, while simultaneously nurturing the native-language development and sociocultural traditions of heterogeneous minority populations.[15] The matter of crucial importance, in Tucker's view, is the attitudes of the community at large toward minority-group members.

It is to be hoped that just as psycholinguistic studies have focused our attention on the importance of attitude in language learning and acquisition, so future research will provide some clues on how best to foster *positive* attitudes. Without this research, our best efforts to improve testing, teaching methodology, and learning strategies are but new coins of no worth.

REFERENCES

1. President's Commission on Foreign Language and International Studies. 1979. Strength through Wisdom. A Critique of U.S. Capability. U.S. Government Printing Office. Washington, D.C.
2. TUCKER, G. R. 1980. Implications for U.S. bilingual education: evidence from Canadian research. *In* FOCUS (2). National Clearinghouse for Bilingual Education. Rosslyn, Va.
3. LAMBERT, W. E. 1967. A social psychology of bilingualism. J. Soc. Issues 13(2): 91–109.
4. GARDNER, R. C. & W. E. LAMBERT. 1972. Students' stereotypes of French-speaking people. *In* Attitudes and Motivation in Second-Language Learning: 97–104. Newbury House Publishers. Rowley, Mass.
5. SCHUMANN, J. H. 1978. The acculturation model for second-language acquisition. *In* Second-Language Acquisition and Foreign-Language Acquisition. R. Gingras, Ed.: 27–50. Center for Applied Linguistics. Arlington, Va.
6. LAMBERT, W. E. 1980. The two faces of bilingual education. *In* FOCUS (3). National Clearinghouse for Bilingual Education. Rosslyn, Va.

7. CHILD, I. L. 1943. Italian or American? The Second Generation in Conflict. Yale University Press. New Haven, Conn.
8. TAYLOR, D. M. 1977. Bilingualism and intergroup relations. *In* Bilingualism: Psychological, Social and Educational Implications. P. A. Hornby, Ed.: 67–75. Academic Press, Inc. New York, N.Y.
9. D'ANGELJAN, A. 1978. Language learning in and out of classrooms. *In* Understanding Second- and Foreign-Language Learning: Issues and Approaches. J. Richards, Ed.: 218–237. Newbury House. Rowley, Mass.
10. COHEN, A. 1976. The case of partial or total immersion education. *In* The Bilingual Child: Research and Analysis of Existing Educational Themes. A. Simoes, Jr., Ed.: 65–89. Academic Press, Inc. New York, N.Y.
11. CUMMINS, J. 1977. Psycholinguistic evidence. *In* Bilingual Education: Current Perspectives. 4: 78–89. Center for Applied Linguistics. Arlington, Va.
12. GENESEE, F., E. POLICH & M. STANLEY. 1977. An experimental French immersion program at the secondary school level 1969 to 1974. Can. Modern Lang. Rev. 33(3): 318–332.
13. TUCKER, G. R. 1977. The linguistic perspective. *In* Bilingual Education: Current Perspectives. 2: 1–40. Center for Applied Linguistics. Arlington, Va.
14. 1981. Foreign-language scholars optimistic that changes are reviving their field. Chronicle of Higher Education 21(18): 1, 14.
15. TUCKER, G. R. 1977. Some observations concerning bilingualism and second-language teaching in developing countries and in North America. *In* Bilingualism: Psychological, Social and Educational Implications. Peter A. Hornby, Ed.: 141–146. Academic Press, Inc. New York, N.Y.

BILINGUALISM AND LANGUAGE ACQUISITION

Wallace E. Lambert

Department of Psychology
McGill University
Montreal, Quebec, Canada H3A 1B1

This conference is unique in my experience because it brings together two relatively unacquainted groups of behavioral scientists, one comprising those who specialize in the fascinating and still largely mysterious process of first-language acquisition and the other comprising those who specialize in the doubly fascinating and mysterious process of second-language acquisition and bilingualism. What links these two groups is a common interest in the developmental sweep of events that characterizes infancy and youth. The hope of the conference planners is that our interchange of experiences will form a new basis of attack on the many mysteries that still exist in both research domains. I share that hope because there are prospects now that an interchange can be mutually beneficial. For a long time, those of us interested in second languages and bilingualism had few models to turn to except those dealing with first-language acquisition; but times have changed, and we now have some ideas of our own about the language-acquisition process that can be useful to those exploring first language. In fact, I'm biased enough to argue that we in the bilingual domain may be getting into the more interesting and richer aspects of language. This comparative richness and complexity of the bilingual domain, however, takes many of us far away from the microtextures of codes to much broader issues. For instance, as social psychologists, we view language acquisition as inextricably associated with matters like ethnolinguistic identity, with problems of communication between language groups, with membership or quasi membership in more than one cultural group, with ethnolinguistic-group contacts, with shared versus distinctive group values, etc. Then, as psychologists, we view language as one aspect of cognition, inextricably tied to thought. These wider ranging concerns of course can take us too far away from the details of code acquisition, making our work vulnerable to the criticism that we are preoccupied prematurely with macro issues while the associated micro issues still are understood poorly. What I hope to do is demonstrate how necessary both macro and micro approaches are to a real understanding of the developmental sweep of events in which we all share an interest. My plan is to describe bilingualism and language acquisition as separate developmental processes and to focus on the ways in which the two processes interact.

0077–8923/81/0379–0009 $01.75/2 © 1981, NYAS

The Impact of Bilingualism on Thought and Language

Does one pay a price in the development of language competence and thinking for being or becoming bilingual? The data base for answering this question still is spotty in various ways and incomplete, even though serious attention has been given to the matter for nearly a century. However, enough data are available to conclude tentatively that under specified conditions, being bilingual can have tremendous advantages not only in terms of language competencies but also in terms of cognitive and social development. The limiting condition is that the two (or more) languages involved in the bilingualism have enough social value and worth that both can be permitted to flourish as languages of thought and expression. James Cummins puts the same idea another way—that if both languages are given the opportunity to meet and pass some minimum threshold of competence, then one can realize the benefits of being bilingual.[1] When these conditions are met, the evidence is very persuasive.

Our involvement at McGill with this research started in the early 1960s when we compared English-French bilingual and monolingual 10-year-olds, equated for social-class background, on a series of verbal and nonverbal tests of intelligence and tests of language competencies in each of the bilingual's two languages.[2] A host of earlier studies from various world settings had turned up mainly deficits of various sorts associated with bilingualism. But we found the bulk of these inadequate in design; they had, for example, neglected to control for social-class background in their comparisons of bi- and monolingual groups, and they rarely measured degree of bilingualism. To our surprise, our bilingual youngsters in Montreal scored significantly higher than did carefully matched monolinguals on both verbal and nonverbal measures of intelligence; they were further advanced in school grade than were the monolinguals; and they performed as well or better on various tests of competence in French (the language of schooling) than did the monolingual controls, at the same time as they outperformed the controls by far on all tests of competence in English. Furthermore, their pattern of test results indicated that they, relative to monolinguals, had developed a more diversified structure of intelligence and more flexibility in thought, those very features of cognition that very likely determine the depth and breadth of language competence.

Since that 1962 research, confirmations have emerged from carefully conducted research in different parts of the world, from Singapore, Switzerland, South Africa, Israel and New York, Western Canada, and Montreal.[3-8] All of these studies (and we have found no others in the recent literature to contradict them) indicate that bilingual young people, relative to monolingual controls, show definite cognitive and linguistic advantages as these are reflected in measures of "cognitive flexibility," "creativity," "divergent thought," or "problem solving," etc. Ben-Zeev's study, for example, involved Hebrew-English bilingual children in New York and Israel; her results strongly support the conclusion that bilinguals have greater "cognitive flexibility" in the sense that her bilinguals had greater skill at auditory reorganization of verbal material, a much more "flexible manipulation of the linguistic code," and more sophistication in "concrete operational thinking," as these were measured in her investigation.[6] Ianco-Worrall's study involved Afrikaans-English bilingual children in Pretoria, South Africa, and it lends equally strong support for a somewhat different form of cognitive flexibility, an advantage bilinguals show over monolingual controls in separating word meaning from word sound.[5] Worrall's bilinguals were some two years more advanced in this feature of cognitive development, one that Leopold felt to be so characteristic of the "liberated thought" of bilinguals.[9] Worrall also found a bilingual precocity in the realization of the arbitrariness of assignments of names to referents, a feature of thinking that Vygotsky believed was a reflection of insight and sophistication.[10] The study by Scott of French-English bilinguals in Montreal is important because it involved a comparison of two groups of young children; one group had been given the opportunity to become bilingual over a period of years, while the second group of comparable youngsters had not been given this opportunity.[8] Scott worked with data collected over a seven-year period from two groups of English-Canadian children; one group had become functionally bilingual in French during the time period through "immersion schooling" in French, while the second group had followed a conventional English-language education program. Scott focused on the possible effects that becoming bilingual might have on "divergent thinking," a special type of cognitive flexibility.[11,12] Measures of divergent thinking provide the subject with a starting point for thought—"think of a paper clip"— and ask the subject to generate a whole series of permissible solutions—"tell me all the things one could do with it." Some researchers have considered divergent thinking as an index of creativity,[13] or at least an index of a rich imagination and an ability to scan rapidly a host of possible solutions. The results, based on a multivariate analysis, showed that the functionally bilingual youngsters were, at grades five and six, substantially higher scorers than the monolinguals with whom they had been equated for IQ and social-class background at the first-grade level. Although the numbers of children in each group are small, this study supports the causal link between bilingualism and flexibility, with bilingualism apparently the factor that enhances flexibility.

There is, then, an impressive array of evidence accumulating that argues plainly against the commonsense notion that becoming bilingual—having two linguistic systems within one's brain—naturally divides a person's cognitive resources and reduces his efficiency of thought or language. Instead, one now can put forth a very strong argument that there are definite cognitive and language advantages to being bilingual. Only further research will tell us how this advantage, assuming it is a reliable phenomenon, actually works. Perhaps it is a matter of bilinguals being better able to store information; perhaps it is the greater separation of linguistic symbols from their referents or the ability to separate word meaning from word sound; perhaps it is the contrasts of linguistic systems that bilinguals continually make that aids them in the development of general conceptual thought. My own working hypothesis is that bilingualism provides a person with a comparative, three-dimensional insight into language, a type of stereolinguistic optic on communication that the monolingual rarely experiences. Bilingualism also helps protect a person against "reification," the human tendency to attribute thing qualities to all non-things that happen to have names (like soul, spirit, kindness, etc.). The protection comes in the form of the bilingual person's better realization that names are essentially arbitrary assignments. This realization along with the distance bilinguals can keep between names and referents makes them better able to play with words and their meanings, in other words, to be creative. Whatever the ultimate explanation, this new trend in research should give second thoughts to those who have used the bilingual-deficit notion as an argument for melting down ethnic groups. Hopefully, too, it will provide a new perspective for members of ethnolinguistic groups who may have been led to believe that bilingualism is nothing but a handicap.

Additive versus Subtractive Forms of Bilingualism

One feature of the studies just reviewed merits special attention. In each of the settings referred to (Singapore, South Africa, Switzerland, Israel, New York, Montreal), we are dealing with bilinguals for whom the two languages involved have social value and respect. Knowing Afrikaans and English in South Africa, Hebrew and English in New York and Israel, or French as well as English in Montreal would in each case be adding a second, socially relevant language to one's repertory of skills. In none of these settings would the learning of the second language necessarily portend the slow replacement of the first, or "home," language, as would be the case for most linguistic minority groups in the United States and Canada who are pressured to develop high-level skills in English at the expense of their home languages. We refer to the former instances as examples of "additive" bilingualism, and we draw a sharp contrast with the "subtractive" form of bilingualism experienced by ethnolinguistic minority groups who, because of national educational policies and social pressures of various sorts, feel forced to put aside or subtract out their ethnic languages for a more necessary and prestigious national language.[14] In the subtractive case, one's degree of biliguality at any time would likely reflect a stage in the disuse of the ethnic home language and its associated cultural accompaniments, and its replacement with another, more "necessary" language. This form of bilingualism can be devastating because it usually places youngsters in a psycholinguistic limbo where neither language is useful as a tool of thought and expression—a type of "semi-lingualism," as Skutnegg-Kangas and Toukomaa put it.[15]

The case of French and English in Montreal is interesting because both additive and subtractive features are involved. For anglophone Quebecers, learning French clearly is additive in nature, with no fear of a loss of identity or of French eradicating English-language competence. Since francophone Quebecers comprise some 80% of the population and have their own French-language school system from kindergarten to the most advanced professional institutions, learning English also might be thought of as additive. From a North American perspective, however, Quebec is a small French-speaking enclave that is bombarded continuously by English-language media, with pressures on its children to prepare themselves for life in an otherwise English-speaking semicontinent. For francophone Canadians outside Quebec, the chances of keeping French alive as a home, school, and work language are slim. This fear of a subtractive loss of Frenchness is real for many French-speaking Quebecers as well: a too ardent move toward Englishness might well subtract out Frenchness.

In my mind, the aim of education in North America should be to brighten the outlook for ethnolinguistic-minority-group children by preparing them to compete better in educational and occupational pursuits. As potential bilinguals, they certainly have the cognitive and linguistic potential, as shown by the research already mentioned. The best way I can see to release that potential is to transform their subtractive experiences with bilingualism and biculturalism into additive ones. We already have a few research-based examples of how this transformation might work. The first is the case of Franco-Americans in northern New England who recently were given a chance to be schooled partly in their home language.[16-19] Some 85% of families in the northern regions of Maine have kept French alive as the home language or as one of the two home languages, even though traditionally all schooling has been conducted in English. We participated in an experiment wherein a random selection of schools and of classes in the area were permitted to offer about a third of the elementary curriculum in French, and where a second sample of schools—with children of comparable intelligence scores and socioeconomic backgrounds—served as a control or comparison in that all their instruction was in English. After a five-year run, the children in the "partial French" classes clearly outperformed those in the control classes in various aspects of *English*-language skills and in academic content, such as math, learned partly via French. At the same time, French had become for them something more than an audiolingual language because of the reading and writing requirements of the French schooling. These results mean that the French-trained Franco-American children were given a better chance to compete in occupations or professions calling for high-level educational training; they had been lifted from the typical low standing on scholastic-achievement measures that characterizes so many ethnolinguistic groups in North America. An important element in this transformation was the change in the self-views of the French-trained youngsters, who, we found, began to reflect a deep pride in being French and a realization that their language was as important a medium for education as was English.[18]

Similar community-based studies are under way in the American Southwest, and these, too, are based on the belief that ethnolinguistic minorities need a strong educational experience in their own languages and traditions before they can cope in an "all-American" society or before they will want to cope in such a society.

A second example of a transformation of subtractive to additive bilingualism is provided by Carolyn Kessler and Mary Quinn.[20] In their study, Spanish-speaking Texas grade-six students were given the opportunity in elementary school to learn subject matters via Spanish while learning English, that is, like the Franco-Americans in the first example, to use their home language—the language through which their basic conceptual thinking developed in infancy—as one of the linguistic media for further conceptual growth. The Hispanic-American students were compared with a much more privileged sample of middle-class, white, monolingual English-speaking American pupils of the same age. Both groups were given an extensive training program in "science inquiry" through films and discussion of physical science problems and hypothesis testing. In tests given after the training, it was found that the Spanish-English bilinguals generated hypotheses of a much higher quality and complexity than did the monolinguals. This problem-solving quality was reflected also in the language used, as indexed by a "syntactic complexity" measure, so that the bilinguals clearly were using more complex linguistic structures as well. Kessler and Quinn also found substantial correlations between their measures of hypothesis quality and syntactic complexity, thereby providing an important link between problem-solving capacity and linguistic skills.

The research by Kessler and Quinn jibes nicely with other findings. For example, Padilla and Long found that Spanish-American children and adolescents can acquire English better and adjust more effectively to the educational and occupational demands of American society if their linguistic and cultural ties with the Spanish-speaking world are kept alive and active from infancy on [21] (see also Reference 22). There are in fact numerous recent examples that point in the same direction.[23-26] G. R. Tucker recently summarized these studies and concluded that there is "a cumulative and positive impact of bilingual education on all youngsters when they are allowed to remain in bilingual programs for a period of time greater than two or three or even five years and when there is an active attempt to provide nurturance and sustenance of their mother tongue in addition to introducing teaching via the language of wider communication." [27]

The Inception of Bilingualism: Early versus Late

The forms of bilingualism just described are controlled mainly by events and exigencies within families or communities that have the effect of making children bilingual. Bilingualism can start early or late. At its earliest, bilingualism can, as Merrill Swain so nicely put it, be the child's "first language." [28] When both languages are given the chance to develop, these "infant" bilinguals show full command of the two (or more) codes, as though they were double monolinguals. There are various ways in which the two languages might be acquired. For instance, both could be introduced as family languages when a child is born, one language emanating from one parent, the second from the other parent, with no requirement that either parent be bilingual in both of the partners' languages. In such a family, strong emotional attachments to each language are initiated. Both parents usually want to have a hand in the linguistic socialization so that their child is not a stranger to them. In this way the child builds up parental associations with each language. In the process the child becomes ethnolinguistically something more than either parent because he or she has a better opportunity to belong to both feed-in cultural groups than does either parent. To the extent that both parents keep up a socializing role, they can regulate and modulate the bilingualism and the biculturalism of the child, making it either balanced or lopsided. The child also has the means, through ethnic and linguistic ploys, to control the parents and the ethnic and linguistic atmosphere of the whole family.

By way of contrast, if both parents know the two relevant languages when a child is born, different emotional and identity demands are placed on the child. Their shared bilinguality usually reflects common background experiences for the parents and suggests that in some previous generation, some other set of parents had initiated the bilinguality. The more the child in this type of family becomes bilingual, the more he or she becomes similar in important respects to both parents.

Bilingualism that starts after infancy also can take various forms. A monolingual child can encounter a second language as a community or commerce language outside the home. Or a second language can be the medium of schooling for an otherwise monolingual child. The shifting of residences through emigration can delay the start of bilingualism to even later age levels. And one can develop full bilingualism at any age through the intensive study of a second language. Current research indicates that these differences in starting points have significant effects on the linguistic, cognitive, and emotional development of a child; apparently the ultimate form of bilingualism is shaped, in part, by the age of inception.

The more formal routes to postinfancy bilingualism that take place through second-language study in school can provide learners with the building blocks for functional bilingualism. We will examine briefly two versions of such programs, one at the high-school level, the other at the elementary, because they throw light on the general nature of language acquisition and its normal developmental course.

Secondary-School Second-Language Learning

The traditional approach to foreign-language (FL) teaching in North America is to provide three or four years of training in an FL at the high-school level, typically as part of a college preparatory course. This approach has left many generations of Americans very poorly prepared to use the FL in any meaningful way. Still, there is much variability in the results produced by such programs: a small minority of students are turned on by the training and make great progress in the FL; the majority seem to just get started as the training ends, and they later look back on it as just another high-school sequence; and another minority are bored and demoralized by what they feel is a sheer waste of time. Robert Gardner and I became interested in this variance of outcomes. To explore it, we designed a series of research studies to determine what is needed to be successful in FL learning.[29,30] The research literature on the topic of FL success or failure goes back to the turn of the century, and most of it deals with a search for special abilities or aptitudes, like having "an ear for languages." That tradition led to the work of Carroll and Sapon on the development of the Modern Language Aptitude Test (MLAT), an interesting compilation of subtests, each of which contributes a unique element to a highly predictive and reliable battery.[31] As of the 1950s, success or failure in FL study was thought to be determined mainly by language aptitude plus certain components of verbal IQ. As social psychologists, Gardner and I wondered whether other factors also might be involved, especially attitudinal and motivational factors. Our design called for pretesting, at the start of an FL-learning program, for aptitude and IQ, along with measures of attitudes towards the cultural group whose language was to be studied, general ethnocentric attitudes, reasons for taking FL training (instrumental and/or integrative reasons), and interest, motivation, and effort put into FL study. This design, with regular checks on achievement in the FL, permits one to observe the language-acquisition process more closely than one can with first-language acquisition, which runs its course so swiftly. What we found is that tests of aptitude and verbal intelligence form a statistical cluster that predicts fairly well one's achievement in FL study over a fixed period of time, but that measures of attitudes toward the other group and its language and measures of one's zeal and interest in learning the FL form a totally separate cluster that predicts equally well the degree of achievement reached in FL study. Recently, Gardner and his colleagues have found that persistence in FL study (e.g., wanting to take more advanced training in the FL) and involvement in FL classroom activities are determined clearly by this set of attitude and motivation variables.

What is significant in this research is the finding that a second, unexpected route to successful FL study is available. This means that if one doesn't have a rich endowment in aptitude for FL, one can compensate through a favorable set of attitudes, orientations, and motivation. This finding changes substantively certain widely held views about language acquisition, first language or second. A new set of questions comes to mind: How much of FL achievement is based on wired-in, genetically based endowment and how much is attitudinal and motivational? And if these questions can be asked about second-language acquisition, then the same questions can be asked about mathematical, musical, and athletic "endowments" and even about first-language endowment.

"Immersion" Programs at Elementary School

We have learned much about the developmental course of language acquisition from our longitudinal studies of early "immersion" programs in elementary schools. In North America, "immersion" programs are intended mainly for English-speaking children who, from their first day in kindergarten or grade one, find themselves with a teacher who speaks only some foreign language (e.g., French, Ukrainian, Hebrew, Spanish, German) and starts conversing and interacting, slowly and considerately, in that language. The foreign language (L2) is used as the sole medium of instruction for kindergarten and grades one and two, when English is introduced for language arts only. By grades five and six, half of the curriculum is taught via L2 and half via L1. The rather dramatic results of early-immersion schooling have been described elsewhere.[32-34] Briefly, we find that by the end of elementary school, students in immersion have developed a functional bilinguality in L2, which is learned mainly in an incidental fashion through its use as a language of instruction. The functional bilinguality attained by grades five and six does not impair in any way the development of language skills in L1. In fact, L1 competencies generally are enriched when comparisons are made with carefully matched control (nonimmersion) groups. Thus, immersion pupils who learn to read via L2 keep up with the nonimmersion controls in English-language reading as well as all other aspects of English. Likewise, skills in content matter (such as math, science, social studies) taught through L2 are as well developed for immersion as for control pupils.

Thus, much transfer from L2 to L1 seems to take place naturally in these programs, as though what is learned through L2 with regard to content matters and with regard to reading skills and language development percolates down to the first language. The immersion children seem to attack the L2 demands of the program with all the thinking and language abilities they have, and this apparently promotes a continuous, mutually beneficial interplay between L2—the instructional code—and L1—the basic language of thought and expression for the children at the start of the experience. This fascinating transfer of skills from L2 to L1 and vice versa holds also for Jewish youngsters whose only home language is English and who follow a double-immersion program where Hebrew and French are used by separate teachers as the sole media of instruction from kindergarten through grade three.[35] The interplay in this case is among L2-H, L2-F, and L1. The main finding here is that language acquisition can proceed at a normal pace even though it involves one or more second languages, for these can interact supportively with first-language development. It also has been found that those with early immersion experiences are more anxious to learn a third language than are the controls who have experienced mainly French-as-a-second-language training.[36] Apparently because they have had success with one foreign language, they are confident and inquisitive about learning others.

Neuropsychological Correlates of Bilingual Language Acquisition

Interest in the age of inception of bilingualism has prompted some of us at McGill to explore the neuropsychology of this aspect of language acquisition. In several respects, this is an extension of earlier research on the contrasts between "compound" and "coordinate" forms of bilingualism.[37] The age of becoming bilingual is one criterion of the compound-coordinate distinction. In this research, comparisons are made between "early" bilinguals (those who are bilingual from infancy on, who are likely to develop compound linguistic systems) and "late" bilinguals (those who became bilingual in the childhood or adolescent years, who are most likely to develop coordinate systems). This turns out to be an extremely interesting and promising research domain.

The behavioral evidence for substantive differences between early and late bilingualism is fairly convincing, suggesting that late bilinguals are more inclined than early bilinguals to keep their two linguistic systems functionally distinctive and segregated. For example, late French-English bilinguals were found to be less able than early bilinguals to draw on mixed-language associational clues (such as *chaise, food, desk, bois, manger*) to arrive at the core concept *table,* which unites the separate cues.[38] On tests of free recall, late bilinguals also were less able than early bilinguals to categorize or cluster mixed-language strings of exemplars (such as *apple, pamplemousse, pear, citron*).[37] However, late bilinguals were *better* able to "gate out" the meaning system of one of their languages when the task (a bilingual version of the Stroop Color Word Test) required them to function, with a minimum of interlanguage interplay, in their other language.[37] These studies indicate that those who develop their binguality early are more inclined to process the deeper meaning of linguistic information than are those who become bilingual at some later developmental period. Put in other terms, the early bilinguals seem to develop relatively more pervasive, superordinate meaning systems that subserve both languages. In contrast, late bilinguals seem to have relatively more compartmentalized semantic systems for each of their languages, and the two language systems seem to be more functionally independent. There may be more than semantic differences involved here, however. In a recent study, Alan Paivio and I have found that late bilinguals are more likely than early ones to evoke mental images as they translate words from one language to another.[39]

The corresponding neuropsychological evidence on the early-late bilingual distinction is becoming convincing (see Reference 40). One McGill study dealt with young adults who had become perfectly bilingual in French and English in either infancy, childhood, or adolescence.[41] They were given very simple linguistic tasks to perform (e.g., to indicate whether the words they heard through earphones were English or French). At the same time the electroencephalographic (EEG) activity in their left and right cerebral hemispheres was monitored and converted into average evoked reactions. It turned out that early bilinguals (those bilingual from infancy or childhood) processed the input information more quickly in their left than in their right hemispheres, while late bilinguals (the adolescent subgroup) processed the input information faster in their right than in their left hemispheres. We interpreted the results in terms of strategy differences: the early bilinguals apparently had a proclivity for a left-hemisphere strategy, one based more on semantic analysis, while the late bilinguals had a right-hemisphere proclivity, using a processing strategy based more on the gestaltlike or melodic properties of the input.

A second McGill study focused on the processing of meaning in early and late bilinguals, with verbal information presented through either the left or right ear.[42] The assumption in this case, too, was that there is a more direct and efficient neurological route from one ear to the contralateral cerebral hemisphere. The findings suggest that bilinguals tend to involve their right hemispheres more in the encoding and decoding of meaning than do monolinguals. But the degree of right-hemisphere involvement is determined by the sex of the subjects as well as by the age of onset of their bilinguality. Thus, male monolinguals are more confined to the left hemisphere for the processing of meaning, whereas male bilinguals involve both right and left hemispheres if their bilinguality starts in infancy but mainly the right hemisphere if the bilinguality dates from adolescence. Female monolinguals start with a balanced involvement of both right and left hemispheres, and bilinguality, whether early or late in its origin, shifts the control of meaning mainly to the right hemisphere.

Two recent studies outside McGill have come to similar conclusions: a greater right-hemisphere involvement in late than in early bilinguals during linguistic processing. One of these investigations was conducted by Hal Gordon using a dichotic listening design with Hebrew-English bilingual adults in Israel, the other by Bella Kotik using the EEG design with Polish-Russian bilinguals in Russia.[43,44]

Harvey Sussman and colleagues at the University of Texas have arrived at similar conclusions from a quite different probing approach.[45] They have bilingual subjects tap on a table with a left- or right-hand finger while speaking in one or the other of their languages. Right-hand tapping, they find, is disrupted for monolingual controls when tapping is concurrent with speech, whereas both right- and left-hand tapping is disrupted for bilinguals. This presumed greater involvement of the right hemisphere is most pronounced for late bilinguals when using their non-native language. All told, then, there is a solid accumulation of evidence for a relationship between early-late bilingualism and left-right hemisphere involvement; but as Vaid and Genesee mention, the concomitant influences of such factors as sex, formal vs. informal modes of language acquisition, and stage of bilinguality have yet to be given appropriate attention in these studies.[40] Nonetheless, we now can ask more penetrating questions about the different patterns of language acquisition experienced by bilinguals, especially the differences between early and late beginnings of bilingualism. For instance: Might there be some connection between the symptoms of flexibility of thought among bilinguals, discussed earlier, and greater right-hemisphere involvement? Why are there such marked early-late differences in degree of right-hemisphere involvement among bilinguals? Why are male bilinguals so special?

REFERENCES

1. CUMMINS, J. 1978. Educational implications of mother tongue maintenance in minority-language groups. Can. Mod. Lang. Rev. **34:** 395–416.
2. PEAL, E. & W. E. LAMBERT. 1962. The relation of bilingualism to intelligence. Psychol. Monogr. **76:** 1–23.
3. TORRANCE, E. P., J. C. GOWAN, J. M. WU & N. C. ALIOTTI. 1970. Creative functioning of monolingual and bilingual children in Singapore. J. Educ. Psychol. **61:** 72–75.
4. BALKAN, L. 1970. Les Effets du Bilinguisme Français-Anglais sur les Aptitudes Intellectuelles. Aimav. Brussels, Belgium.
5. IANCO-WORRALL, A. D. 1972. Bilingualism and cognitive development. Child Dev. **43:** 1390–1400.
6. BEN ZEEV, S. 1972. The influence of bilingualism on cognitive development and cognitive strategy. Doctoral Dissertation. University of Chicago. Chicago, Ill.
7. CUMMINS, J. & M. GULUTSAN. 1973. Some effects of bilingualism on cognitive functioning. University of Alberta. Edmonton, Alberta, Canada. (Unpublished.)
8. SCOTT, S. 1973. The relation of divergent thinking to bilingualism: cause or effect? McGill University. Montreal, Quebec, Canada. (Unpublished research report.)
9. LEOPOLD, W. F. 1949. Speech Development of a Bilingual Child. Northwestern University Press. Evanston, Ill.
10. VYGOTSKY, L. S. 1962. Thought and Language. MIT Press. Cambridge, Mass.
11. GUILFORD, J. P. 1950. Creativity. Am. Psychol. **5:** 444–454.
12. GUILFORD, J. P. 1956. The structure of intellect. Psychol. Bull. **53:** 267–293.
13. GETZELS, J. W. & P. W. JACKSON. 1962. Creativity and Intelligence. John Wiley & Sons, Inc. New York, N.Y.
14. LAMBERT, W. E. 1974. Culture and language as factors in learning and education. Paper presented at the Fifth Western Symposium on Learning, Western Washington State College, Bellingham, Wash.
15. SKUTNEGG-KANGAS, R. & P. TOUKOMAA. 1976. Teaching Migrant Children's Mother Tongue and Learning the Language of the Host Country in the Context of the Socio-Cultural Situation of the Migrant Family. The Finnish National Commission for UNESCO. Helsinki, Finland.
16. DUBÉ, N. C. & G. HERBERT. 1975. St. John Valley Bilingual Education Project. U.S. Department of Health, Education and Welfare. Washington, D.C.
17. DUBÉ, N. C. & G. HERBERT. 1975. Evaluation of the St. John Valley Title VII Bilingual Education Program, 1970–1975. Madawaska, Maine. (Unpublished.)

18. LAMBERT, W. E., H. GILES & O. PICARD. 1975. Language attitudes in a French-American community. Int. J. Sociol. Lang. **4:** 127–152.
19. LAMBERT, W. E., H. GILES & A. ALBERT. 1976. Language attitudes in a rural city in northern Maine. McGill University. Montreal, Quebec, Canada. (Unpublished.)
20. KESSLER, C. & M. QUINN. 1980. Bilingualism and science problem-solving ability. Paper presented at the 14th Annual International Convention of Teachers of English to Speakers of Other Languages, San Francisco, Calif.
21. PADILLA, A. M. & K. K. LONG. 1969. An assessment of successful Spanish-American students at the University of New Mexico. Paper presented to the Annual Meeting of the American Association for the Advancement of Science, Rocky Mountain Division, Colorado Springs, Colo.
22. LONG, K. K. & A. M. PADILLA. 1970. Evidence for bilingual antecedents of academic success in a group of Spanish-American college students. Western Washington State College. Bellingham, Wash. (Unpublished research report.)
23. HANSON, G. 1979. The position of the second generation of Finnish immigrants in Sweden: the importance of education in the home language. Spitz, Sweden. (Symposium report.)
24. McCONNELL, B. B. 1980. Effectiveness of individualized bilingual instruction for migrant students. Ph.D. Dissertation. Washington State University. Pullman, Wash.
25. ROSLER, P. & W. HOLM. 1980. Saad Naaki Bee Na'nitin: Teaching by Means of Two Languages—Navajo and English—at Rock Point Community School. Center for Applied Linguistics. Washington, D.C.
26. TROIKE, R. C. 1978. Research evidence for the effectiveness of bilingual education. Nat. Assoc. Bilingual Educ. J. **3:** 13–24.
27. TUCKER, G. R. 1980. Comments on proposed rules for nondiscrimination under programs receiving federal financial assistance through the Education Department: 5–6. Center for Applied Linguistics. Washington, D.C. (Unpublished.)
28. SWAIN, M. K. 1972. Bilingualism as a first language. Doctoral Dissertation. University of California. Irvine, Calif.
29. GARDNER, R. C. & W. E. LAMBERT. 1972. Attitudes and Motivation in Second-Language Learning. Newbury House Publishers. Rowley, Mass.
30. GARDNER, R. C. 1981. Second language learning. *In* A Canadian Social Psychology of Ethnic Relations. R. C. Gardner & R. Kalin, Eds.: 92–114. Methuen Publications. Toronto, Ontario, Canada.
31. CARROLL, J. B. & S. M. SAPON. 1959. Modern Language Aptitude Test. The Psychological Corporation. New York, N.Y.
32. LAMBERT, W. E. & G. R. TUCKER. 1972. Bilingual Education of Children: The St. Lambert Experiment. Newbury House Publishers. Rowley, Mass.
33. SWAIN, M. 1974. French immersion programs across Canada. Can. Mod. Lang. Rev. **31:** 117–128.
34. GENESEE, F. 1978. Scholastic effects of French immersion: an overview after ten years. Interchange **9:** 20–29.
35. GENESEE, F. & W. E. LAMBERT. 1981. Trilingual education for the majority language child. McGill University. Montreal, Quebec, Canada. (Unpublished.)
36. CZIKO, G., W. E. LAMBERT, N. SIDOTI & G. R. TUCKER. 1980. Graduates of early immersion: retrospective views of grade 11 students and their parents. *In* The Social and Psychological Contexts of Language. R. St. Clair & H. Giles, Eds.: 131–192. Erlbaum Associates. Chicago, Ill.
37. LAMBERT, W. E. 1969. Psychological studies of the interdependencies of the bilingual's two languages. *In* Substance and Structure of Language. J. Puhvel, Ed.: 99–126. University of California Press. Los Angeles, Calif.

38. LAMBERT, W. E. & C. RAWLINGS. 1969. Bilingual processing of mixed-language associative networks. J. Verbal Learning Verbal Behav. **8:** 604–609.
39. PAIVIO, A. & W. E. LAMBERT. 1981. Dual coding and bilingual memory. University of Western Ontario. London, Ontario, Canada. (Unpublished.)
40. VAID, J. & F. GENESEE. 1981. Neuropsychological approaches to bilingualism: a critical review. Can. J. Psychol. (In press.)
41. GENESEE, F., J. HAMERS, W. E. LAMBERT, L. MONONEN, M. SEITZ & R. STARCK. 1978. Language processing in bilinguals. Brain Lang. **5:** 1–12.
42. VAID, J. & W. E. LAMBERT. 1979. Differential cerebral involvement in the cognitive functioning of bilinguals. Brain Lang. **8:** 92–110.
43. GORDON, H. W. 1980. Cerebral organization in bilinguals: lateralization. Brain Lang. (In press.)
44. KOTIK, B. S. 1980. Investigation of speech lateralization in multilinguals. Rostov State University. Rostov, Russia. (Unpublished personal communication of additional research findings.)
45. SUSSMAN, H. M., P. FRANKLIN & T. SIMON. 1980. Bilingual speech: bilateral control? University of Texas. Austin, Tex. (Unpublished.)

DIFFERENCES AND SIMILARITIES BETWEEN FIRST- AND SECOND-LANGUAGE LEARNING

Barry McLaughlin

Psychology Board of Studies
Adlai Stevenson College
University of California
Santa Cruz, California 95064

Comparing first- and second-language development means contrasting different learning situations, different input, and different cognitive and linguistic skills on the part of the learners. To make some sense out of all this, I will distinguish four learning contexts: one context in which both languages are acquired simultaneously, and three contexts in which second-language learning occurs after a first language has been acquired—in preschool children, in school-aged children, and in adults.

Simultaneous Bilingual Acquisition

At the risk of oversimplifying, I think that three generalizations are possible about the simultaneous acquisition of two languages by children learning to speak: [1]

1. Children who experience balanced exposure to two languages develop both languages as do monolingual speakers of either language. Initially children seem to work from a single set of rules and there is a stage of language mixing, especially lexical mixing, but gradually two sets of rules become differentiated.

2. When the exposure to the two languages is less balanced, there may be more persistent linguistic transfer and more frequent introduction of the vocabulary of one language into the grammatical system of the other.

3. There is a single language system that underlies both languages of the bilingual child. It is unparsimonious to postulate separate linguistic systems and more economical to regard the bilingual's two languages as separate linguistic subsystems, analogous to the linguistic codes of a monolingual speaker.

A number of investigators have sought to capitalize on the fact that the bilingual child develops two linguistic subsystems, to make inferences about the structural complexity of the two languages. By observing which of two corresponding structures develops first, it was thought that insight could be gained into the cognitive strategies used to mark specific semantic relations in the two languages. [2]

Such an analysis involves the assumption that the two linguistic subsystems are entirely separate and do not interact with each other—an

23

0077–8923/81/0379–0023 $01.75/2 © 1981, NYAS

assumption that may not be warranted, especially when the languages are not balanced in the input. There is some evidence from research on bilingual children that more complex grammatical constructions can be acquired before less complex ones and that certain grammatical constructions can be acquired in a way that differs from monolingual development and shows the influence of a second language.[3,4] Indeed, if one language is dominant and the other is reduced to subordinate status, transfer between languages usually is noticeable in the child's speech.[1]

Since language balance is a very fragile phenomenon in bilingual children, we are dealing with a question of degree of approximation. The more balanced the input, the more the bilingual child's language development tends to correspond to the pattern found in monolingual children. The one-person-one-language rule and the identification of a language with particular social settings, such as home vs. school, seem to help the child to keep the two languages separate. The more language mixing in persons and places, the more the developmental pattern is likely to diverge from typical patterns observed in monolingual children.

Sequential Acquisition in Preschool Children

I would like to move on now to the situation where the child acquires a second language after having developed basic linguistic skills in a first language. I will refer to this as sequential acquisition of a second language, although the point at which acquisition of a second language becomes sequential is difficult to demarcate with precision. I will assume that this happens at about three years of age; although, since children differ considerably in the rate at which they acquire a first language, a cutoff point based on linguistic and cognitive developmental criteria would be preferable to one based on age. In any event, what can be said about second-language acquisition begun after we are reasonably sure preschool children possess basic communicative and linguistic skills in a first language? How does acquisition of the target second language by such children differ from the developmental pattern found in monolingual speakers of that language? Or does it?

A considerable body of data has accumulated that suggests that the possession of a first language has less influence on the acquisition of a second than one might expect.[1] Indeed there is some evidence that the same developmental sequences can be found in the acquisition data for both first- and second-language learners of a target language. These sequences appear to be the same in second-language learners no matter what their first language. I am thinking here of the research of Ravem, Dato, and others on such constructions as the negative, interrogative, and modal auxiliary in English and other languages.[5,6] For example, Wode studied the development of the negative in four English-speaking children aged 3 to 7½ who were acquiring German as a second language, and found a developmental sequence very similar to that found in monolingual German children.[7] The evidence ran counter to the notion that the children were building on their first language; instead, there seemed to be structural regularities in the target language that determined the course of learning for both first- and second-language learners.

Nonetheless, Wode also noted that his research on German-speaking children learning English as a second language revealed developmental sequences different from those observed in English monolingual children. He argued that these differences result from first-language transfer and overgeneralization, but do so in a systematic way that reflects "general acquisitional principles." [7] For example, he reported a stage in the acquisition of the negative in which the negative form was placed after the verb, a structure that heavily reflected the child's first-language (German) word order. As Wode pointed out, the same error could result from analogy with the English rule for negative placement after auxiliaries. Another possibility is that the two factors—transfer and overgeneralization—actually are interacting in such cases.[8]

This interaction between first- and second-language acquisitional principles has been discussed by Hakuta in his study of a five-year-old Japanese girl acquiring English as a second language.[9] Hakuta concluded that second-language acquisition is a dynamic, fluid process in which the learner's system is shifting constantly, as he put it, "toward the maintenance of an internal consistency within the structures which the learner possesses, or in the direction of an external consistency, where the learner attempts to fit the internal system into what is heard in the input." [9] In this process, the children use what they have—what information they have about the second language and knowledge of their first language—to crack the code of the second language.

If one examines the so-called morpheme studies—studies of the accuracy of use of English grammatical morphemes—one finds consistent regularities in accuracy of use of these morphemes in cross-sectional research with speakers of different first languages, but the order does not exactly parallel that observed in monolingual English-speaking children. Furthermore, there also have been reports of first-language influence. For example, Dulay and Burt found differences in the accuracy orders obtained in Spanish- and Cantonese-speaking children for the article and short plural forms.[10] Fathman found differences in accuracy order for the article for Korean- and Spanish-speaking groups.[11] Kessler and Idar found a somewhat random order in the initial stages of the speech of a Vietnamese child, and only later did the accuracy order approximate that found in the majority of other studies.[12] Thus, while the morpheme studies show definite regularities, there is evidence of deviations from these regularities for groups and individuals.

Indeed, the cross-sectional method used in the morpheme studies has the drawback of minimizing individual variation. Averaging scores across subjects obscures the pattern for any one subject. A number of investigators have reported developmental sequences for individual second-language learners based on longitudinal data that differ considerably from the accuracy orders obtained in most cross-sectional research.[13,8] This does not mean, however, that the accuracy-order data are trivial. In fact, as Andersen has shown, if implicational analysis is performed on cross-sectional data, it is possible to derive information about both regularities and individual variation.[14]

Recent research with immigrant workers' children in Germany by Meisel and his coworkers has indicated that developmental regularities are found in the speech of these children that parallel those observed in younger German monolingual children.[15,16] At the same time, there is evidence that different learners take different routes toward the target language without violating the postulated developmental sequences. That is, while going through ordered sequences of developmental stages, individual learners display within-stage variation depending on learning strategies. This implies the need for a multidimensional approach—one that allows for variation due to learner idiosyncrasies within the context of developmental regularities.

Where does this leave us with respect to the question of differences and similarities in first- and second-language acquisition? My own preference in tangling with the intricacies of this problem is to draw a distinction between those processes that are universal in all language learning—perhaps because they utilize language-specific cognitive mechanisms as well as general cognitive mechanisms—and those processes that are idiosyncratic to individual learners. I have called the universal processes "acquisition heuristics" and the idiosyncratic ones "operating procedures." [17] More recently, Seliger has made a similar distinction, using the more felicitous terms "strategies" and "tactics." [18]

Strategies are superordinate, abstract, constant, and long-term cognitive processes. They are thought to be employed by all language learners regardless of language background, age, or acquisitional context. Examples of such cognitive processes include hypothesis testing, simplification, and overgeneralization. To meet the demands of specific learning tasks, individuals use tactics—short-term processes used to overcome temporary and immediate obstacles to the achievement of the long-range goal of language acquisition. Examples include use of rules, memorization, and various input-generating devices.

In children, one of the differences between first- and second-language learners is in the frequency of formulaic expressions, which are employed more by second-language learners,[8] who are older and more capable, cognitively, of using a tactic that involves imitatively stringing words together. Another tactic is the use of the first language, especially in dealing with intractable problems in the second.[7] On the other hand, because these older children approach the second language with the same set of general language-learning strategies they used for acquiring their first language, one may find similar patterns in the development of formal structures, if these are not obscured by the tactics used in particular contexts.

In short, the hypothesis here is that what is common to first- and second-language acquisition can be attributed to strategies, and differences can be attributed to the tactics of individual learners in specific learning situations. Of course, to attribute common developmental sequences to the use of universal strategies does not solve the problem of similarity unless we can be more precise about the cognitive and linguistic processes that are involved. Nor does the postulated use of idiosyncratic tactics solve the problem of diversity unless more specific data are on hand concerning the way person variables and situational factors interact. I suppose this is another way of saying we have an interesting field of study.

Sequential Acquisition in School-Age Children

At this point I would like to turn to the question of sequential acquisition in school-age children. Not that the picture gets any clearer. Here we encounter the additional complexity of the demands of the classroom. When a child starts to learn a second language in the classroom, the situation certainly is different from the situation in which that child learned his or her first language. For one thing the child is older and hence brings different cognitive and linguistic skills to the task. The input is different, as is what one is expected to talk about.

The last point is critical: language use in the classroom is very different from language use outside the classroom. As Margaret Donaldson put it so well:

> The normal child comes to school with well-established skills as a thinker. But his thinking is *directed outwards* on to the real, meaningful, shifting, distracting world. What is going to be required for success in our educational system is that he should learn to turn language and thought in upon themselves. He must become able to direct his own thought processes in a thoughtful manner. He must become able not just to talk but to choose what he will say, not just to interpret but to weigh possible interpretations. His conceptual system must expand in the direction of increasing ability to represent itself. He must become capable of manipulating symbols.[19]

In short, the child has to develop generalized competencies in abstraction, verbal reasoning, and metalinguistic ability. He or she does this through contact with the language of the school, which Calfee and Freedman have called *formal language*—a language that is highly explicit, context free, logical, and expository—and which they distinguish from the child's highly implicit, context-bound, intuitive, and sequential *informal language*.[20]

The situation of course is compounded when the language of the school is a second language for the child. In this case the child is both "learning a second language" and "learning a second language for school use." Children from literate middle-class backgrounds, who have been sensitized to decontextualized language, can deal with this dual task more readily, as the experience of children in Canadian immersion programs demonstrates. Children from lower-class backgrounds, who have had little experience with decontextualized language, have more difficulty, as the experience of American ethnic minorities demonstrates.[1]

These results are best explained, to my mind, by Cummins' *language interdependence hypothesis,* according to which the cognitive-academic aspects of a first and second language are thought to be interdependent, and proficiency in a second language in a school setting is predicted to depend largely on previous learning of literacy-related functions of language.[21] The literacy-related functions of language, or Cummins' CALP (cognitive/ academic language proficiency), are seen to be distinguishable empirically from the use of language for natural communication, or what Cummins refers to as BICS (basic interpersonal communicative skills), and it is this distinction that accounts for the so-called linguistic facade phenomenon, whereby children who have surface fluency in a second language—an aspect of BICS—do poorly when transferred to a second-language classroom where a premium is placed on CALP.

In other words, second-language learning in the classroom involves skills that are quite different from those involved in second-language learning outside the classroom. The classroom learning context is different both in function and frequency of structure. The semantic task is more complex, and it is not surprising that the child has frequent recourse to first-language structures.[22] Even in highly successful immersion programs, more language transfer is reported than is typically true of children who have acquired the second language outside of the classroom.[1,23]

Nonetheless, children who have been exposed to a second language in the classroom display many of the same developmental sequences that are found in younger children and that reveal relatively little dependence on the child's first language. In a recent study of German 10- and 11-year-old children learning English in a classroom setting where there was almost no naturalistic exposure, Felix found considerable evidence for structural parallels between classroom second-language learning and those developmental sequences observed in monolingual English-speaking children.[24] This was especially true for negative and interrogative structures, where the children followed a developmental path very similar to that observed in naturalistic learners. Particularly striking was their use of incorrect constructions that they had never heard but that represented simplification and overgeneralization strategies identical to those used by monolingual first-language learners.

There were, on the other hand, important differences between the way in which these children learned their second language and naturalistic language acquisition. For one thing, the children were forced in the first few weeks to learn English syntactic structures that do not emerge until a comparatively late developmental stage in naturalistic language acquisition. This resulted in errors not typically found in monolingual speakers, especially in the use of personal and possessive pronouns.

Felix's data suggest to me that two things are happening in this situation. On the one hand, the children are using universal "strategies" of language acquisition to solve the riddle of the foreign language. The use of these general language-learning strategies results in constructions that are quite similar to those found in monolingual children acquiring the target language. On the other hand, the teacher's didactic efforts lead the students to evolve "tactics" for dealing with this particular learning situation, especially when forced to produce utterances before developing the appropriate structural features of the sentence involved. These tactics are idiosyncratic and lead to a somewhat random pattern of errors.

Such a consequence results, I believe, from "learning a second language for school use"—a task that imposes its own demands on the child. Ultimately, schooling may make the individual a more efficient language learner, at least with respect to CALP skills. The school experience teaches the child to become aware of language as a separate structure, to reflect on language itself, and thereby to free language from its embeddedness in events. Schoolchildren become aware of what it is that they talk with—the individual words—and of the rules that govern how words are put together. This heightened metalinguistic awareness affects the way the child approaches language. Children in French immersion programs, for example, have been reported to be quite concerned about the formal properties of the French language as early as the second grade.[25]

Adult Second-Language Learning

This concern with formal properties of language becomes even more pronounced in adolescent and adult second-language learners. This presumably is the result of the attainment of literacy and a school experience that has taught them to reflect upon language and its grammatical structure. Many adults approach a second language deliberately, preferring deductive methods to inductive ones. In fact, it has been shown that for one rule system at least, a deductive approach produces greater long-term performance than do inductive methods.[26] Perhaps prior knowledge of rule systems has a greater facilitative effect on complex grammatical structures than on simpler ones. In any event, the deductive use of formal rules is a tactic employed by most literate adults in learning a second language.

In addition, of course, an adult comes to the task of learning a second language with greater cognitive maturity than the child possesses. The adult has more efficient information-processing techniques and superior mnemonic devices. Adults are more skilled at planning, monitoring, and integrating speech into the real-time flow of information. Adults also have a more elaborate conceptual repertoire and more extensive previous learning than do children. These obvious differences in cognitive ability mean that the experience of the adult learning a second language is different from that of the child.

Some evidence in support of this contention was reported recently by Fathman and Precup.[27] They compared children and adults learning English as a second language in both formal and informal settings and found that more speech planning occurred in adult speech. Adults also repeated and corrected themselves more frequently than did children. Such differences were most pronounced for morphology and syntax and in the groups receiving formal instruction. Fathman and Precup concluded their study by describing the differences as reflections of a continuum, with child-informal learners at one extreme and adult-formal learners at the other. The child-informal learners showed little concern for structural errors, little hesitation, and a definite concern for communicating the intended message. The adult-formal learners showed less concern for message communication, were more hesitant in speaking, and paid more attention to structural correctness.

When direct comparisons are made between adult and child second-language learners, results usually indicate that adult learners perform better on measures of morphology and syntax.[1] Krashen, Long, and Scarcella have argued that adults acquire the morphology and syntax of a second language faster than do young children, but that child learners ultimately will attain higher proficiency.[28] They endorsed a "younger-is-better" position, according to which child second-language learners are expected to be superior to adolescents and adults in terms of ultimate achievement. If anything, however, the evidence they cited suggests that ultimate proficiency in morphology and syntax is highest among learners who have begun acquisition during adolescence.[11,29] The younger-is-better hypothesis also is contradicted by research with children in Foreign Languages in the Elementary Schools (FLES) programs, which shows that children starting a second language in later grades catch up quickly with those beginning earlier. Thus in certain circumstances it may be more economical to capitalize on the superior cognitive and metalinguistic skills of older learners, especially when the second language is introduced through formal instruction in the school and when grammatical accuracy rather than communicative fluency is stressed.

I should note here that I am not arguing that second-language learning in older children and adults is necessarily *qualitatively* different from language learning in younger children. Young children also approach second-language learning by using the information-processing capacities and mnemonic devices at their disposal. They build on what they know about language and on the strategies and tactics that they have accumulated through experience with language. The point is simply that the adolescent and the adult possess more developed processing capacities and this makes their experience different and, in certain respects, potentially easier than may be true for a young child.

Having said all this, what can one conclude about similarities and differences in first- and second-language learning? It depends, I have been arguing, on the age of the learners, on their cognitive abilities, and on situational demands. A good working hypothesis, it seems to me, is that the younger the learner and the more the situation is focused on communication, the more likely the learner is to resort to universal (possibly language-specific) strategies common to first- and second-language learning and the more similar the products. The older the learner and the more situational demands require specific problem-solving tactics, the more variation one will find in second-language learning and the more the product will differ from that of first-language learning.

REFERENCES

1. McLaughlin, B. 1978. Second Language Acquisition in Childhood. Erlbaum. Hillsdale, N.J.
2. Slobin, D. I. 1971. Developmental psycholinguistics. In A Survey of Linguistic Science. W. O. Dingwall, Ed.: 298–410. University of Maryland Press. College Park, Md.
3. Ruke-Dravina, V. 1967. Mehrsprachigkeit im Vorschulalter. Gleerup. Lund, Sweden.
4. Aikyama, M. 1976. Negative questions in Japanese-speaking, English-speaking, and Japanese-English bilingual children. Pap. Rep. Child Lang. Dev. 12: 23–30.
5. Ravem, R. 1974. The development of Wh- questions in first and second language learners. In Error Analysis: Perspectives on Second Language Acquisition. J. Richards, Ed.: 124–155. Longmans. London, England.
6. Dato, D. P. 1970. American Children's Acquisition of Spanish Syntax in the Madrid Environment: Preliminary Edition. U.S. Office of Education, Institute of International Studies. Washington, D.C. (Project No. 3036. Contract No. OEC 2–7–002637.)
7. Wode, H. 1976. Developmental principles in naturalistic L2 acquisition. Arbeitspapiere zum Spracherwerb, Englisches Seminar der Universitaet Kiel.
8. Vihman, M. M. & B. McLaughlin. Bilingualism and second language acquisition in preschool children. In Progress in Cognitive Development Research. C. J. Brainerd, Ed. Springer-Verlag. New York, N.Y. (In press.)
9. Hakuta, K. 1976. A case study of a Japanese child learning English as a second language. Lang. Learn. 26: 321–351.
10. Dulay, H. & M. Burt. 1975. Creative construction in second language learning and teaching. In New Directions in Second Language Learning, Teaching, and Bilingual Education. M. Burt & H. Dulay, Eds.: 21–32. TESOL. Washington, D.C.
11. Fathman, A. 1975. The relationship between age and second language productive ability. Lang. Learn. 25: 245–253.
12. Kessler, C. & I. Idar. 1977. The acquisition of English syntactic structures by a Vietnamese child. Paper presented at the Los Angeles Second Language Research Forum.
13. Rosansky, E. 1976. Methods and morphemes in second language acquisition research. Lang. Learn. 26: 409–425.
14. Andersen, R. 1978. An implicational model for second language research. Lang. Learn. 28: 1–35.
15. Meisel, J., H. Clahsen & M. Pienemann. 1980. On determining developmental stages in natural second language acquisition. Stud. Second Lang. Acquisition. (In press.)
16. Pienemann, M. 1979. Der Zweitspracherwerb auslaendischer Arbeiterkinder. Ph.D. Dissertation. Wuppertal, Federal Republic of Germany.
17. McLaughlin, B. 1978. The monitor model: some methodological considerations. Lang. Learn. 28: 309–332.
18. Seliger, H. 1980. Strategy and tactic in second language acquisition. Paper presented at Los Angeles Second Language Research Forum.

19. DONALDSON, M. 1978. Children's Minds: 87–88. Fontana/Croom Helm. London, England.
20. CALFEE, R. & S. FREEDMAN. 1980. Understanding and comprehending. Paper presented at Center for Study of Reading. Urbana, Ill.
21. CUMMINS, J. 1980. The construct of language proficiency in bilingual education. Paper presented at the Georgetown Round Table on Languages and Linguistics. Washington, D.C.
22. ERVIN-TRIPP, S. 1974. Is second language learning like the first? TESOL Q. 8: 111–127.
23. SELINKER, L., M. SWAIN & G. DUMAS. 1975. The interlanguage hypothesis extended to children. Lang. Learn. 25: 139–152.
24. FELIX, S. W. 1980. The effect of formal instruction on second language acquisition. Paper presented at the Los Angeles Second Language Research Forum.
25. PAULSTON, C. B. 1977. Research. In Bilingual Education: Current Perspectives: Linguistics. Center for Applied Linguistics. Arlington, Va.
26. SELIGER, H. 1975. Inductive method and deductive method in language teaching: a re-examination. IRAL 13: 1–18.
27. FATHMAN, A. & L. PRECUP. 1980. Influences of age and setting on second language oral proficiency. Paper presented at Los Angeles Second Language Research Forum.
28. KRASHEN, S., M. LONG & R. SCARCELLA. 1979. Age, rate, and eventual attainment in second language acquisition. TESOL Q. 13: 573–582.
29. SNOW, C. & M. HOEFNAGEL-HÖHLE. 1978. The critical period for language acquisition: evidence from second language learning. Child Dev. 49: 1114–1128.
30. BURSTALL, C. 1975. Primary French in the balance. Educ. Res. 17: 193–198.

SOCIAL PROCESS IN FIRST- AND SECOND-LANGUAGE LEARNING *

Susan Ervin-Tripp

Psychology Department
University of California
Berkeley, California 94720

TRANSFER

What is the relationship between first- and second-language learning? When we say they are alike, or not alike, what is it that we compare? The most common comparisons are between *outcomes,* such as errors, or orders of acquisition in which certain skills reach a criterion of correctness.[3,6] Since the order of acquisition is a complex outcome of many factors, all must be alike to generate identical orders. A second domain of comparison might be *conditions* for successful learning. These might be such factors as those discussed in the research on mother-tongue acquisition—such as hearing the target language while the meaning is made clear by the context, hearing it in reduced input forms, hearing enough repetition to allow discovery of patterns.[8] A third topic of comparison might be *inferred cognitive strategies,* such as those discussed by Slobin as "operating principles." [19] It is quite possible that the strategies could be the same, and yet the outcomes not be the same because of the intervention of prior knowledge to accelerate some learning in the case of second language.

There is no reason to believe that the language-acquisition system that is effective in mother-tongue development suddenly atrophies; indeed, recent data suggest that adolescents learn extremely rapidly.[22] To test, however, whether there is any specific effect of prior learning requires focused and specific studies. For example, one of Slobin's operating principles proposes "pay attention to the ends of words" and hunt for meaning correlates.[20] This principle derives from the finding that simple suffix information for case, not confused by gender or other "noise," is acquired extremely quickly and almost without error by Turkish children, more quickly than even case information indicated by word order in English.[20] If the same principle applies in second-language learning, we would predict that regardless of first language, Turkish case suffixes should be learned rapidly.

But even the strongest advocate of a common language-acquisition system for both first and second language would have to admit that the starting points are not the same. Learners of second languages, for example, already know how to converse, and they know how to classify.

* The data reported in this paper come from Reference 10 and from two currently funded projects: NSF BNS-78-26539 and NIE 6-79-0118. A few examples are from my own earlier research in France.

0077–8923/81/0379–0033 $01.75/2 © 1981, NYAS

A baby learning language has to learn what to talk about. A baby has to learn the categories that words represent. The baby has to learn how to participate in conversational turns, what to do with language to symbolize and change the world. But a second-language learner already knows how to do these things. In the simplest sense, the second-language learner could be said to be learning new forms for old conversational uses and ideas.

SEMANTICS

Mother-tongue learners spend a fair amount of time sorting out categories, learning names and boundaries. In the texts we have, children are told that superheroes are not dolls in toy stores, that coats are not jackets. In each of these cases, the learner has extended a frequent name to represent a larger category. In each case the correction supplies not the name of the larger category but the taxonomic contrast, creating a new boundary.

We know that second-language learners already have preorganized categories. The second-language learner relabels at first, retaining the well-structured system of categories for things, actions, attributes, relations, and abstractions. We would be quite surprised if a Spanish speaker learning English kept referring to both dogs and cats as "cats" without discomfort, on occasions when the norms of usage are specificity. Yet older learners, with their well-developed semantic system, have a significant advantage *if there is a good cultural match*.

But of course we know that cultures *don't* always have the same categories, and that new boundaries sometimes must be learned.[4,8] Categories learned by verbal context or dependent on social assumptions are the most different between cultures, the slowest to be changed, and the most common in adult speech. Renegotiation of meaning will be the easiest for the observable referents, if they are talked about. Youngsters can alter their semantic system readily because of the frequency of these here-and-now referents, and the directive and expressive words of play.

Particularly problematic for older learners are the general semantic orientations made obligatory by certain languages. These appear to be difficult to restructure after childhood—definiteness, aspect, gender, arbitrary classifiers. Whether this is a critical period of linguistic or cognitive development is unknown.

CONVERSATIONAL ROUTINES

Semantic mismatches and relearning have been discussed in the classic linguistic studies of bilingual interference. Less familiar is the analogous domain of sociolinguistic knowledge and conversational structure. Conversation and discourse also involve latent structure, categories, background assumptions. As in semantic development, the change in conversational skills between ages two and five is very great. Even those rudimentary skills of a two-year-old to attract attention, establish a topic, respond to check questions, state what is wanted, are realized at a later age by more elaborate and varied tactics. The ability to create and sustain elaborate role playing is absent at two but by five reveals stylistic subtlety and range.[1] The intricate web of relevance, allowing focused elliptical replies and extensions of the partner's speech, grows greatly at four and five.

What happens when a beginner enters a conversational exchange? Is there a transfer of conversational skills fleshed out with the available linguistic resources? or must the learner start over? This is the principle issue of this section, going further with some arguments in the important work of Linnakylä.[16]

Let us take a simple example. A newcomer to France readily notices the words spoken at greetings and farewells: *salut, bonjour, au revoir.* If these words alone were mapped onto the English *hi, goodbye, so long,* the result would be defective, since address terms are obligatory in polite greetings to adult strangers or superiors, not optional as in English. In addition, French friends shake hands at meetings and farewells, all around the group. Teenage girls exchange cheek pecks, boys handshakes with face averted. These gestural exchanges are learned very rapidly by newcomers.

What can we learn from this example? (a) Greetings and farewells are among the earliest, most transparent social-exchange events, among the first learned by children even in the first year, since their cue is the arrival or departure of a person. (b) Reciprocal forms are easier to learn than adjacency pairs that are complementary, since they can be acquired by repetition and initiated by a native speaker who provides a model. (c) Invariant parts of formulae are easier to produce than variants requiring semantic choice—in this example, the address term that calls on the complex structure of the social rules of address. (d) Optional items in first-language structures that are obligatory and invariant in the second language will be learned idiomatically as part of the second-language formula. Optional items that are variable (such as the address term) will be regarded as optional by learners. Exceptions will be situation-specific cases like "bonjour madame" to the teacher, which will generalize to similar adults.

The parallel to first-language learning is clear: obviousness of the appropriate situation, ease of reciprocal forms and gestures, semantic decision in address terms. But the transfer of the optionality of address is a specifically second-language issue. And there are latent issues of transfer in who and when to greet, in who initiates, and certainly in the semantics of address.

A GENERAL FRAMEWORK

Let us step back for a moment. In examining the conversational basis of mother-tongue acquisition, we need to take into account (a) the learner's interaction network—to whom the learner listens and talks; (b) the speech activities and genres in which the learner participates; (c) local discourse structure—relations between nearby utterances; (d) social variation to which the learner is exposed, such as bilingualism and dialect or register contrast; and (e) beliefs, explicit teaching, and prescriptive attitudes about language.† But if we turn to second-language acquisition, we find exactly the same set of considerations to be fundamental to understanding acquisition. While individual and cultural variations in the development of the mother tongue have been noticed increasingly, it appears that second-language learning is even more varied. The reason lies in the greater diversity in interaction networks and speech activities of second-language learners—with whom, how often, and for what purpose the target language is depended on uniquely for understanding of what is happening. A timid second-language learner, especially one out of school, may avoid even hearing the second language. An infant may be silent, but with rare exceptions can't help hearing the mother tongue in obvious and repetitive circumstances.

Local Discourse

Children must learn to get into and maintain interaction if they want to play effectively. Local discourse development in novice second-language learners, as pointed out by Hatch, is strikingly parallel to early mother-tongue use.[12] We find child second-language learners using *calls* or *attention getters* within the first month to establish talk. The means are *names, lookit, hey,* French *regarde, ici.* Strage and I found the French examples within the first month of learning. Fillmore found the English examples in the first month for four out of five Spanish speakers; the fifth did not initiate interaction until the second month, when he used these forms.[10]

Repairs are more interesting, because mother-tongue learners respond to repetition requests early, though in my data, four children did not initiate repair requests until near the end of the third year. Yet Fillmore, in her second-language sample of five-year-olds, found repetition requests in the first month: "Huh? What? What you say?"[10] And later, clarification requests, as in the following: ‡

(1) Spanish 6 years old, 8 months in English:
        T: Well, hurry up, cause we're gonna have to go.
            Put these things up, right away.
        Sp: *Now?*

---

† To be discussed in Reference 21.
‡ In the examples, Spanish 6 years, 7 months in English (N) means that child N is a Spanish-speaking 6-year-old with 7 months of school English. In the dialogue, S: and E: refer to the speaker's dominant language, T: to an adult at school.
*** Identifies overlaps or interruptions.

Adjacency pairs refer to utterances that are yoked, often next to each other, but sometimes separated by clarification requests or other disruptions. Examples are question-answer, order-acknowledgment, permission request–permission, summons-reply. Questions and replies were found within the first month formulae of all of the children in Fillmore's study of five-year-olds, for instance: "what happen?" "I know," "I dunno," "all right," "wait." [10] All the children knew "I dunno." [10]

Patsy Lightbown compared first- and second-language acquisition.[15] She pointed out that first-language research—such as the studies of Ervin-Tripp and Tyack and Ingram [7,25]—had shown that locative, person, and thing answers (as to *where, who,* and *what* questions) preceded time, manner, and cause replies. She found no such order in second-language *comprehension,* implying that the result is based on cognitive development. This finding fits well with the similar result for Genie, the child who learned English as a first language during adolescence.

On the other hand, Lightbown reports that the order in *production* was similar in the second language, that is, questions of place and thing were first.[15] Questions of *who,* then *why,* then *when* and *how* emerged after. Swain and Felix found similar orders.[9,24] Lightbown noted that while the words used were acquired in this order, conceptually the children sometimes tried to express the more advanced category with the question-word vocabulary already at hand. What we see, then, is semantic and functional transfer from the knowledge the child already has, but a slow formal development as vocabulary is acquired to express what the child knows.

(2) Two anglophone six-year-olds playing memory, matching pairs in scrambled cards with face down.
   a. *Ça, c'est quoi? Ah. Ça c'est pas ça.* (turns card)
   [This one? It's what? Ah. This, it's not it.]

(3) Anglophone playing teacher. 7 years 2 months. (N)
   a. *C'est quoi, le nom à toi?* (It's what, the name of yours?)
   b. French: Pourquoi? E: *Parce que* . . . [Because . . .]
   c. Spanish 5 years old, 7 months in English. (M)
      Dat whistle, what is for?

In Fillmore and Strage's studies, questions of surprising length appeared within the first two or three months. Some were restricted situationally, like "Hey, what a your name" and "What time you my house," which can't be used repeatedly. Others were important in keeping the conversation moving, like "What happened" and "Whatsa matter." In the first months, there were "What do you think," "Hey, what's going on here," and "How do you do these." And by seven months in English, we can find not only complex questions but complex inferred replies:

(4) Where'd you find it? (M)
   Sp: *Ah, Vera give it to me.*

SPEECH ACTS

The most dramatic contrast in the first- and second-language conversations can be seen in the wider range of interpersonal functions in the older second-language-learning children. Because they are aware of more complex ways to interact, because they are familiar with the structure of games, and because many play cues are nonverbal, these children can discover the meaning of the many forms they hear repeated during play, as in (21) and (22) below.§

In first-language learners between two and two-and-a-half years of age, we can find examples in which children point out, name, state, describe, deny, comment about their own ongoing activity, and mark completion of acts (there!). They express wants and commands; they boast, claim, offer, prohibit, reject, and refuse. They request, correct, question names and places, and acknowledge. As their speech develops, the acts become more varied both in type and in expression. In addition to all of these acts, in the second-language texts for the first seven months, we also find more complicated acts than would occur in children of two. They *persuade:*

(5) Spanish 5 years, 7 months in English. (Sy)
    S: (E is getting into doctor kit) *Don't get it.*
    E: Mine
    S: *OK, you get one. Oh, getta glasses.*
    E: No, I need em.
    S: *I need em, too.*
    E: Both need em.

In such conversations, the English- and Spanish-speaking partners appear well matched in the level of play and talk, probably in part because of accommodation to the new learner.
The children can *joke:*

(6) Spanish 6 years old, 8 months in English. (R)
    S: *My name is Elba* (giggles)
    E: My name is Sabrina! (giggles) (has switched their names)
    T: Y'all are just making fun now.

---

§ After his first few weeks in a French school, my six-year-old described (in English) to me a complex new playground game involving many conditionals. Since his French contained only a few isolated words and formulas, and I assumed such learning was through verbal instruction, I was very puzzled. The French semiotician, Greimas, pointed out that games are structurally alike, so that on the basis of relatively little observation my child could have induced the system. This knowledge not only permitted him to play, but also to learn the relevant language. Now, after a year of taping language learning in this age group during games, I understand what Greimas meant. The game structure has to be induced, but it then becomes available as a here-and-now referent for talk. Besides, an active learner can negotiate the game structure if the group is small enough.

They can *offer praise:*

> (7) Spanish 5 years old, 7 months in English. (M)
>   a. *It's pretty things in here!*
>   b. *How pretty she look with that!* (shoes)

They can *give warnings:*

> (8) English 5 years old, 1 month. (French context) (C)
>   *Attention. Attention, Arthur!* (to baby) [Watch out]

They can *plan:*

> (9) Spanish 5 years, 7 months in English. (M)
>   S: *You gonna put it over here?*
>   E: Yeah.
>   S: *And nobody can play.* (with play shoes)

They announce intentions:

> (10) Chinese 5 years, 7 months in English.
>   C: *Miss Smith, I'm getting out of here.* (climbing away from
>   teacher's group)

They solicit more complex information than do two-year-olds:

> (11) Spanish 5 years, 7 months in English. (M)
>   *How does shiu work?* (A toy spring, a Slinky®)
>   *Where you buy all dese things? I gunna tell my mom to buy
>   me one of these.*
> (12) Spanish 5 years, 7 months in English. (Sy)
>   *Who lives in there?* (empty cage)

They can ask permission indirectly:

> (13) Spanish 5 years, 7 months in English. (M)
>   *Those things are put in there. Those things are yours? Or you
>   put it to play?*

They can *contradict* by questioning assumptions. Keller-Cohen, Chalmer,
and Remler provide other examples.[14]

> (14) Spanish 5, 8 months in English. (Sh)
>   E: Go on. Here's a place. We could play telephone.
>   S: *No. It's no play telephone.*
>   E: Is this a play telephone?
>   T: It's not a play telephone. It's real, but there's no plug.

They can give explanations:

> (15) Spanish 5 years, 5 months in English. (N)
>   E: I like your earrings, Nora.
>   S: *Mm, and I, and I, and I, like your hair, because your hair is
>   beautiful. Looky, look here.* (twists E's curls)

(16) Spanish 5 years, 5 months in English. (N)
   T: Hey, there was a tamalada here at school. Did your mommy come?
   S: *It was great. My mommy was not there because she don't like to go.*

If they try more complex speech acts, they sometimes cannot carry them out because of lack of linguistic resources. Lightbown mentioned that in asking temporal questions, children might use *where,* as in "où est ton fête?" (Where's your birthday party?).[15]

These limitations can come about because an adult pushes too far, as in the following:

(17) Spanish 6 years, 8 months in English. (R)
   T: Is he a good driver?
   S: *No.*
   T: Why not?
   S: *Cause he's going uh uh uh.*
   T: Cause why, why isn't he a good driver?
   S: *Cause he drink, cause he go boom.*
   An cause he cruzo.

SPEECH ACTIVITIES AND GENRES

The most persuasive indicator of the marked difference in the abilities between a young mother-tongue learner and a five-year-old is in the structure of play. The older learners are able to organize play, to negotiate, to set the stage, and to enact a variety of fuller activities, such as teaching a lesson, making a pretend phone call, playing a game, telling a story, playing with a puppet, role playing, or arguing. In enacting these activities, the children's discourse skills were far more complex than those of children at the comparable level of mother-tongue formal knowledge.

Here is a child organizing a game of doctor-patient:

(18) Spanish 5 years, 7 months in English. (C)
   S: *Here. Oh, it's a doctor toy. Look. Hey, look . . .*
   E: What's this for?
   S: *I dunno.*
   E: What over here.
   S: *Oh look. Enrique. Hey, lemme see you tongue.*
   Lemme see you tongue. Lemme see.
   E: (You're dumb/your tongue)
   S: *Gimme your feet.* (holding hammer)
   E: Ouch. Now, lemme do you. (hits S's knee and both laugh)

The children are able to negotiate roles and claims to objects, an important facet of play for youngsters of three to seven. Strage has other examples too.[23]

(19) Spanish 5 years, 7 months in English. (Sy)
  S: *That not mine. Yours. That for boys, not for girls.* (robot)
  E: That for boys. Hey, lookit this.
  S: *This for girls, this for girl, huh?* (doctor kit).
(20) Spanish 5 years, 8 months in English. (Sh)
  E: Gonna sit at the table.
  S: *Yeah.*
  E: What do you wanna eat tonight?
  S: *I'm the mother. I'm the mother.*
  E: Pretend you're the sister. You're helping me.
  S: *Yeh.*

They rapidly learn the special vocabulary of games. Here is a vivid board game of soccer, full of excitement:

(21) English 11 years, 1 month in French. (C)
  E: *Bravo, très bien, dégage. Oh bravo! Bien joué!*
   [Bravo, very good, clear. Oh bravo. Well played.]
(22) English 11 years, 2 months in French. (C)
  F: Bon, allez, une touche pour les bleus.
   [All right! Go, go! A goal for the blues.]
  E: *Un zéro pour Marcel et moi.*
   [A zero for Marcel and me.]
  F: Un centre et les rouges qui ont la balle.
   [A center and the reds have the ball.]
  E: *Toi devant.*
   [You're ahead.]

At this age, the children are capable of complicated role playing. But role playing usually is highly verbal and depends on linguistic skill and formulaic repertoire:

(23) Spanish 5 years, 7 months in English. (Sy)
  S: *I get the bowls out.*
  E: You cook, right? You cook. Where's the table?
   We need one . . .
  S: *This is for the food.*
  E: Oh. This is, too. This is for cake . . .
  S: *Spoon. Spoon. Fork.*
  E: Coffee.
  S: *I need a spoon . . . I making egg.*
  E: Huh?
  S: *I making egg.*
  E: Eggs?
  S: *Eggs. Look the eggs. Hey, you don't need this.*
   You don't need this. This is for the cake.
  E: I know.
  S: *This is for the eggs.*

In example (23) there has been a successful collaboration, ending with a presentation of cake and coffee by S and a discussion about the meal. The correction by E of *egg* was established by S as a new version of her play assertions. Here we can see how an active learner can get information by engaging peers in play, and getting their help to enlarge their knowledge.

In the following example, a child who had been in France only a few months was able to set up and manage successfully the enactment of a classroom role-playing scene, playing the role of teacher and teaching commutation. The scene ends with physical punishment, which she had seen in the French village school.

(24) English 7 years, 2 months in French. (N)

    E: *C'est moi la maîtresse. Alors, excusez moi, tu viens ici . . . Derrière les enfants. Tu viens ici.* (Giggles, shows seat in front of her. She has slate.) *Et quoi, C'est quoi, toi. C'est quoi, le nom à toi?*
    [I'm the teacher then, pardon me, you come here? Behind the children. You come here. And what, it's what, you, it's what, the name of yours?]

    F: Stéphanie . . . (big negotiation on names)

    E: *Sept. Attends, attends, c'est ça, bon. Mais deux fois sept égale—* [Seven. Wait, wait, that's it, good. But two times seven equals—]

    F: Quatorze. [14.]

    E: *Ou?* [Or?]

    F: Sept fois sept— [7×7—]

    E: *Sept fois deux égale quatorze . . .* [$7 \times 2 = 14$ . . .]

    E: *Mais, tu comprends, eh?* [But you understand, hunh?]

    F: Oui.

    E: *Non, tu viens là! Tu, tu, tu attends là. Viens par là. Stéphanie, Stéphanie, allez vite. À toi. À toi. Non!*
    [No, you come here! You, you, you wait here. Come here! Stephanie, Stephanie, come quickly. It's your turn. No!]
    (runs after her with a little stick while both laugh)

The child-teacher in (24) already knew a good deal about classroom structure from English. She adopted linking forms comparable to English "okay, now, good" that can initiate new units.[18] She knew eliciting tricks, such as unfinished sentences and rising "Or?" Yet the assembly of these parts is new. As Andersen found, role playing is a combination of stereotyped, imitated, and invented parts.[1]

The bare bones of a sequential structure are revealed in numerous play phone conversations of the five-year-olds:

(25) Spanish 5 years, 7 months in English. (Y)
    a. S: *Hello.*
    b. E: What's you doin?

    c. S: *Fine.*
    d. E: My mommy told me to go to school.
    e. S: *Me too . . .*
    f. E: Okay, bye. I'll call you back tomorrow.
    g. S: *Okay, bye.*

In this conversation, only the rudiments are present: greetings (a); opener (b–c) [two possibilities: adult "How are you?" or "How you doing?—Fine" versus child "What're you doing?" (which has no fixed reply)]; conversation (d–e); and farewell (f–g). While E does more initiating except in the greeting, S clearly knows a set of appropriate replies.

How this structure is taught is revealed in the following from Fillmore: [10]

   (26) Spanish 5 years, 5 months in English. (N)
     a. S: *Hello. Come to my house, please.*
     b. E: Who are you?
     c. S: *Nora!*
     d. E: Nora, you've got to say, "What are you doing?"
     e. S: *What are you doing?*
     f. E: Making cookies. What are you doing?
     g. S: *Making cookies, too.*
     h. E: Okay, bye.
     i. S: *Bye.*

In this text, Nora moved directly from the greeting into a conversation or even a precloser in (a) without any opener. Her partner corrects her in (d), which allows a successful exchange since the conversation then can be about the reply to (e). The fact that the child opener "What you doin?" is open allows it to lead to conventional conversational content. I will end with an example that makes clear that the level of skill displayed by the children in English still is restricted by language. After numerous offences, C stole the class crackers and he was undergoing group criticism most of the day, direct and indirect. At the time the first switch from Cantonese to English occurred, there had been a 15-minute dispute in progress.

   (27) Chinese 5 years, 8 months in English (3 Chinese speakers, KG, KH, WF)
     A. *I hit you. You don't keep me orange* [marker] *this time go to outside—I hit you.*
     B. *I tell my ma—tonight my father coming. I tell my father hit you.*
     C. *My father is mmmm.* (makes fist)
     B. *My father is s—*
     A. ****You father big big big big big!* (pretends drinking from bottle)
     B. (giggles) *My father, bigger your father.*

C. *You father big big big big big.* (giggles)
B. *My father, uh, bigger you father.*
C. *My father my father like that!* (stands up, reaches for height)
B. ****My father—*
B. *My father stronger your father.*
C. *My father like that!* (arms wide).
C. *My father—*
B. ****Hunh-unh! My father—*
C. ****Hunh-unh! My father stronger, faster.*
D. (in Cantonese to C) Have you gone to the balloon store?
C. *Hunh-unh!*
B. *Don't talk for—I hit you!*

At this point, the argument had not yet run its course and was escalated in Cantonese until B left:

B. I'm gonna tell your father that you steal things.
C. When have I stolen things?
B. You, you stole Arthur's getting married thing [ring] . . .
C. Hunh-unh.
B. You stole, you stole my car and give it to Arthur.
C. Your car! (sarcastic)
B. You, I hit you. Hit you! When we go outside, I'm gonna hit you. (pointing to his forehead)
C. Well, you'll have to run very fast.
B. When you grow up and you steal, your wife isn't going to like you. (taps table, then his arm)
A. C. dropped in the ocean and no one helps him. C. dropped in the ocean and he doesn't know how to swim! (repeats about eight times, showing picture of event)
B. Yehehehe (taunting tune, laughs, rolls eyes, sticks out tongue)
A. He dropped in the ocean and he can't swim.
B. No one is going to play with you.
C. So you don't play with me—who cares?
B. I'm not gonna play with you. I'm not gonna play with you any more.
C. Who cares if you don't play with me. (cocks head)
B. *So* [English], I'm not gonna play with you.
C. So big deal, so what if you don't play with me. I'll just play with my friends.
B. What friends? Your friends are damned friends.
C. I've got friends. My friend is my big brother.
B. Your friend is your big brother. What kind of friend is a brother! (waggling a finger before C)
C. Big brothers are friends. (B takes her things and stomps off)

The structure of this argument can be compared with the relatively simple and repetitive exchanges of two-year-olds observed by Keenan and those reported by Brenneis and Lein in children at school age.[2,13] The conceptual difference is obvious, both in terms of complexity and in the culture-relevant content and the reference to specific past events. The syntactic demands in English were for comparatives. The Chinese statements make conditional predictions. Why the language switch? The reasons might be syntactic or they might be rhetorical, the threat of ostracism being more Chinese.¶

CONCLUSIONS

The argument in this paper is a simple one. New learners gain significant time advantages by assuming semantic and discourse similarity. They come to a new language assuming that they can learn new names for old categories, and that they can carry on the same kinds of activities and the same kinds of conversational exchanges in the new language.

The evidence that the older learners bring their older conversational knowledge to bear, has been a series of examples (but without the examples from two-year-olds, for which there was not enough space). These examples show that the children use more mature speech acts than do two-year-olds and more complex and indirect versions. They reveal that the genres and speech activities that the older children construct are closer to those of their age-mates than to children at the same linguistic stage.

But linguistic constraints must play a role. We need to explore the specific knowledge needed for the activities into which the learners enter. We might find, for instance, that the language needed for a soccer game (or an assembly line) is very limited, that it is sufficiently simple structurally to be learned fast from its match with action, and that its learning has relatively little generalizability. In the argument (27) we saw that constraints on linguistic complexity might shut the learner out from the full expression of intentions, ideas, and feelings. But of course this is precisely the impetus that can drive new learning. The relation between knowledge of social frames, cognitive growth, and the linguistic means that the learner can deploy is what motivates rapid learning in both the first and second languages.

I argued earlier that the basic reason for the great individual difference in success in second-language learning is the wide range in speech activities that different learners enter. It is clear from our examples that the activity structure and the role of language in activity probably change with age. For example, there is a powerful shift in the structure and content of peer

¶ For further discussion of the relation between language and content in bilinguals see Reference 8, and for rhetorical uses of switching see Reference 11.

interaction at adolescence that may have strong effects on linguistic learning from this source.

The learner's familiarity with complex trajectories of activity and interaction allows recognition of meaning from a few cues, and therefore quick learning of relatively appropriate meanings for complex situated formulae like "whatsa matter" and "what happened" even within the first month. Peck and Strage have many examples of such learning.[17,23]

Because the learners know more than two-year-olds do, they are able to guess what is going on. They can guess meanings of phrases and, if they are socially active, will try them out. This participation in turn provides them with replies, which are shaped directly by instruction as in (26) or more commonly through accommodation by the partner, who changes speech and actions towards what the learner seems to know. These relevant, tailored replies are the kind of contingent replies that Cazden found most likely to foster development in young children.[5] The learner who launches into age-appropriate exchanges keeps partners, is exposed more quickly to new vocabulary, and negotiates both semantic and pragmatic changes of meaning where old categories and conversational structures don't fit. Thus knowledge of conversation, like knowledge of semantic systems, can give older learners a significant advantage over the novice in the mother tongue.

ACKNOWLEDGMENTS

I am grateful to Lily Fillmore for locating and translating some bilingual examples, as well as for discussion of the issues in the paper, and to Amy Strage for giving detailed criticisms.

REFERENCES

1. ANDERSEN, E. 1977. Learning to speak with style: a study of the sociolinguistic skills of young children. Ph.D. Dissertation. Stanford University. Stanford, Calif.
2. BRENNEIS, D. & L. LEIN. 1979. "You fruithead": a sociolinguistic approach to children's dispute settlement. *In* Child Discourse. C. Mitchell-Kernan & S. Ervin-Tripp, Eds.: 49–66. Academic Press, Inc. New York, N.Y.
3. CANCINO, H., E. J. ROSANSKY & J. H. SCHUMANN. 1975. The acquisition of the auxiliary system by native Spanish speakers. TESOL Q. **9:** 421–430.
4. CATFORD, I. 1963. A Linguistic Theory of Translation. Oxford University Press. London, England.
5. CAZDEN, C. 1965. Environmental assistance to the child's acquisition of grammar. Doctoral Dissertation. Graduate School of Education. Harvard University. Cambridge, Mass.
6. DULAY, H. C. & M. K. BURT. 1972. Goofing: an indicator of children's second language learning strategies. Lang. Learn. **22:** 235–252.
7. ERVIN-TRIPP, S. M. 1970. Discourse agreement: how children answer questions. *In* Cognition and Language Learning. R. Hayes, Ed.: 79–108. John Wiley & Sons, Inc. New York, N.Y.

8. ERVIN-TRIPP, S. M. 1973. Language Acquisition and Communicative Choice. Stanford University Press. Stanford, Calif.
9. FELIX, S. 1977. Wh-pronouns in first and second language acquisition. Linguistiche Ber. **43:** 43–59.
10. FILLMORE, L. W. 1976. The second time around: cognitive and social strategies in second language learning. Doctoral Dissertation. Stanford University. Stanford, Calif.
11. GUMPERZ, J. & E. HERNANDEZ-CHAVEZ. 1971. Bilingualism, bidialectalism, and classroom interaction. *In* The Function of Language in the Classroom. C. Cazden, D. Hymes & V. John, Eds.: 235–283. Teachers College Press. New York, N.Y.
12. HATCH, E. 1978. Discourse analysis and second language acquisition. *In* Second Language Acquisition. E. Hatch, Ed.: 401–435. Newbury House. Rowley, Mass.
13. KEENAN, E. O. 1974. Conversational competence in children. J. Child Lang. **1:** 163–184.
14. KELLER-COHEN, D., K. C. CHALMER & J. E. REMLER. 1979. The development of discourse negation in the nonnative child. *In* Developmental Pragmatics. E. Ochs & B. Schieffelin, Eds.: 305–324. Academic Press, Inc. New York, N.Y.
15. LIGHTBOWN, P. M. 1978. Question form and question function in the speech of young French L_2 learners. *In* Aspects of Bilingualism. Michel Paradis, Ed.: 25–42. Hornbeam Press. Columbia, S.C.
16. LINNAKYLÄ, P. 1980. "Hi Superman: What is most functional English for a Finnish five-year-old." J. Pragmatics **4:** 367–392.
17. PECK, S. 1978. Child-child discourse in second language acquisition. *In* Second Language Acquisition. E. Hatch, Ed.: 383–400. Newbury House. Rowley, Mass.
18. SINCLAIR, J. & R. M. COULTHARD. 1975. Towards an Analysis of Discourse: The English Used by Teachers and Pupils. Oxford University Press. London, England.
19. SLOBIN, D. I. 1973. Cognitive prerequisites for the development of grammar. *In* Studies of Child Language Development. C. A. Ferguson & D. I. Slobin, Eds.: 175–208. Holt, Rinehart & Winston. New York, N.Y.
20. SLOBIN, D. I. Universal and particular in the acquisition of language: *In* Language Acquisition: State of the Art. L. R. Gleitman & E. Wanner, Eds. Cambridge University Press. Cambridge, Mass. (In press.)
21. SLOBIN, D. I., Ed. Crosslinguistic Studies of Child Language. Lawrence Earlbaum. Hillsdale, N.J. (In preparation.)
22. SNOW, C. & M. HOEFNAGEL-HÖHLE. 1978. Age differences in second language acquisition. *In* Second Language Acquisition. E. Hatch, Ed.: 333–346. Newbury House. Rowley, Mass.
23. STRAGE, A. 1980. Communicative and analytic strategies in naturalistic second language acquisition. Paper presented at the Fifth Annual Conference on Language Development, Boston, Mass., October.
24. SWAIN, M. 1972. Bilingualism as a first language. Doctoral Dissertation. University of California. Irvine, Calif.
25. TYACK, D. & D. INGRAM. 1977. Children's production and comprehension of questions. J. Child Lang. **4:** 211–224.

DIFFERENCES AND SIMILARITIES BETWEEN FIRST-AND SECOND-LANGUAGE ACQUISITION: GENERAL DISCUSSION

Moderator: Charles A. Ferguson

Department of Linguistics
Stanford University
Stanford, California 94305

H. W. SELIGER (*Queens College, Flushing, N.Y.*): My question is addressed to Dr. Lambert. Cummins has written about the idea of a threshold theory for second-language acquisition, which would seem to predict that certain kinds of children would have cognitive deficits if they had not fully developed cognitively in at least one language before the onset of a second language. Could you comment on that?

W. E. LAMBERT (*McGill University, Montreal, Quebec, Canada*): You're referring to James Cummins' research. I think that there's both a fascination and a practical importance to what Jim Cummins is advocating. For me, it means that there is a responsibility to be met; that we not let home languages slide away and become, if you like, subtracted from the lives of the children involved. It looks to me as if Cummins' research— and others related to it—indicates the responsibility educators have to continue conceptual development along the lines begun with the infant's first language. This is particularly important for those who are members of ethnolinguistic-minority groups. Once the conceptual language is brought up to threshold, then a second language can be added comfortably and without harm.

The contrast that I am drawing here is one between those who are privileged because they are sure that their home language—as in the case of English speakers in North America—will not be replaced or bypassed as a language of conceptual thought, and those who run the risk of having to put their first, concept-laden language aside for a more prestigious or useful national language. In one case, a second language can be added with no trouble because the first language is the language of schooling, with much usefulness and prestige. In the other case, one puts the first language aside in order to learn a second one for schooling and learning. The latter case poses a tremendous handicap.

M. PATKOWSKI (*Hostos Community College, Bronx, N.Y.*): Did I understand you to say, Dr. McLaughlin, that you believe long-term proficiency is higher for those who acquire second languages as adults?

B. McLAUGHLIN (*Stevenson College, University of California, Santa Cruz, Calif.*): What I said is that I think the evidence cited in the report by Krashin, Long, and Scarcella [see Reference 28 of Dr. McLaughlin's paper] doesn't prove the opposite hypothesis, the younger-is-better notion.

In fact it seems to me, looking at the data from the Snow and Hoefnagle-Höhle study, if anything, the older learners (12–15 year age group) do better [see Table II in Reference 29].

M. PATKOWSKI: Snow's study included an interval of about one year; that is not long-term research.

B. McLAUGHLIN: Right, but the older learners attained a ceiling of almost 95% proficiency in syntax and morphology.

H. WODE (*University of Kiel, Kiel, Federal Republic of Germany*): Dr. Ervin-Tripp, you have convincingly illustrated that learners can manage to get through a great variety of situations and that they do so by applying various techniques. It seems that these individual techniques are closely linked to the respective situations. My question relates to the learner utterances and the processing that they result from. Do the learner structures, for example, the interrogative structures, found in some situations differ from those found in others? And if so, would you conclude from this that the processing mechanisms used to learn languages differ or do not differ depending on the situation?

S. ERVIN-TRIPP (*University of California, Berkeley, Calif.*): I would say that the critical element is how formulaic, how fixed, language use is in a situation. Structural transfer would probably not take place until there is evidence of analytic rather than formulaic knowledge. For example, if you learn "how are you" in a series of phone conversations, you are unlikely to recombine "how" at first. You may need to hear a variety of contexts of "how" or "how are . . ." to figure out the composition of the phrase. Lily Fillmore's dissertation contains many such examples [see Reference 10 in Dr. Ervin-Tripp's paper]. We do not recognize relationships between structures until we have enough information from a variety of contexts to isolate similarities. So there is continual reorganization, in both first- and second-language learning.

H. WODE: The situations in which people learn languages may differ vastly, almost infinitely. On the other hand, the processing abilities of the human brain are finite. What is the solution? Does this imply that the processing systems and mechanisms differ as a function of the learning situations, or are the processing mechanisms the same but flexible enough to handle differences in the situations? This is the fundamental question about the language-learning capacity of the human.

NEUROPSYCHOLOGICAL ASPECTS OF BILINGUALISM

Marcel Kinsbourne

Eunice Kennedy Shriver Center
for Mental Retardation, Inc.
Harvard University
Waltham, Massachusetts 02254

The types of hypotheses that are formulated and tested against neuropsychological data reflect the investigators' implicit assumptions about how the brain works. As no one knows how the brain works, it can be instructive to see how certain hypotheses have fared. If the facts obstinately fail to conform to expectations, then one at least can make some inferences about how the brain does *not* work. Recent investigations of bilingualism afford such an opportunity.

Second-language (L2) learning differs from first (L1) in that it is superimposed on, and in potential competition with, an already substantially acquired system. Depending on its timing, it may invoke the cognitive skills and strategies proper to a different developmental stage. It may be acquired in a different context and for a different motive. Can all L1-L2 differences be attributed to such experiential factors, or must differences in brain bases also be involved?

People's ability to learn two languages, and use both with "native" or near-"native" ability, offers an opportunity to test several assumptions about how the brain supports cognitive processes. By comparing language lateralization in bilinguals to lateralization in monolinguals, one can determine whether "more" language uses up more, or different, cerebral territory. By comparing lateralization of first and second language in bilinguals, one can attempt to extend the application of the concept of neuroplasticity beyond the phenomena of compensation for nervous-system damage, to those of acquisition of skill by people with intact nervous systems.[19] Does a cerebral territory become committed to an early acquired skill, leaving an alternative rendition of that skill to find a neural substrate elsewhere in the brain? Or does later language learning use different territories for quite another reason: when early language acquisition has failed to occur, causing "disuse atrophy" of the language area, which becomes inhospitable to late efforts to acquire even a first language?

The two substantial sources of evidence derive from (a) observation following hemisphere lesions affecting language in bilinguals (and polylinguals); and (b) measuring (1) behavioral and (2) electrophysiological asymmetries for L1 and L2 in comparison to those found in monolinguals. These will be discussed in detail.

50

0077–8923/81/0379–0050 $01.75/2 © 1981, **NYAS**

Hemisphere-Lesion Effects

Had the literature afforded instances of double dissociation with involvement of one brain area affecting L1 only and another affecting L2 only, the interpretations would be clear. But no such claim has been made, and attempts to establish a different brain base for L1 and L2 therefore necessarily are based on relatively indeterminate grounds. Galloway has commented on a greater relative incidence of aphasia resulting from right-hemisphere damage in bilingual than in monolingual patients (14.6% as compared to the expected 2.4% based on data from Rasmussen and Milner).[9,24] In such cases both L1 and L2 were involved. Galloway's postulate was that—as in left handers, so in bilinguals—language representation is spread thin across both hemispheres. Bilinguals should, therefore, exhibit a higher incidence of aphasia after cortical damage than would monolinguals (as left handers do compared to right handers). Whether this is so remains to be determined.

Gloning and Gloning found three of four left-handed bilinguals who were aphasic to have sustained right-hemisphere damage (this proportion of 75% is higher than the supposed incidence of right-hemisphere language in left handers).[11] They suggested right-hemisphere lateralization of language in bilinguals. But with such a small sample size, the finding could have been fortuitous.

Other illustrations of the differential role of L1 and L2 after brain damage exist: the patient used L1 in one context, L2 in another, even deteriorated in his use of one while recovering the other.[1] These rare patterns do not necessarily call for anatomical theorizing. Where two languages are mingled, this could be due to reduction of language capability to an automatic level: automatic utterance and unattended words are mingled across languages even by some normal bilinguals. There is no need to suppose that some language "switch" is malfunctioning, as there is no need to posit such a switch in the first place. Bilinguals use the language that suits the prevailing context. If a metaphor is called for, that of state dependence is preferable. Depending on context and adaptive need, the bilingual assumes either the L1 or the L2 state.

The bulk of group data from polyglot aphasia support the simple view that the brain base is the same for the first and subsequently acquired languages.[5,12,20] Those findings that deviate could reflect chance effects or measurement error. But it is not impossible that a subgroup of bilinguals exists whose brain organization does differ for L1 and L2. If so, this could be a manifestation of individual variation in anatomy, or perhaps some yet to be discovered organizing principle could predict members of the minority group. A parameter that has been invoked is age of acquisition of L2.[10,30,32]

Although L2 learning may coincide with L1 acquisition or follow it by a variable period of time, we shall adopt Lambert's simplifying dichotomy between "compound" bilinguals who learned L2 early and "coordinate" bilinguals who learned it late.[18] We may now list hypotheses that have been offered:

1. L1 and L2 use the same cerebral territory, which is (a) greater or (b) no greater than that committed to language in monolinguals.
2. L1 and L2 use overlapping territories, with (a) L2 more extensive; (b) L2 not more extensive.
3. L1 and L2 are separate territories, if they are (a) compound; (b) coordinate; or (c) either compound or coordinate.

One can complicate these conjectures even further by entertaining different outcomes for the two sexes.

Clearly, the matrix of possibilities is rich enough to accommodate, in one or another model, virtually every nook and cranny of an investigator's data. Therefore, replication is needed before any divergence from the null hypothesis of "same brain base" is considered seriously for some subgroup of bilinguals. No such replication has been published.

In the case of brain lesions, conclusions have been drawn for differential deficit in L1 and L2 and for differential rate of recovery. Two laws have been offered: by Ribot claiming more resistance to disruption of L1;[25] and by Pitres, claiming more resistance by the currently more habitually used language (be it L1 or L2).[23] The data, highly inconclusive, favor a combination of these two principles. Predominance of recent use outweighs any primacy effect, but some primacy effect perhaps is present also. Methodological difficulties still to be overcome relate to the generally *post hoc* nature of information about relative use of L1 and L2 at different stages of the life span, and factors operating at the time of test. They are:

1. Contextual—that language is favored that generally is used in the patient's vicinity;
2. Instructional—that language is favored in which the patient is given the most remedial help;
3. Emotional—that language is favored that evokes in the patient emotional reactions pertinent to his present context and predicament.

No study claiming a brain-based dissociation between L1 and L2 successfully has held constant all these potentially biasing variables. Certainly, the *differential* vulnerability of L1 and L2, where demonstrable, does not indicate the *dissociation* of separate linguistic brain territories. For such conclusions to be justifiable, one would need additional corroboration, for instance, different aphasic symptoms in each language. One such case has been reported by Albert and Obler and two by Silverberg and Gordon.[1,28] However, in each case the language that the patient knew better (L1) was the one subject to the milder syndrome (Broca's versus Wernicke's aphasia in Albert and Obler's case and in Silverberg and Gordon's case one, and anomic versus global aphasia in Silverberg and Gordon's case two).[1,28] So it remains possible that within a single neural system, a lesion causes less disruption of the more overlearned language (or permits it to recover faster).

The issue of disuse atrophy is raised by the well-publicized case of Genie, whose language acquisition after social isolation up to age 13 seems to be following a normal, albeit slow, course.[6,8] Suggestions that Genie is using the right hemisphere for language functions rely on an inadequate data base of laterality testing. Even if this were true, it happens once or twice for each hundred right handers. In a single case study, one cannot determine whether the lateralization was brought about by the abnormal environment, or represents this particular person's genotype. Buddenhagen reported successful establishment of language in a previously mute, mentally retarded, mongoloid child at age 18.[2] The limited evidence to date does not compel belief in functional "atrophy" of a disused language hemisphere (or, indeed, in the more general notion of a "critical period" for language acquisition, as formulated by Lenneberg; see also Snow and Hoefnagel-Höhle).[19,29]

In contrast to cases published as individual demonstrations, as a general rule both languages suffer proportionately after lateral brain lesions (for example, References 5 and 12). This is consistent with the simple proposition that the same brain territory caters for two languages as caters for one.

Particularly convincing is the negative outcome of Watamori and Sasanuma.[34] They found that Japanese-English bilinguals with left-hemisphere damage suffered comparable aphasic impairments in their two languages. If there were any substance to the view that L1 and L2 are lateralized differently, this should be the clearest instance, as these two languages are very dissimilar and could call for different processing strategies that are lateralized differently. Nonetheless, no differences in the aphasic outcomes for Japanese and English were noted.

Within what territory are the two languages represented in an identical configuration of neuronal involvement? Ojeman and Whitaker and Whitaker et al. have explored conscious patients' ability to name objects during brain stimulation at surgery.[22,35] The overall wide territory within which the electrical current blocked the patient's attempt to name was similar for L1 and L2, but there was a miscellany of combinations, such that at some loci, naming was blocked for L1 only, for L2 only, or for both. This suggests disparity in the neural substrate for naming in the two languages; but pending knowledge about the stability and generalizability of the language maps that result, we cannot interpret this finding.

The literature on polyglot aphasia does not compel rejection of the most economical view, that the same neural substrate serves L2 and L1. These "natural experiments" necessarily are uncontrolled and, absent a double dissociation, hard to interpret. But one form of possible anatomical dissociation between languages in bilinguals also can be studied experimentally in normal people. That is dissociation of language representation between the two cerebral hemispheres.

Asymmetries

Behavioral Asymmetries

Laterality testing for first and second languages potentially is biased by aptitude and by strategy differences between the two languages.

There is reason to suppose that automatized skills (for example, fluent language use) call for the use, if not of different brain territories, at least of less territory within the relevant part of the brain. Aptitude differences might be indexed by differences in degree of selective hemisphere activation and therefore of perceptual asymmetry. Strategy differences might exist, both between beginning and skilled users of a given language and between users, at a comparable skill level, of languages that differ widely in their nature. It has been suggested that beginning readers use holistic strategies, implying that these are right hemispheric. This is a pretentious way of saying that such readers may guess at meaning, not yet having efficient analytic processes at their disposal. That does not, in fact, imply a right-hemisphere role: the right hemisphere's proven function is no less analytic than that of the left, merely analytic with respect to different variables. It would, however, be apt to lead to less lateralized and therefore less asymmetric functioning.

Even when he has mastered both languages, the user may expend more effort on one. Insofar as different degrees of difficulty experienced with the same material may generate different laterality outcomes (cf. Reference 3), the attempt to infer stable (structural) properties from laterality measurements must hold "task difficulty" constant. This has not been done.

It also is true that the conventional means of assessing laterality—dichotic and hemifield techniques—have little ecological validity, and may not be a good way of representing L1 and L2 behavior. Lateral eye movement, priming, and voice-hand interference paradigms are less subject to this criticism, as they at least use sentences. Also, half-field-viewing techniques are questionable for languages that use nonalphabetic scripts, which may call for various degrees of right-hemisphere processing, whether they are L1 or L2.

In any event, the most competent laterality studies show little difference between L1 and L2 asymmetries, both in the compound and the coordinate situations.[14,33] A few studies do show divergences for particular subgroups, but the pattern of findings is different in each one, leaving it unclear what their implications are for brain organization. They probably represent, in varying proportion, sampling variability and failure to control systematically biasing variables; for instance, Scott *et al.* and Hynd and Scott reported for adults and children, respectively, opposite dichotic ear advantages for English and Navajo listeners, using English consonant vowel syllables.[13,27] The left-ear advantage exhibited by the Navajo listeners is reminiscent of a similar finding by Damasio *et al.*[7] They found that the same phonetically similar words that yielded a right-ear advantage for normal listeners tended toward a reversal (left) ear advantage for illiterate listeners. Of course, this does not imply that illiterates are right lateralized for language: on easier (phonetically dissimilar) verbal material, they showed the usual right-ear advantage; but for a discrimination that they found difficult, they apparently used right-hemisphere strategies.[7] Navajos listening to dichotic messages in English might well do the same. Indeed, Navajos highly proficient in English did not show the left-ear advantage.[4]

The most supportive evidence of differential L1 and L2 lateralization arises from Sussman *et al.*'s use of the verbal-manual interference paradigm to lateralize L1-L2 speech output.[31] When subjects speak while performing a unimanual task, there will be maximal interference between speaking and performance by the hand controlled by the same hemisphere (that is, left hemisphere for speech and for right-hand control in right handers; cf. References 16 and 17). For monolinguals, Sussman *et al.* found only right-hand finger-tapping disruption during speaking, suggesting left speech lateralization—and the same applied to both languages of early (pre–age 6) bilinguals.[31] But late bilinguals revealed left laterality for the L1 area and a bilateral tapping decrement during speaking in L2, implying bihemispheric involvement. This result calls for replication, with speech-task-difficulty control and attention to the possibility of differential trade-offs between the verbal and manual performance for L1 and L2 in the late bilingual group (which could have generated the obtained result artifactually).

Electrophysiological Asymmetries

The attempt to use *electrophysiological indices* appears premature, since it is uncertain what the waveforms that are studied indicate.[10] The study by Rogers *et al.* will serve to illustrate this.[26] They had 16 Hopi Indian children listen to children's stories both in Hopi and in English. Spectral analysis of electroencephalographic data recorded while the children were listening revealed more alpha desynchronization over the right hemisphere while the Hopi story was being told. The children all had learned English as a second language, and apparently were not expert in that language. It seems reasonable to suppose that when listening to the English narrative, they were confronting a relatively difficult language task, calling for substantial selective activation of the left hemisphere. When listening to their own native language, the children would have been more free to pay attention to story content and to form corresponding images, thus using the right as well as the left hemisphere. Thus, the findings tell us nothing differential about the two languages, and certainly nothing differential about their lateralization. This illustration reminds us that when we measure relative activation of parts of the brain, we tap not only what we asked the subject to do, but also what else he is thinking about. Not only should task difficulty be held constant between languages, but also the relevant aspect of the task should fully engage the subject's attentional resources.

The phenomenon of polylingualism has proved tantalizing to those who assume that the brain can be likened usefully to a limited capacity channel for information transmission: hence the eagerness to delimit how much a particular part of the brain can do and how long it remains capable of doing it. None of the hypothesized boundaries have withstood the experimental test. Perhaps the capacity of the part of the brain that subserves language to enlarge its repertoire is no more limited than the brain's capacity to remember things. The capacity metaphor may be wrong. The limit may be not on the total number of responses but on differentiating them (cf. References 15 and 21). At any rate, the literature on brain basis of bilingualism teaches us to be as sparing of hypotheses as nature is of organizing principles. In phylogeny, the same mechanism is used over and over again to meet new and different adaptive needs. In language acquisition, matters also appear to be simpler than believed and the following null hypotheses have not been disconfirmed as yet. Second and subsequent languages are acquired much as is the first, making allowance only for known differences in cognitive strategies at different stages in the life span. The same brain territories are involved in all language acquisition. The aging of the brain during childhood does not diminish ability to learn the vocabulary, syntax, or pronunciation of a second language, and no period of the life span is critical to such acquisition. The well-documented greater plasticity of the immature than the mature brain relates to the ability to compensate for structural loss of brain tissue; it has not been shown to affect the functioning of the brain while it is intact.

REFERENCES

1. ALBERT, M. L. & L. K. OBLER. 1978. The Bilingual Brain: Neuropsychological and Neurolinguistic Aspects of Bilingualism. Academic Press, Inc. New York, N.Y.
2. BUDDENHAGEN, R. G. 1971. Establishing Vocal Verbalizations in Mute Mongoloid Children. Research Press. Champaign, Ill.
3. BYRD, M. & M. KINSBOURNE. Hemispheric priming and interference by a concurrent lateralized task: its relation to age. (Submitted.)
4. CARROLL, F. 1980. Neurolinguistic processing of a second language: experimental evidence. In Research in Second Language Acquisition. R. Scarcella & S. Krashen, Eds. Newbury House. Rowley, Mass.
5. CHARLTON, M. H. 1964. Aphasia in bilingual and polyglot patients—a neurological and psychological study. J. Speech Hear. Disord. 29: 307–311.
6. CURTISS, S., V. FROMKIN, D. RIGLER, M. RIGLER & S. KRASHEN. 1975. An update on the linguistic development of Genie. In Developmental Psycholinguistics: Theory and Applications. D. Dato, Ed.: 145–157. Georgetown University Press. Washington, D.C.
7. DAMASIO, H., A. R. DAMASIO, A. CASTIO-CALDAS & K. DES HAMSHER. 1979. Reversal of ear advantage for phonetically similar words in illiterates. J. Clin. Psychol. 4: 331–338.
8. FROMKIN, V., S. KRASHEN, S. CURTISS, D. RIGLER & M. RIGLER. 1974. The development of language in Genie: a case of language acquisition beyond the critical period. Brain Lang. 1: 81–107.
9. GALLOWAY, L. Towards a neuropsychological model of bilingualism and second language performance: a theoretical article with a critical review of

current research and some new hypotheses. *In* Research in Second Language Acquisition. M. Long, S. Peck & K. Bailey, Eds. Newbury House. Rowley, Mass. (In press.)

10. GENESEE, F., J. HAMERS, W. E. LAMBERT, L. MONONEN, M. SEITZ & R. STARCK. 1978. Language processing in bilinguals. Brain Lang. **5:** 1–12.

11. GLONING, I. & K. GLONING. 1965. Aphasien bei polyglotten. Beitrag zur Dynamik des Sprachabbaus sowie zur Localisationsfrage dieser Storungen. Wien. Z. Nervenheilkd. **22:** 362–397.

12. GORDON, H. W. 1980. Cerebral organization in bilinguals. I. Lateralization. Brain Lang. **9:** 255–268.

13. HYND, G. W. & S. A. SCOTT. 1980. Propositional and appositional modes of thought and differential speech lateralization in Navajo Indian and Anglo children. Child. Dev. **51:** 909–911.

14. KERSHNER, J. & H. G.-R. JENG. 1972. Dual functional asymmetry in visual perception. Effects of ocular dominance and post exposural processes. Neuropsychologia **10:** 437–445.

15. KINSBOURNE, M. 1981. Single channel theory. *In* Human Skills. D. Holding, Ed.: 65–89. John Wiley & Sons, Inc. New York, N.Y.

16. KINSBOURNE, M. & J. COOK. 1971. Generalized and lateralized effect of concurrent verbalization on a unimanual skill. Q. J. Exp. Psychol. **23:** 341–345.

17. KINSBOURNE, M. & R. F. HICKS. 1978. Functional cerebral space: a model for overflow, transfer, and interference effects in human performance. *In* Attention and Performance. J. Requin, Ed. **7:** 345–362. Lawrence Erlbaum. Hillsdale, N.J.

18. LAMBERT, W. E. 1969. Psychological studies of interdependencies of the bilingual's two languages. *In* Substance and Structure of Language. J. Puhvel, Ed.: 99–126. University of California Press. Los Angeles, Calif.

19. LENNEBERG, E. H. 1967. The Biological Foundations of Language. John Wiley & Sons, Inc. New York, N.Y.

20. L'HERMITTE, R., H. HECAEN, J. DUBOIS, A. CULIOLI & A. TABOURRET-KELLY. 1966. Le probleme de l'aphasie des polyglottes: remarques sur quelques observations. Neuropsychologia **4:** 315–329.

21. NEISSER, U. 1980. The limits of cognition. *In* On the Nature of Thought: Essays in Honor of D. O. Hebb. P. W. Juszyk & R. M. Klein, Eds. Lawrence Erlbaum Associates. Hillsdale, N.J.

22. OJEMAN, G. A. & H. A. WHITAKER. 1978. The bilingual brain. Arch. Neurol. **35:** 409–412.

23. PITRES, A. 1980. A study of aphasia in polyglots (1895). *In* Readings in Aphasia in Bilinguals and Polyglots. M. Paradis, Ed. Didier. Montreal, Quebec, Canada.

24. RASMUSSEN, T. & B. MILNER. 1975. Clinical and surgical studies of the cerebral speech areas in man. *In* Cerebral Lateralization. K. J. Zulch, O. Creutzfeldt & G. C. Galbraith, Eds.: 1–18. Springer-Verlag. Berlin, Federal Republic of Germany.

25. RIBOT, T. 1881. Diseases of Memory: An Essay in the Positive Psychology. Paul. London, England.

26. ROGERS, L., W. TER HOUTEN, C. KAPLAN & M. GARDINER. 1977. Hemispheric specialization of language: an EEG study of bilingual Hopi Indian children. Int. J. Neurosci. **8:** 1–6.

27. SCOTT, S., G. W. HYND, L. HUNT & W. WEED. 1979. Cerebral speech lateralization in the native American Navajo. Neuropsychologia **17:** 89–92.

28. SILVERBERG, R. & H. W. GORDON. 1979. Differential aphasia in two bilingual individuals. Neurology **29:** 51–55.

29. SNOW, C. E. & M. HOEFNAGEL-HÖHLE. 1978. The critical period for language

acquisition: evidence from second language learning. Child Dev. **49:** 1114–1128.

30. STARK, R., F. GENESEE, W. E. LAMBERT & M. SEITZ. 1977. Multiple language experience and the development of cerebral dominance. *In* Language Development and Neurological Theory. S. J. Segalowitz & F. A. Gruber, Eds.: 48–58. Academic Press, Inc. New York, N.Y.
31. SUSSMAN, H., P. FRANKLIN & T. SIMON. Bilingual speech: bilateral control. Brain Lang. (In press.)
32. VAID, J. & W. E. LAMBERT. 1979. Differential cerebral involvement in the cognitive functioning of bilinguals. Brain Lang. **8:** 92–110.
33. WALTERS, J. & R. ZATORRE. 1978. Laterality differences for word identification in bilinguals. Brain Lang. **2:** 158–167.
34. WATAMORI, T. S. & S. SASANUMA. 1978. The recovery processes of two English-Japanese bilingual aphasics. Brain Lang. **6:** 127–140.
35. WHITAKER, H. A., D. BUB & S. LEVENTER. Neurolinguistic aspects of language acquisition and bilingualism. Ann. N.Y. Acad. Sci. (This volume.)

NEUROLINGUISTIC ASPECTS OF LANGUAGE ACQUISITION AND BILINGUALISM

Harry A. Whitaker

Department of Hearing and Speech Sciences
University of Maryland
College Park, Maryland 20742

Daniel Bub and Susan Leventer

Department of Psychology
University of Rochester
Rochester, New York 14627

Two general questions are addressed in this paper: (a) Have the parameters of brain maturation contributed to our understanding of either monolingual or bilingual language acquisition? and (b) What do the current data on language representation in the brains of adult monolingual and multilingual speakers suggest by way of a neurolinguistic model? To anticipate the gist of this paper, the outlook is somewhat on the bleak side. First, brain maturation does not appear to be a monolithic event to which the milestones of language acquisition can be correlated easily. Second, nonlocalizationist models of brain-language relationships simply are a silly way to do neurolinguistic science; unfortunately, most current localizationist models do not do an adequate job of accounting for the known facts. On the other hand, the fact that we have at least this much understanding of neurolinguistic aspects of language acquisition and bilingualism is rather direct testimony to the progress that has been made in the field.

In 1967 Lenneberg assembled an extensive body of research and ideas and proposed a number of now-familiar hypotheses concerning the neurological aspects of language.[1] He suggested that the two cerebral hemispheres initially are equipotential for language, that cerebral lateralization gradually develops until it is complete at puberty, and that there is a critical period for language acquisition from two years of age to puberty that is limited and determined by the maturation of the brain. The specific concomitants of physical maturation of the brain to which he referred were changes in cell-body volume, in neurodensity, and in some of the neurochemical components of the brain. Lenneberg's analysis of these criteria led him to postulate a rapid rate of growth until age two, followed by a slow rise, asymptoting at puberty. His view of brain maturation as a single process was quite explicit: "Since the various aspects of cerebral maturation are so highly correlated we may think of maturation of the brain as a relatively unitary phenomenon." [1]

The hypotheses of equipotentiality, the development of lateralization or dominance (currently being discussed in terms of both specialization and

0077–8923/81/0379–0059 $01.75/2 © 1981, NYAS

plasticity), and the critical period have been given extensive and accessible coverage in the literature. On some points there is a reasonable amount of agreement that Lenneberg was mistaken: the cerebral hemispheres are not equipotential for language at any time, and lateralization is present in the neonate (if not earlier) and does not in any simple sense "develop." And in agreement with Lenneberg, it is accepted that plasticity of the brain gradually decreases with age. There is less agreement on the hypothesis of a critical period for language acquisition, particularly in terms of the predictions that such a hypothesis makes for second-language acquisition. Krashen presented evidence in favor of the view that after puberty, second-language acquisition differs in important respects from first-language acquisition; [2] Ekstrand on the other hand rejected the hypotheses of a critical period and an optimum age, and cited evidence in favor of a continued ontogenetic development beyond puberty for both language and cognitive skills. [3]

Lenneberg's hypothesis of the monolithic nature of brain maturation, however, has not been subjected to extensive analysis in the literature over the past 14 years. In view of the key role that brain maturation has played in most discussions of the neurolinguistics of language acquisition, we think that this hypothesis merits some further analysis.

If one uses a crude measure of maturation, such as the relationship between the surface of the cortex and the volume of the brain, then it will appear that a stable growth ratio is achieved by the second year of postnatal life. But even gross measurement of the surface of the cortex reveals differences: between the second trimester and birth, the frontal association region grows about 140%, the inferior parietal association region grows about 330%, and the temporal association region grows about 460%. [4] At birth these phylogenetically new regions of the cortex comprise 11–13% of their adult values, and after birth the surface measurements increase about equally (600–800%). However, the surfaces of these neocortical zones associated with higher mental processes show a far greater degree of enlargement over their birth measurements (about 9 times) than do those of the primary motor and sensory areas (about 5 times) and those of the phylogenetically older insular and limbic regions (about 4 times). As soon as one examines brain development by more than such a gross measure as the ratio of entire cortical surface to entire volume, the notion of a unitary process of brain development begins to collapse.

Lenneberg, in his evidence for the claim of a single pattern of structural change, includes an analysis of some data from Schadé and van Groenigen on the neurodensity of the middle frontal gyrus of the developing cortex. It should be noted that, under the unitary hypothesis, the growth factors of the middle frontal gyrus are taken as representative of the entire brain's growth patterns. Lenneberg states that the data show "how the packing density decreases at a rapid rate during the first two years, at a very slow rate thereafter, with complete stabilization after the early teens." [1] But these data are open to another, quite different interpretation. First, from

Lenneberg's own graph, the period of rapid decrease in neurodensity ends at about 6 months, not 2 years of age. Second, the gray-cell coefficient takes on a wholly different developmental pattern. The gray-cell coefficient is the volume of gray matter divided by the volume of the bodies of nerve cells in it; it depends not only upon the packing density but also upon the size and thus the volume of cells. The gray-cell coefficient does not asymptote "at or around puberty" as claimed, but increases steadily from birth to at least 20 years of age. One would infer from this fact that there is a steady growth in dendritic arborization through at least the first two decades of life.

But what of changes in postnatal neurodensity alone? To some extent, decreased neural density reflects development of the dendrites of the neurons, the sizes of the cell bodies, and the development of the axons. For example, neurodensity is high in the visual cortex due to a predominance of layer-IV axosomatic synapses (perhaps related to analysis of information from subcortical afferent projections), and it is low in the precentral cortex due to extensive receptive surfaces of the large pyramidal cells of layers III and V and their highly developed dendrites. Contrary to a unitary interpretation of this criterion of brain maturation, there are important differences in different cortical regions over time. For example, in the primary motor cortex the average decrease in the number of cells per unit volume of cortex between birth and maturity is approximately 70%, whereas in Broca's area it is only about 50%. Furthermore, neurodensity falls until 12 years of age in the primary motor region, but only until about 2½ years of age in other frontal regions including Broca's area.[4] Since the dimensions of the cells are related to neurodensity, one should note that for the pyramidal cells of the frontal lobe, the dimensions of the cells at birth are closest to their adult values, i.e., they enlarge the least, in the precentral cortex and are farthest from their adult values, i.e., they enlarge the most, in other regions including Broca's area.[4]

Even within a single brain region, there are notable differences in the growth patterns of the different types of cell structures that characterize each of the six different cortical layers. Cytoarchitectonic areas of the cortex were determined by visual classification not only of the neurodensity and the size of cells in the individual layers, but also by the width of the six cortical layers. According to Yakovlev, the width of the cortex as an average increases from birth to maturity (defined in terms of the average brain of a 28-year-old) as follows: layer I increases 136%, layer II increases 150%, layer III increases 170%, layer IV increases 66%, layer V increases 133%, and layer VI increases 194%.[5] However, the evidence from Yakovlev's data indicates that the rate of growth of each of the six cortical layers in any one of the different cytoarchitectonic divisions varies greatly in ontogenesis. FIGURES 1–6 show the percentage increase over values at birth of cortical layers for each of the four areas important in language processing. An inspection of these figures reveals that the average increase value just mentioned masks considerable differences, variations,

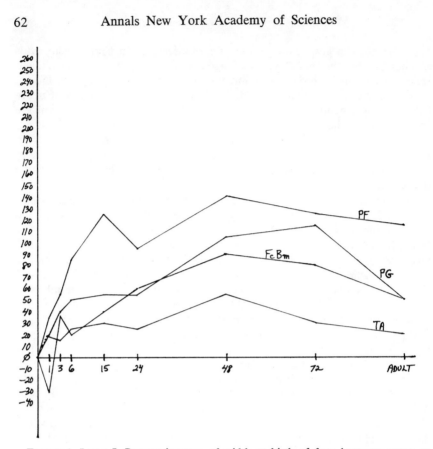

FIGURE 1. Layer I. Percent increase of width at birth of four language zones as a function of chronological age in months. (See text for definitions of abbreviations used in this and other figures.)

and fluctuations between birth and adult age in the four language zones. In each graph, the symbols for the zones are as follows: FcBm refers to Broca's area, TA refers to Wernicke's area, PF refers to the supramarginal gyrus, and PG refers to the angular gyrus.

Notice the greater than average enlargement of layer II in Broca's area (FIGURE 2) and of layer IV in both the supramarginal and angular gyri (FIGURE 4), compared to the far less than average enlargement of layers III, IV, and V in Wernicke's area (FIGURES 3, 4, and 5). While some of the growth patterns are similar in all four language areas, others are not. An opposite pattern for Wernicke's area compared to the other posterior language areas can be seen in layer V between 15 months and 4 years of age (FIGURE 5). Likewise, between 2 and 4 years of age, both Broca's area and Wernicke's area have a growth pattern opposite that of the supramarginal and angular gyri in layer IV (FIGURE 4).

We may consider further extrapolations of these data in order to evaluate the general maturational trends for each of the four language areas, keeping in mind that the parameter being considered is the relative percent of increase in width of each cortical layer compared to values at birth. The width of the cortex, as a measurement of brain development, is limited by the variability introduced by brain shrinkage during fixation, by the variability of differently shaped gyri, and by individual differences. Nevertheless, the width of each cortical layer does depend in part upon dendritic arborization, and thus provides some indication of the development of structural complexity of the cortex.

Let us first consider the patterns reflected in each of the six cortical layers, collapsing across all four language areas, in terms of the peaks and drops in the width ratios.

Layer I: all four language areas peak at 4 years of age.

Layer II: three-fourths of the language areas have a peak at 15 months of age, a drop at 2 years of age, and a peak again at 4 years of age.

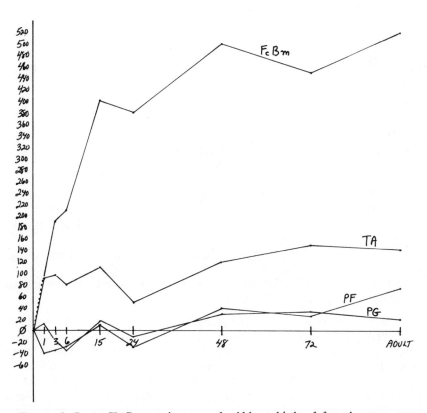

FIGURE 2. Layer II. Percent increase of width at birth of four language zones as a function of chronological age in months.

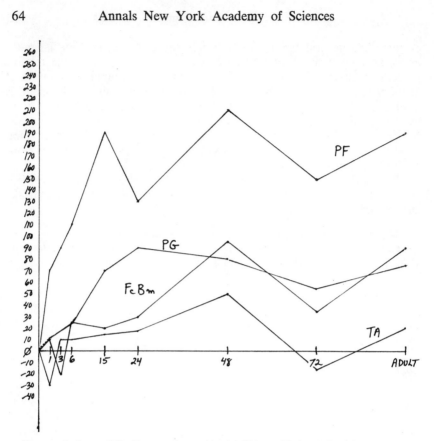

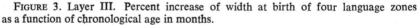

FIGURE 3. Layer III. Percent increase of width at birth of four language zones as a function of chronological age in months.

   Layer III: three-fourths of the language areas peak at 4 years of age and show a drop at 6 years of age.
   Layer IV: three-fourths of the language areas show a peak at 6 months of age and a drop at 2 years of age.
   Layer V: three-fourths of the language areas peak at 6 months of age and show a drop at 2 years of age.
   Layer VI: all of the language areas peak at 15 months of age and all of the areas show a drop at 2 years of age.

   These patterns may be summarized as follows: layers I, II, and III, the outermost laminae of the cortex, typically show a peak in growth at 4 years of age. Layers IV, V, and VI, the innermost laminae, have a more mixed pattern as well as an earlier one: half of the areas peak at 6 months of age, almost half of them peak again at 15 months of age, and almost all of them show a drop at 2 years of age. The differences in the outer and inner layers shown in these data are consistent with other maturational trends as reported by Conel[8] and others—that the cortex matures from the

innermost layers first to the outermost layers last, a fact that lends credence
to these extrapolations from Yakovlev's data.

Considering the four language areas now, we find the following trends:
Broca's area and the supramarginal gyrus have earlier peaks than do the
other areas, at 6 and 15 months respectively, for a slight majority of their
layers. Wernicke's area and the angular gyrus have a peak at 4 years of age
for the majority of their layers. All four language areas show a drop at
2 years of age for most of the layers; and the angular gyrus shows a drop
at 6 years of age for half of its layers. From this analysis only one conclusion is possible: maturation within and across the language areas of the
cortex is a multidimensional process, varying temporally and spatially from
birth through to adult ages.

Myelination is a commonly cited criterion of brain maturation and thus
merits some discussion. Although it is well known that unmyelinated fibers
are capable of carrying nerve impulses, Lecours notes that "the development of myelin in the sheaths of a fiber system may be taken as an indication

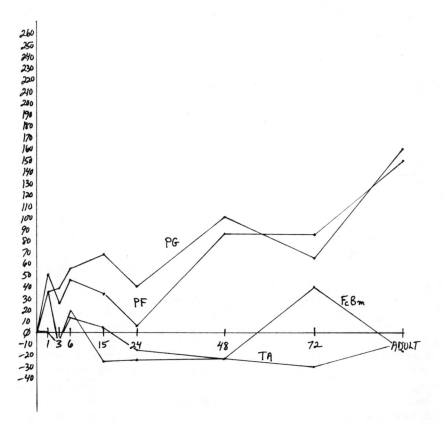

FIGURE 4. Layer IV. Percent increase of width at birth of four language zones
as a function of chronological age in months.

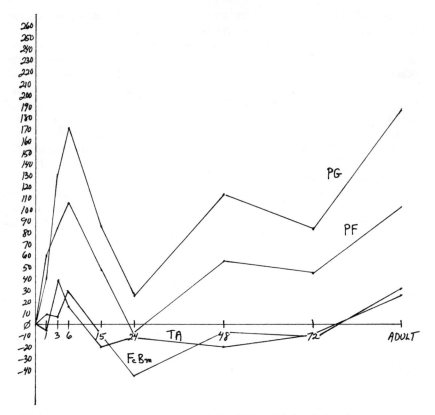

FIGURE 5. Layer V. Percent increase of width at birth of four language zones as a function of chronological age in months.

that the impulse conduction in this system has become space-committed in an invariable path; correspondingly, the fiber system that has completed its myelogenetic cycle may be assumed to have reached functional maturity." [6] Flechsig's early work established the patterns of myelination across the cerebral cortex.[6] In his analysis, the primordial fields develop myelin first: the pre- and postcentral gyri, the calcarine cortex, the transverse gyri of Heschl, and the retrosplenial, subcallosal, and septal areas. Intermediate fields begin myelinating during the first three postnatal months. The terminal fields (the classical association areas) myelinate after the fourth postnatal month. Yakovlev and Lecours extended this early work on the onset of myelination to include the notion of a cycle of myelination, a highly variable onset-to-adult-status period of myelination.[7] The important distinction between onset of myelination and the cycle of myelination is evident in a comparison of the primary visual and auditory areas. Although both the optic and acoustic radiations begin to myelinate in the perinatal period (onset), the optic radiations complete their myelination by the fourth postnatal *month* (short cycle), whereas the acoustic radiations are not myelinated until the fifth postnatal *year* (long cycle).

Conel's detailed anatomical studies of the postnatal cortex show that, overall, brain development proceeds from the primary motor and sensory areas (Rolandic cortex, calcarine cortex, Heschl's gyri, and the planum temporale) outward to the secondary and association areas.[8] On most criteria, the motor cortex develops earliest and maturation within the frontal lobe progresses toward the frontal pole, with the frontal eye field ahead of Broca's area; the somatosensory cortex generally is next in overall maturity, and development within the parietal lobe proceeds posteriorly from the postcentral gyrus; the primary visual cortex matures earlier than the primary auditory cortex (consistent with the myelination pattern of the optic and acoustic radiations); development in the occipital lobe proceeds through areas 17, 18, and 19 in that order, and development in the temporal lobe proceeds through the superior, then the middle, and finally the inferior temporal gyri. An extrapolation of both the myelination

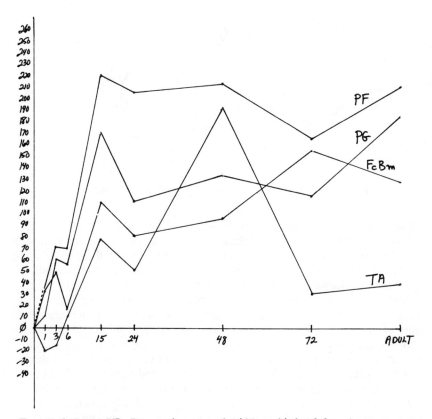

FIGURE 6. Layer VI. Percent increase of width at birth of four language zones as a function of chronological age in months.

and the cytoarchitectonic studies of brain maturation just reviewed leads to a cortical developmental pattern, which is shown in FIGURE 7. The numbers 1–4 indicate the points at which cortical maturation begins, and the arrows indicate the direction across the cortical mantle in which maturation proceeds. Once again it is obvious that brain maturation is a multidimensional process rather than a monolithic one.

It is almost trite to point out that language acquisition itself, whether first or second, is a multidimensional process, too. For example, articulatory and phonological development continue well after basic sentence structure is mastered, vocabulary development is virtually a life-long process, etc. Since these facts are consistent with the maturational facts, a natural question to ask is whether it still is possible to correlate brain maturation with language acquisition in a predictive, albeit complex, multidimensional model. One plausible answer to that question is "possibly," but in a manner that is interesting only marginally for primary-language

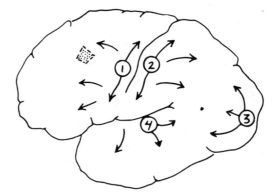

FIGURE 7. Maturation of the cortex. (See text for explanation.)

acquisition and of no interest to later second-language acquisition. Our reason for coming to such a conclusion is a simple one: using the currently available criteria of neural maturation, the brain is at virtually 90% of adult values by the age of six years, by a very conservative estimate; and by more liberal estimates, it has reached that point by five years of age. Consider some of the data that Lenneberg published: there are no significant changes in either packing density or neuron volume after two years of age; the weight of the brain reaches 80% of adult values shortly after three years of age; his summary of all of the maturational factors presented in his book indicates that 90% of adult values are reached shortly after four years of age and 80% of them are reached by three years of age.[1]

If one makes the reasonable assumption that the final 10% of all the maturational processes, which evidently occur in a slowly changing pattern over the following two or three decades of life, are unlikely to make a crucial difference for any milestones of linguistic or cognitive development, then the conclusion is obvious. The factors of brain maturation may correlate in interesting ways with early phonological development and some limited aspects of early syntactic development in primary-language acquisition; they are not likely to correlate with any aspects of acquisition after 5–6 years of age. We also must conclude that second-language acquisition, when it occurs after primary-language acquisition, is even less likely to be explicated by the factors of brain maturation as presently understood.

In order to develop hypotheses about the brain mechanisms of bilingualism then, we must turn to a different set of data, that of neurolinguistic studies of adults. There are at least two distinct questions to ask: (a) What do we know about the representation of language in the brain of the monolingual speaker? and (b) Is there evidence that the brain's representation of more than one language is different from that for a single language? Our understanding of the monolingual brain will provide one framework, which may or may not be adequate to account for the multilingual brain.

Neurolinguistic research has been reviewed more than adequately in the current literature; inferences about brain and language relationships have been derived from studies of brain-damaged patients with and without aphasia, from the use of electroencephalographic measures, from the injection of sodium amytal into the brain's blood supply (Wada test), from the sampling of local changes in metabolic rates in the brain (the regional cerebral blood flow technique and positron emission tomography), from electrical stimulation of the exposed cortex during neurosurgical procedures, from studies of other neurosurgical patients such as hemispherectomy or commissurotomy patients, and from studies of normal subjects using such techniques as the dichotic listening method or the visual half-field method. Some general conclusions to be drawn from this research can be expressed in terms of the issues of lateralization and localization, which is where we begin.

Visual half-field and dichotic listening techniques on non-brain-damaged monolingual and multilingual subjects have not produced consistent results. Rather than enter into yet another discussion of why this is the case, we take the conservative view that the different results obtained from this kind of research may very well characterize a range of laterality patterns found in the population (although perhaps not with the frequency that these studies seem to report). As reviewed by Vaid and Genesee and Albert and Obler, there are some studies that show an equivalent degree of lateralization for both languages of bilingual subjects and other studies that show one language less lateralized than the other in bilingual subjects.[9,10] Analogous studies of monolingual subjects have shown greater or lesser degrees of lateralization for a variety of independent language variables, suggesting that different aspects of language processing may make different demands upon left- or right-hemisphere functions.

In one sense, the ambiguity and uncertainty of the results of laterality studies on non-brain-damaged subjects don't really matter, because the results of some studies of brain-damaged subjects have demonstrated unequivocally that a variety of dominance patterns may in fact exist. Although not a common occurrence, it is quite clear that *right*-hemisphere lesions may cause aphasia in the same manner and to the same degree as left-hemisphere lesions. Wada test results also have shown unequivocally that there exist subjects with exclusively right-hemisphere language, and further that there are subjects who have language representation in both hemispheres,[11] in addition to the most common, left-hemisphere situation. Using electrical stimulation of the exposed cortex, Ojemann and Whitaker showed that in two cases of right-hemisphere language representation, there was no particular difference between the stimulation maps of those subjects and of other subjects with left-hemisphere representation, beyond what was expected due to individual differences.[11] However, in the one case of bilateral language representation, the stimulation map was not comparable to the other subjects. Since we also know from the studies of early hemispherectomy subjects that either hemisphere is capable of supporting language processing when it is isolated (although there are likely differences in certain linguistic capacities between the two, under these circumstances),[12] the conclusion about the possible model of brain lateralization for language is quite clear: any pattern of right-to-left dominance may occur. Therefore, although we expect that the typical case will be left-hemisphere language dominance in the multilingual brain (a view supported by Paradis' review of polyglot aphasia),[13] it is possible that a multilingual may have any combination of left- and right-hemisphere dominance; logically, these patterns could differ for each of the languages spoken.

If the range of possible left-to-right variations in language laterality is impressive, then the range of possible variations of the intrahemispheric localization of language is even more so. Neurosurgeons and neurologists long have been aware of the fact that left-hemisphere lesions outside of the classical language zones occasionally will result in aphasic sequelae. Infarctions of the anterior cerebral artery or the posterior cerebral artery occasionally are the cause of aphasia, when the lesion is on the mesial surface of the frontal or parietal lobes or when it is in the posterior, inferior temporal lobe, for example. Parasagittal and tentorial tumors are other classes of lesions that may lead to aphasia, and which are not in the classical language zones. In most of the current literature on brain and language relationships, these anomalous aphasia-producing lesions either are ignored or dismissed. In this connection, it is most interesting to note that the recent use of computerized tomography scans to localize lesions that are causing aphasia has provided some interesting data, too. For the most part, the lesions that cause aphasia have been quite large and have extended beyond the textbook versions of the classical language zones.

The electrical stimulation data of Ojemann and Whitaker and of Van Buren, Fedio, and Frederick have provided a new insight into the question of just how much language cortex there may be in one hemisphere.[14,15] If we make the reasonable assumption that there is language representation within the sulci as well as on the tops of the gyri (the latter is the part of the cortex that typically is stimulated in these studies), then one must conclude that the language system easily may occupy 50% of the cortex of one hemisphere. We emphasize *may occupy* that much; since these studies are conducted on patients with preexisting brain lesions, it is not possible to know, for example, whether all of us make use of the insula cortex for language processes or whether that cortex may just be recruitable as part of the brain's plasticity response to a lesion. But, just as in the case of the laterality research, we are forced to accept the fact that the potential exists for at least this range of language cortex: almost all of the parietal lobe, almost all of the temporal lobe except the pole, the latter half of the second and third frontal gyri and the mesial surface of the frontal lobe, the pre- and postcentral gyri, the insula, and very likely half or more of the occipital lobe.

Given the potential variation in spatial localization within a hemisphere for the language mechanisms, it is not surprising to find that electrical stimulation studies of the bilingual brain reveal differential localization for the different languages. Ojemann and Whitaker studied two bilingual subjects, one a speaker of Dutch and English and the other a speaker of English and Spanish.[11] These patients were undergoing neurosurgical remediation for pharmacologically uncontrollable seizure activity, and as a routine part of these procedures, language mapping of the exposed cortical surface was undertaken with bipolar electrodes, using a small electrical current. The results of this mapping are shown in FIGURE 8.

The circles indicate the points that were stimulated electrically; they are divided into an upper and a lower half to represent each of the two languages being tested in separate blocked trials. The solid black half-circle indicates a point at which stimulation interfered with naming on every trial; the black-and-white-striped half-circles indicate points at which stimulation interfered with naming significantly more frequently than by chance; and the half-circles with asterisks in them indicate points at which stimulation interfered with naming, but not reliably differently from chance.

The data clearly indicate that the two languages of each of these subjects only partially overlap; there are sites at which one or the other language is represented exclusively, and other sites at which both languages are represented, though not necessarily to the same degree. In a study that currently is in preparation, Rapport, Tan, and Whitaker studied four multilingual patients using this same procedure; these patients all were at least trilingual, variously speaking English, Cantonese, Mandarin, Hokkien, and Malay.[16] The same pattern of partially overlapping language representation was found, lending some credence to a model of multilingual language representation that does not require the languages to occupy, so to speak, the same pieces of brain. Incidentally, neither the study by Ojemann and Whitaker nor the study by Rapport, Tan, and Whitaker produced any evidence from the Wada test results that the opposite hemisphere supported any primary or secondary language functions.

As we asserted at the beginning of this paper, it simply is unproductive

to reject the hypothesis of localization out of hand and it is equally unproductive to reject the hypothesis of lateral dominance. However, the above
discussion certainly suggests that these hypotheses be stated with some care.
It is likely that there is a spatially flexible (plastic, if you will) range of
cortex that may be recruited for language functions within one hemisphere,
as well as a flexible distribution of processing strategies to allocate between

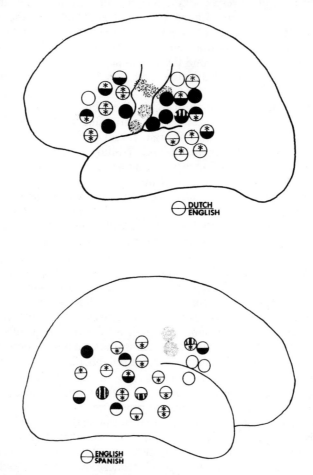

FIGURE 8. Language mapping of the cortical surface in two bilingual subjects.
(Data from Reference 11.) (See text for definition of symbols used.)

the two hemispheres. This is a situation that one would expect if the
localization and representation of a behavior in a nervous system were
determined more by experience than by genetics. Cortical functions may
be specified genetically in only the broadest possible manner, for example,
in the manner of the frontal lobe being designated broadly for output pro-

gramming or the parietal lobe being designated broadly for integrative programming of behavior, within the characteristics of that hemisphere's processing capacities. The specific localization of the cortical representation of language may be the result of a variety of experiential factors, in ways well described in the current neuroscience literature (as for example in papers in Reference 17). In this view, what is remarkable is that there is as much consistency in localization as has been demonstrated in the literature, a point we have noted before in the context of a commentary on individual differences in brain structure and function.[18] No extant model of brain-language relationships encompasses these hypotheses as yet, but perhaps some of the directions one might take to develop such a model have been partially elucidated.

REFERENCES

1. LENNEBERG, E. H. 1967. Biological Foundations of Language. John Wiley & Sons, Inc. New York, N.Y.
2. KRASHEN, S. 1975. The critical period for language acquisition and its possible causes. Ann. N.Y. Acad. Sci. **263:** 211–224.
3. EKSTRAND, L. H. 1978. Replacing the critical period and optimum age theories of second language acquisition with ontogenetic development beyond puberty. Paper presented at the Fourteenth International Congress of Applied Psychology, Munich, Federal Republic of Germany.
4. BLINKOV, S. M. & I. I. GLEZER. 1968. The Human Brain in Figures and Tables. Plenum Press. New York, N.Y.
5. YAKOVLEV, P. 1962. Morphological criteria of growth and maturation of the nervous system in man. Res. Publ. Assoc. Res. Nerv. Ment. Dis. **39:** 3–46.
6. LECOURS, A. R. 1975. Myelogenetic correlates of the development of speech and language. *In* Foundations of Language Development. E. H. Lenneberg & E. Lenneberg, Eds.: 121–135. Academic Press, Inc. New York, N.Y.
7. YAKOVLEV, P. & A. R. LECOURS. 1967. The myelogenetic cycles of regional maturation of the brain. *In* Regional Development of the Brain in Early Life: 3–70. Blackwell. Oxford, England.
8. CONEL, J. L. 1939–1967. The Postnatal Development of the Human Cerebral Cortex. Harvard University. Cambridge, Mass.
9. VAID, J. & F. GENESEE. Neuropsychological approaches to bilingualism: a critical review. Can. J. Psychol. (In press.)
10. ALBERT, M. L. & L. OBLER. 1978. The Bilingual Brain. Academic Press, Inc. New York, N.Y.
11. OJEMANN, G. & H. A. WHITAKER. 1978. The bilingual brain. Arch. Neurol. **35:** 409–412.
12. DENNIS, M. & H. A. WHITAKER. 1976. Language acquisition following hemi-decortication: linguistic superiority of the left over the right hemisphere. Brain Lang. **3:** 404–433.
13. PARADIS, M. 1977. Bilingualism and aphasia. *In* Studies in Neurolinguistics. H. Whitaker & H. A. Whitaker, Eds. **3:** 65–122. Academic Press, Inc. New York, N.Y.
14. OJEMANN, G. & H. A. WHITAKER. 1978. Language localization and variability. Brain Lang. **6:** 239–260.
15. VAN BUREN, J. M., P. FEDIO & G. C. FREDERICK. 1978. Mechanism and localization of speech in parietotemporal cortex. Neurosurgery **2:** 233–239.
16. RAPPORT, R. L., C. T. TAN & H. A. WHITAKER. 1980. Language Function

and Dysfunction among Chinese and English-Speaking Polyglots: Cortical Stimulation, Wada Testing and Clinical Studies. Academy of Aphasia. South Yarmouth, Mass.

17. ROSENZWEIG, M. R. & E. L. BENNETT, Eds. 1976. Neural Mechanisms of Learning and Memory. MIT Press. Cambridge, Mass.

18. WHITAKER, H. A. & O. A. SELNES. 1976. Anatomic variations in the cortex: individual differences and the problem of the localization of language functions. Ann. N.Y. Acad. Sci. 280: 844–854.

"NATURAL METHODS" OF FOREIGN-LANGUAGE TEACHING: CAN THEY EXIST? WHAT CRITERIA MUST THEY MEET?

Karl Diller

Department of English
University of New Hampshire
Durham, New Hampshire 03824

Two persistent and related problems with the study of second-language acquisition involve skepticism. One involves skepticism as to whether second-language acquisition is "natural" in the sense that the learning of the mother tongue might be said to be natural, or even whether second languages can be mastered at all, especially if the acquisition process begins after age six or eight.[1] The second skeptical position involves teaching, and questions not only whether teaching is natural, but whether languages really can be taught at all. In the first part of this paper, I will argue that a large part of this skepticism is a result of misconceptions and faulty reasoning. The word "natural" itself is a very slippery term. Then, in the second part of the paper, I will discuss criteria for teaching methods that will enhance one's natural (i.e., biological) abilities to learn language, arguing that some of the methods labeled "natural" actually may inhibit these natural abilities.

Misconceptions Leading to Skepticism about Learning and Teaching

First, then, to the skepticism about learning. One misconception seems to be the view that if a learned behavior is "natural," it should be quick, easy, and effortless to learn. As I have pointed out elsewhere, vocabulary size alone prevents language learning (native or foreign) from being quick.[2] College students typically know more than half of the 450,000 words in *Webster's Third International Dictionary*. A vocabulary of more than 225,000 words divided over all the days in the life of a 20-year-old averages out to the learning of more than 30 words every day for the native language. With a task of such magnitude, even if it is easy, one should not expect nativelike mastery of a foreign language in a few months even of intense exposure or study. It is reasonable to suppose that some natural processes take a very long time to be completed. Yet much of the skepticism about the naturalness of second-language learning comes from failure of the people involved to master a second language in the short time allotted.

One basic question as to whether second-language learning is natural is a neurolinguistic one, and the most radically skeptical position on second-language acquisition in adults comes from the neurosurgeon Wilder

0077–8923/81/0379–0075 $01.75/2 © 1981, NYAS

Penfield. He writes that "when new languages are taken up for the first time in the second decade of life, it is difficult, though not impossible, to achieve a good result. It is difficult because it is unphysiological." [3] Penfield's argument is that the cortex becomes "committed" by about age six or eight, as seen by the fact that new language centers in the right hemisphere cannot be developed by adolescents and adults who acquire aphasia and by the fact that foreign accents usually develop in adolescents and adults who learn foreign languages. There is overwhelming behavioral evidence, however, that if one disregards the foreign-accent phenomena, adults are much more efficient language learners than are children.[4] One study suggests that college freshmen may be five times faster than nine-year-olds in learning foreign languages.[5]

T. M. Walsh and I have given a neurolinguistic explanation of the apparent contradiction between Penfield's argument and the behavioral data, by considering the recent work on local-circuit neurons that was unavailable to Penfield. Of two major types of neurons, the pyramidal cells develop early—certainly, as Penfield knew, by age six or eight. These are the neurons that make long-distance connections with their long axons, and are crucial in establishing the relations between the language centers and other centers of neural control. We argue that only at a very young age, while the pyramidal cells are still developing, can new language centers be formed in the right hemisphere in response to left-hemisphere injury. The pyramidal cells also are crucial in neuromuscular control, and changes in the plasticity of these cell systems might be reflected in the emergence of pronunciation difficulties and foreign accents. The maturation schedule of the pyramidal cells, then, could explain the changes at age six or eight noted by Penfield.

A second major type of neuron, however, is specially linked with higher order cortical functions, with cognition and learning in particular. These are the stellate cells, or local-circuit neurons. They are short-axon cells, characterized by distinctive postnatal growth, by relatively slow differentiation in the brain, and by continued maturation over at least two to three decades. The continued neuroplasticity of the local-circuit neurons explains why it is *not* "unphysiological" (to use Penfield's expression) to continue to learn new things—including new languages—after age six or eight, and why the cognitive aspects of new languages are learned better by relatively mature people even though the neuromuscular control of pronunciation might present certain difficulties.

The biological and neurological arguments thus do not support skepticism as to whether second-language learning is natural—except possibly in the realm of pronunciation. There are, of course, sizeable individual differences in language-learning aptitude that are biological, and which have to be taken into account;[6] but presumably the chief reasons for widespread failure to learn second languages (and the resultant skepticism as to whether it really is natural for people to succeed) are psychological and social reasons, which takes us to the question of teaching.

The context for skepticism about whether languages really can be taught is Chomskian linguistics, where an important neurolinguistic question bearing on second-language acquisition is the problem of how much language is not learned at all but is universal and innate. As Chomsky puts it, "We must postulate an innate structure that is rich enough to account for the disparity between experience and knowledge." [7] If we use the term *language* in the most general sense, meaning the principles of language, or universal grammar, then we can say that language is not learned but is innate. We still would say, though, that specific languages, insofar as they are culturally determined, have to be learned and are not innate. This point of view should not necessarily lead to skepticism as to whether we can teach foreign languages to adults, for surely if the principles of language are innate, the teacher's task in teaching a given foreign language is lessened considerably. This view *has* led to skepticism about teaching, however, because ever since Wilhelm von Humboldt, linguists have slid from the position that "language is not learned or taught, but is innate" to the notion that "languages are not taught but develop automatically" or that "languages are learned but not taught." Chomsky paraphrases this slip of Humboldt's, with apparent approval, when he writes that Humboldt maintained

> the rationalist view that language is not really learned—certainly not taught—but rather develops "from within," in an essentially predetermined way, when the appropriate environmental conditions exist. One cannot really teach a first language, [Humboldt] argued, but only "provide the thread along which it will develop of its own accord," by processes more like maturation than learning.[7]

Thus Chomsky's Humboldt slips from saying that we can't teach language in the universal sense, to saying that we really don't teach the culturally shaped individual languages either. This second point does not necessarily follow from Chomsky or Humboldt's rationalist position; and while maintaining that rationalist position in this paper, I will argue that the point about not teaching specific languages is false.

One is too easily led, though, to Krashen's suggestion that there is a distinction between a natural process called *acquisition* and an artificial one called *learning* (a distinction hard to maintain in practice),[8] and to Lenneberg's position (clearly counterfactual)[9] that there is such a thing as "automatic acquisition from mere exposure." [10] There is the suggestion that formal instruction in second languages be abandoned altogether, in an article by Spolsky—"The Value of Volunteers in English Language Teaching, or Why Pay for It When You Can Get It for Nothing." [11] And Macnamara, who rightly extolls streets as being in some ways superior to traditional classrooms as environments for language learning,[12] ignores the well-known fact that there are as many bad street environments as good ones, allowing countless Americans overseas and many others in language minorities to avoid quite easily learning the languages spoken in the streets around them, while intensive language programs are relatively successful.

We have said that the chief reasons for failure in learning second languages are psychological and social reasons. Psychological reasons are related to motivation, desire, and perceived need. Since social factors usually are the basis for this motivation, desire, and perceived need, it is the social factors that are crucial. This concern for social factors is reflected in Chomsky's paraphrase of Humboldt (above), which suggested that language would develop "when the appropriate environmental conditions exist." [7]

It is clear that a good environment enhances language learning even in native-language acquisition. Let us consider four pieces of evidence:

1. Mothers speak more distinctly and adjust the complexity of speech and vocabulary when talking with young children;

2. Kagan's data would suggest that the reason why upper-middle-class daughters have the most precocious language development of any category of child is that they get more distinctive verbal stimulation, or more individual teaching, by their mothers; [13]

3. Plumer found that eight-year-old boys of high verbal ability came from families where the parents assumed a markedly didactic role, in the Socratic sense, as contrasted to other parents; [14]

4. In the case of my own son John, 25% of the first 200 words in his spontaneous spoken vocabulary were words taught to him directly out of storybooks (words such as gopher, deer, teepee).

Children do not learn their native language just by overhearing it spoken in their presence. They need direct communication and direct teaching activity by parents or by peers.

Language-Teaching Criteria

If the universal principles of language are innate, and people have natural language-learning abilities, and if these abilities continue into adulthood, as we have argued, then what are the criteria for teaching methods that will enhance our natural ability to learn languages?

It is sometimes thought that the most natural method of language teaching is the most primitive and least structured method. Just put your students in a foreign culture, have them live with a family, and they will pick up the foreign language naturally. One fallacy of this approach may be that it isn't all that natural to be living with a strange family in a foreign culture where you don't know the language. François Gouin was in that type of situation when he went to Hamburg to learn German a century ago. Not knowing how to take advantage of his unstructured environment, he made only sporadic and painful attempts at conversation, and spent a large portion of his time alone in his room memorizing the grammar, the roots, irregular verbs, and basic sentences of German, trying slowly to translate

Goethe and Schiller, and finally, in desperation, memorizing his entire dictionary of 30,000 words. At the end of this effort, he tested his ability by attending a lecture at the university, and found that he was unable to understand a single word.[15,2] Gouin later turned out to be a brilliant linguist, in the practical sense of that word, who mastered German and several other foreign languages and who invented the highly structured Series Method. But his first attempt at learning the German language gave the literature on second-language acquisition one of its most spectacular failures.

Usually we regard Gouin's failure as a failure of the grammar-translation method, but it is just as much a failure of an unstructured, primitive, naturalistic environment, which lacked at least some of the qualities needed for an effective language-learning environment. We should note that Gouin must have heard a great deal of German being spoken in his presence—at meals, in the streets, in shops, etc. Why didn't he learn German from that exposure? Presumably because the German that Gouin heard around him was not often enough directed at him personally, at his own level, so that he could understand it. If Gouin lacked an opportunity for listening comprehension, it was not the opportunity to hear the language but the possibility of comprehending it that he lacked.

One other aspect of Gouin's case is worth examining. The apparent reason that he did not try *speaking* much German was that he was afraid of ridicule. He lived with a hairdresser, and occasionally tried a carefully prepared sentence on the customers, only to be greeted by laughter. One might take this as support for Stevick's position that a warm, nonthreatening, supportive environment is more important than method in language learning and that the teacher's focus should be more on morale than on linguistic content.[16] Yet one has to be careful not to go too far in that direction. It frequently is said that if a man really wants to master a foreign language he should find a girlfriend who speaks that language, but one should not overlook the possibility that this warm, sympathetic, supportive woman might try to learn the man's language instead—just as many perfectly nice language teachers spend too much time using their students' native language for conversations with them.

An environment that will enhance one's natural language-learning abilities, then, must be more than a place where one lives alongside the foreign-language community, no matter how warm, sympathetic, and supportive that environment might be.

To specify the teaching methods that might enhance our natural language-learning capacities, a useful first step is to examine the neurolinguistic foundations of these methods, as T. M. Walsh and I have done in a series of articles.[17,18,4] The localization data from aphasic cases indicate that there are several different language subsystems, which are processed in distinct areas of the brain. In Broca's aphasia, for example, the semantic processes involving content words are virtually intact, whereas there are severe problems with syntactic processes such as the English passive and various constructions involving function words and suffixes. Wernicke's aphasia presents a complementary syndrome, with grammatical fluency and semantic problems.

Walsh and I have argued that different language-teaching methods utilize the different language areas and pathways of the brain in different ways. Some of these methods are rather restrictive in the way in which they emphasize certain areas and pathways. For example, there is the aphasic syndrome of "isolation of the speech area" in which Broca's area and Wernicke's area are spared from damage, as is the arcuate fasciculus connecting them, but the semantic processing areas are not functional.[19] Patients with this syndrome do not initiate meaningful speech and give no indication of understanding anything. What they do is mimic everything said to them ("echolalia"), and sing along with songs that they have memorized. They will continue with their songs once they are started, and they can learn new songs by rote. The extreme form of the so-called audiolingual method—mimicry, memorization, and pattern drill—actually may be very much like this aphasic syndrome in isolating the speech area and in ignoring to an alarming degree the semantic processes, which can make the transition from elementary to intermediate stages of language learning quite difficult in this method. (See FIGURE 1.)

The grammar-translation method likewise makes little attempt to link meaning directly to the spoken or written symbols of the new language, requiring the meaning to be mediated by words in the student's native tongue.

The Winitz and Reeds method of teaching language through listening comprehension with the avoidance of speaking is another method that makes less than complete use of the language areas of the brain,[20] but the process that is missing in mim–mem–pattern drill and in the grammar-translation method is exactly the process on which the Winitz and Reeds method focuses: a link between Wernicke's area for auditory processing and the semantic areas of the supramarginal gyrus. The remarkable success of this method presumably lies in the fact that making this link between sound-symbol and meaning is *the fundamental problem of language acquisition,* with expressive speech being secondary to this symbolic-cognitive process. (See FIGURE 2.)

One additional method that we analyzed was the direct method of Emile de Sauzé. The most salient characteristic of this method is meaningful practice, both in listening comprehension and speaking, with translation avoided almost entirely. Reading and writing are introduced from the beginning as well, and grammatical reasoning—conscious hypothesis formation—is encouraged in postadolescent students. This method thus seems to make use of all the language areas of the left hemisphere plus the auxiliary areas involved in reading and writing. (See FIGURE 3).

From this background discussion, we now can begin to formulate more explicitly the criteria that methods should meet in order to enhance our natural abilities to learn second languages. In assuming that the capac-

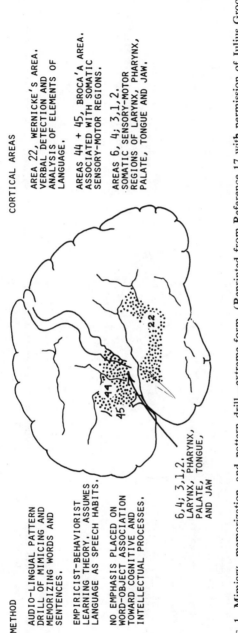
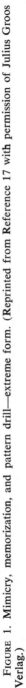

METHOD

AUDIO-LINGUAL PATTERN
DRILL OF MIMICING AND
MEMORIZING WORDS AND
SENTENCES.

EMPIRICIST-BEHAVIORIST
LEARNING THEORY. ASSUMES
LANGUAGE AS SPEECH HABITS.

NO EMPHASIS PLACED ON
WORD-OBJECT ASSOCIATION
TOWARD COGNITIVE AND
INTELLECTUAL PROCESSES.

6,4; 3,1,2.
LARYNX, PHARYNX,
PALATE, TONGUE,
AND JAW

CORTICAL AREAS

AREA 22, WERNICKE'S AREA.
VERBAL DETECTION AND
ANALYSIS OF ELEMENTS OF
LANGUAGE.

AREAS 44 + 45, BROCA'A AREA.
ASSOCIATED WITH SOMATIC
SENSORY-MOTOR REGIONS.

AREAS 6, 4; 3,1,2.
SOMATIC SENSORY-MOTOR
REGIONS OF LARYNX, PHARYNX,
PALATE, TONGUE AND JAW.

FIGURE 1. Mimicry, memorization, and pattern drill—extreme form. (Reprinted from Reference 17 with permission of Julius Groos Verlag.)

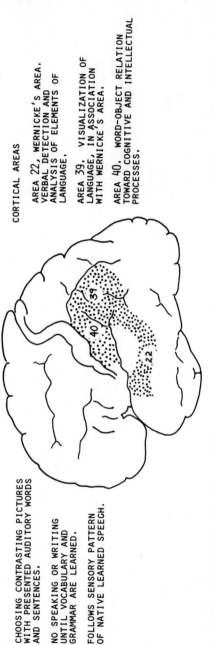

CORTICAL AREAS

AREA 22, WERNICKE'S AREA.
VERBAL DETECTION AND
ANALYSIS OF ELEMENTS OF
LANGUAGE.

AREA 39, VISUALIZATION OF
LANGUAGE, IN ASSOCIATION
WITH WERNICKE'S AREA.

AREA 40, WORD-OBJECT RELATION
TOWARD COGNITIVE AND INTELLECTUAL
PROCESSES.

METHOD

CHOOSING CONTRASTING PICTURES
WITH PRESENTED AUDITORY WORDS
AND SENTENCES.

NO SPEAKING OR WRITING
UNTIL VOCABULARY AND
GRAMMAR ARE LEARNED.

FOLLOWS SENSORY PATTERN
OF NATIVE LEARNED SPEECH.

FIGURE 2. Winitz and Reeds, "Rapid acquisition of a foreign language by the avoidance of speaking." (Reprinted from Reference 17 with permission of Julius Groos Verlag.)

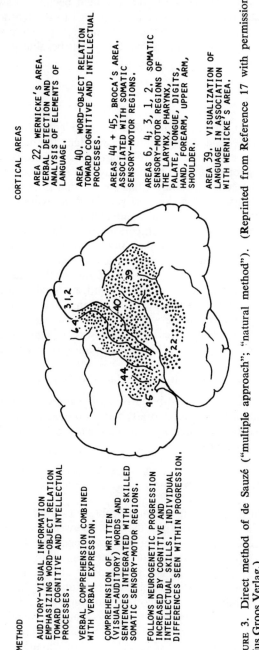

METHOD

AUDITORY-VISUAL INFORMATION
EMPHASIZING WORD-OBJECT RELATION
TOWARD COGNITIVE AND INTELLECTUAL
PROCESSES.

VERBAL COMPREHENSION COMBINED
WITH VERBAL EXPRESSION.

COMPREHENSION OF WRITTEN
(VISUAL-AUDITORY) WORDS AND
SENTENCES INTEGRATED WITH SKILLED
SOMATIC SENSORY-MOTOR REGIONS.

FOLLOWS NEUROGENETIC PROGRESSION
INCREASED BY COGNITIVE AND
INTELLECTUAL SKILLS. INDIVIDUAL
DIFFERENCES SEEN WITHIN PROGRESSION.

CORTICAL AREAS

AREA 22, WERNICKE'S AREA.
VERBAL DETECTION AND
ANALYSIS OF ELEMENTS OF
LANGUAGE.

AREA 40. WORD-OBJECT RELATION
TOWARD COGNITIVE AND INTELLECTUAL
PROCESSES.

AREAS 44 + 45, BROCA'S AREA.
ASSOCIATED WITH SOMATIC
SENSORY-MOTOR REGIONS.

AREAS 6, 4; 3, 1, 2. SOMATIC
SENSORY-MOTOR REGIONS OF
THE LARYNX, PHARYNX,
PALATE, TONGUE, DIGITS,
HAND, FOREARM, UPPER ARM,
SHOULDER.

AREA 39. VISUALIZATION OF
LANGUAGE IN ASSOCIATION
WITH WERNICKE'S AREA.

FIGURE 3. Direct method of de Sauzé ("multiple approach"; "natural method"). (Reprinted from Reference 17 with permission of Julius Groos Verlag.)

ity for language learning is innate, our problem becomes how to transmit the culturally determined aspects of the language to the learner, or how to put the students into contact with the new language in such a way that they (a) will want to learn the language and (b) will be able to learn it most easily.

Motivation

Motivation is a problem with second-language acquisition in a way that it isn't with the native language. Children who lack the motivation to learn their native language are rare and are regarded as pathological, but it is all too common for people to resist both openly and subconsciously the learning of a second language. Lambert has shown that *integrative* motivation results in better learners than does *instrumental* motivation.[21] Part of the issue between integrative and instrumental motivation is one of ends and means; those with instrumental motivation are looking to the end but are not enthusiastic about the means they must take to reach this end. This is where teachers and methods can intervene most effectively. Three factors are important here: the intrinsic interest of the method itself, the socio-cultural content of the teaching materials, and, as Stevick has emphasized so strongly,[16] the quality of human interaction. The human interaction is perhaps most important in the way in which it encourages speaking; but the experience of many indicates that even with listening comprehension materials, it is better to have a live performance with a teacher than to have a recorded voice.

Our first set of criteria, then, those related to motivation, would be:

1. A natural method should be intrinsically interesting, should involve sociocultural content that is appropriate to the students, and should involve high-quality human interaction, so that the means to learning the language will be as satisfying as the end.

Mastering the Linguistic Content

We have said that the fundamental problem in both first- and second-language acquisition was making the link between sound-symbol and meaning. For second-language learning we then should seek listening comprehension opportunities that hold attention both because of·their interest and because they can be comprehended. This means that materials should not be presented in some haphazard fashion, but should be ordered both according to interest and according to linguistic comprehensibility. In some way the materials must be ordered so that the crucial examples are given for inferring the proper meaning of expressions and constructions. Presumably there are many possible orderings of linguistic material that meet this criterion. The first lessons of the Berlitz direct method, for example, are based on questions and answers; total physical response is based at the beginning on commands; the Winitz and Reeds method is based on indicative statements.

If establishment of the sound-meaning connection has a certain priority in language acquisition, the mastery of speech can't be far behind. In fact we might suspect that it is not an accident that motor speech control and grammatical processes are linked anatomically, as seen in Broca's aphasia. Meaningful practice with speech may be necessary for the development of full grammatical competence.

What then about reading and writing? Even in native-language acquisition, it has been shown by Doman and Fuller, with quite different approaches, that brain-damaged low-IQ children gain a great deal in language development and general cognitive development by learning to read as soon as possible.[22,23] Both reading and writing likewise are very helpful in second-language acquisition, especially when dealing with mixed groups with their individual differences.

Our second set of criteria, then, would be that:

2. A natural method presents linguistic material for listening comprehension in an ordered way so that the meaning of both words and grammatical constructions is clear, and it gives opportunities for meaningful practice of speech. When possible, it also involves reading and writing.

Language-teaching methods that enhance our natural language-learning abilities, then, are not the most primitive and haphazard methods. We know enough about human language-learning processes and abilities to accelerate the process and insure a better result by proper ordering of materials according to criteria of motivation and linguistic content; in short, by careful teaching.

REFERENCES

1. PENFIELD, W. 1964. The uncommitted cortex. Atlantic Monthly **214**(1): 77–91.
2. DILLER, K. C. 1978. The Language Teaching Controversy: 128–134, 55–71. Newbury House Publishers. Rowley, Mass.
3. PENFIELD, W. & L. ROBERTS. 1959. Speech and Brain Mechanisms: 255. Princeton University Press. Princeton, N.J.
4. WALSH, T. M. & K. C. DILLER. 1978. Neurolinguistic considerations on the optimum age for second language learning. Proc. Berkeley Linguistics Soc. **5**: 510–524. (Reprinted in Reference 6.)
5. DURRETTE, R. 1972. A five year FLES report. Modern Lang. J. **56**(1): 23–24.
6. DILLER, K. C., Ed. 1981. Individual Differences and Universals in Language Learning Aptitude. Newbury House Publishers. Rowley, Mass.
7. CHOMSKY, N. 1968. Language and Mind: 79, 76. Harcourt Brace Jovanovich. New York, N.Y.
8. KRASHEN, S. 1981. Aptitude and attitude in relation to second language acquisition and learning. In Individual Differences and Universals in Language Learning Aptitude. K. C. Diller, Ed.: 155–175. Newbury House Publishers. Rowley, Mass.

9. DILLER, K. C. 1971. "Resonance" and language learning. Linguistics **70:** 16–24.
10. LENNEBERG, E. 1967. Biological Foundations of Language: 176. John Wiley & Sons, Inc. New York, N.Y.
11. SPOLSKY, B. 1968. The value of volunteers in English language teaching; or why pay for it when you can get it for nothing. Paper presented to National Association of Foreign Student Affairs. San Francisco, Calif.
12. MACNAMARA, J. 1973. Nurseries, streets, and classrooms: some comparisons and deductions. Modern Lang. J. **57**(5–6): 254–258.
13. KAGAN, J. 1967. On cultural deprivation. A paper presented to a conference on biology and behavior. Rockefeller University. New York, N.Y.
14. PLUMER, D. 1970. Parent-child verbal interaction: a study of dialogue strategies and verbal ability. Doctoral Thesis. Harvard University. Cambridge, Mass.
15. GOUIN, F. 1880. L'art d'enseigner et d'étudier les langues. Libraire Fischbacher. Paris, France.
16. STEVICK, E. 1976. Memory, Meaning, and Method. Newbury House Publishers. Rowley, Mass.
17. WALSH, T. M. & K. C. DILLER. 1978. Neurolinguistic foundations to methods of teaching a second language. IRAL **16**(1): 1–14.
18. DILLER, K. C. & T. M. WALSH. 1978. "Living" and "dead" languages: a neurolinguistic distinction. Actes du Congrès, Fifth International Congress of Applied Linguistics. Montreal, Quebec, Canada.
19. GESCHWIND, N., F. A. QUADFASEL & J. M. SEGARRA. 1968. Isolation of the speech area. Neuropsychologia **6:** 327–340.
20. WINITZ, H. & J. REEDS. 1975. Comprehension and Problem Solving as Strategies for Language Training. Mouton. The Hague, the Netherlands.
21. LAMBERT, W. 1969. Psychological aspects of motivation in language. (As reprinted in DILL, A. S., Ed. 1972. Language Psychology and Culture: Papers by Wallace Lambert. Stanford University Press. Palo Alto, Calif.)
22. DOMAN, G. 1963. How to Teach Your Baby to Read. Random House. New York, N.Y.
23. FULLER, R. 1974. Breaking down the IQ walls: severely retarded people *can* learn to read. Psychology Today (October): 97–102.

NEUROPHYSIOLOGICAL PROCESSES IN LANGUAGE ACQUISITION: GENERAL DISCUSSION

Moderator: Samuel Anderson

New York State Psychiatric Institute
New York, New York 10032

A. V. RAY (*Burlington, Ontario, Canada*): Dr. Kinsbourne, I hope I may add some information on lateralization. A patient of mine suffered from a big intracranial extracerebral tumor (meningioma, 180 grams). He was a highly educated priest having a perfect command of Latin, German, French, Italian, and Spanish. The typical symptomatology of progressively increasing intracranial pressure involved an early, progressive dysphasia equally affecting all his languages. It was the "anomic" type of aphasia (Gerstmann syndrome), that is, speech and written language but not comprehension or repetition affected. We removed the tumor impressed in the brain, filled the resulting space with a gauze strip, and subsequently allowed the brain to expand by pulling the gauze strip out in steps of every two or three days. With the brain expanding, the patient's capacity to speak and write all his languages returned dramatically and progressively to normal.

This experience shows, in accordance with many other experiences and data, that there is no particular localization or lateralization or centers for different languages in the brain.

In teaching languages, we always have to consider the total activity of the brain resulting from the coordinated activity of its individual parts and, consequently, the fact that such activity is subjected to favorable as well as adverse influences related to all sorts of conditions of and around the learning individual. They occupy a whole spectrum from the student's physiological state, environmental conditions, pedagogic methods used, and so forth, up to last, but not least, interpersonal relations with the teacher.

There is no way that we could or should address ourselves exclusively to any particular part or center of the brain, as was suggested in one of the presentations. Obviously a sensory signal, following its nature, is received primarily in a specific center or centers in the brain, but its further elaboration is a matter of the integral brain function, that is, coordinated functions of the brain centers that are known and defined by us, or which still are unknown.

M. KINSBOURNE (*Eunice Kennedy Shriver Center for Mental Retardation, Inc., Harvard University, Waltham, Mass.*): I appreciate your beautiful illustration. Thank you.

M. PATKOWSKI (*Hostos Community College, Bronx, New York*): I think it is relatively well established that childhood aphasia is different from

0077–8923/81/0379–0087 $01.75/2 © 1981, NYAS

adult aphasia. Lesions in the same areas of the brain in children and adults do not result in similar symptoms. Couldn't we infer something from that?

M. KINSBOURNE: Yes, let me tell you what I think we can infer. There are two differences between childhood and later aphasias. They hold for most cases, but not for all of them. The children more often have an output problem without a comprehension problem, whereas in adults, the comprehension problem often accompanies the output problem. The second is that children tend to recover faster than adults do. Neither of these differences tells us what the hemispheres were doing languagewise before the damage. What they tell us is interesting but totally different—it is about plasticity in recovery. It is a general neurobiological principle that the immature nervous system recovers better, or better compensates for damage to parts of it. This seems to be the case also in humans. If the damage to the left hemisphere is very early, language development may proceed entirely in the right hemisphere and may differ only in a subtle way from that based in the usual left hemisphere.

Now this propensity for the right hemisphere to take over when the left is damaged is available to all of us no matter how old we are. I have published, and others have confirmed, that in adults who are aphasic, quite frequently the language that is aphasic is not coming from the damaged left hemisphere at all, it is coming from the intact right hemisphere, which is compensating. So we see here a very interesting issue in plasticity in recovery or compensation of function but nothing relevant to any difference between language lateralization in the child and the adult. I have made the latter issue the subject of a major research program, and I have found reason after reason to suppose that, contrary to Lenneberg's assertion, those of us who are left lateralized for language were so even from the first unspoken word, and that the precursors of language are left lateralized even at birth. The idea that language lateralization is progressive from bisymmetry to left seems to be totally misconceived.

R. W. RIEBER (*John Jay College of Criminal Justice, New York, N.Y.*): I just want to make a comment on the critical period. I remember talking to Eric Lenneberg during one of his critical periods. I am not referring to when we were children. He did say some things that were perhaps worth reflecting on. It is sometimes forgotten that at least in the modern literature, the concept of the critical period was first suggested as having a much more extensive meaning than most researchers give it today. Penfield—a Canadian living in a bilingual district of Canada where English is now somewhat unfashionable—was one of the first to suggest this notion. The motivation that Penfield had when he wrote on this subject was pedagogical and oriented toward social-cultural issues, even though he was a famous brain surgeon. The question centered upon when to teach children L2 or L1 [second or first language] in their educational development. The purpose of his contribution was to give some rationale for the notion of teaching L1 to young children at the earliest possible age. Lenneberg was familiar with Penfield's work and was influenced by it. In his enthusiasm, he tried to develop a hypothesis of a more specific nature and came up with the critical-period hypothesis.

I do believe, however, that if he were alive today, he would be willing to revise it in such a way as to incorporate the broader social implications that I just alluded to.

H. WODE (*University of Kiel, Kiel, Federal Republic of Germany*): Dr. Whitaker, I have just an information question about the little circles on your diagrams [see FIGURE 8, page 72]. As I understood your talk, these circles indicate areas that are dysfunctioning, including overlap between the two languages. My question would be, Exactly what kind of test could one devise to check on this? What kind of overlap did you get? The point that I am driving at is this. One may either start with nonlinguistic variables, like asking for names of objects and so on. On the other hand, one might want to check on the formal properties of linguistic devices, for example, word order, the voicing distinction, the plosives, etc. This has important implications for determining the nature of the dysfunctioning, namely, whether it is due to nonlinguistic phenomena or to linguistic properties in the narrower sense, like word order and so forth.

H. A. WHITAKER (*University of Maryland, College Park, Md.*): Yes. I will try to elaborate on that very quickly. The data that I reported here are based on a naming test. As you can appreciate, in the operating room there are some restrictions on the sort of testing one can do. We use a slide that has an easily identifiable picture on it, and the patent is asked to read a phrase up above that. The phrase varies, such as "this is a" or "that is a," and so forth. The patient reads the test phrase and names the picture. The data that you see are based upon the ability to name a picture and a retained ability to read and speak, so that we are not interfering with motor function per se or with visual processing at least to that degree. The reason we use naming data is that naming appears to be ubiquitous to the language cortex. Just about any piece of brain that is used in the language system appears to be able to cause anomia when it isn't functioning right, and so naming gives you a good measure of how much brain might be involved in a language system.

We are now beginning to look at phoneme perception, practice movements, pronunciation, reading, various grammatical factors, and so on. It turns out that these functions are much more restricted in their localization, and appear to give you a different sort of representation, as you might expect. The purpose of the naming is not to identify what is different about an area so much as it is to look at the degree of commitment of those areas to a general, more global kind of linguistic function.

S. ANDERSON: Does Dr. Kinsbourne wish to comment on the evidence for double dissociation?

M. KINSBOURNE: My comment would be that if the differential patterning within the language area that Dr. Whitaker so eloquently presented had stability across patients, and if one could make predictions from case to case, then double dissociation would be established.

H. A. WHITAKER: The naming itself is not likely to accomplish that, by virtue of the fact that it seems to be tapping a rather different process. As far as I can see, it doesn't uniquely relate to any of the separate pieces of the brain, but when you get into things like looking at syntactic functions—as George Ojemann did, in a paper published in *Science* two years ago with Katy Meteer—you find that across patients there is in fact a systematic zone, if you will, for syntactic processing and outside of that there is a memory zone. There is a separate zone that is even closer in toward the Sylvian fissure for phoneme perception and articulatory production and so forth. The differentiation that you would find in these patients seems to relate to other kinds of functions, but what the naming data are looking at is really a degree of commitment to a global language process.

When we find that on five stimulation trials in this spot, naming is interfered with in English and that on none of the trials is it interfered with in Dutch, we are prepared to say that language processes are not represented for one language in that spot, but they are for the other. The only other way to infer the reliability of these data is to note that all the monolingual studies that we have done produce maps that look like this.

M. KINSBOURNE: The point is well taken. It is a different point than the one usually addressed in the bilingualism literature. It makes the point that within a dedicated area, different types of information—in this case, languages—are present in not exactly the same pattern. In other words, while the same general area is used, the specific configurations are not exactly superimposed.

H. A. WHITAKER: I agree. There is another level of consequences that I am in the process of working on now, and that is to raise the question as to whether biology is going to contribute anything to our notion of language universals. If this particular trend holds up for other factors when we actually are measuring empirically the functions in the brain, I would be willing to speculate that before very long we will abandon the notion of language universals—certainly abandon them as a biological construct. You could then do a fast retreat and argue that language universals accrue because of communication and behavioral demands; that is another matter. It is beginning to look as if biology is not going to make much of a contribution in that direction.

S. ERVIN-TRIPP (*University of California, Berkeley, Calif.*): Dr. Diller, your comment about needing possibly oral practice for grammar learning made me think about passive bilinguals, such as the grandchild who understands the grandmother. I wonder if anybody here has actually done detailed enough work to know whether we overestimate their grammatical understanding because they would seem to be a violation of that principle.

K. DILLER (*University of New Hampshire, Durham, N.H.*): I think that a certain amount of grammar can be learned passively. However, it's very easy to be misled. Broca's aphasics seem to understand ordinary conversation pretty well, until you test them on reversible passives and other

difficult grammatical constructions. The children who had left hemispherec-
tomies reported on by Dr. Harry Whitaker also had similar problems but
seemed relatively normal to the nonsophisticated people who heard them.

H. A. WHITAKER: Dr. Diller, I have more of a discussion comment
than a direct question. The use of some of the aphasic data to extrapolate
to second-language-teaching methods could lead someone astray if we
didn't extend it a little bit further. I realize you were constrained by time,
and so I'm going to take the liberty to extend it a bit further and tie it
back into your first comments on the stellate cells, or the local neuron cells.

I think that one ought to think of the changes in stellate cells, which
certainly go on for a lifetime as long as one remains healthy, not as a
function of maturation but as a function of interacting with the environment
and learning. I think what you want to do then is to go back in terms of this
neurolinguistic model and talk not so much about the aphasias, where
pieces of the brain are damaged and cannot work, but about areas of the
brain and their contributions to language functioning. In the normal intact
brain, you cannot do something that would, say, activate just Wernicke's
area. The supramarginal gyrus and Broca's area are attached to it and are
going to do something anyway regardless of whether you have specifically
trained it, so to speak.

So that the best way of viewing your model, I think, would be to put
it back in terms of learning parameters and argue that certain kinds of
second-language-teaching methods would have more of a modifying effect
on particular areas of the brain, leaving some areas of the brain not directly
approached. The brain is capable of modifying itself in a variety of un-
predicted and perhaps unwanted directions because, as I said, the normal
healthy brain is completely attached in all places and there is going to be a
myriad of influences from one part to another, no matter what you try to do.
Teaching methods that you've identified would be thought of best in terms
of focusing their attention on modifying only parts of the language system
rather than modifying all of it.

K. DILLER: Yes, your point is well taken. However, blood-flow
studies show that for reading aloud, for example, certain language areas are
clearly involved more than others. Although areas may be interconnected,
some areas are used in certain specific activities much more than are other
areas.

PERCEPTION OF FLUENT SPEECH BY CHILDREN AND ADULTS

Ronald A. Cole

Department of Computer Science
Carnegie-Mellon University
Pittsburgh, Pennsylvania 15213

What does it mean to acquire a language? In practical terms, we have acquired a language when we can use it to communicate like a native speaker. One aspect of this skill is the ability to translate our thoughts into speech. The other aspect is the ability to understand everyday, conversational speech—the ability to transform a continuous stream of sound into an ordered sequence of words.

This paper examines the process by which children and adults understand natural continuous speech. The paper begins with a brief description of some of the problems that a listener must overcome in order to understand fluent speech. A model of speech perception is presented, which describes the strategies that listeners use to overcome these problems. Three experiments then are described that investigate children's speech perception. Finally, the results of the experiments will be considered in terms of the model.

PROBLEMS INVOLVED IN UNDERSTANDING SPEECH

The problems involved in recognizing words from fluent speech can be described best by analogy to printed text. The words on this page are separated by spaces. While reading, these spaces are used to segment the text into words. If the spaces between words are removed, the resulting text is difficult to read; youcanseethatthisismoredifficultthannormaltext. In fluent speech, there are no physical cues that consistently and reliably indicate where one word ends and the next begins. It is up to the listener to segment speech into words. Secondly, in printed text, a particular word is physically the same whenever it appears, except for occasional changes in type font. By contrast, fluent speech is characterized by substantial phonological variation. The sound pattern of a word may change from one utterance to the next. Consider, for example, the different realizations of "what" in "What time is it?" "Whacha doin?" and "Whadaya say?" These two factors—lack of word boundaries and phonological variation—combine to make fluent speech a highly ambiguous stimulus. A given stretch of speech can often be segmented into words in more than one way. For example, the words "grew eyes" can be heard as "grew wise" and the sentence "We fed the catatonic" can be heard as "We fed the cat a tonic."

92

0077–8923/81/0379–0092 $01.75/2 © 1981, NYAS

A MODEL OF SPEECH PERCEPTION

Unless we are in the presence of a prolific punster, we rarely notice the ambiguity inherent in fluent speech. We almost always hear just those words that the speaker intended us to hear. How do we do it? Cole and Jakimik have attempted to answer this question within the framework of a model of word recognition from fluent speech.[2] The model consists of three assumptions, each of which has received support from a number of different experiments. The first assumption is that words are recognized through the interaction of sound and knowledge. That is, we recognize words by combining information that is present in the speech signal with our knowledge of the phonological, syntactic, semantic, and pragmatic structure of our language.

Cole and Perfetti have supported this claim by demonstrating that college students and children from preschool through fifth grade use various sources of knowledge to recognize words from fluent speech.[5] Cole and Perfetti recorded a 20-minute story in which some of the words were mispronounced by changing a single consonant sound to produce a non-sense word. Each word was mispronounced twice in the story—once when it was highly predictable from the preceding context and once when it was unpredictable. The results showed that all children detected mispronunciations more accurately and more rapidly when they occurred in predictable contexts. These results show that children and adults use contextual information to recognize words from fluent speech.

A second assumption of the model is that words in fluent speech are recognized sequentially, one after another. As each word is recognized, it provides syntactic and semantic constraints that are used to recognize the immediately following word. The assumption of word-by-word recognition helps to explain how speech is segmented into words; each word's recognition defines the beginning of the next word, and provides syntactic and semantic constraints that can be used during recognition. Cole and Perfetti have shown that both children and adults are able to use constraints provided by one word to help recognize an immediately following word while listening to fluent speech.[5] Their study included a set of words for which predictability was determined by the word immediately preceding the mispronunciation (e.g., "fried jicken" versus "dried jicken"; "hall ploset" versus "tall ploset"). All of the mispronunciations of the predictable words in this set were detected faster than the unpredictable words, showing that children as well as adults can use information from one word to facilitate recognition of an immediately following word.

Syntactic information that accompanies a word's recognition also can be used to guide the segmentation of speech into words. Consider the phrase "nosedrops will help the cold." When this phrase is spoken, it also can be heard as "knows drops will help the cold." Cole, Jakimik, and Cooper recorded a number of such ambiguous phrases, and then by means of tape splicing produced sentences that differed only by a single word, which preceded the ambiguous phrase.[4] For example, the ambiguous sequence "nosedrops (knows drops) will help the cold" was preceded by "The Doctor said he" and "The Doctor said that." When these sentences were presented to subjects, they all were heard as naturally spoken sentences without ambiguity, and in all cases, segmentation was consistent with the syntactic constraints provided by "that" and "he." Thus, if subjects heard "The Doctor said that," they then perceived "nosedrops will help the cold." If subjects heard "The Doctor said he," the rest of the sentence was heard as "knows drops will help the cold." Thus, segmentation of the same physical stimulus was determined solely by syntactic constraints provided by the word occurring just before the ambiguous sequence. These results, considered together with those reported by Cole and Perfetti,[5] show that syntactic and semantic information that accompanies a word's recognition can be used to guide segmentation or recognition of the incoming speech.

The third assumption of the model, suggested by Marslen-Wilson and Welsh, concerns the way in which phonetic information is used to recognize words.[11] According to Marslen-Wilson and Welsh, the sounds that begin a word are used to activate a set of word candidates. For example, if the listener hears the word-initial sequence "st," in the sentence "I like st—," the words "steak," "steel," "stew," "straw," and "stupid" are activated subconsciously, along with all other words in the listener's vocabulary that begin with "st." As additional phonetic information is processed, word candidates are eliminated until only one candidate remains. It is at this point that the word is recognized. Thus, phonetic information is used first to suggest word candidates, and then to eliminate them. The role of context is to speed up the process of choosing only one word. If a word is highly predictable, the listener can recognize it before it is specified uniquely by the acoustic input. A number of studies using different experimental tasks (e.g., phoneme monitoring, detection of mispronunciations, shadowing of continuous speech, gating of speech) now have provided strong support for the assumption that words are recognized through the sequential use of sound.[4,7,8,10] Moreover, experiments by Jakimik and Grosjean have confirmed that sound and knowledge interact during word recognition in the manner described by the model.[7,8]

To summarize, there is strong experimental support for the following assumptions about perception of fluent speech:

1. Words are recognized through the interaction of sound and knowledge. Listeners combine what they hear with what they know to recognize words.

2. Words are recognized in order. Each word's recognition helps locate and constrain recognition of the following word.

3. The sounds in a word are used sequentially to suggest and then eliminate word candidates until a single candidate emerges.

Taken together, these assumptions provide a fairly detailed description of the moment-by-moment processing that is involved in the perception of fluent speech. For a more detailed description of the model and its experimental support, the interested reader is referred to Cole and Jakimik.[2]

EXPERIMENTS IN SPEECH PERCEPTION

Now that we have considered the manner in which adults recognize words from fluent speech, we can turn our attention to children's speech perception. The experiment by Cole and Perfetti suggests that two of the assumptions of the model are relevant to children's speech perception. Recall that in this experiment, children detected mispronunciations in a recorded story more rapidly when the mispronounced word was predicted by prior context, and that this result was observed when predictability was determined by the word just before the mispronunciation.[5] These results suggest that children perceive speech word by word, and that children combine acoustic information with contextual information during word recognition.

The present experiments use the "listening for mispronunciations" task to investigate the manner in which children use phonetic information during word recognition from fluent speech.[1] Experiments 1 and 2 examine children's ability to perceive phonetic distinctions in word-initial, -medial, and -final position. Experiment 3 investigates whether children are able to use knowledge about the order in which phonetic segments can occur within words during recognition.

Experiment 1

In a series of six experiments, Cole, Jakimik, and Cooper examined college students' ability to detect mispronounced words in recorded stories.[3] The purpose of these experiments was to examine the detectability of phonetic distinctions in fluent speech. Mispronunciations were produced by substituting one consonant sound for another to produce a nonsense word (e.g., "boy" to "doy," "many" to "nany"). The results of these experiments can be summarized as follows:

1. The stop consonants /b/, /d/, /g/, /p/, /t/, and /k/ were more perceptible than were other consonants. In all six experiments, substitutions of stop consonants were detected more often than were substitutions of other consonants.

2. Changes involving the place of articulation of a stop consonant (e.g., "boy" to "doy") were more perceptible than were changes involving only the voicing of the consonant (e.g., "boy" to "poy").

3. In one-syllable words, word-initial mispronunciations were more detectable than were changes in word-final position. This result was observed for changes in place of articulation of the voiced stops /b/ and /d/ and the nasals /m/ and /n/. For nasals, the superior detectability of

word-initial changes is especially interesting, since the acoustic cues for the place distinction are at least as salient in final position as in initial position. This result suggests that listeners pay more attention to beginnings of words than to ends of words while listening to fluent speech.

Experiment 1 uses the listening for mispronunciations (LM) task to examine the detectability of a variety of phonetic features in word-initial, -medial, and -final position. In the LM task, subjects are presented with recorded prose and are instructed to respond (usually by pushing a button) whenever they detect a mispronounced word. In Experiments 1 and 2, mispronunciations were produced by changing a single consonant sound in a word to produce a nonsense word (e.g., "boy" to "doy" or "boy" to "poy").

The detection of a mispronunciation demonstrates the subject's ability to discriminate among two phonetic segments. In order to detect "poy" as a mispronunciation of "boy," the listener must be able to discriminate between /b/ and /d/. Within a particular experiment, the task provides a measure of the relative perceptibility of different phonetic contrasts. For example, if listeners consistently detect mispronunciations involving substitution of /d/ for /b/ but fail to detect mispronunciations involving substitution of /p/ for /b/, we can conclude that /b/–/p/ is a more difficult discrimination than /b/–/d/.

Method

Stimuli. Since the 22 consonants and semivowels of English yield $22 \times 21 = 462$ possible mispronunciations, it was not possible to examine all possible phonetic substitutions in Experiment 1. Consequently, the decision was made to limit substitutions to segments that differed by only a single phonetic feature, and to examine a representative sample of stop consonants, nasals, fricatives, and semivowels. The selection of mispronunciations also was motivated by the results of previous research; for example, fricative voicing changes were not examined, since Cole *et al.* had shown that these changes seldom are detected by adults.[3]

Children were presented with a total of 52 mispronunciations; 29 in word-initial position, 11 in word-medial position, and 12 in word-final position. The mispronunciations included changes of stops in initial, medial, and final position; manner of articulation changes of stops in initial position (e.g., "bird" to "vird"); manner and place changes of the fricatives /s/, /sh/, /f/, and /θ/ in initial, medial, and final position; substitution of /w/ and /r/ for /l/ in initial and medial position; and a single substitution of the affricate /ǰ/ in initial position.

In order to eliminate the effect of a word's familiarity or predictability on detection performance, the mispronunciations were presented in spoken versions of three familiar songs. Approximately six weeks before subjects were tested, I taught these songs to the four- and five-year-old children at the Carnegie-Mellon University Children's School. The songs were sung by the children at least twice a week before the experiment was begun. Although there is no guarantee that a given child actually knew all of the words in each song, it was at least certain that each child had heard each word spoken correctly a number of times in the context of the song before participating in the experiment.

The songs were recorded in a normal speaking voice by the author, who has had extensive practice recording stories with mispronunciations. When producing a mispronunciation, the altered word was pronounced exactly as if it were a real word, so that the resulting speech had a natural prosodic structure.

Procedure. The children were tested individually in a small room in a session lasting approximately 20 minutes. They were taught to clap their hands whenever a word was "said the wrong way." The training procedure consisted of two parts. First, the experimenter pointed to parts of her face while mispronouncing the names of some of the parts (e.g., "dose" instead of "nose," "peeth" instead of "teeth"). All children were able to learn to clap their hands to mispronunciations during this part of the experiment. The child then was told to listen for "silly words" in nursery rhymes. The nursery rhymes were presented at a comfortable listening level over a loud-speaker situated about one meter in front of the child. Each nursery rhyme was presented first without any mispronunciations to familiarize the child with both the rhyme and the speaker's voice. If the child failed to detect either of the two mispronunciations in the first rhyme ("Mary had a little lamb"), the experimenter pointed out what the mispronunciations had been, told the child to listen for them, and presented the nursery rhyme a second time. By the end of six nursery rhymes, all but two children (one four-year-old and one five-year-old) consistently detected mispronunciations in fluent speech. Following the training procedure, the spoken versions of the songs were presented over the loudspeaker without interruption while the child listened for mispronunciations.

Subjects. A total of 18 four-year-olds, 12 five-year-olds, and 20 college students were tested. College students did not receive the training procedure; instead, they were presented with spoken versions of each song without mispronunciations before listening to the experimental tape. This was done in order to familiarize them with the material and eliminate the potential effect of a word's familiarity or predictability on detection performance.

Results·

The main result to emerge from this experiment was that children rarely detected mispronunciations at the ends of words. Five-year-olds detected mispronunciations in initial, medial, and final position, respectively, 51%, 27%, and 12% of the time, while four-year-olds produced corresponding detection rates of 46%, 23%, and 13%. These compare to detection percentages of 95%, 86%, and 71% produced by college students. Thus, all groups of subjects detected mispronunciations most often in word-initial position and least often in word-final position. Children were between three and five times more likely to detect a word-initial mispronunciation than a word-final one. Note that when the data are viewed in terms of the proportion of total errors made at each position, the results are equivalent for children and adults.

The effect of word position on detection performance is extremely robust, since it was observed no matter how the stimuli were subdivided. For example, when only the most detectable word-final mispronunciations were considered—those detected over 90% of the time by college students—detection performance still was only 27% by both four- and five-year-olds. It seems safe to conclude, then, that four- and five-year-old children are most sensitive to phonetic information in word-initial position in fluent speech.

Detection performance also was affected by the type of phonetic substitution. TABLE 1 displays detection performance for all word-initial mispronunciations grouped according to the type of phonetic substitution. Note first that college students detected all word-initial mispronunciations with at least 90% accuracy. By adult standards, all of the phonetic substitutions are highly detectable. Inspection of TABLE 1 reveals that children's detection performance was influenced by the type of phonetic substitution that produced the mispronunciation. In general, the most detectable mispronunciations involved the substitution of one stop consonant for another or the substitution of a nasal for a stop. By contrast, substitutions among nasals and fricatives were detected 20% to 30% less often than were substitutions among stops.

TABLE 1 reveals one interesting exception to this pattern of results—the three mispronunciations that were produced by changing a voiceless plosive to its voiced counterpart were detected only 42% of the time by five-year-olds and 24% of the time by four-year-olds. This compares to over 70% detection of all other stop-consonant substitutions. As we will see, this result is replicated in the next experiment using three additional speakers.

A final result of interest in Experiment 1 was that children almost never detected substitutions of /r/ or /l/ for /w/ in medial position. No child detected "swawwowed," and only one child detected "swarrowed." College students detected "swawwowed" 55% of the time and "swarrowed" 85% of the time.

To summarize, Experiment 1 has shown that children attend to beginnings of words rather than to ends of words in fluent speech, and that children perceive some phonetic distinctions better than others. These results are in excellent agreement with those reported by Cole et al. for college students.[3] At a more general level, Experiment 1 demonstrates that the LM task can be used to examine children's phoneme perception using natural continuous speech.

Experiment 2

Experiment 2 was performed in order to provide a more detailed examination of children's phoneme perception. The experiment was designed for two reasons: (a) to compare children's detection of mispronunciations in isolated words and in fluent speech, and (b) to compare detection of the same mispronunciations produced by different speakers.

In Experiment 2, four-year-old children were presented with mispronunciations both in isolated words and in fluent speech. Each child first listened for mispronunciations of words spoken in isolation, and then listened for mispronunciations in nursery rhymes. Although the words that were mispronounced were different in the two parts of the experiment, the phonetic substitutions were exactly the same.

TABLE 1

PERCENT DETECTION OF WORD-INITIAL MISPRONUNCIATIONS FOR DIFFERENT PHONETIC SUBSTITUTIONS

	Four-Year-Olds	Five-Year-Olds	College Students
Stop Place Changes			
Voiced Stops	69	74	98
Voiceless Stops	50	70	97
Stop Voicing Changes			
Voiced to Voiceless	83	61	97.5
Voiceless to Voiced	42	24	92
Stop to Nasal	71	69.5	97.5
Nasal to Stop	37.5	30.5	92.5
Nasal to Nasal	41.5	36	97.5
Fricative to Fricative	42	40	90
/l/ to /r/	50	22	100
/r/ to /l/	58	56	100

Method

Stimuli. The substitutions used in Experiment 2 are shown in TABLE 2. It can be seen that the stimuli can be grouped into categories consisting of substitutions among stop consonants, among fricatives, and among semivowels. In addition, there were two nasal-plosive substitutions and three substitutions commonly observed in the speech of children with functional articulatory disorders. Mispronunciations in both isolated words and nursery rhymes always occurred in word-initial position in a stressed syllable.

Procedure. In the isolated word condition, children were taught to clap their hands if an object shown in a colored photograph was "said the wrong way." Stimuli in the isolated word test included photographs of objects presented in the following order: hat, chair, table, fish, lamp, dog, pencil, ring, saw, cat, matches, goat, bell, shoe, knife, and wagon. As the pictures were shown to the child, the object shown in the picture was named several times, sometimes correctly and sometimes with a word-initial mispronunciation. The number of mispronunciations that accompanied each picture was dictated by the number of phonetic substitutions involving the word-initial segment. Thus, the photograph of a table was accompanied by the sequence "table," "cable" (/t/ to /k/), "table," "dable" (/t/ to /d/).

The pictures of the hat and the chair were used to teach children to detect mispronunciations of words spoken in isolation. The children were told to clap their hands if "the thing shown in the picture is said the wrong way." The experimenter then placed the photograph of the hat in front of

TABLE 2

MISPRONUNCIATIONS IN NINE NURSERY RHYMES

Stop Consonant Place Changes		
/b/ to /d/	/d/ to /g/	/g/ to /d/
/p/ to /t/	/t/ to /k/	/k/ to /t/
Stop Consonant Voicing Changes		
/b/ to /p/	/d/ to /t/	/g/ to /k/
/p/ to /b/	/t/ to /d/	/k/ to /g/
Nasal to Stop Changes		
/m/ to /b/	/n/ to /d/	
Fricative Substitutions		
/f/ to /s/	/s/ to /f/	/sh/ to /f/
/f/ to /sh/	/s/ to /sh/	/sh/ to /s/
Semivowel Substitutions		
/l/ to /r/	/r/ to /l/	/w/ to /r/
/l/ to /w/	/r/ to /w/	/w/ to /l/
Common Articulatory Substitutions		
/sh/ to /t/	/s/ to /t/	/f/ to /p/

her face (to obscure speechreading cues) and said "pat." If the child failed to clap upon hearing the mispronunciation, the experimenter said: "I said 'hat' the wrong way; I said 'pat' instead of 'hat.' You were supposed to clap your hands when I said 'pat.' Let's try it again." The experimenter then proceeded through the sequence "pat," "hat," "hat," "gat," "zat." The sequence was repeated until the child clapped to each mispronunciation of "hat" and produced no false alarms to correct pronunciations. The training procedure was continued with a photograph of a chair accompanied by the spoken sequence "chair," "bair," "mair," "chair." All children were able to complete the training procedure.

Following the training procedure for isolated words, the experimenter informed the child that she would hold up "pictures of things," one at a time, and that the name of the thing shown in the picture would be spoken over the loudspeaker. The child was told to clap if the name was said the wrong way. The experimenter then held up the first photograph, and the child listened for mispronunciations of the expected word.

After the last photograph was presented, the experimenter trained the child to listen for mispronunciations in nursery rhymes. The child was trained as in Experiment 1, using the nursery rhyme "Jack and Jill," which contained two mispronunciations. The child was required to detect both of the mispronunciations in this rhyme before listening to the nine recorded rhymes.

Subjects. Four groups of four-year-old children were tested; each group of children listened to a different speaker's voice. Thirty-six children listened to speaker RC (male), 18 children listened to speaker MS (female), 12 children listened to speaker BJ (female), and 12 children listened to speaker GB (male). For speakers MS, BJ, and GB, the isolated words and nursery rhymes were recorded on tape and presented to the children over a loudspeaker. For speaker RC, only the nursery rhymes were recorded. This group of children heard the pictures named by either of two female experimenters.

Results

The results showed that children detect mispronunciations in isolated words much more accurately than in fluent speech. Across all groups, mispronunciations of words spoken in isolation were detected 95% of the time, compared to 59% detection of mispronunciations in nursery rhymes. This result certainly is not surprising, since segment durations of words spoken in isolation are approximately twice as long as segment durations of words in fluent speech.[9] Unfortunately, we cannot conclude that superior detection performance for isolated words was due to acoustic factors, since these words also were accompanied by a picture. It is likely that children were more confident that a mispronunciation had occurred (and thus were more likely to respond) when they were able to match the spoken word to the object shown in the picture. Because of this confound, we can conclude only that mispronounced words presented along with a visual referent are detected about twice as often as are mispronounced words in fluent speech. However, even this conclusion is interesting, since most tests of phoneme perception require children to point to an object or a picture of an object after hearing it named. The present experiment clearly shows that this situation maximizes discrimination performance. We can conclude, then, that most clinical tests of phonetic discrimination overestimate a listener's ability to perceive phonetic differences while listening to conversational speech.

Children's detection of mispronunciations in nursery rhymes is shown in TABLE 3 for each speaker for the different types of phonetic substitutions. For all speakers, children were most accurate in detecting "articulatory substitutions"—mispronunciations like those observed in the speech of children with articulatory disorders. On acoustic grounds, this result is not surprising, since the segments /s/–/t/, /f/–/p/, and /sh/–/t/ have different onset characteristics and therefore are perceptually distinct.

In Experiment 1, it was noted that children did not detect mispronunciations involving a change in voicing of a word-initial voiceless stop. This result was replicated in Experiment 2. For all speakers, children had the most difficulty detecting a change from a voiceless stop to its voiced cognate (e.g., "tails" to "dails"). This result is especially interesting in view of the fact that children in all four groups had no difficulty detecting a change in the opposite direction—from voiced to voiceless (e.g., "diamond" to "tiamond").

Why should children have more difficulty detecting a change from /t/ to /d/ or /p/ to /b/ than a change from /d/ to /t/ or /b/ to /p/? One possibility is that children ignore voiceless to voiced changes because the

TABLE 3

PERCENT DETECTION OF MISPRONUNCIATIONS PRODUCED BY FOUR
SPEAKERS FOR DIFFERENT PHONETIC SUBSTITUTIONS

	Speaker			
	RC	GB	BJ	MS
Stop Consonants				
Voiced Place Change	60	53	53	54
Voiceless Place Change	78	64	47	83
Voiced to Voiceless	78	72	58	65
Voiceless to Voiced	20	42	39	30
Nasal to Stop	62	42	54	78
Fricative Substitutions	47	51	55	53
Semivowel Substitutions	52	60	55	90
Articulatory Substitutions	85	75	83	85

voiceless stops /p/, /t/, and /k/ undergo substantial allophonic variation in fluent speech. For example, in word-initial position, the voiceless stops are aspirated, but they are unaspirated in /s/-stop clusters (e.g., "spill," "stop," "skip"). In fact, if the initial /s/ is removed from a word like "spill," English speakers hear "bill" rather than "pill." Moreover, the duration of a voiceless stop is affected greatly by the stress of the syllable in which it occurs, whereas voiced stops are relatively unaffected by syllable stress. Because of this variation, children may not assign much importance to the duration of a voiceless stop, and therefore fail to detect mispronunciations in which voiceless stops are changed to their voiced cognates.

Thus far we have examined the similarities in children's detection performance across the four speakers. These results may be summarized as follows: (a) the common articulatory substitutions /s/ to /t/, /f/ to /p/, and /sh/ to /t/ are most detectable; (b) the voiceless to voiced stop consonant substitutions /p/ to /b/, /t/ to /d/, and /k/ to /g/ are poorly detected; and (c) the voiced to voiceless stop consonant substitutions /b/ to /p/, /d/ to /t/, and /g/ to /k/ are highly detectable.

Beyond these similarities, the results are best described as "speaker dependent." That is, children's detections of the different types of phonetic substitutions varied across speakers. The results for speaker RC were similar to those obtained in the previous experiment—changes involving stop consonants were detected more often than were fricative or semi-vowel substitutions. For speakers GB and BJ, detections were quite similar across the different types of substitutions. Speaker MS produced the most interesting pattern of results in that detections of her mispronunciations differed from the other three speakers. For MS alone, the semivowel substitutions were detected more often than any other type of mispronunciation. This variation across speakers is most interesting, since it suggests that different phonetic classes are most salient in the speech of different speakers. The possibility exists that across a wide range of speakers, children are presented with an acoustically well-defined specification of each phonetic class.

Experiment 3

In Experiments 1 and 2, the detection of a mispronunciation required two sources of knowledge: knowledge about the phonemes of English and knowledge about the words of English. In order to determine that "top" is mispronounced in the sentence "Johnny spun his dop," the listener must be able to tell that "dop" is not "top," that is, that /d/ and /t/ are different, and that "dop" is not an English word. Experiment 3 looks at children's ability to use a third source of knowledge about spoken English—knowledge about the order in which phonetic segments can occur within words. Experiment 3 examines children's ability to use phonotactic knowledge—knowledge of phoneme-sequence constraints—during word recognition from fluent speech.

The order in which phonetic segments can occur in English words is highly constrained. For example, in English, a word-initial cluster of three consonants must begin with /s/, be followed by /p/, /t/, or /k/, and end with /r/, /l/, or /w/ (e.g., "split," spring," "street," "screw," "squeeze"). Speakers of English implicitly know the phonotactic structure of their language. When playing Scrabble, an English speaker might bluff with "blit," "shrats," or "fren," but would never bluff with "dlit," "srats," or "vren." The player knows that English words cannot begin with /dl/, /sr/, or /vr/ and that other English speakers share this knowledge.

In a classic experiment, Greenberg and Jenkins verified that linguistic competence includes detailed knowledge about the phonotactic structure of one's language.[6] Using a formal substitution algorithm, they generated a set of 24 CCVC* syllables that formed a continuum representing deviation

* Consonant-consonant-vowel-consonant.

from the phonotactic structure of English. Syllables at one end of the continuum were real English words, while syllables at the other end represented maximum deviation from English. English-speaking adults listened to the syllables and rated each one according to its similarity to English. The results showed that English speakers not only are able to distinguish "legal" nonsense words from "illegal" ones, but are able to discriminate subtle differences among nonsense words in terms of their deviation from the phonotactic structure of English.[6]

Whorf has described the phoneme sequence constraints for one-syllable English words in a single formula.[14] According to Whorf, every child between the ages of two and five who is learning to speak English is engaged in learning the pattern expressed by this formula. In his words:

> By the time the child is six, the formula has become ingrained and automatic; even the little nonsense words the child makes up conform to it, exploring its possibilities but not venturing a jot beyond them. At an early age the formula becomes for the child what it is for the adult; no sequence of sounds that deviates from it can even be articulated without the greatest difficulty. New words like "blurb," nonsense words like Lewis Carroll's "mome raths," combinations intended to suggest languages of savages or animal cries, like "glub" and "squonk"—all come out of the mold of this formula.[14]

Experiments by Menyuk and by Messer support these speculations.[12,13] Menyuk examined the ability of children between the ages of four and eight to discriminate and reproduce legal and illegal nonsense words.[12] In the first phase of the experiment, the experimenter pointed to colored balls and named each one. The names consisted of legal nonsense words such as "trid," "drid," "stid," "glid," and "kwid" or illegal words such as "tsid," "dlid," "srid," "gzid," and "kvid." Menyuk found that children were equally adept at learning to point to the appropriate ball when legal and illegal names were used. This result is not surprising since the five words in each condition began with a different consonant, so the child had only to match the appropriate word-initial sound to the appropriate ball. The more interesting result occurred in the second stage of the study, when children were asked to reproduce the nonsense words immediately after hearing the experimenter say them. It was found that children had much more difficulty reproducing the illegal words than the legal ones. Pre-school children averaged 15% correct reproduction of the illegal nonsense words, compared to 45% correct reproduction of legal nonsense words. The corresponding percentages for second graders were 35% versus 65%.[12] These results show that even eight-year-old children have trouble remembering and reproducing words that violate the phonotactic structure of their language.

Messer asked three- and four-year-old children which of two spoken items sounded "more like a word."[13] The words pairs consisted of legal and illegal nonsense words (e.g., "frul" vs. "mrul"). Messer found that children chose legal nonsense words to be more English-like significantly more often than illegal ones. Interestingly, on those occasions when children said the illegal nonsense word as their choice, they usually mispronounced it. Messer reports significantly more mispronunciations of illegal words than legal words, and that over 90% of these mispronunciations produced forms that were more English-like.[13] Thus, both Menyuk and Messer found that children have difficulty producing words that violate the phonotactic structure of their language, while Messer showed that children as young as three years of age are able to make decisions about spoken words based on their similarity to the sound pattern of English.

Experiment 3 uses the LM task to determine whether four- and five-year-old children use phonotactic structure to recognize words in fluent speech. To investigate this hypothesis, children were presented with a recorded story that contained both legal and illegal mispronunciations. They were taught to push a response button as quickly as possible whenever they heard a mispronunciation. The dependent variable in this experiment was the time required to detect a mispronunciation, measured from the beginning of the mispronounced word.

If children use phonotactic knowledge during speech perception, we should expect to find faster recognition of illegal mispronunciations than of legal ones. Consider the mispronunciation of "love" in the sentence "I know you will shlove it." After recognizing the words "I know you will," an English speaker can determine that a mispronunciation has occurred as soon as "shl" is heard, since English words do not begin with this cluster. By contrast, when presented with a legal mispronunciation such as "slove," the listener must wait for additional acoustic information in order to determine that a mispronunciation has occurred, since many English words begin with "sl." Thus, if children use phonotactic knowledge during word recognition, they should detect illegal mispronunciations faster than legal ones.

Method

Stimuli. A total of 32 mispronunciations were presented in a 12-minute story. Eight legal mispronunciations were produced by adding a word-initial /s/ to words beginning with /l/ (e.g., "slong," "slady"), and 8 illegal mispronunciations were produced by adding a word-initial /sh/ to eight additional words beginning with /l/ (e.g., "shliked," "shleaned"). Similarly, 8 legal mispronunciations were produced by adding a word-initial /s/ to words beginning with /w/ (e.g., "swould," "sworked") while 8 illegal mispronunciations were produced by adding a word-initial /f/ to words beginning with /w/ (e.g., "fwish," "fwheel"). As in the previous experiments, mispronunciations were produced by saying each mispronounced word as if it were a real word while recording the story.

Procedure. During the experiment, the children first listened to a recorded version of the story with no mispronunciations. This was done to familiarize them with the story. After listening to the story, they were taught to press a response button as soon as they heard a word "said the wrong way." The training procedure was similar to that used in the previous two experiments; children first learned to push the button to mispronunciations of isolated words, and then to mispronunciations of words in a nursery rhyme. After the training procedure, the children were presented with the story version containing the mispronunciations, and were told to push the button as fast as they could whenever they detected a mispronunciation.

A tone was placed at the onset of each mispronounced word on the alternate channel of the recording tape. This tone, which was inaudible to the subject, was used to trigger a millisecond timer. The timer was stopped when the subject pushed the response button, indicating that a mispronunciation had been heard.

Subjects. The story was presented to 18 four-year-olds and 16 five-year-olds at the Carnegie-Mellon University Children's School, and to 18 college students. None of the children in the present experiment had participated in the previous experiments.

Results

The results will be considered in terms of both detection accuracy and response latencies. A detection was defined as a button press that occurred within two seconds of a mispronunciation—reaction times longer than two seconds were scored as nondetections. Overall detection accuracy in the present experiment was higher than in the previous two experiments. Four-year-olds, five-year-olds, and college students, respectively, detected 84%, 81%, and 99% of the mispronunciations in the story. It appears that the addition of a word-initial segment produces a highly detectable mispronunciation, since the detection percentages for four-year-olds in the present experiment were equivalent to the highest detection percentages observed in the previous experiment.

The percentage of legal and illegal mispronunciations detected by each group of subjects for words beginning with /l/ and /w/ is shown in TABLE 4. It can be seen that children detected words beginning with /shl/ about 10% more often than words beginning with /sl/, and that words beginning with /sw/ were detected about 10% more often than words beginning with /fw/. The lower detection percentages for words beginning with /fw/ probably is due to the fact that the frication noise for /f/ is extremely weak. Because of this, children may have had some difficulty hearing the /fw/ cluster, resulting in fewer detections or longer response times.

The reaction-time data are displayed in TABLE 5. Inspection of this table reveals that illegal mispronunciations were detected faster than legal ones by four-year-olds, five-year-olds, and college students. Separate analyses of variance were performed on the reaction-time data, using both subjects and words as random effects. The only significant effects to emerge

TABLE 4

PERCENT DETECTION OF LEGAL AND ILLEGAL MISPRONUNCIATIONS
IN WORDS BEGINNING WITH "L" AND "W"

	/sl/	/shl/	/sw/	/fw/
Four-Year-Olds	78	92	88	79
Five-Year-Olds	82	89	80	71
College Students	100	100	98	99

across both analyses were age and phonotactic structure. Thus, college students detected mispronunciations faster than did children, and all subjects detected illegal mispronunciations faster than legal ones ($p < 0.01$ in both cases). As TABLE 5 shows, the only exception to this pattern of results was that four-year-olds were equally fast at detecting mispronunciations of words beginning with /sw/ and /fw/. As noted above, the weak frication noise for /f/ relative to /s/ may have produced longer reaction times to words beginning with /fw/. TABLE 5 shows that the effect of phonotactic structure was greater for /shl/ versus /sl/ than for /fw/ versus /sw/ for all groups of subjects. The interaction between phonotactic structure and word-initial segment (/l/ versus /w/) was significant in the analysis of variance with subjects as the random effect, but failed to reach significance in the analysis with words as the random effect ($p = 0.16$).

The results of Experiment 3 clearly support the hypothesis that children use phonotactic structure to recognize words from fluent speech. Mispronunciations that violated phoneme-sequence constraints in English words were detected faster by both four- and five-year-olds than were mispronunciations that did not violate these constraints.

DISCUSSION

The results of these experiments can be summarized as follows:

1. Children pay more attention to phonetic information in word-initial position in fluent speech than to phonetic information in word-medial or word-final position.

TABLE 5

REACTION TIMES TO LEGAL AND ILLEGAL MISPRONUNCIATIONS

	Words Beginning with /L/		Words Beginning with /W/	
	Legal (/sl/)	Illegal (/shl/)	Legal (/sw/)	Illegal (/fw/)
Four-Year-Olds	1139	975	1130	1127
Five-Year-Olds	1143	990	1204	1106
College Students	698	577	693	630

2. Children detect mispronunciations of words spoken in isolation (and accompanied by a picture of the object that is misnamed) more accurately than mispronunciations of words in fluent speech.

3. Some phonetic substitutions are more detectable than others.

4. Children use knowledge of phoneme-sequence constraints to recognize words from fluent speech.

The results of these experiments suggest that children rely mainly on word-initial information to recognize words from fluent speech. Children detected mispronunciations more accurately in word-initial position than in word-final position, and were able to use knowledge about word-initial phoneme-sequence constraints to facilitate the detection of mispronunciations. Let us consider these results in terms of the assumption that children recognize words by using phonetic information to first suggest and then eliminate word candidates.

Marslen-Wilson and Welsh performed an experiment in which subjects were required to shadow (repeat verbatim) connected speech.[11] Some of the words in the speech were mispronounced, and mispronunciations occurred either in word-initial or word-final position. Analysis of the subjects' speech while shadowing showed that more word-initial mispronunciations were detected than word-final mispronunciations. Marslen-Wilson and Welsh argued that listeners are able to arrive at a single word candidate before processing word-final information, and therefore are less likely to detect mispronunciations in this position. Cole, Jakimik, and Cooper also observed a higher percentage of word-initial mispronunciations than word-final ones,[3] and college students in the present study produced a similar pattern of results. If we apply the same reasoning used by Marslen-Wilson and Welsh to the children's recognition data, we are led to conclude that children are able to combine phonetic information and prior context to recognize words before word-final information has arrived and therefore pay less attention to word-final information.

The finding that illegal mispronunciations are detected faster than legal mispronunciations also is consistent with the assumption that children use phonetic information sequentially during word recognition. According to the model, word-initial information is used to generate a set of word candidates. Thus, when a word begins with /sh/, all words beginning with this sound are activated as candidates; when the listener hears /l/, forming an illegal cluster, a decision can be made that a mispronunciation has occurred, since all word candidates have been eliminated. When a word begins with /s/ followed by /l/, there are many candidates still available, and a decision must await additional phonetic information.

The picture that emerges from the listening for mispronunciations experiments performed to date is that by the time children are four years old, they are able to use the same strategies as adults to recognize words from fluent speech. These strategies include recognizing speech word by word, combining sound and knowledge during word recognition, and recognizing words through the sequential analysis of sound. On the other hand, the present research shows that children may not always hear the same thing as adults while listening to speech. Four- and five-year-old children have great difficulty distinguishing voiceless stops from voiced stops in word-initial position, whereas adults have less difficulty with this discrimination. It appears that five-year-old children have yet to acquire some of the perceptual distinctions that are used by adults during word recognition. The present research shows, however, that children use the phonetic information that is available to them in much the same way as adults do.

References

1. Cole, R. A. 1973. Listening for mispronunciations: a measure of what we hear during speech. Percept. Psychophys. **13:** 153–156.
2. Cole, R. A. & J. Jakimik. 1980. A model of speech perception. *In* Perception and Production of Fluent Speech. R. Cole, Ed. Erlbaum. Hillsdale, N.J.
3. Cole, R. A., J. Jakimik & W. E. Cooper. 1978. Perceptibility of phonetic features in fluent speech. J. Acoust. Soc. Am. **64:** 44–56.
4. Cole, R. A., J. Jakimik & W. Cooper. 1980. Segmenting speech into words. J. Acoust. Soc. Am. **67:** 1323–1332.
5. Cole, R. A. & C. Perfetti. 1980. Listening for mispronunciations in a children's story: the use of context by children and adults. J. Verb. Learn. Verb. Behav. **19:** 297–315.
6. Greenberg, J. H. & J. J. Jenkins. 1964. Studies in the psychological correlates of the sound system of American English. Word **20:** 157–172.
7. Grosjean, F. 1980. Spoken word recognition processes and the gating paradigm. Percept. Psychophys. **28:** 267–283.
8. Jakimik, J. 1980. The interaction of sound and knowledge during word recognition in fluent speech. Doctoral Dissertation. Carnegie-Mellon University. Pittsburgh, Pa.
9. Klatt, D. H. & K. N. Stevens. 1973. On the automatic recognition of continuous speech: implications from a spectrogram-reading experiment. IEEE Trans. Audio Electroacoust. **AU-21:** 210–217.
10. Marslen-Wilson, W. D. 1978. Sequential decision processes during spoken word recognition. Paper presented at the meeting of the Psychonomics Society, San Antonio, Tex.
11. Marslen-Wilson, W. D. & A. Welsh. 1978. Processing interactions and lexical access during word recognition in continuous speech. Cognitive Psychol. **10:** 29–63.
12. Menyuk, P. 1968. Children's learning and reproduction of grammatical and nongrammatical phonological sequences. Child Dev. **39:** 849–859.
13. Messer, S. 1967. Implicit phonology in children. J. Verb. Learn. Verb. Behav. **6:** 609–613.
14. Whorf, B. 1955. Language, Thought and Reality: 223–224. Cambridge Technology Press. Cambridge, Mass.

PHONOLOGICAL UNIVERSALS IN LANGUAGE ACQUISITION *

Marlys A. Macken and Charles A. Ferguson

Department of Linguistics
Stanford University
Stanford, California 94305

The paradox of human language is that it is, at once, both fixed and free; universals of structure and process coexist with diversity and change. True universals are so deeply a part of language, so basic to the ways in which we think about language, that—like fish in water—we find it difficult to recognize them or, when we do, they seem obvious or trivial. Not surprisingly, progress has been slow toward the goal of characterizing human language. In phonology, exceptionless universals include linearity of units that are analyzable into hierarchical structures, rule-governed systems, redundancy, and variation in sounds by context, speaker, social setting, and over time.

Easier to discover are the widespread tendencies of languages to pattern in certain ways. The term "universal" will be used here, as it often is used in linguistics, to describe such cross-language patterns—ones that have a high probability of occurrence but are not without exception, such as Trubetzkoy's typology of vowel systems, Ferguson's universal states and normal tendencies for nasals, and Greenberg's implicational universals for glottalized consonants.[1] In phonology, many such universals derive from universal properties of human articulatory and perceptual systems.[2-5] Yet the hallmark of human language is its range of variation, across particular languages and within the individual. A characterization of the constraints on this variation is as much a part of a theory of human language as is the characterization of the commonly occurring patterns.

The same paradox exists for language development: it too is both fixed and free. The determination of true universals likewise is difficult, the statement of general patterns somewhat easier. And once again, the hallmark is variation, across languages and in the individual. Much research in child phonology is directed toward finding regularities in this variation. The formulation of a theory of acquisition lies in the distant future, and behind us lies a history of the sequential demise of elegant, yet ultimately too simple, acquisitional theories.

We begin this paper by briefly reviewing the major universalist theories, both to provide the necessary framework for the data we discuss and also

* Some of the research reported here was carried out at the Child Phonology Project of Stanford University, under a series of grants from the National Science Foundation, the National Institutes of Health, the National Institute of Education, and the W. T. Grant Foundation.

0077–8923/81/0379–0110 $01.75/2 © 1981, NYAS

to emphasize the point that a discussion of "language universals" (developmental and otherwise) entails a particular theoretical position—one that is not uncontroversial. The philosophical debate over language universals goes back centuries. Although the universal status of the phonological properties we gave earlier (as examples of true universals) is accepted widely in the field, not all phonologists are committed to the view that there exists a set of general patterns (e.g., most early American structuralists and the proponents of the British prosodic school). Likewise, in child phonology, debate continues over the existence of a universal developmental sequence.

In the second section, we give a partial typology of phonological processes that are universal in the probabilistic sense and appear to be due to purely linguistic constraints. In addition to summarizing the major findings of a certain body of research, this review serves to exemplify the nature of linguistically oriented work conducted (explicitly or implicitly) within a universalist framework. Accurately reflecting the general state in the field as a whole, this typology is descriptive, not explanatory.

From general patterns, we take up the issue of variation, exploring a single topic—the acquisition of voicing—in search of universals, methodological explanations for variation, and regularities underlying cross-language differences. Just as cross-cultural, anthropological research on Polynesian navigation systems, iKung San hunting practices, and Kpelle class-inclusion concepts has revealed the cultural context of western theories of cognition including that of Piaget (e.g., Reference 6), cross-linguistic phonological acquisition research has demonstrated that the developmental sequence is affected greatly by both the macro context (the particular language) and the micro context (e.g., the specific input to the child).

In the final section, we turn to variation in the individual child—abstracting away from this linguistic variation to formulate general functional characteristics of the acquisition process that seem to be nonlinguistic in origin: underlying the linguistic variation are regularities that appear to reflect a general process of rule formation, which we refer to as "regularization." Here, as in the section on voicing, we propose that at least some general patterns underlie variation and that insight into the developmental process can be gained by a detailed consideration of variation itself. Together these sections exemplify two directions that research must take if the goal of characterizing constraints on variation is to be met. In discussing regularization, we propose two hypotheses that cast a different light on the nature of at least some developmental universals; these hypotheses, with the data that support them, partially constitute the foundation of a more cognitive model of phonological acquisition.

Throughout this paper, the two themes of pattern and diversity are interwoven. The topic of phonological universals is exceedingly complex: the data we obtain from children are diverse, and many central theoretical issues are not yet well understood (and, in fact, not often discussed). Thus, it is premature for first-language (L1) research to provide answers to questions of importance to second-language (L2) research. A more modest goal is, however, attainable: the purpose of this paper is to present a perspective from normal L1 phonological development in the child that will offer clues for research in L2 phonology acquisition.

UNIVERSALIST THEORIES

During the past 15 years, linguistically oriented research on child phonology has been dominated by three universalist acquisition theories, each related to a particular phonological theory.

In the structuralist tradition, Jakobson's theory formulated several acquisition predictions based on the premise that there is a universal hierarchy of structural laws that determine the inventory of phonemic systems and the relative frequency, combinatorial distribution, and assimilatory power of particular phonemes.[7] Jakobson's predictions include the following: (a) the order of acquisition of minimal consonant and vowel inventories (e.g., p>t>m>n); (b) stops are acquired before nasals, with fricatives next and liquids late; (c) voiceless consonants are acquired before voiced; (d) front consonants are acquired before back; (e) in the early stages, fricatives will be replaced by stops and back consonants by front consonants. Jakobson's theory is by far the most influential of the various universalist models: several researchers have worked from a Jakobsonian framework (e.g., Moskowitz);[8,9] and many cross-linguistic data have been interpreted as providing support for its general outline of development (e.g., Velten, English; Pačesová, Czech; Jeng, Chinese).[10-12]

The universalist/nativist approach to acquisition most often associated with Chomsky, and with it the classic generative phonology paradigm,[13] is represented in the works of Smith (e.g., References 14 and 15). Smith identifies four universal tendencies: the tendencies toward consonant and vowel harmony, consonant cluster reduction, systemic simplification (mostly deletion and substitution rules), and grammatical simplification (e.g., the use of a single CV† syllable for all unstressed syllables). Smith—who is purposely neutral on the nativist issue—views these universal constraints as "part of a universal template which the child has to escape from in order to learn his language."[14]

The third theory is that of Stampe's natural phonology, which emphasizes universal innate natural processes and an associated acquisition theory.[16,17] Stampe's basic assumption is that the phonological system of a language is the residue of a universal system of processes, governed by forces implicit in human articulation and perception. During acquisition, those processes not applicable to the particular language being learned are constrained by the mechanisms of suppression, limitation, and

† C, consonant; V, vowel.

ordering (e.g., Reference 18). Examples of early processes are unstressed syllable deletion, cluster reduction, de-spirantization (i.e., stopping), and depalatalization. A proponent of natural generative phonology (a theory that is based on some aspects from each of the three theories previously mentioned), Hooper takes a strong position on the similarity between the child's phonological system and the adult's [19] (as do Stampe and Smith).

From the early 60s (and especially since 1968, the publication date of the English translation of Jakobson), interest and publication in child phonology have increased dramatically. This period of research—largely universalist and linguistic-theory dominated—has made important contributions to the field in at least two areas. First, a great deal of information has been collected on the sounds and substitutions that children produce and, more generally, the set of simplificational processes that characterize the relation between the adult model and the child replica. Second, this research period has produced insight into issues of central importance to universals and generalizations that underlie cross-linguistic differences. The following two sections summarize selected findings within each of these two areas of contribution. The first section catalogues and interprets a number of universal tendencies; this typology of rules, thus, covers a variety of topics. The second section explores a single topic in greater detail to clarify several factors affecting the developmental sequence.

Throughout this research period, the universalist theories were examined and evaluated, and each was criticized on various empirical and theoretical grounds (e.g., References 20–22). For example, several key points of Jakobson's theory were called into question, most importantly its claim that development is uniform across children (cf. counterexamples to the Jakobsonian order of acquisition in Reference 23) and the claim that the process of acquisition is one of successive acquisition of phonological oppositions (cf. evidence for the early priority of whole word contrasts and effects of word position in Reference 24). A second important body of research challenged the empirical assumptions on which Chomsky's hypothesis of an innate "language acquisition device" was based.[25,26] For example, research has shown that the input to the child is *not* degenerate in quality (e.g., Reference 27) and that language acquisition is not independent of cognitive development.[28] A third important finding is summed up by Harris (in his 1979 critique of Hooper):

> The considerable developmental literature over the last decade suggests that the acquisition process involves a series of successive approximations to adult grammars and that some adjacent stages involve discontinuities that might well be characterized as "radical." [29]

With some notable exceptions, the critiques during this period did not alter substantively the basic premises of the universalist approach. Now, however, a shift is in progress in the field as a whole, toward a new model of acquisition, one that focuses on a new and different type of universals.

This shift mainly is due to the accumulation, over the past several years, of data that cannot be handled within the universalist linguistic models. These data document the existence of significant, widespread individual differences between children acquiring the same language and show that the acquisition process, in certain key aspects, is not a linear progression of unfolding abilities—as assumed by the universalist model. The emerging model recognizes several types of learning (e.g., accretion and tuning) but emphasizes the cognitive aspects of acquisition.[22,30,31] In this view, the child is an active seeker and user of linguistic information who forms hypotheses on the basis of input data, tests and revises these hypotheses, and constructs more complex systems (or "grammars") out of earlier, simpler ones. The shift is away from a deterministic linguistic model toward a flexible model that accommodates variation in development by acknowledging the active role of the child, the diversity of input, and the variety of solutions possible. The contributions of the earlier period of research were to clarify universal tendencies that result from purely linguistic constraints imposed by the nature of human language and human articulatory and perceptual systems. To these universals now is added a set assumed to result from universal cognitive, problem-solving abilities of the human learner—a set that describes how the young child deals with complexity (what Cazden calls universal processing strategies), recognizes patterns, constructs linguistic categories and organizes categories into systems. It is this new set of proposed universals that is the topic of the last section of this paper.

PHONOLOGICAL PROCESSES AGE 1 YEAR 6 MONTHS TO 4 YEARS

One of the best attested facts about child language development is the appearance of systematic relationships between adult speech sounds and the corresponding child speech sounds during the period of greatest phonological development, typically between one and a half and four years of age. Children make systematic "errors" in producing speech sounds, i.e., they regularly tend to produce a particular wrong sound in place of the correct adult sound, as when an English-learning child says *t* for *k* in several words (e.g., *tum* for *come*). The relationships between the target sounds and the child's counterpart sounds ("model" and "replica" sounds) are not random but are phonetically systematic, and in current analyses they are regarded as instances of *phonological processes* (PPs) in operation.[32] Thus, the replacement of *k* by *t* is an example of the PP of "fronting," by which a palatal or velar consonant is replaced by a corresponding dental/alveolar one. Ingram summarizes present knowledge of PPs in children,[33] and his classification is followed here.

In addition to the fact that PPs universally appear in operation at this age, the PP phenomenon has universal significance in that some processes are extremely common across many languages and many children, while others are more likely in particular languages or are favored by particular children. Although the incidence of particular processes cannot be predicted, probability statements of considerable interest can be made. For example, in accordance with the fronting process, it is much more likely that model [k] will be represented by replica [t] than vice versa.

Substitution Processes

The most obvious kind of child PP is the substitution of one segmental sound for another, and such patterns of substitution have been discussed in detail in various places.[7,14,34] One substitution process, *stopping,* will serve as an example of the type: fricatives are replaced by stops of the corresponding place of articulation. Thus, in acquiring their first language, many children will at some stage make "errors" in producing such fricatives as [f v s z . . .], replacing them with corresponding stops [p b t d . . .], as in [dɛ] for English *there* or [to] for French [so] *sceau* (bucket).[35,36]

The stopping process is a good example of a fundamental principle accounting for such varied phenomena as the distribution of phoneme types among the world's languages, the processes of language change over time, language acquisition, and language loss. Jakobson and his successors have sought such fundamental principles. In this instance the principle is one of "markedness": fricatives are more complex articulatorily, more "marked" than stops, and hence their presence in a language or in a child's phonology presupposes the presence of stops in the same system. Any natural human language that has fricative phonemes in its inventory also will have stops but not vice versa, a language typically has more stops than fricatives, and any child who produces fricative consonants also produces stop consonants. Yet in this instance, as in some others, the principle does not carry over directly into sound change: the change of fricative to stop is not nearly as common as stop to fricative in the history of the world's languages.[37]

Other substitution processes operative in child phonology include fronting, gliding, and vocalization.[33]

Assimilation Processes

Another common type of child PP is that in which sounds in the child's production are assimilated to neighboring sounds in the same word or other unit. Thus the affected sound has a phonetic relation not only to the model sound but also to relevant other sounds that occur near it. For example, if a child regularly says *guck* for *duck,* the initial alveolar /d/ is being assimilated to the velar /k/ later in the word, and the same child may say [d] for adult /d/ in words that do not contain a following velar stop.

Assimilatory processes are the commonest type of PPs in operation in synchronic alterations, and they also are common in child phonology. The example we choose here, however, is *consonant harmony,* the assimilation of consonants at a distance within the same word, a **PP** quite frequent in child phonology but extremely rare as a process in the world's languages.[38,39] In a detailed study of 13 children acquiring six different first languages, this **PP** affected over 14% of the words in their vocabulary, with more than half the children showing 12% or more consonant harmony words.[40] Investigators have noted evidence of a strength hierarchy such that velars and labials are most resistant to assimilation and dentals the most likely to assimilate: [gʌk] is more likely than [dʌt] for adult *duck*. It also has been noted that this hierarchy differs from the order-of-acquisition hierarchies, which provide that velars more often are acquired later than anteriors (labials or dentals) and that the control of the voicing parameter typically is achieved earlier in anteriors than in velars.[23,41]

Other assimilation processes operative in child phonology include consonant voicing (in voiced surroundings; devoicing in word-final position) and denasalization.[33]

Syllable Structure Processes

One of the most noticeable phonetic relationships between model and replica sounds is children's omission of segments or whole syllables present in the adult item. Such deletion processes are examples of syllable structure PPs, which affect the phonetic complexity of the speech chain. Such processes range from simple deletions (e.g., [bɛ] for *bed*) to highly idiosyncratic rearrangements (e.g., [kajan] for *chocolate*).[42] The sample process chosen here is *consonant cluster reduction*: a sequence of two or more consonants is replaced by a single consonant (e.g., [dɛs] for *dress*) or is eliminated in some other way.

This PP is extremely widespread; it probably appears in the course of L1 acquisition of any language that has consonant clusters, and it is part of a general trend favoring simple CV syllables as against CCV, CVC, and other, more complex syllable types. It is possible to identify strong statistical trends that hold across languages. For example, clusters of stop plus liquid (e.g., *tr*, *kl*) typically progress through liquid deletion to liquid substitution to correct production (e.g., *tain*, *twain*, *train*).[43] Cluster reduction appears in language phenomena other than L1 acquisition, but the cluster reduction recorded in the history of languages often shows very different trends than in child phonology, e.g., epenthesis, the insertion of a vowel to break up the cluster, is common in language change and borrowing, but not in child phonology.[39] An example of close matching in trends, however, is the treatment of medial clusters of nasal plus stop. In both child phonology and historical change, the most likely outcome is the deletion of the nasal if the stop is voiceless and the deletion of the stop if it is voiced (presumably through an intermediate stage of assimilation, e.g., *nd* → *nn* → *n*).[44]

Other Processes

As is evident from the example of nasal cluster reduction, many PPs in child language combine assimilatory and syllable structure aspects or do not fit neatly into the classification. As an example of such not readily classifiable processes, we choose *reduplication*, i.e., the transformation of model words into structures of repeated identical or partially identical CV syllables. This PP, or family of PPs, may involve extension of adult monosyllables, e.g., *ball* → [bʌbə], modification of adult reduplication, e.g., *bye-bye* → [dɛdɛ], or of an adult nonreduplication model, e.g., *water* → [wɔwɔ]; it may thoroughly transform an adult word, e.g., *window* → [ŋeːŋeː], or it merely may affect the child's choice of which adult words to produce.

This phenomenon is widespread, attested for many children and many languages. Recently it has been the subject of experimental study, as in Schwartz *et al.* from which our examples are taken.[45] The extent of operation of this process varies very much from one child to another,[14] just as the grammatical, lexical, and discourse uses of reduplication and repetition vary from one language to another. Schwartz *et al.* have provided evidence that, for some children at least, reduplication plays an important role in the acquisition of polysyllabic words.[45]

Phonological Processes in L2 Acquisition

Phonological processes operate in L2 acquisition in the sense that there are systematic phonetic relationships between the sounds of the target language and those of the learner's interlanguage. Some of the PPs apparent in L2 acquisition are similar to those of child language development and may be interpreted as a kind of reactivation of L1 strategies and processes. Others are transfer processes representing interference from the structure of the learner's L1. Still others cannot be accounted for by either explanation.

Recent studies of *substitution* processes in L2 acquisition emphasize the interaction of developmental and transfer PPs. Mulford and Hecht explore this interaction in detail in the phonology of a six-year-old Icelandic boy, Steinar, acquiring English.[46] A simple illustration is Steinar's pronunciation of final stops in English: he devoiced them (a common L1 process) and strongly aspirated them (a characteristic of Icelandic). Mulford and Hecht hazard some tentative hypotheses on the interaction, e.g., that "substitutes predicted by both transfer and developmental processes are the ones most likely to appear and to persist." [46] A more interesting hypothesis they offer is that the relative roles of the two kinds of processes differ depending on the part of the phonology involved, along the following continuum:

Vowels	Liquids	Stops	Fricatives and Affricates

◄───►

| Transfer processes predominate | | | Developmental processes predominate |

Wode proposes other hypotheses about the interaction of the two types of processes: that children acquire the L2 phonology "through the grid of their L_1 system" and that the two crucial issues are their developmental stage in the L1 and the matching process by which they identify L2 elements similar to L1 elements, which they substitute for them, and non-similar elements, for which they have natural developmental sequences like those of L1 learners.[47,48] All these hypotheses are steps toward a predictive theory of L1-L2 phonological development, but as their authors acknowledge, they need much more research to confirm or modify.

Assimilation processes in L2 acquisition have not been much studied, although it is very likely that both developmental and transfer processes operate, and that such common L1 assimilation processes as consonant harmony are uncommon in L2 acquisition—one does not expect a foreign learner of English to say [gʌk] for *duck*.

Tarone studied *syllable structure* processes in L2 acquisition.[49] She analyzed the speech of six subjects learning English, two native speakers each of Cantonese, Korean, and Portuguese. About 20% of the syllables attempted by each speaker had syllable structure errors: consonant deletion, epenthesis, and glottal stop insertion (breaking up a vowel sequence). Attributing the changes to transfer of L1 structure whenever possible, Tarone found a residue of nontransfer errors ranging from 47% for one of the Korean speakers to 10% for one of the Portuguese speakers. Much of the consonant deletion could be explained as either transfer or developmental, but the amount of epenthesis was much higher than is found in L1 acquisition, and Tarone attributed it to a universal preference for CV syllables that operated independently of transfer and was manifested differently than in L1 phonological development.

Reduplication seems very much tied to the age of the learner and to L1 rather than L2 acquisition. Certainly reduplication strategies rarely are noted in classroom L2 learning by adolescents or adults. Data on reduplication in L2 acquisition by very young children—if this can be separated from simultaneous acquisition of two languages—would bear directly on the sources and functions of reduplication in language acquisition.

In summary, we can say that PPs operate in both L1 and L2 acquisition. Those common in L1 acquisition presumably reflect universal constraints of human speech perception and production systems, coupled with general developmental characteristics apparent also in nonphonological behavior. They are influenced by the phonological structure of the language being acquired and by the characteristics of the particular vocabulary to which the child is exposed. PPs found in L2 acquisition are similar in part to those of L1 acquisition; such similar processes presumably represent either continued operation of the same universal constraints or reactivation of developmental processes in connection with a new acquisition situation. Other PPs found in L2 acquisition clearly are transfer processes that reflect the phonological structure of the L1, and many may combine both sources or at least not provide unequivocal evidence one way or the other. Still other PPs in L2 acquisition are neither developmental nor transfer. They may represent universal or language-specific constraints operating differently than in L1 acquisition, or they may represent language-external factors such as social constraints.

The central question here is the interaction among these different kinds of processes, and future research directed to this question probably will be highly productive.

ACQUISITION OF THE VOICING CONTRAST

The literature on L1 acquisition of voicing in stops is a particularly rich source of information on the acquisition process and the nature of universals. It is extensive, with data from a wide variety of languages and several age groups. Further, it benefits from the development of sophisticated instrumental analysis techniques and a considerable body of knowledge accumulated by phonologists and phoneticians on the distribution and properties of voicing contrasts in languages of the world and their acoustic and articulatory components. As a result, this research clarifies several issues of central importance to both L1 and L2 research: the appropriate units of analysis, research methodology and its consequences, and the interpretation of cross-language differences.

A Universal

Data from a number of languages provide strong support for Jakobson's proposed universal that "so long as stops in child language are not split according to the behavior of the glottis, they are generally produced as voiceless and unaspirated." [7] Macken provides a general discussion and references on English, Spanish, Cantonese, Garo, Taiwanese, and Hindi. [23] Kewley-Port and Preston claim that voiceless unaspirated stops are used first because they are articulatorily easier to control than either prevoiced or aspirated stops. [50] Characteristics of the English acquisition process provide some support for this claim, [51] since they match the kind of rule change identified by Macken for articulatorily based rules as opposed to perceptually based ones. [52]

In contrast to this universal, we find either individual or language differences in other aspects of voicing acquisition or insufficient data to make further claims. The age at which the voicing contrast is acquired varies by child and by language: for example, the age at which English-speaking children acquire a voicing contrast in initial stops may vary from under age 1;10 ‡ to 2;8,[51,14] while Spanish-speaking children acquire an adultlike phonetic voicing contrast after age 4.[53] For languages with more than two types of voice in stops, only Srivastava's Hindi study is available.[54] He reports the following sequence: voiceless unaspirated stops at 1;1, prevoiced at 1;4, voiceless and voiced aspirates at 2;0. With respect to contrast at different places of articulation, the results of Macken and Barton indicate differences by language (or by voicing type): the English (aspiration) contrast is acquired in the order dental>labial>velar, while the Spanish (true voicing contrast) appears first at the labial place of articulation.[51,53]

Issues

Units of Analysis

There are several reports of apparent counterexamples to Jakobson's proposed universal. For example, in Velten, we find that Joan acquired the "voiced" stops (by 1;1) before the "voiceless" ones (2;1),[10] while in Contreras and Saporta, the child acquiring Spanish acquired the "voiceless" (1;0–1;2) before the "voiced" stops (1;6).[55] The problem here is with the labels "voiced" and "voiceless."

Phonologically contrastive stops produced at the same place of articulation traditionally are said to differ in "voicing." While this description may be sufficient to describe the phonological contrast, it is not the case that all "voicing" contrasts are the same at the phonetic level. In fact, English "voiced" stops generally are voiceless unaspirated at the phonetic level, comparable to Spanish "voiceless" stops. Given this fact and the results of Macken and Barton, who use voiceless unaspirated stops (as measured by voice onset time, VOT) as the unit of analysis,[51,53] it is likely that in the Velten and Contreras and Saporta accounts, language-particular labeling practices obscure the underlying similarity of the acquisition process.[10,55] Thus, the first requirement of L1 and L2 research is the determination of the appropriate phonetic units for analysis, not subject to conflicting interpretation either within or across languages. For the analysis of voicing acquisition, the appropriate units, measured in terms of VOT, are prevoiced, voiceless unaspirated, and voiceless aspirated.[56] Researchers must know the phonetic components of the voicing contrasts under study and should be aware that even the three types given above may differ across languages.[57]

Methodology

In part, the reported differences within and across languages can be attributed to differences in research methodology (see Reference 58). For

‡ 1;10 means 1 year 10 months.

example, the difference in age of acquisition reported in the studies of Macken and Barton on the one hand and Smith on the other is due partly to different criteria used for assigning the point of acquisition and different means of analysis.[51,14] A second point of methodological importance is the value of spectrographic analysis. Because Macken and Barton used this technique, they were able to determine an early stage of acquisition wherein the English-speaking children were making statistically significant contrasts between adult voiced and voiceless phonemes and yet where all the children's productions fell within the adult perceptual boundaries for a single phoneme: the children's productions would have been labeled "voiced" by the nonphonetician and were in fact generally transcribed as "voiceless unaspirated" by the researchers. This example demonstrates the problems involved in the imposition of adult categories on child speech and the importance of supplemental instrumental analysis: without the aid of spectrographic analysis, an important fact about acquisition (i.e., a stage of a "nonadult" contrast) would have been missed (cf. the similar lesson in Williams' study of bilinguals).[59]

Cross-Language Differences

Two of the differences above demonstrate the importance of a close examination of the sound patterns that occur in the language—specifically, the particular lexicon—being acquired by the child. In contrast to the Hindi child reported in Srivastava,[54] the Spanish children in Macken and Barton produced prevoiced stops correctly only after age four.[53] These children, however, already had acquired the Spanish "voicing" contrast by age two as a kind of stop-continuant contrast: voiced stops frequently were produced as glides, while the voiceless stops nearly always were well-formed stops. This language-specific pattern apparently has its roots in the allophony involved in the Spanish voicing system. Second, the differences between the Spanish and English orders of acquisition by place of articulation correlated with differences between the two languages (and in the individual child lexicons) in the distribution of word-initial stop types, i.e., differences between the two languages in the utilization of the voicing contrast (see Reference 23 for a more complete discussion). Several studies over the past several years (e.g., References 60 and 61) similarly have found that "universality is confounded by the particular data the child is confronted with."[62]

In summary, the L1 acquisition process, even for a highly restricted portion of a phonological system (voicing in word-initial stops), is complex. What do these L1 findings suggest for L2 research? First, universals have different etiologies and different implications. If the articulatory ease of voiceless unaspirated stops is not restricted to the speech of very young children (as the distribution of these stops in languages of the world would suggest), then the early acquisition of these stops would be expected also during L2 acquisition. Second, L2 research must take full account of (a) the different phonetic components underlying even superficially similar phonological contrasts, (b) the full set of allophonic and morphophonemic rules in the different phonological systems, and (c) perhaps most important, the phonetic and phonological characteristics of the particular input the child receives. Note that a contrastive analysis based solely on segment inventories would not have been adequate to either predict or explain the cross-language differences discussed here for L1 acquisition. Third, the use of spectrographic techniques—especially for the acquisition of voicing in stops—is particularly valuable for the exploration of nonadult contrasts; thus, instrumental techniques can be used to look for and investigate characteristics unique to a bilingual system or interlanguage. Such techniques can document phenomena that *cannot* be detected by the categorically bound perceptual systems of researchers. We realize that these points are not unknown to L2 researchers,[63] but we repeat them here because they so often are neglected by L1 researchers.

REGULARIZATION

The issue of variation has been addressed in two different ways in the preceding two sections. First, to account for the fact that individual children may provide no evidence for the operation of a particular process or, in some cases, counterevidence, we stated our process universals in terms of statistical probabilities. Second, because we found that there exist some cross-language differences in voicing acquisition, we considered several factors, such as the differential effects of the particular input to the child, that in effect place conditions on the operation of universals.

There remains, however, a substantial residue of variation—individual differences between children acquiring even the same language and in some cases confronted with the same input.[64] These differences are particularly striking in the earliest stages where the number of adult-based words a child produces is small, but they are also apparent throughout the developmental process. Yet the diversity itself reveals regularities— regularities that seem to reflect the processing carried out by the child. Two important hypotheses can be derived from these facts:

Hypothesis 1. Phonological acquisition, like other types of linguistic and nonlinguistic learning, involves a process of discovering patterns, via forming, testing, and revising hypotheses—a process we refer to as "regularization."

Hypothesis 2. At least some linguistic universals are not due to the operation of an innate linguistic language acquisition device but, rather, derive from the interaction of the learner and a patterned input.

With the publication of several multisubject longitudinal studies—each documenting widespread individual differences—researchers began to recognize the active role played by the child. This literature continues to grow (e.g., References 24 and 64). Since a review of the frequency and diversity of such differences is beyond the scope of this paper, three examples from English will suffice: there is no invariant order of acquisition or set of substitution processes for stops or fricatives; [23] early phonotactic patterns are highly varied (e.g., References 65 and 66); later rules for polysyllabic words often are idiosyncratic [e.g., References 14 (page 172) and 42]. On the surface, a certain amount of cross-subject difference could be attributed to random variation; however, underlying these differences, there appears to be a general pattern that demands further explanation.

What seems to cut across such linguistic differences is a general similarity in stages prior to final correct production: early piecemeal, unintegrated data, with occasional isolated accuracy on a few forms ("idioms"); experimentation; regularization where several words are produced the same way for the first time; and a period of overgeneralization, sometimes resulting in the loss of the accuracy of previously correct forms ("regression").

Words that show accurate production (in advance of the other words produced by the child in the same period) and then lose their adultlike accuracy have been called "progressive idioms" by Moskowitz.[9] The classic example is Hildegard Leopold's *pretty*: this word—which was this child's first permanent word (at 10 months)—was produced with near perfect accuracy for almost a year; it subsequently was changed to [pɪti] and then to [bɪdi], at the times when rules of consonant cluster reduction and voicing (respectively) appeared elsewhere in her system. Leopold reports that nine words during the first two years followed a similar development from early accuracy to later reduction (Reference 34, 1: 164–5). It seems that these idioms are unanalyzed wholes for the child. As the child learns to break down whole word shapes into phonetic components, he or she discovers or invents rules that systematize relations between sounds in different contexts.

That this process of building up a phonological system is not an automatic one but rather an active, constructive one can be seen clearly in "experimentation" episodes and "overgeneralization" data. An example of experimentation is one child's attempts to say *boat*, eight attempts scattered throughout a 20-minute session: (1) [pɔpʰ kʰ]; (2) [potʰ]; (3) [pʌpᵕpʰǫkʰ]; (4) [pʌkʰ] (2 times); (5) [pɔkʰ] (2 times); (6) [pɔkʰ kʰ] (2 times); (7) [papʰ kʰ]; and (8) [pʌkʰ kʰ] (at age 1;5.30). Subsequent analysis showed that on the three previous sessions, *boat* was produced as [pɔ] or [pɔʔ] (final consonant deletion or substitution), and that in the following five sessions, it was produced as [pop] (consonant harmony). The fourth session was unusual in several ways: the final consonant varied between [p] and [k] (with one [t] token), sometimes within the same production; the frequency of *boat* was two to six times greater than in any other session; and the productions of *boat* were interpreted at the time of utterance by the adults present (who were unaware of the developmental significance of the final consonant variation) as deliberate effortful attempts by the child to say this word. Sometime between the fourth and fifth sessions, a regular rule of consonant harmony was established, one that affected several words with final stops.

Data from another child's idiosyncratic acquisition of stop+r clusters provide not only an example of regularization (similar in form to the above child's development of a rule of consonant harmony) but also a particularly striking example of overgeneralization. Initially, this child deleted the r from stop+r clusters (1;6–1;10). Subsequently (1;11), she produced initial /tr/ and /dr/ as [f]. Then beginning at 2;0, this child extended her [f] rule to initial /pr/ and /kr/ clusters: from 2;0 to 2;1 (and later), all four clusters were produced as [f] (the stage of overgeneralization and regression). When this child overgeneralized her [f] rule to /pr/ and /kr/, her previous productions for these clusters "regressed": [f] for /pr/ and /kr/ is less adultlike than were her previous productions of [pʰ] and [kʰ] (respectively). These phonetic changes appear to be due to a change in the child's hypothesis about how such clusters should be pronounced. The significance of this example and the other examples does not lie in the specifics of which particular phone is produced in substitution for, e.g., initial stop+r clusters or final alveolar consonants: children may and often do differ in the particular substitutions produced for these and other difficult sounds. Rather, what is significant is what the examples suggest about the underlying process— the process of "regularization."

Cognitive Model (Hypothesis 1)

Regularization (particularly its features of overgeneralization and regression) points to the active role of the child and gives evidence of the universal disposition of the child to discover patterns. Moreover, there is a parallelism between this process of rule formation and stages in the acquisition of nonlinguistic knowledge [67] that suggests that both types of learning share the following features: (a) single-item match; (b) gradual recognition of a pattern; (c) period of exploration; (d) construction of a theory, followed by overgeneralization and loss of ability; (e) gradual recognition of regularity of counterexamples; (f) construction of a new theory, distinct from the first; and (g) gradual development of a single unified theory. Further evidence for the active role of the child are data showing children's creativity (such as invented words and the use of segments or rules plausible given the child or adult system but incorrect from the adult point of view) [41] and data showing children's selectivity (i.e., children's selection or avoidance of words with a particular sound structure). [24]

The process of regularization underlying individual differences in phonological development and the parallel between this process and that seen in the acquisition of nonlinguistic knowledge—together with other evidence for the child's active role (creativity and selectivity)—have led child phonologists to posit a more cognitive model of acquisition—one that focuses on the child's organization of phonological data and the nonautomatic, nonlinear nature of the child's progress toward the adult system. This model is discussed in detail in Ferguson and Macken [31] (see also References 22 and 30). In its current stage, the model has several serious defects and requires elaboration and testing. It signals an important new direction, precisely because the data on which it is based are data (individual differences and regularization) that are difficult for linguistic universalist theories to explain.

Universals (Hypothesis 2)

Early diversity and evidence for a cognitive model of regularization suggest that some "linguistic universals" are due to the interaction between the child's ability to categorize and the child's experience with language: given similar categorization abilities and the broad similarities between the phonological systems of languages of the world, certain regularities necessarily will result. In contrast, only those universals present from the beginning are evidence of innate linguistic universals, and, as we have noted, there seem to be few of these. If we assume that regularization and its components (as described under "Cognitive Model") constitute a set of processing universals—relevant to language learning and other nonlinguistic learning—it seems likely that there exists an associated set of purely linguistic universals that would characterize probable outcomes, given particular linguistic inputs and the child's categorization skills and physiological capabilities at particular stages of development.

The two hypotheses we have proposed here on the basis of the accumulated research of the past 15 years have important implications for L2 acquisition research. First, a model of L2 acquisition necessarily will involve consideration of the L2 learner's stage of cognitive development and prior linguistic knowledge and the context of learning (e.g., the particular input to the child). Second, substantive cross-linguistic similarities of L2 acquisition will be evident primarily in situations where similarities in these factors exist in the L2 situations being compared. Third, probability statements of phonological development do not predict individual cases as exceptionless universals would, and a developmental L2 model based on such probabilities (from L1 research) is correspondingly limited. Finally, a recognition of the child's disposition to recognize patterns (inferred from a consideration of the regularization process) casts doubt on traditional accounts of the motivational force underlying L1 language acquisition (cf. Reference 68): the learner will try out new hypotheses, revise old ones, and progress toward full knowledge in a series of backward and forward steps largely independently of such pressures as adult correction of errors or child self-correction for communication clarity.

REFERENCES

1. GREENBERG, J. H., C. A. FERGUSON & E. A. MORAVCSIK, Eds. 1978. Universals of Human Language. 2. Stanford University Press. Stanford, Calif.
2. OHALA, J. J. 1974. Phonetic explanation in phonology. In Papers from the Parasession on Natural Phonology. A. Bruck et al., Eds.: 251–274. Chicago Linguistics Society, Chicago, Ill.
3. OHALA, J. J. 1980. The application of phonological universals in speech pathology. In Speech and Language: Advances in Basic Research and Practice. N. J. Lass, Ed.: 75–97. Academic Press, Inc. New York, N.Y.
4. LINDBLOM, B. 1979. Some phonetic null hypotheses for a biological theory of language. In Proceedings, Ninth International Congress on Phonetic Science 2: 33–40. University of Copenhagen. Copenhagen, Denmark.
5. LILJENCRANTS, J. & B. LINDBLOM. 1972. Numerical simulation of vowel quality systems: the role of perceptual contrast. Language 48: 839–862.
6. SUPER, C. M. 1979. A cultural perspective on theories of cognitive development. Paper presented at the Society for Research in Child Development Meeting, March, San Francisco, Calif. [Expanded version: Anthropological contributions to theories of child development. In New Trends for Child Development. C. M. Super & S. Harkness, Eds. (In preparation.)]
7. JAKOBSON, R. 1941. Kindersprache, Aphasie und Allgemeine Lautgesetze. (1968. Child Language, Aphasia and Phonological Universals. A. R. Keiler, Trans. Mouton. The Hague, the Netherlands).
8. MOSKOWITZ, B. A. 1970. The two-year-old stage in the acquisition of English phonology. Language 46: 426–441.
9. MOSKOWITZ, B. A. 1973. Acquisition of phonology and syntax. In Approaches to Natural Language. K. J. J. Hintakka, J. M. E. Moravcsik & P. Suppes, Eds.: 48–84. Reidel Publishing Co. Dordrecht, the Netherlands.
10. VELTEN, H. V. 1943. The growth of phonemic and lexical patterns in infant language. Language 19: 281–292.
11. PAČESOVÁ, J. 1968. The Development of Vocabulary in the Child. Universita J. E. Purkyne. Brno, Czechoslovakia.
12. JENG, H.-H. 1979. The acquisition of Chinese phonology in relation to Jakobson's laws of irreversible solidarity. In Proceedings, Ninth International Congress of Phonetic Science 2: 155–161. University of Copenhagen. Copenhagen, Denmark.
13. CHOMSKY, N. & M. HALLE. 1968. The Sound Pattern of English. Harper & Row Publishers, Inc. New York, N.Y.
14. SMITH, N. V. 1973. The Acquisition of Phonology. Cambridge University Press. Cambridge, England.
15. SMITH, N. V. 1975. Universal tendencies in the child's acquisition of phonology. In Language, Cognitive Deficits and Retardation. N. O'Connor, Ed.: 47–65. Butterworths. London, England.
16. STAMPE, D. 1969. The acquisition of phonetic representation. Pap. Fifth Regional Meet. Chicago Linguistics Soc. 5: 443–454.
17. DONEGAN, P. J. & D. STAMPE. 1979. The study of natural phonology. In Current Approaches to Phonological Theory. D. A. Dinnsen, Ed.: 126–173. Indiana University Press. Bloomington, Ind.
18. EDWARDS, M. L. 1971. One child's acquisition of English liquids. Pap. Rep. Child Lang. Dev. 3: 101–109.
19. HOOPER, J. B. 1977. Substantive evidence for linearity: vowel length and nasality in English. Pap. Thirteenth Regional Meet. Chicago Linguistics Soc. 13: 152–164.
20. OLMSTED, D. L. 1971. Out of the Mouth of Babes. Mouton. The Hague, the Netherlands.

21. FERGUSON, C. A. & O. K. GARNICA. 1975. Theories of phonological development. *In* Foundations of Language Development. E. H. Lenneberg & E. Lenneberg, Eds. **2:** 153–180. Academic Press, Inc. New York, N.Y.
22. KIPARSKY, P. & L. MENN. 1977. On the acquisition of phonology. *In* Language Learning and Thought. J. Macnamara, Ed.: 47–78. Academic Press, Inc. New York, N.Y.
23. MACKEN, M. A. 1980. The acquisition of stop systems: a cross-linguistic perspective. *In* Child Phonology: Perception and Production. G. Yeni-Komshian, J. F. Kavanagh & C. A. Ferguson, Eds. **1:** 143–168. Academic Press, Inc. New York, N.Y.
24. FERGUSON, C. A. & C. B. FARWELL. 1975. Words and sounds in early language acquisition. Language **51:** 419–439.
25. LEVELT, W. J. M. 1975. What became of LAD? *In* Ut Videam: Contributions to an Understanding of Linguistics, for Pieter Verburg on the Occasion of his 70th Birthday. Peter de Ridder Press. Lisse, the Netherlands.
26. MCCAWLEY, J. D. 1977. Acquisition models as models of acquisition. *In* Studies in Language Variation. R. Shuy, Ed.: 51–64. Georgetown University Press. Washington, D.C.
27. SNOW, C. E. & C. A. FERGUSON, Eds. 1977. Talking to Children: Language Input and Acquisition. Cambridge University Press. Cambridge, England.
28. CLARK, E. 1973. Non-linguistic strategies and the acquisition of word meanings. Cognition **2:** 161–182.
29. HARRIS, J. W. 1979. Some observations on "substantive principles in natural generative phonology." *In* Current Approaches to Phonological Theory. D A. Dinnsen, Ed.: 281–293. Indiana University Press. Bloomington, Ind.
30. FEY, M. & J. GANDOUR. 1979. Problem-solving in phonology acquisition. Paper presented at the 54th Annual Meeting of the Linguistics Society of America, December 27–29, Los Angeles, Calif.
31. FERGUSON, C. A. & M. A. MACKEN. 1980. Phonological development in children—play and cognition. Pap. Rep. Child Lang. Dev. **18:** 133–177. (To appear in Children's Language. K. E. Nelson, Ed. **4.** Gardner Press. New York, N.Y.).
32. OLLER, D. K. 1975. Simplification as the goal of phonological processes in child speech. Lang. Learn. **24:** 299–303.
33. INGRAM, D. 1979. Phonological patterns in the speech of young children. *In* Language Acquisition. P. Fletcher & M. Garman, Eds.: 133–148. Cambridge University Press. Cambridge, England.
34. LEOPOLD, W. F. 1939–1947. Speech Development of a Bilingual Child. 4 volumes. Northwestern University Press. Evanston, Ill.
35. FERGUSON, C. A. 1978. Fricatives in child language acquisition. *In* Papers on Linguistics and Child Language. V. Honsa & M. J. Hardman-de-Bautista, Eds.: 93–115. Mouton. The Hague, the Netherlands.
36. INGRAM, D. 1978. The production of word-initial fricatives and affricates by normal and linguistically deviant children. *In* Language Acquisition and Language Breakdown. A. Caramazza & E. B. Zurif, Eds.: 63–85. The Johns Hopkins University Press. Baltimore, Md.
37. FERGUSON, C. A. 1978. Phonological processes. *In* Universals of Human Language. J. H. Greenberg *et al.*, Eds. **2:** 403–442. Stanford University Press. Stanford, Calif.
38. DRACHMAN, G. 1978. Child language and language change. *In* Historical Phonology. J. Fisiak, Ed.: 123–144. De Gruyter. Berlin, Federal Republic of Germany.
39. VIHMAN, M. M. 1980. Sound change and child language. *In* Papers from the Fourth International Conference on Historical Linguistics. E. C. Traugott *et al.*, Eds.: 303–320. John Benjamin. Amsterdam, the Netherlands.
40. VIHMAN, M. M. 1978. Consonant harmony: its scope and function in child

language. *In* Universals of Human Language. J. H. Greenberg *et al.*, Eds. **2:** 281–334. Stanford University Press. Stanford, Calif.

41. MACKEN, M. A. 1979. Developmental reorganization of phonology: a hierarchy of basic units of acquisition. Lingua **49:** 11–49.
42. PRIESTLY, T. M. S. 1977. One idiosyncratic strategy in the acquisition of phonology. J. Child Lang. **4:** 45–66.
43. GREENLEE, M. 1974. Interacting processes in the child's acquisition of stop-liquid clusters. Pap. Rep. Child Lang. Dev. **7:** 85–100.
44. GREENLEE, M. & J. OHALA. 1980. Phonologically motivated parallels between child phonology and historical sound change. Lang. Sci. **2:** 283–308.
45. SCHWARTZ, R. G., L. B. LEONARD, M. J. WILCOX & M. K. FOLGER. 1980. Again and again: reduplication in child phonology. J. Child Lang. **7:** 75–87.
46. MULFORD, R. & B. F. HECHT. 1980. Learning to speak without an accent: acquisition of a second-language phonology. Pap. Rep. Child Lang. Dev. **18:** 16–74.
47. WODE, H. 1977. The L₂ acquisition of /r/. Phonetica **34:** 200–217.
48. WODE, H. 1978. The beginnings of non–school room L₂ phonological acquisition. Int. Rev. Appl. Linguistics **16:** 109–125.
49. TARONE, E. 1976. Some influences on interlanguage phonology. Working Pap. Bilingualism **8:** 87–111.
50. KEWLEY-PORT, D. & M. S. PRESTON. 1974. Early apical stop production: a voice onset time analysis. J. Phonetics **2:** 195–210.
51. MACKEN, M. A. & D. BARTON. 1980. A longitudinal study of the acquisition of the voicing contrast in American-English word-initial stops, as measured by voice onset time. J. Child Lang. **7:** 41–74.
52. MACKEN, M. A. 1980. The child's lexical representation: the 'puzzle-puddle-pickle' evidence. J. Linguistics **16:** 1–17.
53 MACKEN, M. A. & D. BARTON. 1979. The acquisition of the voicing contrast in Spanish: a phonetic and phonological study of word-initial stop consonants. Pap. Rep. Child Lang. Dev. **16:** 42–66.
54. SRIVASTAVA, G. P. 1974. A child's acquisition of Hindi consonants. Indian Linguistics **35:** 112–118.
55. CONTRERAS, H. & S. SAPORTA. 1971. Phonological development in the speech of a bilingual child. *In* Language Behavior, a Book of Readings in Communication. J. Akin *et al.*, Eds.: 280–294. Mouton. The Hague, the Netherlands.
56. LISKER, L. & A. S. ABRAMSON. 1964. A cross-language study of voicing in initial stops: acoustical measurements. Word **20:** 384–422.
57. LADEFOGED, P. 1978. Phonetic differences within and between languages. UCLA Working Pap. Phonetics **41:** 32–40.
58. WELLS, G. 1979. Variation in child language. *In* Language Acquisition. P. Fletcher & M. Garman, Eds.: 377–395. Cambridge University Press. Cambridge, England.
59. WILLIAMS, L. 1980. Phonetic variation as a function of second-language learning. *In* Child Phonology G. Yeni-Komshian *et al.*, Eds. **2:** 185–215. Academic Press, Inc. New York, N.Y.
60. LUST, B., S. FLYNN, Y. CHIEN & T. CLIFFORD. 1980. Coordination: the role of syntactic, pragmatic and processing factors in first language acquisition. Pap. Rep. Child Lang. Dev. **18:** 79–87.
61. PETERS, A. M. 1980. Language typology and the segmentation problem in early child language acquisition. Working Pap. Linguistics. University of Hawaii. Manoa, Hawaii. (In preparation.)
62. MENYUK, P. 1979. Speech sound categorization by children. *In* Proceedings, Ninth International Congress of Phonetic Science **2:** 176–182. University of Copenhagen. Copenhagen, Denmark.
63. LEHTONEN, J. & K. SAJAVAARA, Eds. 1979. Papers in Contrastive Phonetics. University of Jyväskylä. Jyväskylä, Finland.

64. LEONARD, L., M. NEWHOFF & L. MESALAM. 1980. Individual differences in early child phonology. J. Appl. Psycholinguistics **1:** 7–30.
65. BRAINE, M. D. S. 1974. On what might constitute a learnable phonology. Language **50:** 270–299.
66. MENN, L. 1976. Pattern, control and contrast in beginning speech, a case study in the development of word form and word function. Ph.D. Dissertation. University of Illinois. Urbana-Champaign, Ill.
67. KARMILOFF-SMITH, A. & B. INHELDER. 1974/75. If you want to get ahead, get a theory. Cognition **3:** 195–212.
68. BOWERMAN, M. Starting to talk worse: clues to language acquisition from children's late speech errors. *In* U-Shaped Behavior Growth. S. Strauss, Ed. Academic Press, Inc. New York, N.Y. (In press.)

THEORIES OF PHONOLOGICAL DEVELOPMENT

Lise Menn

Aphasia Research Center
Boston University School of Medicine
Boston, Massachusetts 02130

"Theories of Phonological Development" also was the title that Ferguson and Garnica used in 1973 for their incisive study of the state of the art of child phonology,[1] and this brief survey will refer heavily to that paper. They began their survey this way:

> Most children, as a normal part of their development, learn to recognize and pronounce the sounds of the language in their speech community so well that their perception and pronunciation reflect in countless details their competence as "native speakers" of the language, and their speech lacks any trace of the foreign accent of people who learn the language later. Starting from crying and early cooing and babbling, children gradually acquire the complex patterns of the adult phonology of their language. Phonological development is just one aspect of the larger process of acquiring full communicative competence in language structure and the use of language, but it merits special attention as an independent field of investigation.[1]

In this paper, I will restrict my attention, as Ferguson and Garnica did, to theories of how children learn to pronounce the sounds and sound sequences of their language, and set aside the other major branch of phonology, morphophonemics, which deals with the grammatically governed choice of allomorphs. I also will omit consideration of the acquisition of the ability to perceive and categorize sounds like a native speaker, for which I refer the reader to the work of Kuhl, Strange and Jenkins, Morse, Studdert-Kennedy, and their several colleagues.[2-5]

Ferguson and Garnica wrote during a period of great ferment in child phonology. They reviewed four leading theories: Jakobson's famous structuralist model, Mowrer and Olmsted's behavioristic model, and then two later linguistic models, Stampe's natural phonology and Waterson's prosodic phonology.[6-10] Now the ferment appears to be settling, not because one of those four has "won," but because a new theory has come to the fore, one with a different notion of the nature of phonological development. In this paper, I do not have the space to present a full history of this change; instead I will first present the essentials of this new theory, and then I will go back to some of the theories presented by Ferguson and Garnica and point out ways in which the genuine insights of those theories have been preserved.

First, why have I claimed that we now have a different notion of phonological development? Because the same shift has taken place in

0077-8923/81/0379-0130 $01.75/2 © 1981, NYAS

developmental phonology as in other developmental fields: we too find development to be active and interactive. And it is not that we are just being fashionable; I will review here some of the data that made the shift appropriate for us.

A decade ago, before that shift took place, what I will call the "implicit defining question" of developmental phonology could be stated as, What linguistic theory will explain the order in which the phonemes of a language develop? Or rather, this was the question as linguists saw it; psychologists had a parallel version, roughly, What psychological theory will explain the order in which children master the sounds of their language? As you see, both of these questions presuppose that there is such an order of acquisition, and that it can be explained by appeal to an existing theory of language or of behavior. But both of these presuppositions have had to be replaced by more subtle and flexible ones.

The new implicit defining question of developmental phonology may be phrased like this: What predispositions and abilities does the child bring to the task of learning to communicate with language, and specifically how does the individual go about solving the articulatory and phonological problems posed by the language to be learned? The school that envisions developmental phonology in this manner should justly be called the Stanford school of child phonology, but for expository purposes we need a name more descriptive of the content of the theory. Ferguson and Macken, in their recent major statement in *Children's Language,* call it the "cognitive" theory; [11] but I have come to like the more concrete term "problem-solving" theory, and it is the one I shall use here.

As we discuss this material, bear in mind that the old theories in large measure were arrived at deductively, from lots of thinking about very few data. That is the inevitable nature of a beginning. Remember, too, that it is not merely the data explosion that has brought about the much better theory that we have now, but also our testing of those data against those early theories; they have served a useful purpose. (It is of course disturbing to find quite recent sources in which the older theories are accepted without question, but Kuhn and Fleck before him have shown how inevitable that is.) [12,13] Here, then, is the core of the present "problem-solving" theory of phonological development as I see it. First, the setting: The young child tries to sound like the adults around her and to communicate messages in the way that they do. But she cannot immediately take in and remember all of the auditory information about a word, or correctly segment all utterances, or sort out the various kinds of significance— lexical, morphological, social, affective, etc.—of the variation in the words addressed to her.

Already at this point, children vary in their responses. Some go after one word at a time, while others make global and more variable attempts to approximate long phrases. [14] Some do both, giving us attempts at isolated identifiable words and also long strings of well-contoured babble that may contain some recognizable lexical items.

Here we will restrict our attention again, to "recognizable lexical items." The child has been discovering over the first year of life what lovely sounds her vocal tract can make, and she has brought some of them under voluntary control, at least enough to be able to imitate some adult words when they are spoken to her. Now she begins to use some of her sound repertoire to signal things, to mean things. To do this, she must be able to store information about how words sound and how to produce them, and the "how to produce them" must first be discovered, by trial and error. (No "language is innate" theory, no matter how strong, claims that there is a prewired connection between the articulators and the auditory system.)

From the fact that some sounds and sound sequences tend to be later in acquisition than others, we are entitled to conclude that these trials are made with loaded dice, rather than fair ones. For it is indeed true that some sounds, such as labial stops and low vowels, are likely to be brought under a child's control sooner than others; but a given child may happen to get the hang of, say, /ʃ/ or /g/ before she gets /a/ or /m/. Again, the orders of sound-production mastery are probabilistic, not fixed.

We also have found out that description in terms of the apparent difficulties of segments is not enough. In a language that permits consonants at the ends of syllables and consonant clusters (blends), it is clear that children can find particular sound patterns difficult even when they have no problem with the same sounds in other patterns. Sometimes it is just the position of a sound in a word that matters: it is quite common for a child to have final fricatives mastered before initial ones, e.g., to be able to give an accurate /f/ in "off" while saying [ɪʃ] or [pɪʃ] for "fish." At other times, the effects of other sounds in a word may be very strong; to take a common example, a child may be able to manage the /j/ in "yes" but have a hard time with the same sound in "yellow." A well-known and systematic type of contextual effect in young children is consonant assimilation: a child who can say, for example, "toy" correctly may produce [bʌb] for "tub" [15]—there is nothing wrong with his ability to pronounce /t/ when no similar sounds are in the same word, but he gets fouled up programming two consonants in the same word if their places of articulation differ. Nasal assimilation—e.g., changing "dance" to [næns]—also is attested frequently,[15] and again this usually has nothing to do with the child's ability to pronounce /d/. If this seems counterintuitive, remember that is hard to pat one's head and rub one's stomach at the same time, yet easy enough to, as they say, walk and chew gum. We can only hypothesize that for most beginning speakers, putting two nonhomorganic stops in the same word is more like patting plus rubbing, while putting, say, a consonant with any desired vowel is much less strain on motor programming. In short, some motor sequences evidently are easier to coordinate than others, for reasons that we should be starting to study.

So this is what we mean when we talk of sound patterns, as well as sounds, having great influence on the accuracy of a child's output. And now we can add that the order of mastery of sound patterns also is probabilistic rather than fixed. Some children master the voicing contrast first in final position, while others get it first in word-initial position, for example. There are tendencies—some very strong—but very few, if any, absolutes.

Menyuk and Menn reflect on what is to be done, given this state of affairs:

> The orderly and universal development of phonemic contrast that previous researchers have suggested does not seem to be supported by the data of the more detailed studies that have been carried out recently. . . . one task (for future researchers) is to determine the limits on the range of strategies that may be employed by children. . . . A second task might be a determination of which aspects of the range of strategies employed are indeed universal and when these occur developmentally.[25]

We have argued that variation from one child to the next requires a probabilistic theory. Now, if we look at a variety of children, we find that the same adult sounds and sound patterns give most of them trouble, but that they apparently react to those troubles in different ways. I think that the data before us make the best sense if we regard children as trying to sound like the adults around them in spite of the booby traps set for them by their tongues.[22] I will take as an example what happens when English-learning children attempt to say words beginning with consonant clusters of "blends." Imagine listening to young children saying words like "sky," "story," "cream," and "snow." We have found that the common wisdom enshrined in conventionalized baby talk and in many textbooks knows only the commonest of several patterns of cluster reduction: retention of the stop. However, besides "towy" for "story," we find [sɔwi], [sʌtɔwi], and even something like [tɔɹis] on occasion. In other words, a cluster can be simplified by omission of either member, or by breaking it up. Furthermore, if we have a word like "spoon" or "sky," where the two elements of the cluster are made with different positions of articulation, children may combine the features, producing a single segment (one from column A, one from column B): /sp/ may be produced as [f] or even as the non-English [ɸ]; /sk/ sometimes may be heard as [x]. You see how difficult it would be, in the face of this, to maintain that uniform maturation of a phonological system is playing a determining role.

It may be objected that there is no real evidence for such an anthropomorphic notion as "problem solving" in these data. Could not this whole picture of variation be due to chance? Yes, of course; to show that a child is trying to solve a problem we must bring in evidence of multiple attempts, awareness and avoidance of failure, and pleasure at success. But these behaviors can be found in diary studies since Weir's *Language in the Crib*,[16] and avoidance of phonological failures has been shown in the laboratory by Schwartz and Leonard.[17] So that completes our argument.

So much for a sketch of where the field is now. Let us look back to where it was in 1973.

In spite of their manifest differences, one flaw shared by all of the older theories has become apparent in the light of the data we now possess. All of those theories would predict smooth progress toward adult competence, whether by maturation or by shaping. And a given child certainly will show some areas of smooth increase of production accuracy. But these cannot be complete theories because they cannot deal with a very common and very "cognitive" phenomenon: overgeneralization. A simple example from one of my cases: my son Daniel had a correctly produced word "down," and he said [don] for "stone," originally.[15] But then he started to use a nasal-harmony rule for all words with final nasals, so that "pin" became [mɪn] and "beans" became [minz]. Shortly after this, there was a period of fluctuation in the forms he used for "down" and "stone," and then these appeared stably as [næwn] and [non]. In formal terms, he developed a rule of nasal assimilation, and then overgeneralized it. This kind of regression from a more correct form to a poorer one obviously is similar to the case of the child who first learns to say "came" as a past tense, but then, upon learning the general weak-verb past-tense ending, overgeneralizes it and says "comed." No theory that relies wholly on notions of either maturation or shaping can deal with such data, as we have known for years.

Now, let us look more closely at some aspects of the older theories that have been worth keeping. First, consider Stampe's "natural phonology."[9] Natural phonology in its original form makes most of the same assumptions as Jakobson's theory and is subject to the same criticisms. However, it does contain one major advance: the effect of context on the "difficulty" of sounds is fully recognized. Briefly, what Stampe suggested is that the beginning speaker is, let us say, tongue-tied by the operation of a set of innate "natural processes" that allow only the simplest sequences of articulatory configurations, like [mamama], and tend to convert all others into these. Acquisition of phonology requires the suppression or limitation of these natural conversion processes. Most developmental phonologists since Stampe have been sure that there was something right about what he said, although there are conceptual problems with the notion of natural process, which lie outside the scope of this paper. Now, we have seen that the unskilled speaker trying to say certain sounds is especially likely to fail in particular ways. Final voiced stops are likely to be produced without voicing, initial fricatives are likely to come out as stops, and so on. And if a speaker does indeed fail in one of these modes, she must learn not to do so in order to become a competent native speaker. So the notion of innate natural process has been adapted—it becomes translated as something like "probable failure mode," and thus fitted into the model of articulatory problems and solutions. (For those who are interested, Ingram's forthcoming handbook of phonological analysis has a useful version of Stampe.)[18] Summarizing: Stampe and Jakobson's theories have in common the view of phonological development as a steady and innately determined process of mastering distinctions, and neither can deal with the apparent regressions and overgeneralizations that appear here just as they do in the acquisition of morphology and syntax. But the vision shared by Stampe and Jakobson has a core that still is accepted completely by the problem-solving theory: the inarticulate child gradually learning to overcome some built-in tendencies of her articulatory apparatus as she attempts to say what she hears.

Let us now turn to the work of Waterson,[10] who is still too little known in this country. Waterson is an established phonologist of the British Firthian school, and therefore was prepared, as the rest of us were not, to seize on the child's word as a phonological whole rather than as a sum of segmental parts. I will give a brief sample of the descriptive mode that she uses. Observing, as did Ingram, that a child's early words tend to fall into little families with similar input and output shapes, Waterson seeks to capture the gestalt of each family by listing the properties shared by its members, emphasizing their similarities rather than their differences. Her subject produced the words "finger," "window," "another," and the name "Randall" all with outputs of the form [ŋVŋV].[10] Waterson notes that these words share syllabic structure, presence of nasal, and stress pattern in both input and output. Now this child certainly did not have a general rule that changed initial /f/ into [ɲ]; it would be possible to write a context-dependent rule to do it, just in the word "finger," but that would miss capturing the tight clustering of these four mildly similar adult words into four output forms distinguished only by their vowel sounds.

Waterson's approach can deal insightfully with much more irregularity in the relation of child word to adult model than can any purely segmental "a is substituted for b," or even "a is substituted for b in context c"; and she has an absolute triumph when it comes to the explanation of such forms as Hildegard Leopold's [dɔιʃ] for "stone" and [lɔιʃ] for "story." Waterson's approach cannot deal with the complex regular rules that some children, such as Smith's subject,[19] invent; and Barton also has criticized Waterson's attempt to explain the sounds that children learn only in terms of auditory salience, leaving articulatory factors out of account (as did Olmsted).[20] But the notion of the word as a member of a set of canonical forms (as Ingram called them)[21] and as the earliest phonological unit has become central to the problem-solving theory, through Waterson's work and through the work of Ingram and almost all the other researchers associated with Stanford.

Finally, and this may surprise you at first, a word about what is useful in the behaviorist approach to language acquisition. As Ferguson and Garnica pointed out,[1] behaviorist theories had goals different from linguistically oriented ones; they were patting a different part of the proverbial elephant. Let us look at their end by asking, Why do children start to talk like their parents—and end up sounding like the kids on their block?

A naive food-and-water behaviorism—which is ethologically inadequate in any case—will not get us even up to saying "mama": baby watchers know that small children don't have to ask for what they want; they can wail for it. But there *is* a reward for talking, which we can see if we look at what early words are used for. Diary studies show that most early words are sociable and ritual tokens, not (in general) demands.[15,23,24] As far as I can see, children talk in order to participate, in order to be human, not in mere imitation but in emulation. And they end up with their intricately patterned native speech for the same reason: as an affirmation of identity. Sociolinguistics begins in the crib.

I have tried to show that a cognitive theory like the Stanford one is necessary to explain how children become native speakers, and Macken and Ferguson have presented in much more detail the patterns of generalization and overgeneralization, which cannot be explained by notions of stimulus and response.[26] But I suggest that speakers find it intrinsically rewarding to sound like those whom they wish to be like; this is why the exuberant overgeneralizations later are pruned back until they nearly match the forms that are used in the surrounding language. I suggest further that this motivational aspect should not be neglected in the study of language acquisition.

REFERENCES

1. FERGUSON, C. A. & O. GARNICA. 1975. Theories of phonological development. *In* Foundations of Language Development. E. Lenneberg & E. Lenneberg, Eds. **1:** 153, 180. Academic Press, Inc. New York, N.Y.
2. KUHL, P. The perception of speech in early infancy. *In* Speech and Language: Research and Theory. N. Lass, Ed. Academic Press, Inc. New York, N.Y. (In press.)
3. STRANGE, W. & J. J. JENKINS. The role of linguistic experience in the perception of speech. *In* Perception and Experience. H. L. Pick & R. D. Walk, Eds. Plenum Press. New York, N.Y. (In press.)
4. MORSE, P. A. 1978. Infant speech perception: origins processes, and *Alpha Centauri*. *In* Communicative and Cognitive Abilities—Early Behavioral Assessment. F. Minifie & L. L. Lloyd, Eds.: 195–227. University Park Press. Baltimore, Md.
5. STUDDERT-KENNEDY, M. 1978. The beginnings of speech. *In* Behavioral Development: The Bielefeld Interdisciplinary Project. G. B. Barlow, K. Immelmann, M. Main & L. Petrinovich, Eds. Cambridge University Press. New York, N.Y.
6. JAKOBSON, R. 1941. Kindersprache, Aphasie und Allgemeine Lautgesetze. (1968. Child Language, Aphasia, and Phonological Universals. A. Keiler, Trans. Mouton & Co. The Hague, the Netherlands.)
7. MOWRER, O. H. 1952. Speech development in the young child: the autism theory of speech development and some clinical applications. J. Speech Hear. Disord. **17:** 263–268.
8. OLMSTED, D. 1966. A theory of the child's learning of phonology. Language **42:** 531–535.
9. STAMPE, D. 1969. The acquisition of phonemic representation. *In* Proceedings of the Fifth Regional Meeting of the Chicago Linguistic Society: 433–444. Linguistics Department. University of Chicago. Chicago, Ill.

10. WATERSON, N. 1971. Child phonology: a prosodic view. J. Linguistics 7: 179–221.
11. FERGUSON, C. A. & M. A. MACKEN. Phonological development in children—play and cognition. In Children's Language. K. E. Nelson, Ed. 4. Gardner Press. New York, N.Y. (In press.)
12. KUHN, T. S. 1962. The Structure of Scientific Revolutions. University of Chicago Press. Chicago, Ill.
13. FLECK, L. 1935. (1979. The Genesis and Development of a Scientific Fact. F. Bradley & T. S. Trenn, Trans. University of Chicago Press. Chicago, Ill.)
14. PETERS, A. 1977. Language-learning strategies. Language 53(3): 560–573.
15. MENN, L. 1971. Phototactic rules in beginning speech. Lingua 26: 225–241.
16. WEIR, R. 1962. Language in the Crib. Mouton & Co. The Hague, the Netherlands.
17. SCHWARTZ, R. & L. B. LEONARD. 1979. Do children pick and choose? An examination of phonological selection and avoidance in early lexical acquisition. Paper presented at the Boston University Conference on Language Development, Boston, Mass., September 14–15.
18. INGRAM, D. Procedures for Phonological Analysis of Children's Language. University Park Press. Baltimore, Md. (In press.)
19. SMITH, N. V. 1973. The Acquisition of Phonology. Cambridge University Press. Cambridge, England.
20. BARTON, D. P. 1976. The role of perception in the acquisition of speech. Doctoral Dissertation. University of London. London, England. (Circulated by Indiana University Linguistic Club, Bloomington, Ind.)
21. INGRAM, D. 1974. Phonological rules in young children. J. Child Lang. 1: 49–64.
22. MENN, L. 1979. Towards a psychology of phonology: child phonology as a first step. In Applications of Linguistic Theory in the Human Sciences: 138–179. Linguistics Department. Michigan State University. Lansing, Mich.
23. MENN, L. 1976. Pattern, control, and contrast in beginning speech: a case study in the development of word form and function. Doctoral Dissertation. University of Illinois. Urbana, Ill. (Circulated by Indiana University Linguistics Club, Bloomington, Ind.)
24. HALLIDAY, M. A. K. 1975. Learning How to Mean—Explorations in the Development of Language. Edward Arnold. London, England.
25. MENYUK, P. & L. MENN. 1979. Early strategies for the perception and production of words and sounds. In Language Acquisition. P. Fletcher & M. Garman, Eds.: 49–70. Cambridge University Press. Cambridge, England.
26. MACKEN, M. A. & C. A. FERGUSON. Phonological universals in language acquisition. Ann. N.Y. Acad. Sci. (This volume.)

SOME CHARACTERISTICS OF DELAYED PHONOLOGICAL SYSTEMS

David Ingram

Department of Linguistics
University of British Columbia
Vancouver, British Columbia, Canada V6T 1W5

A Statement of the Problem

The interest in delayed language patterns often stems from the fact that they may be different from so-called normal ones. The notion of difference, however, is one that has been central in discussions on the nature of linguistic representation in normal as well as language-delayed children. In the area of phonology, it is evident that diversity exists between children at comparable points of development when learning the same language. A primary task of the child phonologist, then, is to formulate a theoretical explanation that accounts for these variations. This may be formulated as two simple questions:

1. What are the differences and similarities between all children as they acquire a first language?
2. Which differences result from environmental factors, and which from alternative innate processing mechanisms?

If our task were confined to the explanation of data from monolingual normal children, it would be a difficult enough enterprise. Some of the most challenging data, however, come from two other kinds of children. First, there is the need to account for the deviant phonological systems of language-delayed children. In some of these cases, the pathological factors presumably push the language-acquisition device to its extremes. Second, there is the issue of bilingual acquisition. Will the young bilingual child show similar patterns or strategies for each language being acquired or will the patterns vary interlinguistically? Most clearly in multilingual contexts, we face the problem of the source of the variation. Is it primarily within the child, in terms of individual preferences and strategies, or the consequence of the input languages?

The points just presented can be exemplified by looking at the well-known phonological process of reduplication. It has been known for some time that young children reduplicate during the earliest stages of development, and a cursory glance at diary data indicates that some children do it more than others. Our developmental theory will need to account for this variation. Also, it may be that language-delayed children reduplicate at a different rate, and possibly in a different way. Lastly, the young child acquiring two languages may reduplicate in both, indicating an inherent

138

0077–8923/81/0379–0138 $01.75/2 © 1981, NYAS

tendency, or may do so only in one but not the other, suggesting important input influences.

In this paper I will address the issue of variation and difference by reviewing recent research of mine in each of these areas, focusing on reduplication. As will be argued, the data suggest that the input language may play a more important role than recent literature indicates as a source for variant patterns and strategies.

THREE HYPOTHESES

To begin, let me present three hypotheses about the variations possible in children's use of reduplication.

H1: Reduplication is a process available to all children as part of their language-acquisition device as a means to represent nonreduplicated multisyllabic adult models. It will occur in the child's first attempts at multisyllabic forms.

H2: Since delayed children are subject to the same genetic limitations as normal ones, they should show no qualitative differences in their use of reduplication.

H3: The use of reduplication will vary from child to child dependent on (1) the number of multisyllabic adult models (reduplicated and non-reduplicated) in the child's lexicon; and (2) the child's inability to move on to more advanced skills in processing multisyllabic models.

Each of these hypotheses (based on early research findings) could be extended to broader statements on phonological development, but this would require the presentation of data and adjustments beyond the scope of this paper. Even so, the general implications are straightforward. H1 and H2 propose that young children share very similar (perhaps identical) strategies or processes for the acquisition of phonology. The sources of variation are explicit. One is the adult models that become part of the child's lexicon, which may vary both inter- and intralinguistically. Thus, both a different language and different linguistic environments within the same language will tend to trigger or stimulate specific processes. If the child plays a more active role here, it is in the choice of lexical items, although to date we know little in this regard. Further variation will occur if one child happens to be better or more adept at moving on to the next level of development.

REDUPLICATION IN CHILD PHONOLOGY

Normal Monolingual Children

Data on the use of reduplication by young monolingual English-learning children is available in Schwartz *et al.* and in Fee and Ingram.[1,2] The former study examined reduplication in 12 children from 1;3 to 2;0, while the latter looked at 24 children from 1;1 to 2;8.* When possible, Fee and Ingram compared data from both studies to enlarge the subject pool to 36. Here, I will limit the discussion to a summary of the results from Fee and Ingram. Regarding H1, it was found that the primary function of reduplication was to reproduce adult nonreduplicated multisyllabic words. Second, there was a significant age effect, i.e., the children who used reduplication most also were the youngest. These two results support the general availability of reduplication at the earliest stages of multisyllabic productions.

Fee and Ingram also present results relevant to H3 regarding sources of variation. Like Schwartz *et al.,* we divided subjects into frequent and infrequent reduplicators, and found that infrequent reduplicators (or nonreduplicators) were significantly better at final-consonant production than were frequent reduplicators. That is, one source of variation was the child's ability to move on to final-consonant production. The other source was the extent to which nonreduplicated multisyllabic adult models were present within the child's lexicon. A frequent reduplicator then, was a child with poor final-consonant productions and a vocabulary with several adult multisyllabic forms. We had no information on the reasons for the latter variation, since features of the child's acquisition of vocabulary and the nature of the parental input were not available. Overall, the results suggest evidence for both H1 and H3.

Phonologically Delayed Children

The only comparative study available on phonologically delayed children is Ingram.[3] There, 15 normal children, 1;5 to 2;2, were matched on articulation scores with 15 phonologically delayed children, 3;11 to 8;0. The articulation score is a measure of the number of sounds a child uses (cf. Reference 4) and is a gross score of development similar to mean length of utterance in grammar. It was found that language-delayed children show wide ranges of variation on a diversity of phonological measures, including those of reduplication, but that matched normals show the same ranges of variation. In other words, there were no significant differences between the groups. In terms of reduplication, then, H2 follows from these results. More generally, such research suggests that deviant or unusual systems, should they occur, are as likely to appear in normal as in language-delayed children.

Bilingual Children

Little research currently exists on phonological development in bilingual children. Vogel, one of the only studies in print, argues that her subject Eileen showed the same development and thus the same phonological

---

* 2;8 means 2 years, 8 months.

system for English and Romanian at 2;0.[5] There are some difficulties with these conclusions, however, as discussed in Ingram.[6] Even if we accept Vogel's results, there still is little there to test H3, since English and Romanian are relatively similar in segmental inventories and syllabic structure. For the study of reduplication, a better case would be one of a child learning one language that is primarily monosyllabic as compared to another language with predominantly multisyllabic words. Also, since reduplication interacts with final-consonant production, another possible distinction would be one of open versus closed syllables. To a degree, such differences exist between English and Italian. English is primarily monosyllabic (approximately 75% of the most frequent words); it also tends to close syllables (also around 75%). Italian, on the other hand, is highly polysyllabic and tends toward open syllables.

In Ingram, I observed the phonological system of a young girl L, age 2;0, learning English in an Italian household.[6] As would be expected, her use of multisyllabic productions in Italian was quite high, with her proportion of multisyllabic forms being 0.90. Also as expected, her proportion of closed syllables was quite low, 0.36. Based on Schwartz et al.,[1] her proportion of reduplication was 0.18. What about her English? Based on Ingram, the above figures for L's Italian are found also for some English-learning children.[4] That is, L's use of similar proportions for English would have been within the range of variation for normal monolingual English children. Her English data, however, showed the opposite. Her proportion of multisyllabic forms was much lower, 0.40 (as compared to 0.90 for Italian), and her use of final consonants was much greater, 0.81 (as compared to 0.36). Her English proportion of reduplication was only 0.05.

The major conclusion from this study was that this bilingual child showed separate phonological systems at a very early point in acquisition. Regarding reduplication, the study also suggests that we cannot talk about children as being inherent reduplicators or nonreduplicators. L showed much more reduplication in Italian than in English. The results show that the patterns imposed by the input language do not influence the child's production of the other language (hence the conclusion regarding separate systems). They do show, though, the influence of the structure of the input on the language of the child. They confirm the claim in H3 that the number of multisyllabic adult models in the lexicon determines the variation between reduplicators and nonreduplicators.

THE ROLE OF INPUT

To date, most statements on the role of input in phonological development have been simplistic, e.g., that children speak the language they hear, or do not acquire grammatical features if they do not occur in the parent's language (cf. Ochs on the nonacquisition of ergativity).[7] Studies on children with alternant strategies of phonological development, such as reduplicators versus nonreduplicators, make little reference to the child's phonological environment, and at least imply an internal source for the variation. In such cases, then, children de facto look like they have numerous internal strategies to choose from. The above, however, suggests otherwise—basically a highly constrained language-acquisition device subject to various environmental influences. The following formula is suggested:

$$\frac{\text{surface}}{\text{variation}} - \frac{\text{variations due to}}{\text{environmental factors}} = \frac{\text{real linguistic}}{\text{universals}}$$

Two obvious environmental influences deserve closer scrutiny in this regard. One concerns the factors involved in the child's acquisition of a phonological vocabulary. What role do the parents play in modeling words and the selection of monosyllabic versus multisyllabic words? Related to this is the role of the parent baby-talk style. Do reduplicators have reduplicating parents, or parents who help support continued reduplication in other ways?

Let me close with an example of what may be the most deviant phonological system I have ever observed. Ingram and Terselic report on a phonologically delayed boy, Eric, age 4;1.[8] Among other things, Eric would produce /s/ ingressively (here symbolized as [s̱], and also move prevocalic /s/ to a postvocalic position. Some examples are "soap" [wow.s̱.p]; "snake" [nei.s̱]; "sunglasses" [wai.s̱.lae.s̱.I.s̱]. One's first response is to marvel at the resourcefulness and creativity of the child's phonological system. A closer look, however, suggests certain predictions leading to this pattern along with possible outside effects. First, we normally would expect a [t] to occur in a case like this. The child, however, appeared quite motivated to produce /s/, the consequence perhaps of sensitivity to outside pressures to get it correct. Oller's research on prelinguistic vocalizations suggests that ingressive sounds of this kind are used by infants around the middle of the first year of life.[9] Eric may be resorting to a previous primitive vocalization under unusual stress to get things right.

While observations like the above are only speculations, they nonetheless suggest a line of thinking that is not often faced. It is proposed that a closer look at environmental phonological influences may help us to explain some of the variation found. Once such factors are isolated, we can discuss with more confidence the inherent processing strategies and their alternatives that young children bring to the task of phonological development.

REFERENCES

1. SCHWARTZ, R., L. LEONARD, M. J. WILCOX & K. FOLGER. 1980. Again and again: reduplication in child phonology. J. Child Lang. **7:** 75–88.
2. FEE, J. & D. INGRAM. Reduplication as a strategy of phonological development. J. Child Lang. (In press.)

3. INGRAM, D. A comparative study of phonological development in normal and linguistically delayed children. J. Appl. Psycholinguistics. (In press.)
4. INGRAM, D. 1981. Procedures for the Phonological Analysis of Children's Language. University Park Press. Baltimore, Md.
5. VOGEL, I. 1975. One system or two: an analysis of a two-year old Romanian-English bilingual's phonology. Pap. Rep. Child Lang. Dev. 9: 43–62.
6. INGRAM, D. The emerging phonological system of an Italian-English bilingual child. (In preparation.)
7. OCHS, E. 1980. Social environment and acquisition of ergative case marking in Samoan. Paper presented to the Twelfth Stanford Child Language Research Forum, Stanford University, Stanford, Calif.
8. INGRAM, D. & B. TERSELIC. A case of deviant child phonology. (In preparation.)
9. OLLER, K. Patterns of infant vocalization. In Language Behavior in Infancy and Early Childhood. R. Stark, Ed. Elsevier–North Holland Biomedical Press. New York, N.Y. (In press.)

PHONOLOGY AND PHONETICS:
GENERAL DISCUSSION

Moderator: Melissa Bowerman

Bureau of Child Research
University of Kansas
Lawrence, Kansas 66044

M. STUDDERT-KENNEDY (*Queens College, Flushing, N.Y.*): Dr. Cole, if we recognize words so quickly, why do they last so long?

R. A. COLE (*Carnegie-Mellon University, Pittsburgh, Pa*): According to Marslen-Wilson and Welsh [see Reference 11 in Dr. Cole's paper], listeners can usually recognize a word in a neutral context after processing the first three or four segments, and recognition is even faster if the word is predictable from prior context. Given this "fact" of perception, why should language contain so many polysyllabic words longer than three or four segments? Note that this question assumes that the duration of words in a language somehow depends upon the time that it takes listeners to recognize words. I do not know of any evidence for or against this interesting hypothesis, but let us assume that there is a causal relationship between the time course of word recognition and the duration of words in a language. The question then becomes, What is the optimal form of this relationship? Your question implies that words should only be as long as listeners need to recognize them. A language of this form, however, would have little redundancy; there would be no "unnecessary" syllables. I suspect that a language of this form would be very difficult to understand—like reading Gertrude Stein poetry, which has little redundancy. Long words, which can be recognized before they are complete, give the listener extra processing time when listening to speech. This time can be used for comprehension, to recover from noisy input or lapses in attention, or to frame a reply.

S. BELASCO (*University of South Carolina, Columbia, S.C.*): Dr. Cole, principally what you said about the acoustic cues of word boundaries is true. However, I believe you overstated the case because it is generally known that acoustic cues are sometimes used to differentiate word boundaries.

UNIDENTIFIED SPEAKER: Dr. Ferguson, the examples you gave were from speech production. In L1 [first-language] acquisition, children sometimes are able to recognize differences they don't make in production. Do you find the same parallelism in adult L2 [second-language] acquisition?

C. A. FERGUSON (*Stanford University, Stanford, Calif.*): This is an important question, the relation between perception and production. Perhaps 85 or 90% of our research has had to do with production, not because we weren't interested in the very kind of question that you are raising, but because we find it very difficult to contrive experimental

0077-8923/81/0379-0144 $01.75/2 © 1981, NYAS

studies of young children that will get us the kind of perceptual data that we want. I wouldn't even be convinced of what you said about young children usually being able to hear that difference. This whole area of research is very important, and we jump from infant perception or discrimination data to adult perception, the stuff in between being very spotty and unreliable, including some of the work that we have done ourselves. Also there is very little research on the relation between perception and production errors in L2 acquisition. What we need are better ways of getting at these questions. I suspect that you will find differences between adults and children and between L1 and L2.

R. A. COLE: Dr. Ferguson, would you care to comment on the fact that some of the patterns that you describe as phonological universals are treated by speech and language pathologists.

C. A. FERGUSON: In the first place, we mostly study normal acquisition and try to understand what that is. That turns out to be a hard job. It is not so easy to decide what is the amount of variation that you are going to call normal. Some people who do research in child phonology, however, are also looking at deviant phonologies. It is reasonable to expect questions of this sort or even more pointed ones, such as to give a list of milestones in normal development. Our problem is that we find so much individual variation that we are very uneasy about offering answers at this time. I am not saying that it may not ultimately be possible to specify some kind of range of normal variation that would be useful to people concerned with speech pathology. For the moment, I would just be very cautious.

H. WINITZ (*University of Missouri, Kansas City, Mo.*): Dr. Menn, in view of your comments on phonological development, do you think L1 learners are more capable than L2 adult learners when it comes to speech sound discrimination and production?

L. MENN (*Boston University School of Medicine, Boston, Mass.*): I have no relevant research experience, but here are some considerations. As we know, L1 learners modify their output over time to bring it closer to the model; some information to the effect that they are not matching the model initially would seem to be getting through, but that flow of information might largely be below the level of consciousness.

As for L2 learners, it is indeed often clear that they do not realize how badly they are mangling the pronunciation of the second language on the level of conscious awareness. But if they are tested to see if they can tell the difference between, say, recordings of their own pronunciations and those of native speakers, they might make this distinction quite well. I don't know if such a study has been done.

Then there's the sociological factor of language as a marker of group membership, brought out earlier by Professor Alatis. Many skilled L2 speakers who have an "accent" can sound like native speakers and can demonstrate this easily on request. The few such people that I have interviewed whose second language was English stated that they do not wish to be mistaken for Americans.

M. STUDDERT-KENNEDY: A comment on some social aspects of language learning. There is an amusing analogy in bird song. Several writers have suggested that bird-song dialects are selective-breeding devices, serving to pair birds that are well matched to an ecological niche. However, the route to selective breeding may be quite devious. Dialects are, in the first instance, social devices. Many birds (such as Bewick's wren) learn the dialect not of their fathers (only the male sings), but of the males that they go to live among. In other words, like the children of non-English-speaking immigrants to the United States, they learn the dialect of their peers rather than of their parents. By analogy, one might suspect that an individual who is well past sexual maturity, when he or she begins a second language, may be constrained by social no less than by motoric habits.

UNIDENTIFIED SPEAKER: Dr. Menn, to me, if phonological acquisition is regarded as variable, then accurate prediction is precluded. I am probably overstating the case. Do you mean variation within specifiable limits?

L. MENN: I think that, for a change, there is an exact analogy between historical change and the situation in language acquisition. In the study of historical change, we know that some events are highly probable—certain kinds of deletions or assimilations, for example—but that does not mean that we can actually predict them. The same is true of the acquisition of phonology. One hesitates even to say that variation is "within specified limits," because exceptions keep turning up. Instead, we say that some events are highly unlikely and others are quite probable.

I think that we have a prejudice in favor of absolute theories that claim to make clean predictions because they give us some illusion of control. But absolute theories are not stronger in the sense of placing more constraints on an explanatory model. A theory must explain the distribution of events, whether they tail off gradually or drop abruptly from probability one to probability zero. Absolute theories are only stronger in the philosopher's sense of being harder to falsify; they are no more stringent than probabilistic ones when it comes to constraining explanatory models, and that's the kind of constraint that we need in psycholinguistics.

I'd like to ask a question of Dr. Ingram. You have certainly demonstrated that the difference in language environment between Italian-learning and English-learning children affects the strategies they use. But Italian and English are very different from one another. Suppose instead we consider the kinds of differences that can be found between two children in the same family. For example, in the early stages of acquisition of phonology, one child may use mostly open syllables, and a sibling mostly closed syllables. Would you expect that difference to be due to environmental factors?

Certainly the state of our other explanations for such strategy differences is at present only guesswork. We invoke some vague notion of the child's "style," but we don't even yet know whether there are any relations between a given child's approach to phonology and his or her approach to syntax.

D. INGRAM (*University of British Columbia, Vancouver, B.C., Canada*): In the case of reduplication, two children from the same family would have it as a strategy for the purpose I stated, that is, for the production of multisyllabic models. The child who produces closed syllables happens to be better, and so has moved beyond the use of reduplication. Of course, we cannot discount the possibility that caretakers speak differently to different children.

ACQUISITION OF WORDS BY
FIRST-LANGUAGE LEARNERS

Katherine Nelson

Developmental Psychology
Graduate Center
City University of New York
New York, New York 10036

The first step in learning any language is to learn a few words with which to begin making oneself understood. Unlike phonological development, syntactic development, or even reading and writing, this basic process continues throughout the life span. The process of word learning has, paradoxically, been considered both transparently simple and so complex as to defy the efforts of linguists, philosophers, and psychologists to understand it sufficiently to produce a coherent theory explaining it. In recent years, the developing vocabularies of very young children have been the focus of attention and the center of theoretical debates. Many issues have been drawn forth, such as the problem of overextension, underextension, and overlapping extensions of meaning, the conceptual structure of meaning, the disparity between comprehension and production, and individual differences in both process and product.

While I cannot hope to resolve all of these issues, I would like to examine them with an eye to (1) determining their importance at different stages in the development of a lexicon; (2) providing a preliminary map of those stages; (3) relating processes at work during these stages to conceptual and linguistic development; and (4) discovering the limitations on their applicability to second-language learning later in life.

To the extent that characteristics of word learning in a first language are related to the child's conceptual development, they are unlikely to characterize the older learner. It is important to bear in mind that the first-language learner begins the process as an infant, a child with no preestablished language skills and with cognitive abilities that are limited but undergoing rapid development. The period between one and three years is one of almost miraculous change in all areas of cognition, some no doubt the result of language, but some clearly independent of it. Thus the process by which a child begins to learn and progresses in the language may be dependent to an unknown degree on the limits of his or her ability to process information about both the world and the language describing it. We understand many of these limits and how they change, but by no means all.

On the other hand, to the extent that characteristics of word learning in a first language are general characteristics of mastering any new linguistic or symbolic system, then we would expect parallel processes to be the rule in learning a first and a second language. The lexicon forms an interface

0077-8923/81/0379-0148 $01.75/2 © 1981, NYAS

between the conceptual system and the semantic system, where language maps words onto meanings. It is difficult to talk about word meanings without talking about concepts, while the reverse is quite possible. Language develops into a system that relates to but is not isomorphic with the individual's conceptual system. The relation between these two at different points in development is the key to unraveling some of the controversial issues in this area.

Word-Learning Processes

Word learning most frequently has been viewed as a simple process, dependent primarily on the association of a word spoken by another person and an object to which the word refers. Hidden behind this description are difficult problems such as: How does the learner know what a word is? [1] How does the learner know to what the word refers, whether to an object, a quality, an action, or even *which* object, quality, or action? [2] What is an association? To solve these problems, it has been suggested that the learner is a hypothesis tester, testing his understanding of the reference of the word against the uses of others, and seeking confirmation of his own use in a novel situation. [3] Assuming then that the reference has been established correctly, is the referent object now the meaning that is established for the word? That is, does the *extension* of the word (all of its identified referents) constitute its *intension* (its meaning components)? Is there such a thing as intension separately considered from extension? [4] What about nonobject, abstract words? How are their meanings established?

Let us posit at the outset that learning word meanings is in general a process of *conceptual inference*. The limits that this sets on the system at any given point have to do with the state of development of the conceptual system in that concepts cannot be attached to words if such concepts lie beyond the current limitations of the developing system. In addition, there are limits to the inferential power of the cognitive system that are set by the stage of general cognitive development in addition to the availability of concepts and words to express them. However, it should be noted that making inferences about word meanings on the basis of their uses appears to be within the power of most children by the middle of the second year of life. The type of inference that is made, however, may shift with development.

There are two basic dimensions along which the learning process may vary. First, there may be more or less direct teaching by a tutor. Second, the context of use of the word may involve the nonverbal situation, the linguistic context, or a combination of both.

Consider the conditions of learning at the very outset of language acquisition, when the child is between 10 and 18 months old. Here, because of limited language understanding, whatever is learned must be derived from the situation of use, not from the verbal context. It is therefore the prototype of situationally determined word learning. Next, note that the child may be taught a word directly by having another person point to an object (or a picture) and repeat the word over and over until the child comes to repeat it reliably in the presence of the stimulus. If the tutor also applies the word to other objects from the same class, as when she may say "car" in the presence of the family car, cars in parking lots, cars in picture books, and so on, the child is faced with the problem of conceptual inference, of going from the word used by another to the formation of a *concept* to be attached to the diversity of uses of that word, in this case the concept of car suitably defined. In the process, the child may make inappropriate overextensions based on the experiences he has had with cars and the word car, or he may underextend the word because no one has yet pointed out unusual instances of cars, such as limousines. With sufficient exposure to the culture, however, the child's concept of car will come to match the uses of the word in the adult community.

On the other hand, the child may have a primitive concept of car already, one involving his experiences with the family car, toy cars, cars seen on the street. At some point and for some as yet unfathomable reasons, he may hear his father say, Do you want to go in the car?, and conclude that "car" is the word that refers to his concept, even though he has not been taught the word specifically. In this case, the word maps onto the preestablished concept. Here the child's experience will be central to the meaning of the word because the concept, embedded in experience, was established before the word referring to it was known.

It is much later that the child comes to be able to learn a word from its linguistic context rather than from its situational context, whether directly taught or not. For example, a parent may say, A zebra is a kind of horse with stripes, and expect the child to set up a meaning on the basis of what he already knows about horses and stripes, even without an example to point to. This is definitional teaching, and it has definite limitations, as teachers can testify and as consulting a dictionary with an eye to learning a new word can demonstrate. Another kind of verbal contextual inference condition exists when the word to be learned is embedded in a verbal context but is not taught explicitly. For example a person may say to the child, That's not a long stick, it's short, and the child may infer that "short" is the opposite of "long," thereby learning a new lexical item for an already available concept. Note that this type of learning depends upon the prior existence of a concept space into which the word can fit.

Although there have been few direct studies, it has been claimed that the vast majority of words that are acquired during early to middle childhood must be acquired from either situational or verbal context, because the numbers acquired by the average child (about 20 new words per day) preclude the special teaching that would be required if this were not the case.[5,6] In turn, this claim rests on the assumption that it is easier to make conceptual inferences from previously established knowledge than to learn new concepts to fit new words.

These different methods of learning and teaching have implications for development. First, learning from situational context is primary in the early stages of vocabulary building. However, such learning does not disappear as the child becomes more facile with language. Ostensive teaching proceeds throughout life, and the individual in a novel situation may form a concept (of a particular type of shellfish found on the beach, for example) before encountering the correct word (horseshoe crab) for it. Second, at all stages, attaching words to concepts or knowledge already acquired is far quicker and easier than forming a new concept to go with a novel word. Finally, the fact that learning from linguistic context becomes possible in the preschool period is an indication that a lexical *system,* a network of relationships, has been established, as Bowerman has demonstrated with independent evidence.[7]

Thus far, nothing has been said about what the word meanings or concepts consist of, or how they are structured. Are they representations of the objects referred to? Are they features or relations? Are they conceptual or semantic components of a type not yet defined, general or specific? What relation do they bear to other words in a semantic domain? These are important and contentious questions of considerable theoretical significance. The evidence at the moment is not strongly favorable to any single position. I tend to lean toward a rather fuzzy conception of meaning as a complex of information that is closely or loosely attached to a concept and that changes—both contracting and expanding—as the conceptual system and the lexical system develop over time.[8] Different semantic domains contain different complexes of information. This conception is similar to that set forth by Miller and Johnson-Laird,[9] but I am not staking anything on it here. The only point that I think is vital and that also is indisputable is that at some point in development (but not, I think, at first), relations between words become established in the lexicon such that a lexical network is set up that is independent of but interacts with the underlying conceptual network.

Some Typical Phenomena of Early Lexical Development

With these considerations in mind, let us consider three phenomena of early development that have presented some controversy and that may or may not be relevant to later learning. The first is the vocabulary spurt that has been observed to occur in the middle of the second year in a number of children. This spurt was identified by many early observers. Stern referred to it as the realization on the child's part that "everything has a name." [10] Similarly, Dore has referred to the "designation hypothesis" and believes it marks the child's way into the language as a truly symbolic system.[11] McShane makes a similar claim.[12] The facts to be considered here are that the child usually has been speaking only a few words for a number of months (3 to 12) and within the space of a month or so— at around 17 to 20 months—accelerates the rate of acquisition of new words from a rate of around 3 or 4 per month to 30–50 per month.[13,14]

(As noted earlier, this rate continues to increase, but the rate of acceleration becomes less dramatic.) Lest we rush to explanations of the phenomena too quickly, it must be pointed out that individual differences are the rule here, as they are in so many phenomena of early language. Some children spurt very early, at 13 or 14 months rather than 17 or 20. Some children do not spurt until 24 or 25 months. And some children never spurt at all, plugging away, adding a few words each week, and gradually increasing their rate of acceleration without ever seeming to go through a period where the "designation hypothesis" drives them to learn the name of everything in sight.

However, considering the processes outlined above, what is the best or most probable explanation for the spurt in vocabulary development? I hypothesize that it indexes an important cognitive development, where the child becomes capable of making conceptual inferences, of leaping from word to concept and from concept to presented word. This development in turn appears to be the result of the establishment of a conceptual system where individual concepts are disembedded from larger contexts and thereby become available for naming. The evidence for this development is too complex to elaborate here.[15] However, the important and interesting corollary is that words used prior to this time, that is, during most of the single-word period, are not conceptually based.

Consider next the common observation that children engage in under-extensions, overextensions, and overlapping meanings in their first-language learning. The frequently discussed overextension of terms involves the application of a word to an object that does not belong to the class of objects that form the referent class for adult speakers. While this phe-nomenon is striking, as when a child calls a horse "doggie," it is not by any means a universal occurrence. A systematic study by Rescorla found that fewer than one-third of the words learned by children between 12 and 20 months ever were overextended.[16] Moreover, she found that during this time period, there was no variation in overextending by age, that is, it did not seem to be a function of cognitive development during this period, as some authors had suggested. The basis for overextensions usually has been found to be perceptual, that is, an object receives a label because it looks like, sounds like, moves like, or feels like the "true" referent. Occa-sionally the extension can be identified as having a functional basis, as when a child puts a bucket on his head and says "hat" or throws an apple and says "ball."

The *function* of overextensions has been speculated by some to be attributable to the economical use of a small vocabulary in the effort to communicate. However, frequently young children do not seem to be attempting to communicate in these uses but simply to be labeling for the child's own sake; no acknowledgment or response seems to be expected. In some cases, what appear to be overextensions can be seen to be efforts to say something *about* an object, for example, "Daddy" in reference to Daddy's shoes. An extension of this explanation may be made to cases where the child labels an object or a series of objects with a term from another semantic class entirely, as when the child says "clock" when she hears water dripping or labels crescent-shaped objects "grapefruit." [16,17] It does not seem too unreasonable to consider that in these cases the child is using one term to point out a similarity (or comparison) of its referent object to a feature of another, but not an identity of the two.[18] Indeed, some data from Winner on children's early analogies in language and action support this interpretation.[19]

In sum, interpretations of the overextension phenomena fall into three categories. First, the linguistic interpretation claims that children need to learn what words refer to, that is, in the case of nouns, a referent class of objects, not the individual features that define those objects. A second explanation based on communicative needs is that children are trying to use their limited language in the most effective way and in so doing stretch its meaning. A third, conceptual explanation is that children are learning simultaneously about language and about object classes in the world— including their similarities and differences. In the course of doing so, they not only label objects that fit their preestablished concepts but also point out these characteristics and relationships (e.g., possession), using the only words at their limited command. I believe the latter explanation explains more of the data than do the first two, although clearly the second may have some validity and is the explanation most likely to be relevant to overextension in second-language learning. If, however, the third explanation is the correct one, the phenomenon of overextension should occur much less frequently among second-language learners since they no longer would be at the stage where object concepts are being basically built up, and perceptual similarities and differences are being compared.

It has been claimed that overextension occurs in the production of terms rather than in comprehension. Several studies (Reference 20, for example) have shown that children will identify correctly the appropriate referents for a term that they mislabel with an overextended term in production. However, a recent study by Kay and Anglin has shown that when appropriately controlled tests are employed, two-year-old children both overextend and underextend newly learned words in both production and comprehension.[21] Since word learning in this task (and others like it) is essentially concept learning, this perhaps is not so surprising. It also supports the contention that the basic phenomenon of overextension (and underextension) is a cognitive one having to do with conceptual inference, not a specifically linguistic or communicative one. Thus, as children pass through the stage of learning basic object concepts and then superordinate classes, these phenomena should be less apparent. Of course, anytime a novel class is acquired, some variability in the extension of its term can be expected.

The disparity between comprehension and production in first-language learning is another phenomenon to be considered. Most children learn to understand some language before they begin to produce it. As with production, they learn to respond in action situations and at first may know only one key word in a sentence, but will use that knowledge to respond with an appropriate action. For example, "where's" uttered by mother may send the child on a search for an object while "what's that?" may produce pointing behavior. An object term will direct the child to pick up or give the named object. In general, the acquisition of receptive vocabulary by children in the second year leads production by about six months.[22]

This lag in production may have two sources. First, the child may begin to understand language in specific situational contexts, as the above examples indicate and as Bruner's studies have shown (e.g., Reference 23). In this case the word may not indicate a concept at all but may only direct the child's action. When mother says Where's the ball?, the child understands the action response called for and the object referred to, but does not attach the word to his own concept of ball (if such exists) and has no reason to produce the word to trigger action on mother's part. Second, the child entering a first language has specific problems in mastering the articulatory and phonological systems that hinder production. Thus the great disparity between comprehension and production may be a phenomen unique to first-language learning.

Variations in Learning within and between Children

In making the argument that word learning primarily rests on the process of conceptual inference, I also pointed out that some types of language, in particular those used and understood early in the second year, need not have a conceptual base. It long has been conventional to distinguish contentive (or substantive) words from grammatical functors. The former include nouns, verbs, and modifiers and generally are the types of words produced first by young children, giving their early sentences a "telegraphic" look. Functors include articles, demonstratives, prepositions, and copular verbs among others. They are acquired later as the grammatical system is developed.

But recently a different category of speech productions has come to be recognized, which resists this type of classification because it consists of preformed units (or formulas) that are used to perform a pragmatic function in a specific situational context. A formula is a conventional construction that is learned and produced as an unanalyzed whole. Formulas range from simple greetings and polite forms (e.g., "hi," "thank you," "how are you?") to complex phrases used in ceremonies ("I pledge allegiance to the flag") and everyday life ("and that's the way it is"). There are two things that make these formulas important in language learning. First, they provide the language learner with a ready-made phrase that is useful in a recurrent context without necessarily being understood in terms of its component parts. Second, they may provide the learner with a repertoire that can be subjected to further analysis and thus serve as a foundation for language development.

However, formulaic speech also highlights a problem that pervades all of language learning, the problem of unitization.[1] Unless pieces are specifically made salient by the teacher, language comes to the child in clumps that are not easily broken apart. Words are not separated neatly by pauses but run into each other. One of the significant problems for the learner then is to identify what *is* a word. Older speakers often help with this by embedding a significant word within one or more repeated formulas, e.g., "Where's the ball?" "Can you get the ball?" "Get the ball." Thus formulas and single substantive words play off against each other.

It is not surprising, given the difficulty of identifying substantive words and the usefulness of pragmatic formulas, that children tend to pick up formulas early in language learning. Indeed, such learning seems to constitute a normal early phase of language development for many children, and for some children formulas continue to play a large role in their speech production throughout the early years.[14,24] Recent studies have shown that second-language learners rely on such formulas even more than do first-language learners.[25]

Children usually begin around the end of the first year to understand a few words in a familiar, gamelike context (References 22 and 23) and to produce a few forms that are identifiable as having conventional word targets. These first words usually are like formulas in that they perform a pragmatic function but do not have referential content. Examples are "byebye" said only in the context of someone's leaving, or "mama" used to request help or food, or "peekaboo" in the conventional game context. As Grieve and Hoogenraad have put it, these terms enable the child to share experience but not to talk about it.[26] This characterization fits the hypothesis that early words are not conceptually based. Two other early speech types also support this hypothesis.

Relational words have been described by Bloom and more recently by Niccolich.[27,28] These are terms—such as "all gone," "more," "here," "open," and "up"—that express general object relations of the type that are beginning to be understood by children toward the end of the infancy period. They tend to accompany the child's own actions, and they refer to *single* object relations, that is, disappearance, reappearance, direction of movement. While these relations can be expressed by speakers at any stage, they tend to decline in the children's spontaneous speech as children get older. Thus, their importance in early vocabularies probably derives from their cognitive significance rather than from any specific linguistic stage or process.

In addition children may learn names for things early in the second year, particularly in the picture-naming game that mothers often engage in and that has been described by Ninio and Bruner.[29] However, these labels usually have a narrow situationally specific reference (like the early formulas) and are not used in the absence of the referent or extended to new instances. Or they may be conceptually unbounded and refer to a wide range of loosely related phenomena.

Thus there appear to be a number of different types of early speech, all of which are conceptually empty but situationally significant. However, late in the second year and into the third, the child begins to build a lexicon that is conceptually based. That is, each word appears to be attached to a concept in the child's growing conceptual system. Several hundred words may be acquired by the time the child is two—enough to provide names for everything in the child's limited conceptual space.

However, the power of the two-year-old's vocabulary is small indeed compared to that of the five- or six-year-old who has learned many thousands of words. In order to account for this later achievement, it is necessary to posit the establishment of a lexical *system* that links words themselves (and not simply a word and the concept associated with it). The establishment of this system depends on finding similar meaning components that are shared by two or more words and thereby defining a semantic space occupied by words of similar but different meanings, that is, that share some meaning components but not others. Note that forming an independent lexical system requires the identification of semantic components, although simply learning words for things does not. That is, the analysis of meanings may take place after the meaning has been acquired.[7]

Because of this evolving semantic network, the child becomes able to place new words into nodes that are already, in a sense, predefined but empty. For example, a child who knows the meaning of "big," "little," and "tall" will already have an empty slot to be filled by "short" and therefore will have no trouble in picking it up at the first opportunity. This seems to be the necessary implication of Susan Carey and Elsa Bartlett's work on the acquisition of a novel color word;[5] and it also fits Carey's finding that, contrary to Donaldson's claim,[31] "less never means more."[30] That is, words are not confused in meaning with their opposites. Rather, the understanding of a word like "more" in its quantitative sense implies a contrasting position that "less" easily can fill. Much more work is needed on the development of these lexical systems in early childhood, but their existence seems reasonably well demonstrated.

While developing a lexical system is by definition a linguistic process, it also is a cognitive one. Once fully developed, the lexical system can operate pretty much autonomously; a new relation between language and thought is established. An older child or adult who already has such a system in a first language would be unlikely to go through the same process of development in learning a second language. Thus the postulation of such a system has implications for the relation between the two languages, depending on the age or stage at which the second is acquired.

In sum, I propose three major periods of lexical development. The first, a preconceptual stage, may begin late in the first year and last through the second year. It usually coincides with but is not coextensive with the period of single-word use. In this period, children use their language performatively, pragmatically, or ritually in situationally specific contexts. They are learning to use language but are not learning what language means.

The second stage usually begins around the middle of the second year but may begin earlier for some children and later for others. Here, substantive words are connected directly with concepts, and in the beginning, concepts are combined directly to form primitive sentences.

The third stage begins early in the preschool period and evolves over a number of years with the establishment of relations between words and eventually an autonomous lexical system. It makes possible the learning of new words from verbal as well as nonverbal contexts.

Implications for Second-Language Acquisition

Throughout this paper I have tried to identify problems and processes that are common to the task of acquiring a lexicon in a first language and in a second language later in life, as well as ones that may be unique to a first language. First-language learners are just emerging from infancy. As they learn a language, they also are undergoing rapid cognitive development, some of it related to language acquisition and some independent. Much of this development has to do with conceptualizing the world and the people, places, events, and objects within it along culturally conventional lines. Learning language terms for these categories aids in this process but also solidifies and reifies the categories. Learning a second language later in life means learning a new set of terms that may only partially fit the categories that now have been established. Moreover, the lexicon of the first language has itself become systematized along conventional lines. Thus the direct concept-word match that is the basis of first word learning is no longer easily accessible. While this conclusion is still somewhat speculative, it may suggest why there are different types of bilingualism that appear to be associated with learning a second language at different points in development.

In short, the problems and processes that are associated with concept and category development implicate differences between word acquisition in a first language and a second. However, those processes that do not depend on conceptual development, for example, the problem of unitization (or the use of formulas for communicative purposes), may be expected to be similar for both. While the first-language learner faces unique problems of articulation, conceptualization, and lexical systematization, the second-language learner faces problems of interference from the previously established conceptual and lexical systems. In addition, the developmental perspective set forth here has implications beyond those of explaining differences and similarities in first- and second-language learning. It suggests also that the very nature of *meaning* may change over time as conceptual and lexical systems change and develop. If this is the case, a theory that explains the structure of word meaning in the adult language will not be directly applicable to the young child's lexicon, and vice versa. In particular, if early word meanings are based on single concepts while later meanings derive from a system of lexical relationships, both the content and structure of meaning for a given word can be expected to change over time.

REFERENCES

1. PETERS, A. M. 1980. The units of language acquisition. Univ. Hawaii Working Pap. Linguistics **12**(1).
2. QUINE, W. V. O. 1960. Word and Object. MIT Press. Cambridge, Mass.
3. BROWN, R. 1958. Words and Things. The Free Press. New York, N.Y.
4. ROSCH, E. 1978. Principles of categorization. *In* Cognition and Categorization. E. Rosch & B. B. Lloyd, Eds.: 28–49. Erlbaum Associates. Hillsdale, N.J.
5. CAREY, S. & E. BARTLETT. 1978. Acquiring a single new word. Pap. Rep. Child Lang. Dev. **15:** 17–29.
6. MILLER, G. 1977. Spontaneous Apprentices. Seabury Press. New York, N.Y.
7. BOWERMAN, M. 1977. The acquisition of rules governing "possible lexical items": evidence from spontaneous speech errors. Pap. Rep. Child Lang. Dev. **13:** 148–156.
8. NELSON, K. 1978. Explorations in the development of a functional semantic system. *In* Children's Language and Communication. W. Collins, Ed. **12:** 47–83. Erlbaum Associates. Hillsdale, N.J.
9. MILLER, G. & P. JOHNSON-LAIRD. 1976. Language and Perception. Harvard University Press. Cambridge, Mass.
10. STERN, W. 1930. Psychology of Early Childhood. Holt. New York, N.Y.
11. DORE, J. 1978. Concepts, communicative acts and the LAD. Paper presented at the Boston Child Language Meetings, Boston, Mass., September 29–30.
12. MCSHANE, J. 1979. The development of naming. Linguistics **17:** 879–905.
13. MCCARTHY, D. 1954. Language development in children. *In* Manual of Child Psychology. L. Carmichael, Ed. 2nd edit.: 492–630. John Wiley & Sons, Inc. New York, N.Y.
14. NELSON, K. 1973. Structure and strategy in learning to talk. Soc. Res. Child Dev. Monogr. **38**(1–2, Serial No. 149).
15. NELSON, K. 1980. The conceptual basis for language. Paper presented at the British Psychological Society Meeting, Edinburgh, Scotland, September 5–7.
16. RESCORLA, L. 1976. Concept formation in word learning. Doctoral Dissertation. Yale University. New Haven, Conn.
17. BOWERMAN, M. 1976. Semantic factors in the acquisition of rules for word use and sentence construction. *In* Directions in Normal and Deficient Child Language. D. Morehead & A. Morehead, Eds.: 99–180. University Park Press. Baltimore, Md.
18. NELSON, K., *et al.* 1977. Lessons from early lexicons. Paper presented to the Society for Research on Child Development Symposium on the Acquisition of Word Meaning, New Orleans, La.
19. WINNER, E. 1978. New names for old things: the emergence of metaphoric language. Pap. Rep. Child Lang. Dev. **15:** 7–16.
20. THOMPSON, J. R. & R. S. CHAPMAN. 1975. Who is "Daddy"? Pap. Rep. Child Lang. Dev. **10:** 59–68.
21. KAY, D. A. & J. M. ANGLIN. 1979. Overextension and underextension in the child's receptive and expressive speech. Paper presented at the Society for Research in Child Development, San Francisco, Calif., March.

22. BENEDICT, H. 1979. Early lexical development: comprehension and production. J. Child Lang. **6:** 183–200.
23. BRUNER, J. S. 1974–5. From communication to language—a psychological perspective. Cognition **3:** 225–287.
24. NELSON, K. 1981. Individual differences in language development: implications for development and language. Dev. Psychol. **17**(2): 170–187.
25. VIHMAN, M. M. 1979. Formulas in first and second language acquisition. Pap. Rep. Child Lang. Dev. **18:** 75–92.
26. GRIEVE, R. & R. HOOGENRAAD. 1979. First words. *In* Language Acquisition. P. Fletcher & M. Garman, Eds. Cambridge University Press. Cambridge, England.
27. BLOOM, L. 1973. One Word at a Time. Mouton. The Hague, the Netherlands.
28. NICOLICH, L. M. 1980. The cognitive bases of relational words in the single word period. Rutgers University. New Brunswick, N.J. (Unpublished manuscript.)
29. NINIO, A. & J. BRUNER. 1978. The achievement and antecedents of labelling. J. Child Lang. **5:** 1–16.
30. CAREY, S. 1978. Less may never mean "more." *In* Recent Advances in the Psychology of Language. R. N. Campbell & P. T. Smith, Eds. **4A:** 109–132. Plenum Publishing Corp. New York, N.Y.
31. DONALDSON, M. & R. J. WALES. 1970. On the acquisition of some relational terms. *In* Cognition and the Development of Language. J. R. Hayes, Ed.: 235–268. John Wiley & Sons, Inc. New York, N.Y.

THE IMPORTANCE OF LANGUAGE FOR LANGUAGE DEVELOPMENT: LINGUISTIC DETERMINISM IN THE 1980s *

Lois Bloom

Teachers College
Columbia University
New York, New York 10027

Many factors contribute to the process of language development. The child's context, for example, is one source of the *meanings* of early utterances, inasmuch as children talk about what they do and what they see. The child's social context is one source of the child's communicative *intentions,* inasmuch as children talk to other persons and learn to use language in the context of social and pragmatic events. And, at the same time, both intentions and meanings are mediated by the child's *cognition;* what children talk about and how they use language to interact with other persons depend upon what they know. These factors, context and cognition, together contribute in by now obvious ways to language development.

However, one factor that necessarily interacts with these and other factors in less obvious ways is the formal structure of the target language that the child is learning: *language* is important for language development. The language that children learn—the target language in the child's community—is, itself, a determining factor in how and when the different structures of the language are acquired.

Linguistic Determinism in Child Language

The importance of language for language development, or linguistic determinism, has been emphasized in different ways in the last several decades. For example, Roger Brown in 1957 demonstrated that the surface forms of the language—in particular, articles *a* and *the,* and morphological inflections in English—help the child to learn basic grammatical categories or the part of speech of individual words.[1] That is, noticing the endings of words, such as *-ing,* will help the child to determine whether a word names an action or an object. In the 1960s, another version of linguistic determinism originated with the theory of generative grammar and the idea that much of language learning was determined by language universals that somehow were innate. This view was expounded by Noam Chomsky in 1965 and taken up by David McNeill in 1966 and 1970.[2-4] And, in the 1970s, the importance of a linguistic determinism that is culturally specific was advanced by Dan Slobin.[5] Slobin pointed out, for example, that even

* Supported by a research grant from the National Science Foundation.

0077–8923/81/0379–0160 $01.75/2 © 1981, NYAS

though cognitive development most probably does advance in similar ways among children growing up in different environments, the sequence in which children learn to express similar ideas about the world will be determined in large part by the accessibility of the surface forms of the language that express those ideas.

There have been, then, different views of linguistic determinism in the last several decades of child language research—views that have emphasized the surface forms of the language that the child hears; [1] or the underlying principles of grammar that are presumed to be universal to all languages; [2-4] or the surface grammars of different languages that influence the ways in which meaning gets expressed and different orders of acquisition.[5,6]

The purpose of this paper is to present another version of linguistic determinism, one that derives from several recent investigations of child language in the period between two and three years of age. There have been three related themes that have emerged from the results of these studies. To begin with, there are many factors that contribute to the process of language acquisition, so that appeals or explanations or theories based only on cognitive or social or pragmatic factors alone are insufficient. Second, one factor that consistently interacts with all of these other factors is the formal structure of the adult target language. And third, the central feature of the target language that the child is learning that influences the acquisition of increasing linguistic complexity is the *verb system,* that is, the syntax and semantics of verbs appear to be a major influence on the acquisition of increasingly complex structures.

Thus, while linguistic determinism in the 1950s emphasized the importance of those linguistic features that identify part-of-speech membership, and linguistic determinism in the 1960s emphasized underlying universal principles of grammar, and linguistic determinism in the 1970s emphasized differences between languages, linguistic determinism in the beginning of the 1980s is pointing to the special role that the verb system plays in acquisition. According to the several studies of child language that are discussed below, the verbs that children learn interact with one or another aspect of linguistic structure to influence how that structure is acquired; in particular, the structure of simple sentences, verb inflections, *wh*-questions, and complex sentences appears to be mediated by the verb system of the target language.

Observational, Descriptive Methodology

The data for these studies consisted of many thousands of dialogues with a small number of children, sometimes four, sometimes up to eight children. Each of the children was visited at home, at periodic intervals, for about five to eight hours of observation. The dialogues of the children with investigators and with parents were recorded and transcribed, with contextual notes, to provide the texts for analysis. The dialogues in these texts were reviewed over and over again so that similarities, consistencies, and recurrences among the language behaviors could be identified. Behaviors that occurred again and again in different contexts and with different participants, or behaviors that shared common elements, were grouped together as a potential category of behaviors. Thus, a taxonomy was formed when categories of recurrent behaviors contrasted with one another along some dimension—such as shared meaning, or syntactic relation, or the sequence in which they appear, or their selective use with different linguistic forms.

There are two important features in such an inferential methodology. First, rather than beginning with an intuitive scheme and imposing that organization on the child's behaviors in order to test one or another a priori theory, one observes and describes regularities among children's behaviors in order to discover their organization and build a theory of the child's language. The taxonomy of observed behaviors that emerges from repeated examination of the data is a result rather than a heuristic. Second, in order to infer a pattern of organization from evidence, frequencies of behaviors are compared—both absolute frequency, or simply the number of times a behavior occurs, and relative frequency, or how often a behavior occurs in proportion to all of the child's other relevant behaviors. What is described, then, is *regularity* among behaviors.

There are four levels of regularity among behaviors. At one level, semantic regularity, utterances are presumed to be semantically similar when there are similarities in the behaviors and situational contexts in the speech events in which they occur. At another level, formal regularity, different forms (such as differences in word order or different *wh*-question words or the different inflections on verbs) are distributed selectively among utterances with different semantic interpretations. At a third level, there is developmental regularity, when the regularities in the behaviors of one child at a single time are systematically related to regularities in the behaviors of the same child at a later time. Finally, at a fourth level, there is regularity among children, when the regularities in behaviors of a single child are consistent with regularities in the behaviors of other children, both at the same developmental level and across time.

An inferential methodology, then, requires observation of large numbers of behaviors—from a single child at one time and at successive times, and from different children. Given a large enough sample of behaviors, patterns of organization can be inferred on the basis of the relative frequencies of different kinds of behaviors and the distribution of behaviors in relation to one another.

From Single Words to Simple Sentences

One of the most straightforward indications of the essential relation of verbs to the acquisition of syntax is the fact that verbs (as defined for the adult model) are rare in single-word vocabularies before children begin to combine words. The underrepresentation of verbs in the single-word utterance period has been well known since Dorothea McCarthy's study of the acquisition of parts of speech.[7] In attempting to explain the preponderance of nouns in early vocabularies, McCarthy and others have pointed to the high frequency of nouns in the language that children hear, the importance of objects to very young children, and the importance of naming objects for the development of symbolization.

More recently, Nelson reported that a preponderance of nouns (or "general nominals") was not necessarily characteristic of all children in the single-word utterance period, but the words that children learn, if they are not nouns, usually are not verbs either.[8] At the same time, Bloom pointed out that while children do learn a large number of different noun forms in the period, the words that tend to be used more frequently and in more different situations are words that refer to transformations of objects or relations of objects.[9] Such relational words in children's vocabularies are not nouns, but they also are not verbs; they include, for example, *uhoh, there, up, gone, more,* etc. And, in the study by Goldin-Meadow, Seligman, and Gelman, verbs were both produced and understood much less often than nouns by the children studied during the single-word period, and both comprehension and production of verbs increased as the children approached the use of multiword utterances.[10]

The reason for the low frequency of verbs as single-word utterances could not be their relative abstractness (in comparison with nouns, which refer to objects that are literal, more salient events perceptually); such frequent relational words as *up, gone, there,* and *away* are as abstract as verbs such as *put, make, do, go,* and *eat.* Rather, verbs appear in syntactic contexts when children begin to combine words for multiword utterances. It appears that it is necessary for children to learn verbs in combination with nouns or pronouns, and knowing something about verbs is necessary for the acquisition of grammar. The evidence reviewed here indicates that there is a close relation between learning verbs and learning the grammar of the basic phrase structure of sentences.

Once multiword utterances begin, the verbs that children learn in syntactic combination appear to be constrained categorically. That is, children do not learn a garden variety assortment of verbs, with combinations of words dependent upon the idiosyncratic possibilities of particular, individual verbs for the relations between words. Rather, children seem to learn global or molar categories of verbs that share syntactic or semantic features, so that there is consistency among the relations between words. For example, the verbs *read, eat,* and *ride* are related to one another because they name actions and participate in the same semantic/syntactic relation with actor nouns (e.g., *Mommy read, Daddy eat, Baby ride*). Further, different relations with the same verb are, themselves, related to one another systematically (for example, *Mommy read, read book, Mommy book; Daddy eat, eat raisin, Daddy raisin;* and *Baby ride, ride bike, Baby bike*). Categorical differences among verbs include, for example, the syntactic distinction between transitive verbs (e.g., *read, eat*) and intransitive verbs (e.g., *dance, run*); the semantic distinction between verbs of action (e.g., *eat, dance, run*) and verbs of state (e.g., *want, know, see*); and the semantic-syntactic difference between verbs that entail locative constituents to complete their meaning (e.g., *put, go, sit*) and those that do not.[13,19]

Transitive and Intransitive Verbs in Simple Sentences

One of the broadest distinctions among verbs, the syntactic difference between transitive and intransitive verbs, appears to differentiate among children in the beginning stages of syntax, when the first sentences with verbs appear with some regularity. Certain children have used intransitive verbs primarily (e.g., *jump, sing, run*).[11,12] The syntax of sentences with such verbs entails only one constituent relation: noun (actor) + verb (intransitive action). In contrast, other children have used transitive verbs primarily (e.g., *eat, read, find*).[13–15] The syntax of sentences with transitive verbs entails the relations among subject, verb, and complement, and more than one constituent relation theoretically is possible. For example, the children studied by Bloom *et al.* produced early sentences with the separate constituent relations subject-verb (*Mommy read*), verb-object (*read book*), and verb-place (*put chair*), object-place (*sweater chair*).[16,13]

Thus, there is some evidence that the first break into syntax appears to be guided by the combinatorial possibilities that several different verbs have in common as either transitive or intransitive verbs. Different children apparently begin syntax by learning to combine words with verbs that share one or the other of these syntactic possibilities, with a generalized rule of grammar that is particular to that class of verbs. The fact that one or another syntactic category of verbs predominates in the early syntax of different children is one indication of the way in which distinctions among verbs in the adult target language influence acquisition.

The distinction between transitive and intransitive verbs in children's early word combinations was apparent when the results of several studies by different investigators were compared. Other indications of the importance of the target language for language development, and, in particular, the importance of verbs, have come from the results of a longitudinal investigation of the language development of eight children, which have been reported elsewhere in the literature by Bloom *et al.*[16,13]

There were three kinds of complexity that the children added to their simple sentences when the mean length of utterance of their sentences passed 2.0 morphemes in the period between two and three years of age. The children began to add inflectional endings to verbs (*-ing, -s, -ed*, and irregular past); they began to ask questions with the *wh*-question words *what, where, who, how, why*, and *when;* and they also began to combine the structures underlying simple sentences in order to form complex sentences with the syntactic connectives *and, then, because, what, but, so*, and *that.* Each of these three kinds of increased complexity in the children's language was influenced by the verbs that the children knew and were learning.

Verb Semantics and Verb Inflections

In a study of the emergence of verb inflections, the relationship between the syntax and semantics of the verbs used in early sentences and the emergence of the inflectional forms of the verb auxiliary (-*ing*, -*s*, -*ed*, or irregular past) was explored.[17] In earlier discussions of the acquisition of grammatical morphemes, only the syntax and semantics of the individual *morphemes* themselves (along with their environmental frequency) had been discussed seriously as contributing to the order in which grammatical morphemes are acquired.[14,18] However, the results of this study suggested that the semantic organization of the *verb* system that children learn is at least as important as the meanings of the morphemes themselves for determining the acquisition of the inflections of verbs.

The different inflections (*ing, s,* and *ed* or irregular past) emerged in the children's speech at the same time when the mean length of utterance (MLU) was about 2.0. However, both the syntax of the children's sentences with different verbs and the semantics of verbs interacted selectively with the use of different inflections. First, with respect to the syntax of sentences, there were several categories of verbs in the children's speech that were identified according to whether a locative constituent was entailed in the meaning of the verb (action and locative action verbs) and according to the semantic relation between different locative action verbs and the sentence subject (whether the sentence subject functioned as agent, mover, or patient in the change of place that was named by the verb).[19] If there was no interaction between the syntax of sentences and the inflections of verbs, then one could expect that the relative frequency of the use of inflections would match the relative frequency of sentences that occurred with these different kinds of verbs. That is, there should not be a difference between the relative distribution of sentences with the different categories of action and location action verbs, and the relative distribution of the use of inflections among these sentences. In fact, however, there were statistically significant differences between the distribution of sentences— or relative frequency of sentences that occurred with different categories of verbs—and the distribution of the use of inflections among those sentences with different verbs. Thus, the syntax of the sentence helped to determine whether the verb was inflected.

Further, only a few of the verbs that were inflected occurred with all of the different verb inflections. These were the verbs *do, go,* and *make,* a small group of verbs that were used with great frequency by all of the children; they were more general in reference than descriptive verbs such as *ride, turn,* and *drink* and appeared to function as pro-verbs. But, while all of the possible verb inflections occurred with these semantically general pro-verbs, each of the inflections occurred selectively with different populations of descriptive verbs. Certain descriptive verbs occurred almost exclusively with -*ing;* certain other verbs occurred almost exclusively with past tense (irregular or regular -*ed*); and certain other verbs occurred only with -*s.*

The selective distribution of descriptive verbs with the different inflections coincided with the intersection of two of the most fundamental distinctions of verb aspect: duration and completion. Aspect is the temporal contour of an event that is named by a particular verb—such as an action that is momentary in time (e.g., *hit* or *jump*) in comparison with an action that is durative and lasts over time (e.g., *eat* or *play*), and an action that entails completion or an end result (e.g., *break*) in comparison with an action that does not entail a result (e.g., *swim*). The verbs that occurred with -*ing* named aspectual events that were both durative (that is, they lasted over time) and noncompletive (in that they did not entail an end result), for example, *playing, riding, reading,* and *swimming.* The verbs that occurred with regular -*ed* or irregular past named events that were both nondurative (or punctual and momentary in time) and completive (with an end result), for example, *broke, found,* and *pushed.* Finally, the verbs that occurred with -*s* named events that were both durative and completive, for example, *goes* and *fits.*

The semantics of verb aspect appeared to be the major factor that governed the emergence of verb inflections in these children's speech. The children's use of inflections was redundant in relation to the inherent aspectual meanings of their verbs inasmuch as the inflections themselves carry the same durative and completive aspectual meanings. That is, adults add -*ing* to a nondurative verb to indicate repetition or duration (e.g., *hitting, jumping*) or use the past form of otherwise durative verbs to indicate completion (as in "she *swam* a mile"). The children learned to use the inflections to mark *tense,* that is, to mark the deictic relations between event time and speech time, sometime after they used the forms for redundant coding of aspect. This developmental sequence of coding aspect before tense is consistent with results reported in experimental studies of the use of inflections by somewhat older children; [20,33,34] and it confirms the general principle of aspect before tense proposed by Eric Woisetschlaeger for the morphology of adult languages.[21] The children's early use of inflections was verb specific in that they learned the different inflections with semantically different populations of verbs.

Verbs and the Sequence of Wh-*Questions*

Yet another interaction between the verb system and the development of complexity in the children's language was observed in the acquisition of *wh*-questions.[22] The children asked about 8,000 *wh*-questions in the period from about 22 to 36 months of age and learned to ask *wh*-questions with verbs in the order *what>where>who>how>why>when.* This essentially is the same order that has been observed in other studies as well (for both answering and asking *wh*-questions). There were structural differences among these questions that corresponded to their sequence of acquisition. The first *wh*-questions, *what, where,* and *who,* are *wh*-pronominals that ask for major sentence constituents—object (*what*), place (*where*), subject (*who*)—and are relatively simple syntactically. In contrast, *why, how,* and *when,* which emerged later, are *wh*-sententials, which do not replace major sentence constituents, but ask for information that pertains to the semantic relations among all the constituents in the sentence. The sequence in which the *wh*-forms were acquired, then, reflected the relative syntactic complexity among different *wh*-forms.

In addition, there also was a differential use of *wh*-questions with different populations of verbs. Apart from questions with the contracted and uncontracted copula, there was a small group of verbs, the pro-verbs *do, go,* and *happen,* that were the most frequent verbs that the children used in *wh*-questions. These general, all-purpose pro-verbs, and the copula, occurred overwhelmingly with the early *wh*-question words *what, where,* and *who.* In contrast, the later-appearing questions *how, why,* and *when* occurred primarily with descriptive verbs that named particular actions and states. Thus, there was an interaction between the syntactic function of the individual *wh*-words and the semantic complexity of the verbs that were used with each question form. The pronominal *wh*-forms that asked for sentence constituents (*what, where, who*) occurred predominantly with pro-verbs, whereas the sentential forms (*how, why, when*) occurred predominantly with descriptive verbs. It was apparent that the order of acquisition of the *wh*-forms covaried with both the syntax of *wh*-questions and the kind and variety of verbs.

It appears that the sequence in which these children learned to ask different *wh*-question forms was determined in part by complications having to do with learning to use main verbs for asking questions. As proforms for major sentence constituents, the earliest-learned *wh*-question forms (*what, where, who*) can be combined more easily with the verb proforms (the copula, *do,* or *go*) without the child having to sort out the individual semantic and syntactic constraints between different descriptive verbs and nouns. In contrast, *why, how,* and *when* are *wh*-sententials that do not replace major sentence constituents; the meaning of these forms interacts with sentential meaning. They were used with descriptive verbs primarily, and they were acquired later. In addition, then, to whatever cognitive constraints and whatever motivational and functional factors contribute to the developmental sequence of *wh*-questions, there evidently are important linguistic constraints: in particular, constraints that operate in the selection of verbs with different *wh*-question words.

Verbs and Complex Sentences

A major feature of the children's later language development (after the development of simple sentences and along with the development of inflections and *wh*-questions that has been discussed so far) is the development of complex sentences with connectives.[23] Three syntactic structures have been observed in the children's complex sentences in the developmental sequence conjunction > complementation > relativization, and each of the syntactic structures developed with essentially different populations of verbs. Examples of conjunction were "maybe you can carry that and I can carry this" (additive conjunction); "you push that up and it turn" (temporal conjunction); "get them cause I want it" (causal conjunction); and "I was tired but now I'm not tired" (adversative conjunction). Conjunction, which was the most frequent kind of complex sentence, occurred with many different action and locative action verbs and with relatively few state verbs.[23]

Relativization—for example, "that's the man who fixes the door"—occurred most often with the contracted or uncontracted copula *is* in the main clause. In contrast with conjunction, which used action and locative action verbs primarily, and relativization, which used the copula primarily, the third complex sentence structure to develop, complementation, used state verbs most of the time—for example, "I don't know what her name is"—or, less often, the contracted copula—for example, "That's what you can do." The complementation that the children learned was constrained by semantically specific state verbs: volitional and intentional verbs (*want, like, need*); epistemic verbs (*know* and *think*); notice verbs (*see, look, show, watch*); and communication verbs (*say, tell*).[24] Complementation verbs were acquired by the children in the order volition > notice > epistemic > communication.[24] Similar complementation verbs have been reported for other children and appear to be the semantic antecedents of the verbs used by adults for complementation.[25,26]

The children's verbs were distributed in complex sentences, then, in the following way: conjunction occurred overwhelmingly with action and locative verbs; relativization occurred primarily with the copula *is*; complementation occurred overwhelmingly with state verbs, with semantic subcategories of state verbs acquired sequentially.

The Importance of Verbs in Child Language

The importance of verbs in language has been underscored in both psychological accounts of sentence processing and linguistic accounts of grammatical theory.[27-31] The results of the several child language studies that have been described here have led to the following conclusions about the importance of verbs in language acquisition. First, the child's mental lexicon probably is different for nouns and verbs. With respect to the child's expanding mental lexicon, the studies reviewed here suggest that there probably are not separate entries for verbs in a mental lexicon as there probably are for nouns. The fact that nouns are learned one by one appears to be preserved in most accounts of the way that information about nouns is stored in memory. If children's knowledge of verbs similarly retains information from the way in which verbs are learned originally, then it may not be appropriate to think in terms of a verb lexicon per se. Lexical verb development and grammatical development appear to be mutually dependent, with the result that the child's verb lexicon is not simply part of a mental dictionary with all the words that a child knows, including nouns. Rather, the results of the studies described here suggest that the verb system in child language may consist of a categorization of verbs on several levels of rules of grammar, with a network of attachments to a noun lexicon. Verbs are learned and exist along with the rules for grammar that determine the basic structure of sentences, and children's knowledge of language structure probably never is independent from the different verbs they know.

The categorization of verbs that has emerged from our studies includes large, molar categories—action/state; locative/nonlocative; durative/nondurative; completive/noncompletive; volitional/epistemic/notice/communication states, etc. The claim for the psychological and linguistic reality of these semantic categories rests on their being coextensive with major grammatical developments in the children's language, or on their sequential development. There has been no evidence that more molecular semantic categories—such as verbs of locomotion (*run, walk, skip, fly,* etc.) or verbs of ingestion (*eat, drink, swallow, slurp, chew,* etc.)—have the same psycholinguistic status in these children's early language learning. Such potential molecular categories appear to be represented in the early child speech data by only one or a few instances (e.g., *eat* for the larger category of ingestion; *ride* and *run* for the larger category of locomotion; *say* and *tell* for the larger category of communication, etc.). Thus, there often were only a few verbs in one or another category that occurred with great frequency, as though the children had learned the relevant linguistic form or structure with a few verb exemplars and the high-frequency proverbs, such as *do* and *go,* which they used generally, as they learned a wider range of more semantically specific verbs. Knowing the structure, the children then would be able to fill in and expand the verb categories to form more molecular categories. Certain molecular categories may be relevant, however, for language learning in other cultures, as for instance appears to be the case for verbs of possession and exchange in the acquisition of Kaluli, a non-Austronesian ergative language of New Guinea, as reported by Bambi Schieffelin.[32]

To conclude, it has become increasingly clear that the structural complexity, both syntactic and semantic, of the target language is a critical factor that contributes to its acquisition.[9,5,6] The results of the several child language studies that have been reviewed here provide substantial support for a model of language development that emphasizes linguistic complexity and, in particular, the syntactic and semantic functions of verbs as major factors that contribute to the cognitive requirements for learning language.

ACKNOWLEDGMENTS

An expanded version of this paper, "The Semantics of Verbs in Child Language," was presented as an Invited Address to the Eastern Psychological Association, Washington, D.C., 1978. The present title leans on the title of the recent paper by Dan I. Slobin, "The Role of Language in Language Acquisition." [6] I thank Joanne Bitetti Capatides for helpful comments on an early draft of the paper.

REFERENCES

1. Brown, R. 1957. Linguistic determinism and the part of speech. J. Abnorm. Psychol. **55:** 1–5.
2. Chomsky, N. 1965. Aspects of the Theory of Syntax. MIT Press. Cambridge, Mass.
3. McNeill, D. 1966. Developmental psycholinguistics. In The Genesis of Language. F. Smith & G. Miller, Eds.: 15–84. MIT Press. Cambridge, Mass.
4. McNeill, D. 1970. The Acquisition of Language: The Study of Developmental Psycholinguistics. Harper and Row Publishers, Inc. New York, N.Y.
5. Slobin, D. 1973. Cognitive prerequisites and the development of grammar. In Studies of Child Language Development. C. Ferguson & D. Slobin, Eds.: 175–208. Holt, Rinehart & Winston. New York, N.Y.
6. Slobin, D. I. 1979. The role of language in language acquisition. Invited Address. Eastern Psychological Association. Washington, D.C.
7. McCarthy, D. 1930. The language development of the preschool child. Institute of Child Welfare Monograph No. 4. University of Minnesota Press. Minneapolis, Minn.
8. Nelson, K. 1973. Structure and strategy in learning to talk. Monogr. Soc. Res. Child Dev. **38.**
9. Bloom, L. 1973. One Word at a Time: The Use of Single-Word Utterances Before Syntax. Mouton. The Hague, the Netherlands.
10. Goldin-Meadow, S., M. Seligman & R. Gelman. 1976. Language in the two-year old: receptive and productive stages. Cognition **4:** 189–202.
11. Bowerman, M. 1973. Early Syntactic Development: A Cross-Linguistic Study with Special Reference to Finnish. Cambridge University Press. Cambridge, England.
12. Lightbown, P. 1977. Consistency and variation in the acquisition of French: a study of first and second language development. Doctoral Dissertation. Teachers College. Columbia University. New York, N.Y.
13. Bloom, L., P. Lightbown & L. Hood. 1975. Structure and variation in child language. Mongr. Soc. Res. Child Dev. **40.**
14. Brown, R. 1973. A First Language, the Early Stages. Harvard University Press. Cambridge, Mass.
15. Park, T. Z. 1970. The acquisition of German syntax. Working Paper. University of Munster. Munster, Federal Republic of Germany.
16. Bloom, L. 1970. Language Development: Form and Function in Emerging Grammars. MIT Press. Cambridge, Mass.
17. Bloom, L., K. Lifter & J. Hafitz. 1980. Semantics of verbs and development of verb inflections in child language. Language **56:** 386–411.
18. de Villiers, J. G. & P. A. de Villiers. 1973. A cross-sectional study of the acquisition of grammatical morphemes. J. Psycholinguistic Res. **2:** 267–278.
19. Bloom, L., P. Miller & L. Hood. 1975. Variation and reduction as aspects of competence in language development. In Minnesota Symposia on Child

Psychology. A. Pick, Ed. **9:** 3–55. University of Minnesota Press. Minneapolis, Minn.

20. BRONCKART, J. P. & H. SINCLAIR. 1973. Time, tense, and aspect. Cognition **2:** 107–130.

21. WOISETSCHLAEGER, E. 1976. A semantic theory of the English auxiliary system. Doctoral Dissertation. Massachusetts Institute of Technology. Cambridge, Mass. (Reproduced by the Indiana University Linguistics Club. Bloomington, Ind.)

22. BLOOM, L., S. MERKIN & J. WOOTTEN. *Wh*-questions: linguistic factors that contribute to the sequence of acquisition. (Submitted.)

23. BLOOM, L., M. LAHEY, L. HOOD, K. LIFTER & K. FIESS. 1980. Complex sentences: acquisition of syntactic connectives and the semantic relations they encode. J. Child Lang. **7:** 235–261.

24. BLOOM, L., J. HAFITZ & B. GARTNER. Development of sentence complementation. (In preparation.)

25. LIMBER, J. 1973. The genesis of complex sentences. *In* Cognitive Development and the Acquisition of Language. T. Moore, Ed.: 169–185. Academic Press, Inc. New York, N.Y.

26. ROSENBAUM, P. S. 1967 The Grammar of English Predicate Complement Constructions. MIT Press. Cambridge, Mass.

27. THORNDYKE, P. W. & G. H. BOWER. 1974. Storage and retrieval processes in sentence memory. Cognitive Psychol. **6:** 515–543.

28. WANNER, E. & M. MARATSOS. 1978. An ATN approach to comprehension. *In* Linguistic Theory and Psychological Reality. M. Halle, J. Bresnan & G. Miller, Eds.: 119–161. MIT Press. Cambridge, Mass.

29. BRESNAN, J. 1978. A realistic transformational grammar. *In* Linguistic Theory and Psychological Reality. M. Halle, J. Bresnan & G. Miller, Eds.: 1–59. MIT Press. Cambridge, Mass.

30. CHAFE, W. 1971. Meaning and Structure of Language. University of Chicago Press. Chicago, Ill.

31. FODOR, J. A., M. GARRETT & T. G. BEVER. 1968. Some syntactic determinants of sentential complexity. II. Verb structure. Percept. Psychophys. **3:** 453–461.

32. SCHIEFFELIN, B. 1979. How Kaluli children learn to think, feel and act. Doctoral Dissertation. Teachers College. Columbia University. New York, N.Y.

33. HARNER, L. Children talk about the time and aspect of action. Child Dev. (In press.)

34. SMITH, C. 1980. The acquisition of time talk: relations between child and adult grammar. J. Child Lang. **7:** 263–278.

THE CHILD'S EXPRESSION OF MEANING: EXPANDING RELATIONSHIPS AMONG LEXICON, SYNTAX, AND MORPHOLOGY*

Melissa Bowerman

Department of Linguistics
Bureau of Child Research
University of Kansas
Lawrence, Kansas 66045

INTRODUCTION

Studies of first-language acquisition typically have shown strong respect for the major components into which linguistic analysis divides language: lexicon, syntax, morphology, and phonology. Thus, researchers explore the acquisition of word meaning (for example), or the characteristics of children's early word combinations, or the acquisition of inflectional morphemes, but only rarely compare the elements of the child's developing linguistic system *across* the major formal categories. The picture of language acquisition built up in this way is fragmented. We may know a great deal about the development of particular subsystems, but we do not yet have a clear understanding of how the different parts fit together, how they interact and are affected by each other in the course of development.

Interrelationships among the components of the child's developing grammar can be approached in various ways. The most studied problem to date is whether children's initial rules for combining and inflecting words are bound to particular words or groups of semantically similar words rather than extended across all words of the relevant part of speech (e.g., References 1 and 2). Limited attention also has been paid to the influence of the infant's phonological system on the "selection" of first words to be learned.[3] The present paper asks still a third question: Given that the child has a certain type of meaning he wants to communicate, what are his lexical, syntactic, and morphological options for encoding that meaning, and how do these options change and affect each other over time? This question is elaborated in the first section below. Two issues raised there are considered in more detail in the next two sections. Finally, some possible implications of these issues for second-language acquisition are discussed in the last section.

ALTERNATIVE ENCODING DEVICES

Useful input to the study of the ontogenetic growth of lexical, syntactic, and morphological options for encoding meaning comes from two relatively

* This research was supported in part by Grant HD 00870 from the National Institute of Child Health and Human Development.

0077–8923/81/0379–0172 $01.75/2 © 1981, NYAS

independent fields of inquiry: linguistic research on variability in the way the same or closely related meanings are expressed in different languages, and sociolinguistic and pragmatic investigations of alternative ways of accomplishing a given speech act within a language.

Cross-Linguistic Perspectives

Languages differ in the devices they employ to express meanings of different kinds. What one language marks syntactically with word order another language encodes morphologically with case endings or phonologically with stress. These cross-linguistic differences mean that the division of labor between lexicon, syntax, and morphology is a matter of discovery for the child. Certain cross-linguistic differences, such as the use of word order vs. case endings to mark grammatical relations, already have been discussed extensively by child language scholars.[4] Other, more subtle differences have yet to be investigated systematically, however. One such unexplored difference concerns the question of "what can be a word."

The fluent monolingual speaker may find this a bizarre question: that certain meanings should be dignified with their own words seems self-evident. But cross-linguistic studies have shown fascinating variability in the way complex meanings are packaged, and this variability is, moreover, patterned, with different languages or language families showing internal consistency. For example, categories of meaning that in one language are expressed routinely with single, monomorphemic lexical items may in another language be obligatorily partitioned into two or more components, each of which is assigned to a different word. Still a third alternative, intermediate between these "synthetic" and "analytic" extremes, involves assigning part of the meaning to a lexical root and another part or parts to inflectional or derivational affixes on this root. Languages differ globally from one another with respect to the degree of analyticity they favor,[5] and they also manifest qualitatively different patterns in what meanings tend to get combined with what other meanings and expressed together as single words.[6,7] An intriguing question is whether in the course of acquiring the lexical items to which he is exposed, the child gradually arrives at an abstract understanding of the characteristic patterns in which semantic material combines to form words in his language.

Within-Language Options

When languages are discussed with an eye toward cross-linguistic comparisons, they tend to be treated as single, monolithic entities: "language X does things like this, language Y does them like that." But sociolinguists and pragmaticists remind us that individual languages are anything but monolithic; rather, they are best seen as complex systems of *linguistic variants,* or alternative ways to encode roughly the same meanings under different linguistic and nonlinguistic conditions.[8] Becoming a fluent speaker, according to this view, requires not only mastering a body of linguistic forms but also learning which ones mean approximately the same thing and which circumstances favor the use of one variant over another.

The speaker's options can be conceptualized at a variety of levels. At a relatively global level, for example, a speech act such as requesting something may be realized by sentences with entirely different semantic contents, cf. *Open the window* vs. *It's hot in here* as alternative methods of getting someone to open a window. At a more molecular level, what is roughly "the same" semantic content can be expressed in different ways. Sometimes options involve items drawn from the same component of the grammar (e.g., two "synonymous" words). What is particularly important for present purposes, however, is that roughly synonymous encoding devices may be very dissimilar structurally, often reflecting the range of variability that is found *across* languages. For example, for certain meanings, English offers both syntactic and lexical choices: compare, for instance, how the notion of causation is expressed in *The news of his death made me sad* vs. *The news of his death saddened me,* and in *John opened the door by kicking it* vs. *John kicked the door open;* how repetition is marked in *He read the book again* vs. *He reread the book;* how mode of travel is indicated in *He drove/flew/bicycled/walked to California* vs. *He went to California by car/plane/bicycle/on foot;* and how location is encoded in *Jack put the wine into bottles* vs. *Jack bottled the wine.*

The within-language availability of alternative devices for expressing given meanings raises a host of interesting questions. Most extensively discussed has been what kinds of linguistic and nonlinguistic factors correlate with the use of one form over another.[8,9] Still relatively unexplored, however, are ongoing psycholinguistic processes at the time of speech: how speakers keep track of the many contextual factors that are relevant to the form of their utterances, how they generate linguistic alternatives that meet as many contextual demands as possible, how they evaluate these alternatives and choose among them, and how they manage to do all this under considerable time pressure in ongoing discourse (see Reference 9 for an excellent theoretical discussion of the problem). One particularly interesting question in this connection is how speakers resolve conflicts when alternative incompatible language forms compete for selection in the same speech context.

ACQUIRING LEXICALIZATION PATTERNS

We return now to the question of whether language-learning children acquire an understanding of underlying regularities in the way their language packages semantic material. In principle they need not. They could become fluent speakers simply by memorizing the words they actually have heard and working out their meanings by observing how they are used.

In fact, however, children appear to go well beyond this bare minimum: they analyze and compare the words they are learning in such a way as to develop expectations that words with certain semantic properties should exist, regardless of whether they have ever heard them, and they develop a feel for the possible morphological properties of these words. The evidence for this process lies in children's systematic use of words to convey meanings that they do not convey in adult speech.

Three representative categories of these novel usages by English-speaking children are illustrated with a few examples each in TABLE 1 (see References 10–12 for more detailed analyses). We shall call these usages "errors," meaning by this term only that they deviate from the conventional adult usage of these words. Most of the data presented in this and subsequent tables come from my two daughters, Christy and Eva, whose language development I followed closely by daily diary notes and periodic tape recording from the time of first words. I have documented each error type with data from a number of other children, however; the processes involved appear to be very general.

Errors 1–11 in TABLE 1 all involve the expression of causal relations, a domain in which particularly rich and interesting cross-linguistic differences in lexicalization patterns have been identified. A succinct summary of these differences has been provided by Fillmore,[5] whose outline we shall follow here (see Reference 6 for a more detailed analysis).

Given a complex, two-part causal event in which one event, act, or situation is seen as bringing about a second event, act, or situation: let X stand for a verb that names the initial event (act, situation) and let Y stand for a verb or adjective that names the resulting situation. How shall a speaker express the total complex causal event? One possibility is for there to be a verb Z (a "lexical causative" or "causative verb") that represents this event. Such verbs are extremely common in English, e.g., *kill* (do something that causes someone to die) and transitive *break* (do something that causes something to break). Causative verbs are rare in some languages, however, where causal events are encoded more typically by syntactic combinations equivalent to English *make die, make break,* etc.

If a language does have Z verbs, there are several possible ways that these verbs can be related morphologically to X and Y. One is "no relationship," e.g., *kill* means roughly "do something that causes to die" but is morphologically unlike either a possible causing act (*shoot, stab,* etc.) or the resulting event (*die* or *dead*). Another possibility is for Z to be identical to Y, the resulting event, as in, for example, *John* OPENED *the door* (cf. the door OPENED) or *Mother* WARMED *the milk* (the milk became WARM). Still another possibility is for Z to be identical to X, the causing event; in this case the resulting event is expressed separately with a word or phrase: *John* KICKED *the door open* (cf. John KICKED the door, which caused it to open, or John caused the door to become open by KICKING it); *Jim* CHOPPED *the tree down* [Jim CHOPPED (on) the tree, which caused it to fall down]; *Mary* WIPED *the table clean* (Mary WIPED the table, which caused it to become

TABLE 1

ERRORS SHOWING GRASP OF LEXICALIZATION PATTERNS *

Use of "caused event" predicate as causative verb:

1. C, 3;1: M: The cow would like to sing but he can't. (As C and M handle broken music box shaped like a cow.)
   C: I'm *singing* him. (Pulling string that used to make cow play.)

2. C, 4;3: It always *sweats* me. That sweater is a sweaty hot sweater. (Doesn't want to wear sweater.)

3. C, 4;6: *Spell* this "buy." *Spell* it "buy." (Wants M to rotate blocks on toy spelling device until word "buy" is formed.)

4. E, 3;2: E: Everybody makes me cry.
   D: I didn't make you cry.
   E: Yes you did, you just *cried* me.

5. E, 3;7: I'm gonna put the washrag in and *disappear* something under the washrag. (Putting washrag into container while playing in tub. Has been pretending to put on a magic act.)

6. E, 3;8: I'm gonna *round* it. (Rolling up piece of thread into a ball.)

Use of "causing event" predicate as causative verb:

7. E, 3;9: A gorilla captured my fingers. I'll *capture* his whole head off. His hands too. (= cause his head to come off by capturing it. As plays with rubber band around fingers.)

8. E, 3;11: She *jumped* it off for Jennifer and Christy. (= caused it to come off by jumping. After someone jumps up to pull icicle off eaves of house and gives it to C and a friend.)

9. E, 3;0: The birdies will find the squirrel and *spank* the squirrel from eating their birdseed . . . with their feet. (= cause the squirrel not to eat . . . by spanking him. After squirrel gets into birdfeeder.)

10. C, 3;6: And the monster would *eat* you in pieces. (= cause you to be in pieces by eating you. Telling M a scary story.)

11. A, 4;3: When you get to her, you *catch* her off. [= cause her to come off by catching her. A is on park merry-go-round with doll (= her) next to her; wants friend standing nearby to remove doll when doll comes around to her.]

Novel verbs of directed motion conflating motion plus manner:

12. E, 3;11: Eon laughed too. He *laughed* all the way † down the hill and he *laughed* on top of the other people. (= moved down the hill while laughing and moved on top of the other people while laughing. Describing event in TV show.)

13. E, 5;0: M: It's time to leave.
   E: OK, then I'm *frowning* out the door. (= move in a frowning manner. E then stomps out in mock anger.)

14. C, 10;5: We *crouched* down the hill. (After M and C go down an embankment in a crouching position.)

* C = Christy, E = Eva, M = Mother, D = Daddy, and A = Andrea. Age given in years;months.

† The insertion of phrases such as "all the way" or "right (up)" + preposition can render some otherwise dubious novel verbs of this type more acceptable; children may use these phrases at times but seem not to recognize that many such verb uses are unacceptable without them.

clean). Still other possibilities are for Z to be derived morphologically, e.g., by affixation, from either X (common in German and Hungarian) or Y (common in Turkish) or for Z to be a compound of X and Y (as in Mandarin).

English is unusual among the languages of the world in possessing many Z verbs—lexical causatives—that are identical morphologically to X or Y. But not every X or Y expression can be used as a Z. In some cases there is indeed a Z term, but it is either morphologically unrelated to X or Y (e.g., *kill*) or derivationally related to Y in ways that are no longer productive in contemporary English (e.g., *sharpen, flatten, legalize, enrich*). In other cases, there simply *is* no Z, no single-word lexical causative.

It is well known that when children discover a patterned way of doing things in language, they regularize forms that are exceptions to this pattern. Apparently the use of X or Y forms as Z—lexical causatives—is prevalent enough in English that the child extracts a pattern from the particular lexical causatives she has encountered and comes to *expect* that X or Y terms can be used, without morphological modification, as lexical causatives regardless of whether she has ever heard them so used. In 1–6 in TABLE 1, the child uses Y (a predicate for the caused event) as a lexical causative where English simply *has* no verb with the meaning of the converted Y (in many equivalent errors, the child's novel Z form replaces an existing Z form, e.g., transitive *die* for *kill*, cf. 7 in TABLE 2). In 7–11 it is X, a predicate specifying the causing act, that is used as a novel lexical causative. Errors of these types are quite analogous to more familiar overregularizations involving inflectional morphology, such as *foots* and *breaked*.

Examples 12–14 in TABLE 1 express not causation but the directed motion of the entity specified by the sentence subject with respect to some other object. Lexicalization patterns involving the simple expression of directed motion have been studied extensively by Talmy.[7] According to Talmy's analyses, there are three basic patterns. English, along with Chinese and most or all Indo-European languages except Romance, follows a pattern whereby the verbs used in sentences encoding such events typically express, in "conflated" or combined fashion, both the *fact* of motion and either its *manner* or its *cause:*

Motion + manner:
1. The ball *slid/rolled/bounced* down the hill.
2. I *limped/stumbled/rushed/groped* my way into the house.

Motion + cause:
3. The napkin *blew* off the table.
4. The bone *pulled* loose from its socket.

The verbs in such sentences frequently have other, more "basic" uses in which the notion of directed motion is absent:

5. The ball *bounced* up and down.
6. I *stumbled* on a rock/*groped* around in the dark.

Sentences like 1–4 are so natural for speakers of English that it is difficult not to see them as the obvious way to encode such events. But in Spanish and other Romance languages, along with Semitic languages among others, the usual pattern is quite different: along with the basic fact of motion, the verb expresses *path,* or the course followed by the moving entity with respect to the background object (English has a few such verbs, mostly borrowed from Romance). If manner or cause is expressed at all it must be given independently, e.g., as an adverbial or

TABLE 2

INTERCHANGEABLE USE OF LEXICAL AND PERIPHRASTIC CAUSATIVES *

Periphrastic causative used where lexical causative is required:

1. C, 2;11:   I *maked* him *dead* on my tricycle. (= *killed* him. Re: imaginary monster she had run over.)

2. C, 3;1:   I don't want you to *make* him *go* off. (= *brush* off, *knock* off. After M tries to brush a moth off C's car seat with her hand.)

3. E, 2;3:   Then I'm going to sit on him and *made* [sic] him *broken*. [= *break* (squash). Looking at ant on seat of her toy tractor.]

Lexical causative where periphrastic causative is required:

4. C, 5;10:   Water *bloomed* these flowers. (=*made* these flowers *bloom*.)

5. C, 4;0:   The machine might *put* him away. (= *make* him *disappear/go* away. C watching "Captain Kangaroo" story about a magic machine that caused Captain Kangaroo to disappear for a while; she's now suggesting same thing may happen to Mr. Greenjeans.)

6. C, 5;8:   It's not worse. But the airplane's *keeping* it. [Re: stomachache C had before boarding plane. Now, as we fly, the plane (ride) is *making* stomachache *continue, go on.*]

Successive use of periphrastic and lexical causatives in same speech context:

7. C, 5;0:   OK. If you want it to die. Eva's gonna *die* it. She's gonna *make* it *die*. (Upset because E is about to touch a moth.)

8. E, 2;8:   *Put* it on her. *Make* it *be* on her. (Wants M to put a dress on her doll.)

9. E, 3;9:   Can you *make* this *flattened* and *round*? You *round* it and then I'll *flatten* it. (To M, as E plays with a piece of play dough.)

10. Em, 2;11:   You *make* me *swing* around. You *swing* me around. (To Melissa, who is rotating chair Emily is sitting in.)

* Names and ages as in TABLE 1. Em = Emily.

gerundive; since this may be awkward it is often simply omitted. For example:

7. La botella *entró*   a la cueva (flotando)
   The bottle moved-in to the cave   (floating)
   "The bottle floated into the cave"

8. La botella *salió*   de la cueva (flotando)
   The bottle moved-out from the cave   (floating)
   "The bottle floated out of the cave"

9. La botella *volvió*   a la orilla (flotando)
   The bottle moved-back to the bank (floating)
   "The bottle floated back to the bank"

10. El globo *subió*   por   la chimenea (flotando)
    The balloon moved-up through the chimney (floating)
    "The balloon floated up the chimney"

In still a third pattern, exemplified by certain American Indian languages such as Navaho and Atsugewi, verb roots express in a conflated manner both motion and the *type* of object that moves. For example, Atsugewi -*lup*- means "for a small shiny spherical object to move (or be located)"; -*qput*- means "for loose dry dirt to move (or be located)," etc. Manner and path are both expressed separately by affixes on the root.

Sentences 12–14 in TABLE 1 fall squarely into the English pattern whereby motion and manner are expressed simultaneously with a single verb. The child has taken a "basic" action term and converted it into a verb that means "to move (with respect to ——) while doing this action." English, however, does not allow quite such a free conversion, and the results sound odd to adult ears. Although to my knowledge there are no relevant data available from children learning Spanish, it seems unlikely that such sentences would occur in their speech. The lexicalization pattern of Spanish simply would not give rise to the expectation that motion and manner could be expressed simultaneously.

It should be noted, but cannot be elaborated here (see References 10–12), that errors like those in TABLE 1 are *not observed* in the early stages of the child's use of the verbs in question. To the contrary, errors of each type are preceded by months or in some cases even years during which usage is syntactically impeccable. This rules out an interpretation according to which the child simply is confused, e.g., does not know yet whether a verb is transitive or intransitive, or whether it can take a locative complement. The period of correct usage before the onset of the errors strengthens the inference that, far from reflecting basic ignorance of the linguistic system, these errors are signs of a rather sophisticated grasp of underlying regularities in the English lexicon.

CONFLICT AND HARMONY AMONG COMPONENTS OF GRAMMAR

The choices that speakers make as they piece together sentences from the lexical, syntactic, and morphological resources of their language are not carried out independently of one other. Rather, choices in one domain can severely restrict or eliminate choices in another domain. Learning how to coordinate the components of grammar is an important aspect of first-language development that may have interesting implications for second-language learning.

Choosing the Right Alternative

There is evidence that early in development, children seek a relatively direct mapping between underlying meanings and overt linguistic forms. That is, a particular meaning will be associated with a unique form (or allomorphs of a form) and, conversely, this form can be seen as the procedure invoked to express this meaning and no other.[4] It is not long, however, before roughly equivalent forms begin to multiply. The child with several forms at his disposal must learn how to make principled choices among them. The learning process can be extended, and marked by many errors.

Consider the child who, like Christy and Eva at 24 months, can express causal events either with single-word causative verbs (e.g., *kill, break,* or novel forms like transitive *die*) or with syntactic ("periphrastic") causatives (*make die, make break*). How does he choose between them? In adult English, the choice hangs on a complex set of distinctions involving, most critically, how directly the "causer" brings about a change of state in the "causee."[13] Children at first may fail to appreciate these distinctions, however. The evidence is that they initially make many errors in which the lexical form is used where the periphrastic is called for, or the other way around, or *both* forms are used within the same context as if they were regarded as interchangeable. Some examples are shown in TABLE 2 (see Reference 12 for further discussion). Further development consists of working out the conditions under which each form is preferred.

A different kind of conflict between roughly equivalent forms is shown in TABLE 3. The semantic domain involved here can be termed "acts of separation." English encodes acts of separation in several ways. In some cases, separation is entailed by the reversal of an action of coming together or fastening, and is expressed with the reversative prefix *un-*: *untie, unbuckle, uncoil, unbutton,* etc. In other cases, separation is encoded by a locative particle following the verb, e.g., *take off/out/apart/ away.* In still other cases, separation is more implicit, incorporated directly into the meaning of a monomorphemic lexical item such as *open, break, peel,* or *split.*

Children initially seem to learn the correct method for each lexical item independently, and make no errors. Later, however—starting around age four for Christy and Eva—they begin to make occasional errors. For example, in 1 and 2 of TABLE 3 the child has prefixed *un-* to verbs that require *off* or *out.* Examples 3 and 4 show the reverse type of error, adding *out* to a verb that requires *un-*. In examples 5 and 6 the child has simultaneously selected both *un-* and a postverb particle. Finally, in 7–9 the child has redundantly and incorrectly prefixed *un-* to a verb that already expresses separation simply by virtue of its lexical meaning.

Errors like these indicate that beyond a certain point in development, the intention to encode a given act of separation does not present itself to the mind as a unit, neatly tagged with a suitable lexical item. Rather, the notion of separation apparently is "pulled out" from the surrounding semantic specifics and mentally represented in a form that is neutral enough to simultaneously activate encoding devices from different components of the grammar. Errors result when the child fails to choose successfully among them.

TABLE 3

ERRORS IN ENCODING ACTS OF SEPARATION *

un- prefixed to verb that requires *off/out,* etc.:

1. E, 4;2:   D: Pull your pants up, Eva. (E has pants sagging down.)
               E: Somebody *unpulled* 'em. (= pulled them down/off.)

2. C, 5;6:   . . . So I had to *untake* the sewing. (= take the sewing/stitches out. Telling about sewing project at school.)

out following verb that requires *un-*:

3. C, 4;5:   (Wants to move electric humidifier): I'll get it after it's *plugged out.* (Shortly after): Mommy, can I *unplug* it?

4. E, 4;5:   M: The end is tucked in. (Discussing state of E's blanket as puts E to bed.)
               E: Will you *tuck* it *out?*

un- and *out/off* both selected:

5. E, 3;5:   How do I *untake* this *off?* (= take this off. Trying to get out of swimsuit.)

6. E, 4;11:   . . . and then *unpress* it *out.* (Showing how she gets play dough out of a mold by pressing it through.)
               M: How do you unpress it out?
               E: You just take it out.

un- prefixed to lexical item that already incorporates notion of separation:

7. C, 4;11:   Will you *unopen* this? (Wants D to take lid off Styrofoam® cooler.)

8. E, 4;7:   E: (Holding up chain of glued paper strips): I know how you take these apart. *Unsplit* them and put 'em on.
               M: How do you unsplit them?
               E: Like this. (Pulling a link apart.)

9. S, 5;2:   How do you *unbreak* this? (Trying to pull sheet of stamps apart.)

* Names and ages as in TABLE 1. S=Scott.

Coordinating Verb Choice and Syntactic Arrangement

When a speaker chooses a certain verb for a simple, active, declarative sentence, she is not free to assign the noun arguments of that verb to any syntactic role she likes. Rather, the verb imposes a certain syntactic arrangement on these arguments. If the verb is *sell,* for example, the noun phrase naming the one who hands over the goods must function as the subject while a name for the recipient of the goods, if present, is the oblique object. *Buy,* in contrast, requires the opposite arrangement:

11. Harry *sold* a car to John/*John *sold* a car from Harry.
12. John *bought* a car from Harry/*Harry *bought* a car to John.

Similarly, but with respect to the direct object, we have a contrast between verbs like *pour* and *fill.* *Pour* requires the name for the moving liquid to be the direct object while the name for the container, if mentioned, is the oblique object; it is precisely the other way around for *fill:*

13. John *poured* water into the cup/*John *poured* the cup with water.
14. John *filled* the cup with water/*John *filled* water into the cup.

On the whole, children do a remarkably good job of learning the syntactic roles associated with the noun arguments of the verbs in their vocabularies. But mistakes do occur, and these give interesting clues to the processes involved in coordinating verb choice and syntax.

In the examples given in TABLE 4, verb choice and syntax do not harmonize. The child has selected the wrong syntactic arrangement for the verb or, to look at it the other way around, the wrong verb for the syntactic arrangement. The precise cause of such errors is not easy to establish. Different errors—even different tokens of the same type of error with a given verb—may have somewhat different causes. Some errors, particularly errors made under the age of about four or five with familiar, high-frequency verbs like *spill* and *fill,* appear to reflect generalizations about the proper or possible syntactic treatment of the noun arguments of "verbs of this semantic type." [14] Others, especially with later-learned verbs of lower frequency that are members of a set of semantically closely related verbs (e.g., *cost/spend/pay/charge; mind/matter/care; rob/steal; enjoy/appeal to*), may stem from "contamination" among members of the set. That is, the differing syntactic requirements of verbs that are semantically very similar may confuse the child. Beyond the age of five or six there is increasing reason to suspect a third cause for error: the child's growing awareness of syntactic structure as a device for conveying perspective and her attempts to actively manipulate it in service of this goal.

"Perspective" is a complex psychological construct having to do with where the speaker mentally places himself with respect to the event described by his sentence.[7,15] One important device through which perspective is conveyed in English is the way in which the noun phrases of a sentence are arranged syntactically with respect to the verb. Those entities referred to by the noun phrases functioning as subject and direct object of the verb are perceived as "in perspective," whereas entities mentioned only as oblique object or omitted entirely are, relatively speaking, perceived as "out of perspective." Thus, a speaker would utter sentence 12 above if he took the perspective of John, the receiver of the car, whereas he would choose 11 if he took the perspective of Harry, who gives over the car. Which entities are chosen for placement "in perspective" is influenced by a variety of factors, such as whether they have been the subject of prior discourse, whether they are animate or inanimate, stationary or moving, definite or indefinite, etc.

Some semantic domains in English are characterized by great flexibility

TABLE 4

ERRORS IN COORDINATING VERB CHOICE WITH ASSIGNMENT
OF SYNTACTIC ROLES TO NOUN ARGUMENTS *

1. C, 7;0: (M has chucked C under chin):
   C: Don't do that. I don't *appeal* to that. (=that doesn't *appeal* to me/I don't *like* that.)
   M: That doesn't appeal to you?
   C: Yeah.

2. E, 6;6: I saw a picture that *enjoyed* me. (=that I *enjoyed*/that *appealed* to me.)

3. C, 8;7: (To M): I have an idea but it won't *approve* to you and Daddy. (= you and Daddy won't *approve* of it/it won't *meet* with your and Daddy's *approval*.)

4. E, 7;7: She doesn't *picture* to me like a "Henrietta." Does she to you? (= I don't *picture* her as—/she doesn't *look like/strike* me *as*—. After telling that a friend's middle name is "Henrietta.")

5. E, 6;3: It didn't *mind* me very much. (= I didn't *mind* it—/it didn't *matter* to me—. While recounting that there had been a storm in the night.)

6. E, 7;2: Does it not *care* if I see the eggs? (= does no one *care* if—/does it not *matter* if—. After M suggests that E and D buy chocolate Easter eggs together; E wondering whether she should see them ahead of time.)

7. C, 6;10: *Feel* your hand to that. (=*feel* that with your hand/*put* your hand on that. Wants M to put her hand on one end of a hose; then she blows into the other end.) †

8. E, 5;0: Can I *fill* some salt into the bear? (= *fill* the bear with—/*pour* some salt into—. Playing with empty bear-shaped saltshaker.) †

9. E, 7;2: (Dipping water out of tub and letting it run down her stomach; has discovered with delight that her navel holds water): My belly holds water! (= belly button).
   Look, Mom, I'm gonna *pour* it with water, my belly. (=*pour* water into my belly button/*fill* my belly button with water.) †

10. E, 4;11: (M sees uneaten toast at end of breakfast, has asked if E plans to eat it):
   I don't want it because I *spilled* it of orange juice. [=*spilled* orange juice on it/*got* it *wet*; (poor choices): *wetted* it, *moistened* it with orange juice.]†

* Names and ages as in TABLE 1.
† See Reference 14 for discussion of errors of this kind.

with respect to the taking of perspective. In some cases this flexibility is due to the availability of a variety of verbs that encode the same meaning from different perspectives (e.g., *buy/sell; give/take; lend/borrow; rob/steal*). Alternatively, it may stem from the presence of syntactically versatile verbs that permit more than one perspective (e.g., *her face radiated joy/joy radiated from her face; the farmer loaded hay into the wagon/the farmer loaded the wagon with hay).* In other semantic domains, however, there is less flexibility and the verb that semantically is ideally suited to the meaning to be conveyed may require a syntactic arrangement that is counter to the desired perspective.

The resources of language are riddled with such gaps; speakers must learn to work around them, to find compromises. Adults have impressive skill at unconsciously and effortlessly striking balances in which one communicative goal is met less satisfactorily than it otherwise could be in the interests of maximizing another goal deemed more important.[9] Children, in contrast, make many errors in which they apparently try to "eat their cake and have it too." That is, they attempt to establish a desired perspective through the manipulation of syntactic roles, they select a verb that on semantic or other grounds is "just right," and they proceed to weave these two choices together without attending to whether the choices can be realized harmoniously in the same sentence.†

Example 9 from TABLE 4 illustrates the genre (as does 10). Here, the child is concentrating on her navel. In the first utterance, she places it maximally in perspective by making it the sentence subject (*belly* apparently is a shorthand for *belly button* in this monologue). In the second utterance, the agent (*I*) takes over the subject slot, but the navel clearly is still more in perspective than the water; its placement as direct object rather than oblique object thus is well motivated pragmatically. But *pour* does not allow this arrangement: *belly* must be the oblique object. If Eva wants *belly* as direct object, she should switch to another verb that allows this. But *fill* is the only plausible candidate, and *fill* is semantically odd here: can one speak of "filling" a "container" as shallow as a navel, which is, moreover, oriented sideways? Under the circumstances, sentence 9 can be seen as well tailored to both the perspectival and semantic requirements of the situation—unfortunately, however, English does not permit this nice combination of goals.

As this example suggests, new problems for the child to resolve are created by her own growing ability to take perspective into account and to manipulate it through syntactic role assignment. A first step in the resolution of such problems is for the child to recognize that conflict exists—that some constraints are binding and that she may not be able to meet all goals satisfactorily with her "first choices" of lexical items and syntactic structures. Beyond this, she must learn how to search for suitable "near synonym" verbs, how to exploit alternative devices for handling perspective such as passivization or clefting, and, when all else fails, how to give up a less important goal in the interests of preserving grammaticality.

---

† An experimental study by A. Karmiloff-Smith indicates that prior discourse does not begin to influence the child's selection of sentence subject until about age six,[16] which is approximately the time at which Christy and Eva began to make errors attributable to manipulation of perspective.

SOME IMPLICATIONS FOR SECOND-LANGUAGE ACQUISITION

The foregoing sections have discussed several ways in which lexical, syntactic, and morphological aspects of grammar begin to interact in first-language acquisition, often causing important problems for the child to resolve. We now look briefly at the possible relevance of these observations for second-language acquisition.

Lexicalization Patterns

I have argued that one aspect of first-language development is the acquisition of a sense of what lexical items are semantically possible and what morphological forms these items can take, relative to other semantically related words. To the extent that a second language (L2) has different lexicalization patterns from the first (L1), the L2 learner may face particular kinds of interference.

Consider, for example, native speakers of English and Spanish trying to learn Spanish and English, respectively. English speakers may expect that verbs like *float, hop,* etc., should be usable as verbs of directed motion (MOVE while floating/hopping, etc.) and may fail to realize that the Spanish translation equivalents are more restricted semantically and syntactically than their English counterparts. Errors would result. Spanish speakers, on the other hand, may fail to recognize the potential of English verbs for these uses and therefore underexploit them, possibly overlooking the systematic preference of English for such constructions over semantically equivalent, technically correct, but uncolloquial expressions, such as *John entered the house (hopping).*

Even more subtle kinds of interference could arise when L1 and L2 fall into the same typological category with respect to certain lexicalization patterns but differ in how freely and unconditionally the pattern can be realized. For example, I have observed that Dutch speakers of English as a second language often have trouble "hearing" the unacceptability or marginality of sentences like 7–11 in TABLE 1. This is because Dutch exploits more fully than English the pattern whereby an X term (predicate representing the causing act) serves as a Z (lexical causative), freely allowing constructions like *drink your tummy full, eat your plate empty,* and *Jip sprayed Janneke wet* that sound distinctly or somewhat odd in English.

It is possible that the ability to extract underlying lexicalization patterns on the basis of exposure to the words of a language diminishes with age or with prior experience with another language. Some suggestive evidence comes from studies of American sign language (ASL) by Newport.[17] Newport found that children who learn ASL as a native language acquire a sensitive feel for the internal morphological structure of signs and create novel forms analogous to those shown in TABLE 1. Speakers who acquire ASL as a second language often achieve considerable fluency, but they appear to learn signs in frozen citation form and rarely exhibit an understanding of the internal structure of these signs and the possibilities for novel recombination. If L2 learners typically have trouble seeing past the individual lexical items they are learning to the more abstract patterns these items reflect, they might benefit from explicit tuition on these patterns and how they differ from those in their own language.

Competing Forms

It was argued that first-language learners may have difficulty sorting out the distinctive uses of alternative forms that express the same or closely related meanings, such as lexical vs. periphrastic causatives or *un-* vs. *off*. Once mastered, however, the L1 system may prove resistant to modification. When a second language offers analogous alternative forms that are not distributed in quite the same way as their L1 counterparts, errors in L2 may result that are quite parallel to those the speaker made earlier in acquiring his first language.

Consider the methods of encoding separation discussed in Choosing the Right Alternative. English *un-* is cognate with Dutch *ont-*, *off* with *af*, and *out* with *uit*. These "translation equivalents" function identically in many contexts, e.g., *I unload = ik ontlaad, I chop off = ik hak af*, and *I cut out = ik knip uit*. Unfortunately for the L2 learner, however, the correspondence is far from perfect: side by side with these matches, we find such unpredictable crossovers as *I unpack = ik pak uit* (I pack out), *I unhook = ik haak af/uit* (I hook off/out), *I undress = ik kleed me uit* (I clothes myself out), *it slips out = het ontglipt* (it unslips), and *I skin* (e.g., my knee) *= ik ontvel* (I unskin). As a recent L2 learner of Dutch, I had considerable difficulty with these apparently arbitrary mismatches, often making incorrect L1-based predictions about the Dutch forms and stammering when well-practiced English units like *unpack* had to be abandoned in favor of more analytic expressions as in *ik pak mijn koffer uit*, literally, "I'm packing my suitcase out."

Verb Choice and Syntactic Arrangement

Mutual constraints between verb choice and the syntactic arrangement of the noun phrases in a sentence may lead to a number of interference problems in learning L2. Most obviously, a verb in L1 may permit or insist on certain role assignments that a translation-equivalent verb in L2 does not allow; conversely, the verb in L2 may be *more* flexible than that in L1. The result could be errors in the first case, underuse of a resource of L2 in the second case.

Consider English *lend*. This verb allows only one syntactic arrangement, whereby the one who gives something is in perspective relative to the receiver:

15. John *lends* Mary a book.

If the speaker desires the receiver to be in perspective, he must use a different verb:

16. Mary *borrows* a book from John.

But many languages have only one verb that is syntactically adaptable to either perspective, e.g., Dutch *lenen:*

17. John *leent* Mary een boek.
    "John lends Mary a book"
18. Mary *leent* een boek van John
    "Mary borrows a book from John"

The Dutch learner of English identifies Enlish *lend* with his *lenen* and assumes an equal flexibility for it; errors of the form *Mary lends a book from John* are common. Conversely, the English speaker identifies Dutch *lenen* with his *lend* and assumes an equal restrictiveness; he therefore tends to overlook *lenen* while searching in vain for a Dutch equivalent for *borrow*. It should be noted that these errors or blockages are due to deeply ingrained habits and persist even when the speaker has had explicit instruction and "knows better."

A second kind of interference is more subtle. A certain language, X, may have considerable flexibility with respect to realizing different perspectives in a given semantic domain, either because it has two or more verbs with different syntactic requirements (e.g., *lend, borrow*) or because the verbs it does have are syntactically flexible (e.g., Dutch *lenen*). A speaker accustomed to X therefore may have developed an implicit sense that "everything is possible"; he is not used to dealing with conflicts between semantic content and perspective-taking in this particular content area. If language Y lacks this flexibility, the native speaker of X may tend to talk himself into a dead end in Y. He starts off, for example, with a certain noun intended as sentence subject, but is drawn up short when he cannot find a verb in the right semantic ball park that can take this noun argument as subject. Blocking, hesitations, false starts, and errors will result as the speaker struggles to recruit the needed linguistic devices. The converse of this situation, of course, faces the speaker who is going from Y to X: this individual will have well-developed habits concerning constraints on what is possible, and he will not think to exploit the flexibility in combining certain perspectives with certain semantic contents that his second language affords him.

Finally, L2 learners, like L1 learners, may have trouble determining or remembering the syntactic role requirements of particular L2 verbs, especially if they are of low frequency or are members of a set of semantically closely related verbs with differing requirements. The following errors collected from Dutch adults speaking English appear to reflect difficulties of this kind: *This kind of reason is very* ACQUAINTED *to me* (= I am very *acquainted* with ——/—— is *well known* to me; cf.

Dutch *Het is me bekend,* "it is to-me beknown"); *I will* SUFFICE *with these examples* [= these examples (which I give) will *suffice;* I will *finish* up with/*limit* myself *to* these examples]; *I don't know what all I robbed; I robbed here and there* ("what all" referred to the stolen objects; hence: I don't know what all I *stole; I stole* here and there).

Conclusions

The above discussions touch on a few potential problem areas in L2 acquisition that reflect differences in how L1 and L2 assign the job of expressing meaning to the lexical, syntactic, and morphological components of grammar. The list is far from exhaustive. However, I hope it is sufficient to indicate that the study of how lexicon, syntax, and morphology come to be interrelated in first-language development can lead to interesting and fruitful questions about second-language learning and perhaps eventually to more effective methods of language teaching.

REFERENCES

1. BRAINE, M. D. S. 1976. Children's first word combinations. Monogr. Soc. Res. Child Dev. **41**(1): Serial No. 164.
2. BLOOM, L., K. LIFTER & J. HAFITZ. 1980. Semantics of verbs and the development of verb inflection in child language. Language **56**: 386–412.
3. FERGUSON, C. A. & C. B. FARWELL. 1975. Words and sounds in early language acquisition. Language **51**: 419–439.
4. SLOBIN, D. I. 1973. Cognitive prerequisites for the development of grammar. *In* Studies of Child Language Development. C. A. Ferguson & D. I. Slobin, Eds.: 175–208. Holt, Rinehart & Winston. New York, N.Y.
5. FILLMORE, C. J. 1978. On the organization of semantic information in the lexicon. *In* Papers from the Parasession on the Lexicon. D. Farkas, W. M. Jacobsen & K. W. Todrys, Eds.: 148–173. Chicago Linguistic Society. University of Chicago. Chicago, Ill.
6. TALMY, L. 1976. Semantic causative types. *In* Syntax and Semantics. M. Shibatani, Ed. **6**: 43–116. Academic Press, Inc. New York N.Y.
7. TALMY, L. Lexicalization patterns: semantic structure in lexical forms. *In* Language Typology and Syntactic Field Work. T. Shopen, Ed. **3**. (In press.)
8. HYMES, D. 1972. Models of the interaction of language and social life. *In* Directions in Sociolinguistics. J. J. Gumperz & D. Hymes, Eds.: 35–71. Holt, Rinehart & Winston. New York, N.Y.
9. TALMY, L. 1976. Communicative aims and means. *In* Working Papers on Language Universals **20**: 153–185. Stanford University. Stanford, Calif.
10. BOWERMAN, M. 1974. Learning the structure of causative verbs: a study in the relationship of cognitive, semantic, and syntactic development. Pap. Rep. Child Lang. Dev. **8**: 142–178.
11. BOWERMAN, M. 1977. The acquisition of rules governing "possible lexical items": evidence from spontaneous speech errors. Pap. Rep. Child Lang. Dev. **13**: 148–158.
12. BOWERMAN, M. Evaluating competing linguistic models with language acquisition data: implications of developmental errors with causative verbs. Quad. Semantica. (In press.)

13. SHIBATANI, M. 1976. The grammar of causative constructions: a conspectus. *In* Syntax and Semantics. M. Shibatani, Ed. **6:** 1–40. Academic Press, Inc. New York, N.Y.

14. BOWERMAN, M. Reorganizational processes in lexical and syntactic development. *In* Language Acquisition: The State of the Art. L. Gleitman & E. Wanner, Eds. Cambridge University Press. London & New York. (In press.)

15. FILLMORE, C. 1977. The case for case reopened. *In* Syntax and Semantics. P. Cole & J. M. Saddock, Eds. **8:** 59–81. Academic Press, Inc. New York, N.Y.

16. KARMILOFF-SMITH, A. Language as a formal problem-space for children. *In* The Child's Construction of Language. W. Deutch, Ed. Academic Press, Inc. New York, N.Y. (In press.)

17. NEWPORT, E. Constraints on structure: evidence from American Sign Language. *In* Minnesota Symposium on Child Psychology. W. A. Collins, Ed. **14.** Erlbaum. Hillsdale, N.J. (In press.)

SECOND-LANGUAGE ACQUISITION FROM A FUNCTIONALIST PERSPECTIVE: PRAGMATIC, SEMANTIC, AND PERCEPTUAL STRATEGIES *

Elizabeth Bates

Department of Psychology
University of Colorado
Boulder, Colorado 80309

Brian MacWhinney

Department of Psychology
Carnegie-Mellon University
Pittsburgh, Pennsylvania 15213

In her 1977 keynote address to the Stanford Child Language Forum, Susan Ervin-Tripp offered some reflections on all the research that has accumulated in the last decade on semantics, pragmatics, discourse structure, and sociolinguistics.[15] As a pioneer in all of these areas, Dr. Ervin-Tripp offered us the following reminder: *we never did solve the problem of how grammar is acquired.* Although studies of meaning and function are valuable in their own right, they need to be taken one step further, to an understanding of how semantic and pragmatic factors influence the discovery and use of grammatical forms.

One way to meet this goal is through the construction of a *performance grammar*—a unified theory of the pragmatic, semantic, and perceptual processing strategies that adults and children use to comprehend and produce sentences, inside and outside of a discourse context. Such a grammar would focus not only on the "possession" of a rule by a language or by an individual, but on the way grammatical information is handled in real time. In monolinguals, we have evidence suggesting that grammatical processing takes place with incredible speed, integrating many different levels of discourse simultaneously. For example, linguistic research on the relationship between discourse and grammar has shown that many different communicative functions are conveyed with every single grammatical decision.[19,20] Psycholinguistic research has shown that listeners integrate information from every level of discourse (phonology, lexical relations, word order, and prior discourse context) rapidly and in parallel, from the very first word presented in on-line sentence-comprehension experiments.[37] Given these constraints, the accomplishments of an adult bilingual seem nothing short of miraculous. First of all, the bilingual is in the unique position of mapping the *same* underlying meanings and intentions onto *two*

* The research cited here was carried out with support from National Science Foundation Grant No. BNS7905755, and with cooperation from the Istituto di Psicologia, Consiglio Nazionale delle Ricerche (CNR), Rome, Italy.

separate (or, at least, separable) sets of surface forms. The potential for interference in real-time processing is tremendous, and yet many investigators have concluded that the evidence for interference and transfer from first language (L1) to second language (L2) is surprisingly small (e.g., Reference 33). Second, the number and variety of discourse functions that grammar must carry for an adult are much larger than the discourse constraints on children. During first-language acquisition, children tend to operate in the "here and now," conveying messages that are of immediate interest without trying to tie that message into a larger, more coherent narrative or text structure.[23] For example, a three-year-old may use the pronoun "he" instead of the phrase "the man," simply to mark the difference between a referent in plain view versus a referent who is out of the room. For older children and adults, pronominalization is a much more complex process, used to mark givenness or newness of referents in regard to a much broader discourse context (e.g., whether this man was talked about several sentences back, and whether other men have been talked about in the meantime). In first-language learning, the many and varied discourse properties of syntax can be acquired gradually across time; new levels of complexity are added when the child becomes sophisticated enough to need them. For the adult second-language learner, *all* of the discourse functions conveyed by grammar are already present; hence the message load, or communicative pressure, on adult second-language learners is much greater than it is for the child. Studies of pragmatic, semantic, and perceptual processing strategies in second-language acquisition may help us to understand how adults deal with all of these competing discourse pressures on grammar—an issue that in turn may be related to problems of literacy, text comprehension, and formal speaking and writing in the adult world.[26]

We have been involved for several years in research on pragmatic and semantic influences on grammar, in children and adults, in several different languages.[1-5,34,35] Using the method of cross-linguistic comparison, we have been trying to develop a performance grammar that can account for the rapid and simultaneous integration of many aspects of discourse during sentence comprehension and production. For reasons that hopefully will become clear below, the theory is called *the competition model*. Although there is relatively little research on processing strategies in second-language learning (cf. Reference 14) and our own pilot results with bilinguals are quite tentative, we suggest that the competition model and its cross-linguistic data base form a useful point of departure for research comparing first- and second-language acquisition.

The competition model is eclectic, representing our own efforts to integrate several linguistic and psycholinguistic proposals. First, the emphasis on processing strategies owes a great deal to Bever,[7] although his own theoretical goals are different. The emphasis on cross-linguistic comparison is inspired by our teacher and colleague Dan Slobin.[44,45] Finally, we share the view of many psycholinguists that more progress can be made in studies of language performance if we are informed by the principles and assumptions of some kind of linguistic theory—a "competence" model, which may be formulated in somewhat different terms from the psychologists' real-time performance theory.[16]

Some clarification may be needed on what "performance grammar" means, and how it relates to a traditional distinction in psycholinguistics between *competence* (the native speaker's abstract knowledge of the rules of his language) and *performance* (actual language use in speaking, understanding, making judgments, etc.). A performance grammar lies somewhere in between these two poles, involving a description of the native speaker's *competence to perform*. In principle, any linguistic theory could be chosen as the basis for a performance grammar. Within linguistics, there is a variety of proposals available that are particularly compatible with the goal of studying semantic and pragmatic effects on grammar.[13,19,20,27,28,31,32,48] Although these theories vary considerably in detail, they all share one common assumption: *the surface conventions of natural languages are created, governed, constrained, acquired, and used in the service of communicative functions.* These relationships between form and function may be complex and often opaque, involving interactions of many different pragmatic, semantic, and perceptual or mnemonic factors. Nevertheless, there is a kind of Darwinian faith that language forms can and should be explained in terms of functional pressures. For this reason, these linguistic theories collectively can be called *functionalist grammars.*[3]

Because functionalist grammars make reference to such psychologically motivated categories as "topic," "animacy," and "point of view," a functionalist theory of competence may not differ greatly from a psychological theory of performance. For some theorists, the separate concepts of competence and performance converge completely within a single theory of competence to perform, as illustrated in the following quote from Lakoff and Thompson:

> We believe that there is a direct and intimate relation between grammars and mechanisms for production and recognition. In fact, we suggest that GRAMMARS ARE JUST COLLECTIONS OF STRATEGIES FOR UNDERSTANDING AND PRODUCING SENTENCES. From this point of view, abstract grammars do not have any separate mental reality; they are just convenient fictions for representing certain processing strategies.[31]

Whether or not we embrace this strong position, it is still clear that processing strategies (and hence performance) must play an important role in any theory of grammar where linguistic forms are explained in terms of the communicative work they do.

There is an alternative and equally valid approach within linguistics and psycholinguistics, emphasizing instead the absolute *independence* of pragmatic, semantic, and syntactic components. As a theory of competence, this approach perhaps is articulated best by Chomsky in his principles of *absolute autonomy* and *blind application of transformations.*[11] Chomsky stresses that no syntactic rule may be motivated by semantic concerns, nor may such a rule be formulated in terms of semantic-pragmatic structures.

The autonomous component approach often proves difficult for non-linguists to understand. Functionalist theories, in which linguistic forms are mapped directly onto meanings and functions, have a more immediate appeal to us as psychologists because they seem to follow our intuitions about how we formulate thoughts into utterances. However, autonomous component theories are equally appealing on formal grounds. Imagine an algebra in which rules for moving x and y were formulated in terms of specific numerical content, e.g., "for any x, unless that x is an even number greater than 7 and less than 104." Such an algebra would be cumbersome, difficult to learn, and difficult to use. By the same token, syntax in an autonomous component theory functions as a kind of linguistic algebra, elegant and useful precisely because it does *not* make reference to semantic or pragmatic content. As a performance theory, this kind of "modular" approach to language is defended by Forster in the following quote:

> The whole point of a language having a syntax is to provide a clear and unmistakable indication of the correct interpretation of the sentence. . . . Any move to allow the syntactic processor to be influenced by pragmatic factors works against the fundamental purpose of syntax. In fact, one might surmise that the evolution of syntax has been influenced by the degree to which it successfully guards against errors introduced by a consideration of pragmatic and semantic facts.[17]

It is an empirical question at this point which approach will prove most useful in helping us to understand first- or second-language acquisition. However, there are two reasons why we prefer to approach the acquisition problem from a functionalist perspective.

The first reason is the *directness of form-function mappings* in functionalist theories (i.e., without a series of intervening transformations or separate components). This close and direct relationship between meaning and form is consistent with a growing literature on rapid, parallel processing of information at every level of discourse in sentence processing.[37] And it also is consistent with our own experience as second-language speakers, i.e., the feeling that we begin with the same familiar set of meanings and intentions that we use in L1, and acquire L2 by seeking out those forms that do the same communicative work (see also Reference 50). If we make the same assumptions of direct mapping in experimental research with bilinguals, we are justified in selecting one or more functional inputs as independent variables (e.g., topic, animacy) and observing their effects on corresponding forms in the speaker's two languages (e.g., word order, noun-verb agreement). In short, the direct-mapping assumption is useful at both the intuitive and the experimental levels. Of course any grammatical theory could describe such intuitions and experimental results *indirectly*. The advantage of functionalist theories for research on processing strategies in second languages is that the functional equivalence of forms in L1 and forms in L2 can be stated so directly.

The second reason involves fuzzy, probabilistic or weighted form-function mappings. In many functionalist theories, the relationship between a particular surface form and its associated functions is stated in probabilistic terms (as we will explain in more detail below). This means that we can talk about the *strength* or *degree* to which a given form and function are tied to one another in a complex interaction. These weights or strengths can change across time (a) in the history of a given language, (b) in the acquisition of a first language, and (c) in the transition from one language to another. Hence what may look superficially like a discrete, discontinuous change may actually reflect a much more gradual and continuous process. Theories that incorporate such "fuzzy" or probabilistic elements are at an advantage in describing subtle patterns of interference or transfer in second-language acquisition. We do not have to talk about the presence or absence of rules, but rather the degree to which a processing strategy applies.

The principle of "fuzzy" or weighted mappings may help us to explain a number of phenomena that are not covered by traditional models of interference and transfer, including why second-language learners sometimes seem pragmatically "odd," even though no obvious grammatical errors are introduced. Let us illustrate with a couple of examples from our own second-language experience. Both of us (E.B. in Italian, B.M. in Hungarian) have become conversationally fluent in languages with much more flexible word orders than English. Although we are at the point where we rarely produce grammatical errors, both of us have been told that we make a rather "peculiar" use of emphatic stress. Because Italian and Hungarian can use word order to express topic-focus relationships, they also make much less use of stress.[35] But we Americans continue to "double mark" topic and focus in our second language by using *both* the word-order variations of Italian and Hungarian and the contrastive stress strategies of English. There is a concomitant transfer of strategies back onto English. For example, after many weeks in Rome speaking little or no English, Bates finds herself making inordinate use of the few word-order variations that are permissible in English (e.g., "him I don't like"), as though an Italian topic-focus mapping strategy still were being applied. Note that these are not "errors" in the strict sense, because they result only in grammatically well-formed utterances. But they could be regarded as errors at the discourse level. These are the kinds of processing comparisons that we hope to capture more precisely with experimental methods from the competition model.

To summarize, we feel that functionalist theories are well suited to cross-linguistic research, and that they offer useful mechanisms for describing what it means to be "in between" two different languages or two different stages in a single language. *The major thrust of our own proposals concerning second language is the assessment and explanation of "in-between status" during the acquisition of a second set of semantic, pragmatic, and perceptual processing strategies.*

To illustrate how the competition model works, we will draw most of our examples from *Italian* and *English,* plus some pilot findings from *German.* These three languages make a particularly interesting contrast for research on bilingualism because they are formally similar, but there are good reasons to expect some marked differences in functional processing strategies. We will concentrate primarily on one aspect of grammar—*the surface role of subject.* In all three languages, this role is defined (at least) by *preverbal position* in pragmatically neutral sentences, *agreement* with the verb in person and number, plus a limited form of *case marking.* This surface role is related to (at least) two underlying functions: *the semantic role of agent* and *the pragmatic role of topic.* Before proceeding, let us briefly consider a few relevant facts about these languages.

Italian, English, and German all have a basic word order of subject-verb-object (SVO) in pragmatically neutral, active declarative sentences. In all three languages, the subject agrees with the verb in person and number, but not in gender (with one small dialectal exception in Italian past-participle constructions, see Reference 49). With regard to case marking, Italian and English are identical: the only case marking available is non-productive, restricted to the personal-pronoun system (e.g., "I" versus "me"). In German, there is a more extensive case system: for example, a nominative-accusative contrast carried on the article preceding a noun phrase. This type of case marking of course is much more limited than the rich case systems of such languages as Hungarian and Russian. Furthermore, case endings in German are not always a reliable cue to basic syntactic-semantic relations. For example, German nouns in the feminine gender have the same article for nominative and accusative.

The other important contrasts among these three languages involve possible deviations from basic SVO order. English is known to be one of the most rigid word order languages in the world. SVO order is followed in main clauses and subordinate clauses, in questions (except for the fronted auxiliary) and declaratives, and in actives and passives alike. Also, subject deletion is possible only in imperatives (where it is obligatory, e.g., "wash the dishes") or in response to questions (e.g., "What did you two guys do last night? Went to the movies."). However, a small amount of word-order variation can occur even in English: OSV, or left-dislocated constructions (e.g., "eggcreams I like"), and VOS, or right-dislocated constructions (e.g., "really gets on my nerves, that guy"). Even in informal conversation, though, other variations are impossible: SOV (e.g., I egg-creams like") and VSO (e.g., "really gets on, that guy, my nerves").

Since German has case marking on nouns and English does not, we might expect Germans to use more word-order variation. Pragmatic variations are possible in German, but they are far from "free." For example, OVS sentences do occur in active declarative form, but only when there is a case contrast on the two nouns. VSO is used in questions and commands, or when a focussed adverbial phrase precedes the verb. VOS does occur under certain pragmatic conditions, but it is very rare. Finally, the obligatory order of constituents in relative clauses is SOV.

Surprisingly, Italian actually has more word-order variation than German does, despite the fact that Italian is equivalent to English in the amount of available case information. In informal conversation, all possible word orders can and do occur—in statements, questions, main clauses, and relative clauses. People actually say things like "the lasagna ate Giovanni" and "Giovanni Maria kissed." Furthermore, Italian (unlike German or English) permits extensive subject deletion (in over 70% of informal conversation, according to Bates).[1] This means that semantic and pragmatic facts must play a central role in a performance grammar of Italian, perhaps even more so than in German. Furthermore, we would expect both Italians and Germans to pay more attention to grammatical cues other than word order, e.g., agreement with the verb. In short, performance grammars for these three languages may look very different, perhaps more distant than we would expect just on the basis of formal grammatical differences.

Most of what we do know about processing strategies in these languages involves research with children. For example, several studies suggest that English-speaking children use a rigid SVO word-order strategy around the age of five (e.g., Reference 7), which leads them into errors in interpreting passives. Ervin-Tripp reports that English children who are losing their English while transferring to French, regress to such a first-noun strategy to interpret English sentences but show no such errors in their new language.[14] Slobin and Bever report that English and Italian children both use SVO strategies by (at least) the age of five; however, this word-order strategy seems to be stronger in the American group.[46] Finally, Roeper has argued that German children pay considerable attention to word order, even when case information is available.[39] Much less is known about word-order strategies in adults, even in English. For example, Forster predicts that English adults should use a first-noun strategy to "guess" the meaning of noun-noun-verb (NNV) sentences like "doctor patient cure." [17] However, as we shall see later, this prediction is not borne out by our own comprehension experiments in English.

Let us turn now to the theoretical framework for our cross-linguistic studies. A more complete description of the competition model is presented elsewhere.[3] We will provide a much briefer summary here, hopefully enough for the design and interpretation of our experiments to be clear.

The Competition Model: Basic Tenets

Competition and Coalitions

We begin with the assumption that the resources of the acoustic-articulatory channel are so limited (by the number of things that we can do at all, and by perceptual and memory constraints in real time) that functional categories (e.g., topic and agent) must compete for control of surface grammatical resources. The more important a category (e.g., high frequency, high information value), the stronger its claim on channel resources. Because of this competition for "surface territory," there is a pressure in all natural languages toward "doubling up" wherever possible.

Natural languages recognize the need for doubling up, by exploiting situations of natural overlap (i.e., functions that cooccur most of the time) and assigning surface devices not to *one* function but to a *coalition of associated functions*. For example, we humans tend to talk about ourselves a great deal. As a result, the two functions of topic and agent overlap in natural discourse (e.g., Reference 13). One way to exploit this overlap is to create a "high-priority" surface category like "subject," which may be governed *jointly* by a coalition or category comprised of both topic and agent.

Another result of forming *joint functional categories* is the creation of *joint surface categories,* or coalitions of surface forms that may have served separate functions at some earlier point in the history of the language. The surface category of subject illustrates this principle also. For example, many functionalists have discussed reasons why preverbal position should be associated with the discourse notion of topic: specifically, it is useful for our listeners if we make our topic explicit before we deliver a comment on it (e.g., Reference 27). It is also clear why the semantic role of agent or actor should be closely associated with its corresponding action verb. As Slobin has noted, processing is more efficient when semantically related units occur close together in an utterance.[44] Givon has offered some interesting arguments on why these different surface solutions (topic first, agent close to the verb, topic close to its comment) might have merged together naturally to form a set of devices that operate as a block: preverbal position, subject-verb agreement, semantic case markings for agency.[19,20] Keenan has reviewed evidence across many different languages for a "special" surface role corresponding to subject.[24] He reports that the exact makeup of this heterogeneous surface category varies from one language to another but that all languages seem to draw from the same universal set of possibilities (including topic-related and agent-related phenomena).

To summarize, the complete performance grammar that results from these assumptions comprises a large and interrelated set of *surface categories containing coalitions of forms* and *functional categories containing coalitions of meanings and intentions.*

Category Membership

When an utterance is produced, the decision to assign a surface role to a particular element would be triggered by the membership of that element at the functional level. Hence the element that provides the "best fit" to a joint topic-agent would be assigned the surface role of subject. In comprehension, the process works in reverse. As summarized in Bates and MacWhinney, a number of problems concerning categorization processes are solved if we assume that grammatical categories at both levels are structured in a manner similar to the category structures proposed in Rosch's theory of prototypes.[3,40] Categories are defined in terms of an idealized "best member," or prototype, which may have a heterogeneous internal structure (as with the above coalitions). Category membership is a function of *degree of resemblance* to this prototype, from central "best instances" to peripheral instances at the "fuzzy" outer boundaries. In processing terms, Rosch has shown that reaction times are faster for prototypes, that information learned about the prototype spreads faster through the category than information learned about peripheral members, and that prototypes are confused much less easily with members of neighboring categories.[40] All of these predictions would apply to a grammar organized around the prototype model. This theory has been used to explain a number of grammatical phenomena, e.g., some syntactic differences between active verbs ("good") and stative verbs ("peripheral") in Ross.[41] (For further discussions of prototype theory in grammar, see References 8, 12, 30, and 42, among others.)

Vector Weighting and the Breakdown of Coalitions

What happens when two converging elements in a functional category do *not* overlap, for example, if we want to topicalize the patient of an active verb? One solution is to assign an alternative (although perhaps less efficient or more complex) surface form. For example, in English we can topicalize the patient with a passive ("the ball was hit by John"), or focus on the subject through contrastive stress ("*John* hit the ball"). In either case, *the unity of the surface subject coalition* is retained: the same element receives preverbal position, agreement, etc.

In Italian, both of these options are available. However, Italians usually elect a very different solution to patient topicalization—break the surface subject coalition down into its component parts and assign those parts separately. Hence first position is assigned to the topic, but verb agreement is retained for the agent (e.g., "the apples eats Giovanni"). Another way of saying this is that the unity of the surface subject coalition, i.e., its tendency to operate as a block, is greater in English than it is in Italian. Word order can be "broken out" of the set fairly easily in Italian, but not in English.

We have already introduced one quantitative notion: the degree to which a surface coalition sticks together. We need another one as well, to decide which element of a functional coalition "wins" assignment of shared surface privileges when overlap breaks down. We assume that coalitions of functions operate like coalitions of parties in a parliamentary system, so that distribution of resources when an alliance is suspended is determined by relative power or strength in different sectors. In the competition model, individual functions within a coalition carry *canonical weights* or *vectors* (i.e., a determining force of measurable magnitude and direction) that state their degree of association with the surface coalition as a whole, and with components within that surface coalition. For example, word order and agreement *both* are associated with topic and agent, in English and Italian. However, word order seems to be tied more strongly to topic in Italian, while it is tied more strongly to agency in English. In other words, two languages can have the same configuration of forms and functions, but assign different weights. We would expect these differences to show up in the processing strategies used in cross-linguistic experiments.

Conventionalization

In the competition model, the line between *probabilistic tendencies* and *determinate rules* becomes a matter of degree. In fact, two rules that are treated as obligatory in some competence models actually may carry different psychological weights (e.g., a hypothetical difference of 100% versus 97%).

To illustrate how two apparently obligatory rules might differ in degree of conventionalization, consider an experiment in Hebrew by Frankel and Arbel.[18] In a sentence interpretation experiment, these authors presented Hebrew listeners with simple sentences consisting of a verb and two nouns. These sentences reflected all possible converging and competing combinations of basic NVN order, number agreement, and gender agreement. Both the interpretations and the reaction times are consistent with the view that "not all rules are created equal." The fastest and clearest responses were of course obtained when all three cues converged on the same interpretation (i.e., the prototype). Otherwise, the three cues added and subtracted in a probabilistic fashion. When word order competed with both number and gender agreement, the two morphological cues clearly won out (i.e., listeners rarely chose the first noun). When word order allied with gender, number still won (but at low levels, with slower reaction times). When word order allied with number, gender lost (although this "standoff" still produced slow reaction times and some inconsistent responses). In other words, we can rank order the determining value of grammatical cues in Hebrew as follows: number agreement, gender agreement, and word order. Such probabilistic results could not be predicted or explained by a grammatical theory that views all rules as completely obligatory.

Processing Claims

To summarize so far, the competition model involves direct mappings of coalitions of functions onto coalitions of surface forms. The speed and clarity of these mappings are a function of converging and competing vector weights from each form-function relationship within the coalitions: prototypic combinations yield fast and clear responses, but two cues can compete with one another or "conspire" together to "gang up" on some stronger or weaker cue. Cases of competition and conspiracy should take longer to resolve, depending on the difference in strength on both sides of the competition. *We make the further claim that this mapping process takes place through simultaneous, parallel weighting of cues.* This parallel-processing assumption is compatible with research on language processing by Marslen-Wilson and Tyler,[37] and with certain models for visual pattern recognition including the classic "pandemonium model."[43] The notion of direct and parallel mapping of surface forms is also compatible with several linguistic theories, including some that do not believe in functionally defined grammatical categories (e.g., References 9 and 38).

In the experiments that we are about to describe with monolinguals and bilinguals, we have tried to evaluate the competition model by setting up competition experiments, that is, experiments in which forms and functions are set into competing and converging combinations so that we can evaluate the relative strength of cues from one language to another. An analogy to the Gestalt perceptual literature may be useful here. Because our perceptual organizing principles evolved to fit world events, we may not notice how they interact unless they are set in competition—in Necker cubes, Escher prints, and other ambiguous or internally contradictory stimuli. When speakers are asked to describe an unnatural event (e.g., a cartoon with an inanimate object chasing around a given or "topicalized" animal), or when listeners are asked to interpret an internally contradictory or unlikely utterance (e.g., "a pencil chased the cow"), we can use their responses and reaction times to understand the separate and interacting contributions of different forms and functions to language processing. If we waited for such "conspiracies" among cues to occur in natural conversation, we might have to wait a very long time.

Some Cross-Linguistic Experiments

The largest experiment that we have completed so far is a sentence interpretation study with Americans and Italians.[4] The method is similar to the Frankel and Arbel study reported above, except that we included semantic and pragmatic cues in the converging and competing item sets.

Subjects were 30 Italians and 30 Americans. All were middle-class, college-educated adults—an important point, since Gleitman and Gleitman have shown that processing strategies may vary as a function of social class.[21] Each subject heard a total of 81 sentences (English and Italian versions were exact translations of one another), and each subject received a unique random order and a unique combination of specific lexical items. This means that specific lexical effects (e.g., sheep are more likely than cats to kick a pencil) were homogenized as much as possible across the design. The 81 sentences represent a complete orthogonal combination of four factors at three levels each: *word order* (NVN, NNV, VNN), *animacy* (reversibles, nonreversibles with animate first, nonreversibles with animate second), *contrastive stress* (default stress, first noun stressed, second noun stressed), and *topicalization* (no topic, first noun topicalized, second noun topicalized). The topic manipulation involved introducing one of the nouns first (e.g., "here is a cow"), and then referring to it with a definite article in the target sentence, while the other noun was indefinite (e.g., "the cow a horse kicked"). TABLE 1 lists some corresponding examples from English and Italian. The two dependent variables were *percent choice first noun* and *reaction time*.

TABLE 1

SOME SAMPLE ITEMS FROM TWO COMPREHENSION EXPERIMENTS

Experiment 1	
English	Italian
1. The horse hits the cow.	Il cavallo colpisce la vacca.
2. The pencil hits the cow.	La matita colpisce la vacca.
3. The cow the eraser kisses.	La vacca la gomma bacia.
4. *The eraser* the dog grabs.	*La gomma* il cane afferra.
5. Here is a ball. Kisses the ball a camel.	Ecco una palla. Bacia la palla un cammello.
6. Here is a lamb. *The lamb* a dog pats.	Ecco un agnellino. *L'agnellino* un cane carezza.
7. Here is a cube. Sniffs the cube *a monkey.*	Ecco un cubo. Annusa il cubo *una scimmia.*

Experiment 2		
English	Italian	German *
1. The horse is kissing the cow.	Il cavallo bacia la vacca.	Die Ratte kuesst die Kuh.
2. *The balls* are eating the camels.	*Le palle* mangiano cammelli.	*Die Kerzen* fressen die Eidechsen.
3. Is grabbing *the cat* the cigarettes.	Afferra *il gatto* le sigarette.	Ergreift *die Katze* die Zigaretten.
4. Are licking the pens *the cat.*	Leccano le penne *il gatto.*	Lecken die Zengen die Katze.

* German lexical items were changed to insure ambiguity of case, so that feminine gender nouns are substituted randomly for items used in the English and Italian versions.

Since this procedure yields a 2 (language) $\times 3 \times 3 \times 3 \times 3$ design, the results were extremely complex, involving a large number of main effects and interactions down to the four-way level. But we can at least summarize the most important results:

1. Italians and Americans showed *completely opposite processing strategies.* Americans relied primarily on word-order cues, while Italians relied primarily on animacy (see FIGURE 1).

2. The American reliance on word order extended not only to NVN,

but also to a powerful second-noun strategy in interpreting VNN and NNV items. As far as we know, this second-noun strategy has never been described in the literature (and is the opposite of Forster's prediction for English). However, it is perfectly consistent with our earlier comments about pragmatic reordering in English: VOS and OSV do occur in informal conversation, but VSO and SOV do not.

3. By contrast, Italian use of word order was relatively weak even on NVNs. On reversible items, with no competition from their preferred animacy strategy, Italians still chose the first noun only 84% of the time (compared with 96% for the Americans)—and it took them much longer

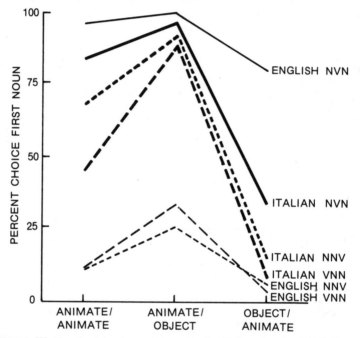

FIGURE 1. Word order × animacy interaction in 30 American and 30 Italian native speakers.

to reach those decisions. On VNN their performance was completely random when there were no semantic or pragmatic cues, and on NNV there was only a slight bias in the opposite direction from Americans, toward SOV. It seems fair to conclude that Italian is *quantitatively less* of a word-order language than English, even when there is no competition from semantic or pragmatic information.

4. Finally, stress and topic were much weaker cues in this experiment—not surprisingly, since we were emphasizing interpretation of agent rather than interpretation of topic. Nevertheless, the evidence on how stress and topic interact with order and animacy strongly supports our theory of

coalitions and competition. We made a series of 24 specific predictions about how pragmatic cues should converge to shore up a high-probability interpretation, or conspire to shore up a weak one. For example, default stress should strengthen use of a pragmatically neutral SVO interpretation, while contrastive stress should increase the acceptability of a marked OVS interpretation. Nineteen of the 24 predictions were supported—good evidence for a coalition model in which cues converge in parallel to determine a response.

The main conclusion from this experiment seems to be that lexical contrasts (animacy) are at the "core" of Italian processing to the same degree that order information is at the "core" of English. Any processing theory that gives universal priority to either type of information would have difficulty accounting for these data. Furthermore, the probabilistic results (competition, convergence, conspiracy) fit in a principled way with a processing theory that makes use of weighted form-function mappings. We see no way that a theory based on determinate, obligatory, 100% rules could account for these findings.

However, these results do not necessarily mean that Italians ignore syntax! We now are carrying out a new version of the experiment using competing and converging combinations of order, animacy, stress, and noun-verb agreement, e.g., "are kissing the cows the pencil" (see TABLE 1 for more examples). This experiment is being carried out in English, Italian, and German (using feminine nouns in German so that number agreement can vary without using case contrasts). Although the results are preliminary (involving three to four subjects per language), they again suggest strong and consistent differences among languages in weighting of cues.

FIGURE 2 illustrates the word-order strategies in all three languages, for items where animacy and agreement both are ambiguous. It is clear that German and Italian are more similar to one another than to English: they both make slightly less use of SVO than English does, and there are no clear and unambiguous strategies for dealing with nonstandard word orders.

FIGURE 3 illustrates the effects of animacy, summing across word orders, for items where agreement is ambiguous. Once again, Italian and German are more like one another than like English: they make very consistent use of the lexical contrast (slightly less in German than in Italian), compared with much smaller animacy effects in English.

Finally, FIGURE 4 illustrates the effect of agreement, summing across word orders and animacy conditions. This graph looks strikingly like the results for animacy, with German and Italian clustering close together in their extensive use of agreement, against much smaller effects in English. We have said that Italian is "less" of a word-order language than English. It also appears to operate "more" like a case-inflected language. We have not graphed the $order \times animacy \times agreement$ interactions for these languages, because they are so complex. However, it looks as though the order of importance of cues in English is word order first, followed

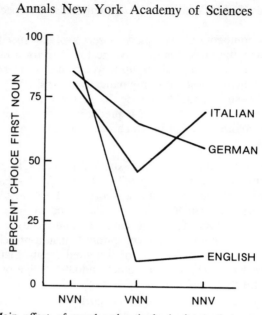

FIGURE 2. Main effect of word order (only in items that are ambiguous with regard to animacy and subject-verb agreement) in English, Italian, and German native speakers (Germans include only a pilot sample of three subjects).

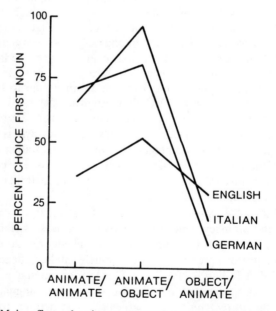

FIGURE 3. Main effect of animacy summed across word orders (only in items that are ambiguous with regard to subject-verb agreement) in English, Italian, and German native speakers (Germans include only a pilot sample of three subjects).

by agreement and animacy. The order of importance of cues in both German and Italian is agreement first, followed by animacy and order.

We seem to have found a continuum here in the use of morphological versus syntactic information in sentence interpretation. The two languages that make the most use of morphology also make more use of lexical information (as though bound- and unbound-morpheme strategies hang together somehow). The English reliance on word order operates at the expense of attention to either inflectional morphology or lexical contrasts. The idea that this is a continuum rather than a bipolar classification rests on the fact that German seems to be located somewhere in between English and Italian—although it is closer to Italian.

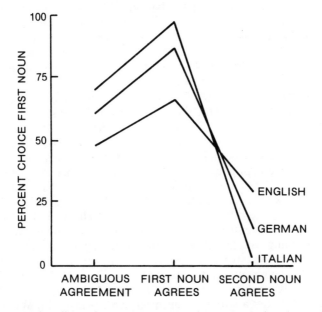

FIGURE 4. Main effect of agreement summed across word order and animacy conditions, in English, Italian, and German native speakers (pilot samples for all three languages).

If it is possible to talk about languages as being "in between" one another on a continuum of processing strategies, what about bilingual speakers? We have given the order-animacy-agreement version of our comprehension experiment to one Italian bilingual, and to several native speakers of German with varying degrees of fluency in English. Although the findings are tentative, they are very clear in showing evidence for a transfer of L1 processing strategies onto the second language.

First a brief introduction to our bilinguals. The Italian, UR, is a graduate student in his 40s, a northern Italian who has spent most of the last 18 years in the United States while working for an Italian company. He writes English well, his accent is noticeable but slight, and he claims that he now "thinks in English." English was acquired first in school, after puberty. The Germans include a group of three "new bilinguals," southern-German graduate students who are in their first year of study in the United States. Their English was acquired in school, and has a long way to go before it could be called fluent (although it is possible to hold a conversation on any topic). The other two Germans have used English as their primary language for many years. WK is a native-born Austrian, a professor of psychology who learned his English in European schools. He has lived in this country for over 25 years, writes English very well, but speaks with a pronounced German accent. He and his American-born wife speak both English and German in the home. Finally, IB has a Ph.D. in psychology and has lived in this country or England for 22 years. She and her British husband have always spoken English. IB writes flawless technical English prose, and Americans can detect no German in her accent (although British speakers of English are aware that she is not a native speaker). She acquired English in school and spent one year as an exchange student in the United States when she was 15.

The left graphs in FIGURES 5, 6, and 7 plot the main effects in English for our German bilinguals (the three new bilinguals are summed together). Starting with the word-order strategies, it is clear that only IB shows an English pattern: strong first noun on NVN, strong second noun on the nonstandard orders (especially OSV). The new bilinguals are much closer, instead, to the German pattern. WK lies partway in between, but certainly is closer to the German end. In other words, all the German bilinguals show German word-order strategies in English, except for IB. This distribution holds in the other two main effects as well. In FIGURE 6, we can see that IB overlaps entirely with the English plot for animacy. Both WK and the new bilinguals cling closely to the German pattern, making extensive use of animacy contrasts when agreement is ambiguous. Finally, FIGURE 7 illustrates the agreement effects. IB once again clings to the English pattern almost perfectly, making relatively little use of agreement. WK and the new bilinguals show a strong reliance on agreement—with WK even surpassing the struggling new foreign students in his use of German strategies. *In sum, of the four German bilinguals tested, three very clearly are using German processing strategies to interpret English sentences.* It is interesting to speculate on the relationship of these data to differences in accent: IB, whose accent is barely detectable, uses English strategies in grammar as well; WK, whose accent is nothing short of notorious, uses German strategies in grammar. We have begun to test some English bilinguals who have acquired German as a second language. Again, the data are quite tentative, but they are completely consistent with the transfer hypothesis—in the opposite direction, as we would expect, with strong use of word order and very little use of agreement or animacy in German.

The right graphs in FIGURES 5, 6, and 7 present our one Italian bilingual plotted against the norms for English and Italian. Although UR feels that he thinks in English, the data clearly show that he applies Italian strategies

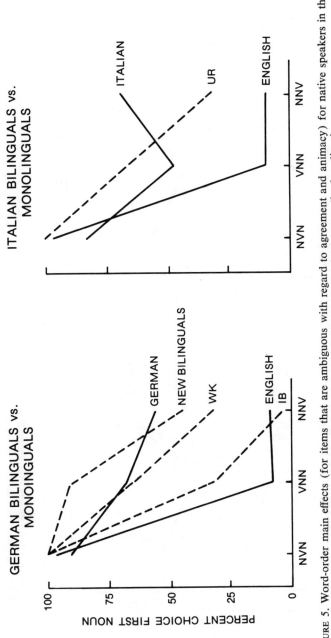

FIGURE 5. Word-order main effects (for items that are ambiguous with regard to agreement and animacy) for native speakers in their first languages (filled lines) and for bilinguals tested in English as a second language (broken lines).

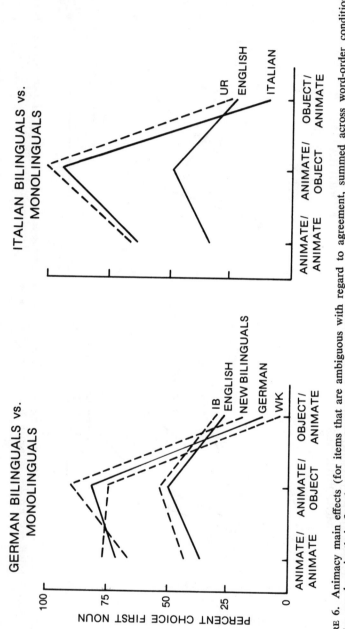

FIGURE 6. Animacy main effects (for items that are ambiguous with regard to agreement, summed across word-order conditions) for native speakers in their first languages (filled lines) and for bilinguals tested in English as a second language (broken lines).

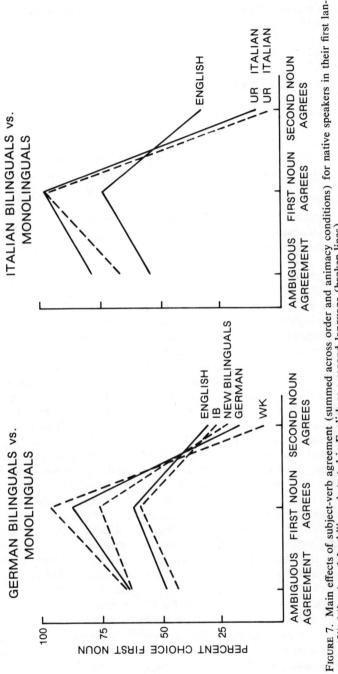

FIGURE 7. Main effects of subject-verb agreement (summed across order and animacy conditions) for native speakers in their first languages (filled lines) and for bilinguals tested in English as a second language (broken lines).

to English sentences: strong use of animacy and agreement, much less use of word order. However, UR does show one interesting differentiation, in that he has moved in the direction of a second-noun strategy in NNV items (OSV) while his VNN performance remains close to chance.

We said earlier that according to some investigators, the evidence for interference and transfer from L1 to L2 is surprisingly small.[33] This may be true when we are using a narrow definition of grammar, looking only for clear-cut examples of grammatical errors, lexical substitution, etc. These competition experiments seem to expose a deeper level of processing, where transfer and "in-between status" are more clearly evident. We suggest that differences at this level of processing, where grammatical forms are mapped directly onto forms like topic and agent, may be involved in subtle difficulties that second-language learners have with discourse structure and with that nebulous area called "stylistics."

We can say much less right now about our production experiments using the competition model, but the general research strategy is the same. We have constructed animated films that set up converging and competing combinations of several factors that are known to affect the selection of sentence subjects (and a variety of related syntactic constructions). These include *animacy* (chairs versus zebras, etc.), *actual movement* (e.g., the chair chases a zebra), *point of view* (induced, for example, through camera angle), and *givenness* (how often and how recently has this animal or object been seen, and did it serve as an actor or as a patient of an action in earlier frames). Subjects include adults, and children from three to seven. In the first experiment, we are asking them simply to describe what they see after each segment. In a second experiment, their descriptions are constrained further by discourse, including questions like "What happened to the chair?" In a third set of experiments, the very same films will be used for comprehension and verification. That is, subjects will view a segment and then be asked to verify whether or not a given sentence (e.g., "*the chair* chased the zebra" or "the chair chased *the zebra*") corresponds to what they have just seen. In all of these studies, reaction time data as well as the responses themselves will serve as dependent variables.

The goal of these production studies is not to show simply that a given function does have an effect. For example, we already know that English speakers tend to mark given information with definite articles. We do not need experiments to prove what is obvious to any native speaker. Instead, our goals are similar to those in an earlier production study comparing English, Hungarian, and Italian children and adults in the effects of givenness and newness on picture description (in sequences of pictures where one element systematically changed and the others remained constant).[35] Our focus there was the *degree* to which a given form was controlled by givenness or newness, in *language × age interactions*. This includes the finding that Americans tend to use contrastive stress at those points where Italians and Hungarians adopt word-order variations, or the finding concerning points where Americans use pronouns while Italians and Hungarians use ellipsis.

We were interested also in the developmental process of *differentiation*: children begin looking more similar to one another in the way that surface forms are controlled by givenness; gradually, they diverge from one another in the direction of adults in their respective languages. Language × age interactions like these are not at all obvious without experimentation, and attest to the value of cross-linguistic research on psycholinguistic issues.

Using the same sentence-production techniques, we now would like to examine the degree to which adult bilingual speakers fit the processing strategies of L1 versus L2 in free production and in response to discourse constraints (e.g., "What happened to the chair?"). With this method, we should be able to investigate more precisely the kinds of transfer that we ourselves experience in moving between the rigid word order of English and the more flexible orders of Italian and Hungarian (overuse of contrastive stress in Hungarian, overuse of topic-focus reorderings in English, etc.). The same differentiation process that we have examined in monolingual children may occur in second-language learning as well, as speakers become more and more skillful in integrating pragmatic and semantic information across discourse.

Finally, for both the comprehension and production experiments, we are beginning to move away from an analysis-of-variance format. Analysis-of-variance designs greatly restrict the number of variables that can be considered together in a given experiment (something that became very clear to us in trying to interpret four-way interactions in Bates *et al.*).[4] Yet the competition model is built around the simultaneous interaction of many different forms and functions in sentence comprehension and production. The method of choice in evaluating such a theory is *structural equation modeling*. We can build a quantitative model of all the hypothetical vectors that impinge on, for example, interpretation of agency in comprehension or subject assignment in production. The weights attached to each vector can be specified in advance, or adjusted empirically to reflect a first round of experiments. We can test the reliability of such models by examining their goodness of fit to a second sample of subjects in the same language group. And we also can derive goodness-of-fit statistics for models of two or more languages—a way of testing the result that seems intuitively right from FIGURES 2 to 4, that Italian and German are closer to one another than to English. The implications of this approach for second-language learning are clear. If we have structural equation models for both L1 and L2, it should be possible to determine the goodness of fit of a given second-language learner to either or both of his two languages, in terms of the processing strategies that he uses in comprehension and production (see Reference 36 for examples of structural equation modeling in cross-linguistic data).

We have claimed that these processing strategies provide a missing link between acquisition of grammar and all the research that has accumulated in the last decade on pragmatics, semantics, discourse structure, and sociolinguistics. If that is the case, the acquisition of the processing strategies in a second language should accompany an increased sophistication in many subtle pragmatic, semantic, and discourse phenomena that are often the last barrier to true possession of a second language.

ACKNOWLEDGMENTS

Thanks are due to Antonella Devescovi and Reinhold Kliegl for assistance in data collection.

REFERENCES

1. BATES, E. 1976. Language and Context: The Acquisition of Pragmatics. Academic Press, Inc. New York, N.Y.
2. BATES, E. & B. MacWHINNEY. 1979. A functionalist approach to the acquisition of grammar. *In* Developmental Pragmatics. E. Ochs & B. Schieffelin, Eds. Academic Press, Inc. New York, N.Y.
3. BATES, E. & B. MacWHINNEY. Functionalist approaches to grammar. *In* Language Acquisition: The State of the Art. L. Gleitman & E. Wanner, Eds. Cambridge University Press. New York, N.Y. (In press.)
4. BATES, E., S. McNEW, B. MacWHINNEY, A. DEVESCOVI & S. SMITH. Functional constraints on sentence processing: a cross-linguistic study. Cognition. (In press.)
5. BATES, E., B. MacWHINNEY & V. VOLTERRA. 1981. A cross-linguistic study of the development of sentence interpretation strategies. Paper presented at the Biennial Meeting of the Society for Research in Child Development, Boston, Mass., April.
6. BERNSTEIN, B. 1970. A sociolinguistic approach to socialization: with some reference to educability. *In* Language and Poverty: Perspectives on a Theme. F. Williams, Ed. Markham Publishing Company. Chicago, Ill.
7. BEVER, T. G. 1970. The cognitive basis for linguistic structures. *In* Cognition and the Development of Language. J. R. Hayes, Ed. John Wiley & Sons, Inc. New York, N.Y.
8. BRAINE, M. D. S. & R. S. WELLS. 1978. Case-like categories in children: the actor and some related categories. Cognitive Psychol. **10:** 100–122.
9. BRESNAN, J. 1978. A realistic transformational grammar. *In* Linguistic Theory and Psychological Reality. Morris Halle, J. Bresnan & G. Miller, Eds. MIT Press. Cambridge, Mass.
10. CEDERGREN, H. J. & D. SANKOFF. 1974. Variable rules: performance as a statistical reflection of competence. Language **50:** 333–355.
11. CHOMSKY, N. 1975. Reflections on Language. Pantheon Books. New York, N.Y.
12. DEVILLIERS, J. 1981. Prototype theory and the acquisition of grammar. *In* Language Development: Syntax and Semantics. S. Kuczaj, Ed. Lawrence Erlbaum. Hillsdale, N.J.
13. DIK, S. 1978. Functional Grammar. North-Holland. New York, N.Y.
14. ERVIN-TRIPP, S. 1974. Is second language learning like first? TESOL Q. **8:** 111–127.
15. ERVIN-TRIPP, S. 1976. Keynote address to the Stanford Child Language Forum. Pap. Rep. Child Lang. Dev.
16. FODOR, J., T. BEVER & M. GARRETT. 1974. The Psychology of Language. McGraw-Hill Book Company. New York, N.Y.
17. FORSTER, K. I. 1979. Levels of processing and the structure of the language

processor. *In* Sentence Processing: Psycholinguistic Studies Presented to Merrill Garrett. W. Cooper & E. Walker, Eds.: 55–56. Erlbaum. Hillsdale, N.J.

18. FRANKEL, D. G. & T. ARBEL. 1980. Probabilistic assignments of sentence relations on the basis of differentially-weighted interpretive cues. (Unpublished manuscript.)

19. GIVON, T. 1980. On Understanding Grammar. Academic Press, Inc. New York, N.Y.

20. GIVON, T., Ed. 1980. Syntax and Semantics. **12**. Discourse and Syntax. Academic Press, Inc. New York, N.Y.

21. GLEITMAN, L. & H. GLEITMAN. 1970. Phrase and Paraphrase. W. W. Norton & Company, Inc. New York, N.Y.

22. HATCH, E. 1978. Discourse analysis and second language acquisition. *In* Second Language Acquisition: A Book of Readings. E. Hatch, Ed. Newbury Publishing. Rowley, Mass.

23. KARMILOFF-SMITH, A. 1979. A Functional Approach to Child Language. Cambridge University Press. Cambridge, England.

24. KEENAN, E. 1976. Towards a universal definition of "subject." *In* Subject and Topic. C. Li & S. S. Thompson, Eds. Academic Press, Inc. New York, N.Y.

25. KINTSCH, K. 1974. The Representation of Meaning in Memory. Erlbaum. Hillsdale, N.J.

26. KINTSCH, K. 1980. Psychological Processes in Discourse Production. Technical Report 99. Institute of Cognitive Science. University of Colorado. Boulder, Colo. (Paper presented to the workshop on Psycholinguistic Models of Production, Kassel, Federal Republic of Germany, July, 1980.)

27. KUNO, S. 1975. Three perspectives in the functional approach to syntax. *In* Papers from the Parasession on Functionalism. R. Grossman, Ed. Chicago Linguistic Society. Chicago, Ill.

28. KUNO, S. 1980. Functional syntax. *In* Current Approaches to Syntax: Syntax and Semantics. E. Moravcsik & J. Wirth, Eds. **13**. Academic Press, Inc. New York, N.Y.

29. LABOV, W. 1969. Contraction, deletion, and inherent variability of the English copula. Language **45**: 715–762.

30. LAKOFF, G. 1977. On linguistic gestalts. *In* Proceedings of the 13th Regional Meeting of the Chicago Linguistic Society. University of Chicago. Chicago, Ill.

31. LAKOFF, G. & H. THOMPSON. 1977. Introducing cognitive grammar. Pap. Berkeley Linguistic Soc. **3**.

32. LI, C. & S. THOMPSON, Eds. 1976. Subject and Topic: A New Typology of Language. Academic Press, Inc. New York, N.Y.

33. MCLAUGHLIN, B. 1977. Second language learning in children. Psychol. Bull. **84**: 3, 438–459.

34. MACWHINNEY, B. 1974. How Hungarian children learn to speak. Doctoral Dissertation. University of California. Berkeley, Calif.

35. MACWHINNEY, B. & E. BATES. 1978. Sentential devices for conveying givenness and newness: a cross-cultural developmental study. J. Verbal Learn. Verbal Behav. **17**: 539–558.

36. MACWHINNEY, B. & J. O'CONNELL. A functionalist model of the development of point-making. (In preparation.)

37. MARSLEN-WILSON, W. & L. TYLER. 1980. The temporal structure of spoken language understanding. Cognition **8**: 1–71.

38. PERLMUTTER, D. & P. POSTAL. 1977. Toward a universal characterization of passive. *In* Papers from the Third Annual Meeting of the Berkeley Linguistic Society. University of California. Berkeley, Calif.

39. ROEPER, T. 1973. Theoretical implications of word order, topicalization and

inflections in German language acquisition. *In* Studies in Child Language Development. D. Slobin & C. Ferguson, Eds. Holt, Rinehart & Winston. New York, N.Y.

40. ROSCH, E. 1977. Human categorization. *In* Studies in Cross-Cultural Psychology. N. Warren, Ed. Academic Press, Inc. New York, N.Y.

41. ROSS, J. 1972. The category squish: Edstation Hauptwort. *In* Proceedings of the Eighth Regional Meeting of the Chicago Linguistic Society. University of Chicago. Chicago, Ill.

42. SCHLESINGER, I. M. 1977. Production and Comprehension of Utterances. Lawrence Erlbaum. Hillsdale, N.J.

43. SELFRIDGE, O. 1959. Pandemonium: a paradigm for learning. *In* Symposium on the Mechanization of Thought Processes. HM Stationery Office. London, England.

44. SLOBIN, D. 1973. Cognitive prerequisites for the development of grammar. *In* Studies in Child Language Development. D. Slobin & C. Ferguson, Eds. Holt, Rinehart & Winston. New York, N.Y.

45. SLOBIN, D. 1979. Psycholinguistics. 2nd edit. Scott-Foresman. New York, N.Y.

46. SLOBIN, D. & T. BEVER. 1980. A cross-linguistic study of sentence comprehension in children. University of California. Berkeley, Calif. (Unpublished manuscript.)

47. STROHNER, H. & K. NELSON. 1974. The young child's development of sentence comprehension: influence of event probability, nonverbal context, syntactic form, and their strategies. Child Dev. **45:** 567–576.

48. VAN VALIN, R. & W. FOLEY. 1980. Role and reference grammar. *In* Current Approaches to Syntax: Syntax and Semantics. E. Moravcsik & J. Wirth, Eds. **13**. Academic Press, Inc. New York, N.Y.

49. VOLTERRA, V. 1972. Nota in margine sul participio passato nel linguaggio infantile. Istituto di Psicologia/CNR. Rome, Italy. (Unpublished manuscript.)

50. WONG-FILLMORE, L. 1976. The second time around: cognitive and social strategies in second language learning. Ph.D. Dissertation. Stanford University. Stanford, Calif.

SYNTAX, SEMANTICS, AND PRAGMATICS—FIRST
LANGUAGE: GENERAL DISCUSSION

Moderator: Catherine E. Snow

Graduate School of Education
Harvard University
Cambridge, Massachusetts 02138

UNIDENTIFIED SPEAKER: Dr. Nelson, in L2 [second-language] acquisition we have a problem called avoidance. Some learners will not attempt to speak even though they are capable. Is this particular phenomenon being given attention in L1 [first-language] acquisition, that is, studying children who may be able to speak, but simply don't?

K. NELSON (*Graduate Center, City University of New York, New York, N.Y.*): That is a very interesting question. Very little attention has been given to this issue in first-language learning. However, one reason is that most investigators study children who are speaking and, therefore, tend to avoid children who are not speaking. We have all observed children who go virtually through the second birthday, or even later, without producing any language and then sometime around 25 months begin to produce sentences that are roughly equivalent to those of children who have been producing right along.

Individual differences in language acquisition are probably related to the cognitive style that is used to approach a learning task. We don't have enough information at this time, but we can speculate that the approach that is used to acquire early language is applied later on by the same children when learning to read or learning a second language.

L. MENN (*Boston University School of Medicine, Boston, Mass.*): Just a word in for phonology. With regard to the often-observed spurt in vocabulary growth, it may be that some children who are learning to understand object names are not saying them because they haven't mastered the required sounds of the words. Children avoid saying sounds they cannot produce. It is an early language-acquisition strategy. It is often difficult, of course, to show that a child is avoiding certain sounds. You need to be able to compare the words attempted with the words that the child understands and apparently has opportunity to use, and, additionally, look for systematic absences of attempts at words containing certain sounds or sound patterns.

K. NELSON: I referred to that in terms of the comprehension-production disparity. However, I don't think it explains all of the spurt phenomenon.

UNIDENTIFIED SPEAKER: Dr. Bloom, I don't think you mean to imply that the focus you have given to verbs suggests in language acquisition that communication or the pragmatic use of language is largely irrelevant.

L. BLOOM (*Teachers College, Columbia University, New York, N.Y.*): My presentation addressed the issue of verb development and its implications for language development, and I proposed that children's knowledge of verbs is an important factor in language acquisition. This position certainly does not negate the considerable importance of communicative processes in language acquisition.

UNIDENTIFIED SPEAKER: Dr. Bloom, I was wondering if you would speculate on whether or not children with motor problems, such as cerebral-palsied children, have the same categories for verbs, and the same patterns of development.

L. BLOOM: I think your question implies that there is a correspondence between motor activity and whatever is printed out in the language. I think that what I am trying to say is that it is the structure of the language itself that determines that certain aspects of the language are more readily learned at certain times in development. I am not sure it has to do with a child's motor activity at any particular time. While cerebral-palsied children may not be able to perform certain actions themselves, they observe others participating in actions. It is an issue that should be examined.

H. W. SELIGER (*Queens College, Flushing, N.Y.*): Dr. Bowerman, with regard to the categories of syntactic and lexical verbs that you spoke about in the third part of your presentation—verbs that you call syntactic, I would call lexical. For example, in the typical two-word verbs, the preposition doesn't add any particular information other than lexical content, as in "take off the sweater," where "off" would never be deleted, leaving "take the sweater," simply because it is part of lexical content. This construction is in contrast to one in which a preposition is attached to a verb and that indicates the prepositional relationship. For example, "give the book to Harry" becomes "give Harry the book" by deleting "to" and applying a rearrangement transformation. I am wondering why you call a verb-plus-particle combination like "take off" syntactic?

M. BOWERMAN (*Bureau of Child Research, University of Kansas, Lawrence, Kans.*): Many linguists have indeed treated verb-plus-particle combinations lexically, as two-part verbs, but other linguists, such as Fillmore, have treated them syntactically. It is the latter approach I am following because I believe it captures various developmental phenomena more accurately. According to this approach, superficially simple sentences like "Johnny pulled his socks up" have two underlying propositions. The main verb comes from what Fillmore calls the "causing event" clause, for example, "Johnny pulled on his socks," and the particle comes from the "resulting event" clause, for example, "his socks came up." So the two elements are more independent than in the lexical account; they get together only through transformations. But even if you prefer a lexical account of verb-plus-particle combinations, they are clearly different kinds of lexical items from single-word verbs in which the notion of "separation" is only implicit, like "break" or "open." So I would still want to make the claim that there is competition among very different kinds of formal devices for expressing meaning.

UNIDENTIFIED SPEAKER: Dr. Bowerman, I found your explanation of lexicalization patterns in children insightful, but I was wondering why you introduced the notion of "error" or "mistake" into it. It seems to me that there is no necessity to call these "errors," because the notion of error is a prescriptive concept.

M. BOWERMAN: Yes. I agree with you in a way, since my intent is certainly not to be prescriptive. Other people have also said, Why call them errors? I sometimes call them "deviations from adult norms," but that gets awfully long and the term "errors" is easier. What I want to highlight, by calling them deviations or errors, is that adults do not say these things. Children's utterances differ in specific ways from what they hear in the speech around them, and even from their own previous usage. This allows you to infer that there is something creative going on, that some processing or analyzing on the child's part is taking place. The discrepancy between the linguistic model and the child's form is important to stress. Some of the phenomena that I have been calling "errors" I think are not actually errors from the standpoint of the child's own system. For example, for the young child it may be perfectly acceptable to derive novel causative verbs at will from noncausative intransitive predicates. But other things I have called errors—like "How do you untake this off?"—I think probably do have the status of errors even in the child's own system. This is because they are relatively rare; normally the child does it in the adult way. I think that these very occasional errors suggest that the child's self-editing and monitoring system is not quite up to adult standards. The child makes mistakes more often, that is, selects the wrong item, or two mutually exclusive items at the same time. But even though these utterances may well be simply slips, not the output of the child's rule system, they are still very revealing about how things are organized in that system. For example, they tell us what meanings are similar enough to what other meanings in the child's head that the forms expressing them may be simultaneously activated by the child's intention to talk about a certain event.

E. BATES (*University of Colorado, Boulder, Colo.*): In the few remaining minutes I would like to add that we have extended our research to children. Research on English-speaking children would lead one to believe that a semantic strategy is more primitive than a word-order strategy because English four-year-olds, given sentences like "the pencil kicked the cow," will tell you that the cow did it. Somewhere around five, they switch.

What we are finding is that at five years of age, English children make less use of word order than do English adults, and more use of animacy than do English adults. However, Italian children make more use of word order than do Italian adults, and less use of lexical information than do Italian adults.

From an Italian point of view, if the psycholinguistic literature were "Italo-centered" instead of "Anglo-centered," one might argue that word-order strategies are primitive, simpleminded things that children do until they acquire the lexical sophistication of the adult.

No doubt children use all the information they can get from any source. Gradually they acquire a system, which they differentiate in the direction of their adult language. The idea of differentiating in two different directions could be applied, of course, to second-language learners.

LANGUAGE-ACQUISITIONAL UNIVERSALS: A UNIFIED VIEW OF LANGUAGE ACQUISITION

Henning Wode

English Department
University of Kiel
2300 Kiel, Federal Republic of Germany

The Need for a Comprehensive Language-Learning Theory

There is a strange mismatch between what human beings can achieve with respect to learning languages and the way these achievements have been dealt with by the social sciences, including linguistics and psychology. Normal human beings can learn more than one language; they can learn them simultaneously or successively; with or without schoolroom instruction; they can forget a language, and they can relearn it. This ability is unique to *Homo sapiens*. Yet past research on language acquisition and, in particular, on language-acquisitional universals is dominated by a strange type of self-imposed methodological limitation that creates the impression that people use different and functionally unrelated mechanisms each time they learn a language in a different situation. The question of whether there are universal acquisitional regularities in the sense that they are available for all acquisitional situations was not raised. For example, Jakobson's classic study on phonological acquisition (1941) probably is the best known among the early proposals concerning acquisitional universals.[24] But it never occurred to Jakobson to consider, for example, foreign-language teaching or naturalistic second-language (L2) acquisition. Jakobson's approach was limited to first-language (L1) acquisition and phonology. During the 1960s his approach was carried over to syntax and other structural areas, but it still was limited to L1 acquisition.[8–10,19,29,35] This research failed to show how universal the proposed universals really were.

On the other hand, foreign-language-teaching researchers failed, or refused, to see any links extending toward L1 acquisition. In fact, there are many references in the literature to the effect that foreign-language teaching must be regarded as something totally different from L1 acquisition, because the learning situation is so—obviously—different (for example, References 11 and 25). However, how learning a language in the classroom differs from learning one without instruction has not been investigated empirically so far. The question is whether the foreign-language-learning student applies totally different neuropsychological language processing and learning mechanisms when he is taught a language as opposed to when he learns it without instruction.

The situation improved during the early 1970s, due to the rise of

0077-8923/81/0379-0218 $01.75/2 © 1981, NYAS

research on naturalistic, i.e., untutored, L2 acquisition. (Surveys in References 17, 28, and 46.) Among other things, this research has been concerned, from its beginning, with the question of to what extent naturalistic L2 acquisition parallels L1 acquisition. L2 research also has always stressed its implications for foreign-language teaching, although it is not, at present, very clear at all what these implications are. It seems to me, however, that we have to advance further and consider all types of language acquisition and check them all for differences and commonalities, if we are ever to arrive at a satisfactory understanding of how human beings learn languages.

What is needed is an integrated theory of language acquisition that characterizes the overall ability of human beings to learn languages. This theory must state the commonalities as well as the differences among all types of language acquisition, including learning a language in the classroom. The task, therefore, is to determine whether human beings do, in fact, employ totally different and unrelated language-learning mechanisms in different learning situations and at different age levels. Such a view is highly unlikely on both theoretical and empirical grounds. For all practical purposes there are infinitely many different external situations in which languages are learned. Yet the capacity of the human brain is finite. It is more likely, therefore, that human beings have one language-learning system that is flexible enough to cope with differences in the external situations. This is where the universals issue rearises, this time, however, in a truly universal (dis)guise. What is needed is to check whether there are acquisitional regularities that apply to all acquisitional types and all age groups, or only to some, and whether and to what extent these universals can be influenced or manipulated, for example, by instruction.

Fascinating theoretical perspectives derive from adopting such a view. I assume that what happens when people learn languages is that input, i.e., speech, is processed by the brain or mind to result in learner languages that, ultimately, may or may not fully approach the target languages. The structure of learner languages, therefore, reflects the processing abilities of the brain. It follows, first, that languages can be structured only such that they are learnable, i.e., that they can be processed by the brain; second, that languages can change only in such a way that they remain learnable; and, third, that the typological peculiarities of natural languages also must be constrained by the processing abilities of the brain. All this means that, eventually, it should be possible to provide a more unified perspective for various domains involving languages that, at the present state of the art, appear as unrelated phenomena, namely, language learning, borrowing, (imperfect) code switching by bilinguals and bidialectals, etc. Although the theoretical arguments may be quite convincing, the actual challenge, of course, is to develop research designs that make it possible to study such issues empirically.

The empirical evidence summarized in this paper results from an attempt to devise such a methodology.* I think the available data clearly point to the existence of the sort of universals speculated on above. The focus in this paper is on universals rather than on the differences between acquisitional types, because most researchers are convinced that there are such differences. However, it will be necessary to present a few theoretical considerations pertaining to various aspects of the nature and the domain of an integrated language-learning theory, before the empirical data can be reviewed and before some implications inherent in my approach can be discussed.

On the Nature and the Cognitive Basis of a Language-Learning Theory

The approach advocated here deviates in certain ways from much of current thinking—notably, concerning the relationships between language learning and social interaction and between language learning and the development of general cognition.

It is a truism that a language is, generally, not acquired for its own sake. People learn languages for social reasons, namely, to be able to communicate, to take part in social interactions, to be a member of a group. This does not mean that a theory of the development of communication and interactional competence also automatically accounts for the way in which the linguistic structures are learned. Such a view would be highly erroneous.

The initial truism merely indicates that the learner does not discover the input to his learning system, i.e., the linguistic structures, in a vacuum, but that, instead, the language data to be learned occur together with, and are part of, complex social events. Since there can be no communication via speech unless the speakers know the linguistic structures, it follows that a language-learning theory must be centrally directed to the linguistic structures. On the other hand, it is obvious that such an approach also must indicate how the learner sorts out the complex social events, and how interactional, communicative, and other variables interact with the acquisition of the linguistic system in the narrower sense.

The ability to learn languages is unique to *Homo sapiens*. It follows that he must be equipped with special abilities that enable him to process speech data for the purpose of learning linguistic structures, hence lan-

* The approach was developed in a project initiated in 1968. Its core is a typology of acquisitional situations providing for monolingualism, bilingualism, etc.; L1, L2, L3 . . ., i.e., nonsimultaneous acquisition; language teaching vs. naturalistic, i.e., untutored acquisition; relearning of languages; and others. We systematically trace the acquisition of selected structural areas across these acquisitional types. We now have data on L1 German, L1 English, L2 German (acquired by speakers of L1 English), naturalistic L2 English (L1, German), naturalistic relearning of L2 English (L1, German), foreign-language-teaching L2 English (L1, German), and some pidgins and creoles. The age ranges are from infancy to adulthood. (For details on the design of this project see References 40 and 46.)

guages. I assume that these abilities, whatever their nature, are part of, and integrated into, man's overall cognitive functioning. Recent research has made it reasonably clear that general conceptual development, the development of logical thinking, the development of pragmatic skills, or how to handle complex social interactions, fail to explain the intricacies of how learners process the formal properties of the linguistic devices used in natural languages, such as word order, inflections, embeddings, suprasegmental vs. segmental markings, phonological features, etc.[40,46] Consequently, I assume that integrated into man's overall cognitive functioning, there is a subsystem, perhaps a set of subsystems, especially geared to, and laid out to, handle the formal properties of the linguistic devices of natural languages. I therefore call this the linguocognitive system(s).[46]

I shall attempt to characterize the process of learning a language in terms of three basic notions: developmental sequence, decomposition of target structures, and individual variation. The notion of developmental sequence refers to the relative chronology in which the elements of the target language are learned. The notion of decomposition refers to the fact that target structures are not necessarily acquired all at once. Complex structural areas are at first decomposed, as it were, into various elements that later are reintegrated, step by step, into the target structure, as reflected in the errors observable in the speech of learners. The notion of individual variation refers to the fact that the linguistic structure of learner utterances within a given developmental sequence may vary to some extent among different learners of the same acquisitional types. This variation is not infinite; its range is limited relative to the acquisitional type(s) and the target structure(s) (details on these notions in References 45 and 46).

The Acquisition of Negation in Several Types of Language Acquisition

The points developed above—that is, focusing on the formal properties of linguistic devices, decomposition, developmental sequences, and individual variation among developmental structures—can be substantiated as we inspect the cross-cultural data on negation collected from different acquisitional types.

For the present purposes, the most convenient way of presenting the results of such comparisons across acquisitional types is to tabulate the developmental sequences. In addition to the chronological ordering as mirrored in the developmental sequences, these tables also quickly reveal the nature of the decomposition and whether and to what extent a developmental structure or peculiarity is universal or restricted to L1, L2, etc. Individual variation is displayed in separate tables.

Minor idiosyncrasies apart, TABLE 1 contrasts the (major) early non-anaphoric learner structures that have been observed in the acquisition of the negation system of English as L1, naturalistic L2, and L2 relearning. Foreign-language-teaching L2 English and pidgins will be considered later.

TABLE 1

SOME STRUCTURAL TYPES IN THE DEVELOPMENT OF NEGATION IN L1 ENGLISH, SEVERAL TYPES OF L2 ENGLISH, AND RELEARNING OF L2 ENGLISH ACQUIRED BY SPEAKERS OF VARIOUS AGE GROUPS AND FROM DIFFERENT L1 BACKGROUNDS *

	L1 English		L2 English							Relearning of L2 English
	Bellugi[5]	Bloom[8]	Wode[46] L1 German	Ravem[32] L1 Norwegian	Fillmore[20] L1 Spanish	Schumann[34] L1 Spanish	Adams[1] L1 Spanish	Butterworth[12] L1 Spanish	Milon[30] L1 Japanese	Allendorf[2] L1 German
Age Range at First Exposure to L2 †			3;11–8;11	3;9–6;6	5;6–8;0	5;0–33;0	4;11–5;9	13;0	7;0	5;11–10;11
Number of subjects	3	3	4	2	5	5	10‡	1	1	4
External *no*										
no Adj/V/N	++++	++++	++	+	++	++		+++?	+	++
no VP										
no S			+		+					
X no	++	+	++	+	++				++	++
Internal *be* negation										
X (be) no Y								+		
X (be) not Y							+	+		
X no be Y						+?				

Internal V negation
Postverbal no/not
  Subj V no X
  Subj V not X
  Sub V Pron not (X)
  Subj V a not N
  Subj V a no N
Preverbal no/not
  Subj no VP
  Subj not VP
PreAux no
  Subj no Aux VP

* Expanded from Reference 46. Plus (+) indicates that the structural type was observed in the respective study; ? means occurrence not quite clear. Items in parenthesis are optional.

† 3;11 means 3 years, 11 months.

‡ The number of subjects studied by Adams is 10. The structural types have been extracted from the protocols of one subject, because the records of the others are not provided.

The order of listing corresponds roughly to the developmental sequence of naturalistic L2 acquisition. The plus sign (+) indicates that the respective structural type has been observed in the respective study.

As for the concept of decomposition, even a quick glance at the illustrative examples shows that this notion is well motivated. The respective learner structure(s) can be used to infer which property of the target structure, if any, was decomposed to lead to such developmental structures. (Such an attempt is carried out in detail in Reference 46 for L1 and naturalistic L2 English.) Moreover, there are some restrictions among the developmental learner structures and the various acquisitional types. Thus, the type *pre-Aux no* is not reported so far for L1, but is reported for L2 and L2 relearning. The types with sentence-internal *post-V negation no/not* are reported only in those L2 combinations where the respective L1 has post-V negation—obviously, a clear case of interference. The other developmental structures are common to L1, L2, and L2 relearning. Note that this also holds for the adolescents and the adults in the survey (i.e., References 12 and 34).

In order to determine whether there are any truly universal acquisitional universals, it must be shown that the respective developmental structures also recur in other acquisitional types, for example, in foreign-language teaching and pidgins, and in the acquisition of other languages. Not enough data are available to follow such questions for every learner structure of TABLE 1. But we can go a long way for two of them, namely, for *external no* and *Subj no/not VP*. In more general terms, the corresponding types in other languages would be *external neg,* more precisely, *neg X* and *Subj neg VP*. TABLE 2 summarizes a survey across various studies on L1 monolingualism other than English. Note that both structures are well attested.

As for pidgins and creoles, the two negation structures are among those most frequently cited to illustrate the peculiar nature of (early) pidgins and creoles. TABLE 3 is a small excerpt from a survey of reports on pidgins and creoles. Note here, too, that both negation structures are well attested, even in those pidgins and creoles that do not involve Indo-European languages or that arose without contact with each other (further details in Reference 46).

As for the developmental sequences, they are not fully identical across the acquisitional types, but they are not totally without parallels either (cf. TABLE 4). First, the developmental types differ as a function of the structure of the languages involved. For example, postverbal negative placement appears in the L2 types only if the target L2 or the learner's L1 has it, as in German or Norwegian (recall TABLE 1). Second, the sequencing in terms of stages differs across the acquisitional types. For example, one-word anaphoric negations may cooccur in L2 acquisition; in L1 acquisition, they do not. Internal *be*-negation tends to arise before sentence-internal full verb negation in L2 acquisition; but there is no such difference in L1 acquisition. In the L2 relearning data, it is even more

TABLE 2

NEGATION TYPES *neg X ~ X neg* AND *Subj neg VP* IN MONOLINGUAL L1 ACQUISITION *

Target Language	Source	Neg X	X neg	Subj neg VP
German	Wode [42]	nein sauber "no clean" nein schaff ich "no manage I" (I can't manage)		Heiko nicht darf "Heiko is allowed to not" hier nicht beide wohnen "here not both live"
	Preyer [31]		Kaffee nein "no coffee"	
Swedish	Lange & Larsson [27]	nej kossa "no moo-cow"		Embla inte ha täcket "Emble not have quilt"
Russian	Gvozdev [21]	njet kavo "nobody [there]"		nima njet oski "me no spoon"
Dutch	Schaerlaekens [38]	nee drinken "no drink" niet op "not on"		not mentioned
Latvian	Wode & Ruke-Dravina [47]	nav s, tu s "[there] is no ruler, there ruler" ne mimimi "no pencil"	aci nav "[the book about the] bear isn't there" gib nē "want no"	te nav bilda "here are no pictures" ipupu nē ita "bathroom no go"
Finnish	Toivainen [38]	en laula "I won't sing" ei tyy "no like"		not mentioned

* Adapted from Reference 46.

difficult to clearly delimit stages such as I–IV of L1 and L2. But all three acquisitional types agree in that the first stages or utterance types are marked by the use of free-form negators. The rise of the enclitic negation -*n't* is later in all three types. Of course, a division into stages is impossible for foreign-language teaching. Here the notion of developmental sequence is useful in allowing us to characterize foreign-language teaching as not showing such strict ordering as found in the naturalistic types. But even so,

TABLE 3

NEGATION TYPES *Neg X ~ X Neg* AND *Subj neg VP*
IN VARIOUS PIDGINS AND CREOLES *

	neg X ~ X neg	Subj neg VP
Hawaiian Pidgin (Carr)[18]	my father, no take care me "my father, [he] didn't take care of me"	baby name, me no like "I don't like my baby name"
Tok Pisin (Bauer)[4]	(not mentioned)	mi no lukim "I haven't seen him"
Chinese Pidgin (Hall)[22]	no can pe dog chicken bone "you can't give the dog a chicken bone"	tomollow maj no can come "tomorrow I can't come"
Chinese Pidgin (Bauer)[4]	can do? no can do? "can't you do that?"	he no belong handsome "he isn't handsome"
Jamaican Creole (Bailey)[3]	no sliip pan da bed "don't sleep on that bed"	nobody no gaan a puos yet "nobody has gone to the post office yet"
Beach-la-mar (Hall)[22]	no water stop "there is no water"	my belly no got kaikai "my belly isn't hungry"
Guyanese Creole (Bickerton)[7]		bod an ting na most pik am "birds and such mustn't eat it"
Freetown Krio (Todd)[37]	no do "don't do"	I no do "I don't do"
Russonorsk (Hall)[22]		moja njet snai "I don't know"
Ewondo Populaire (Todd)[37]	ke boo "don't do"	me ke boo "I don't do"

* Adapted from Reference 46.

the result is that the structure of the developmental sequences should be predictable provided individual variation is appropriately allowed for.

As for individual variation among learner structures within a given developmental sequence, there can be no doubt at all that such a phenomenon does exist. The crucial point is to determine its nature. TABLE 5 displays some types of structural variation for four child learners of L2 English (L1, German). Note that the learner structures of TABLE 5 differ

TABLE 4

MAJOR STAGES IN THE DEVELOPMENTAL SEQUENCES FOR THREE TYPES
OF LANGUAGE ACQUISITION: L1, L2, AND L2 RELEARNING *

| | | Acquisitional Type and Stages | | |
| | | L2 Based on | | L2 Relearning |
Structural Type	L1	L1 Preverbal	L1 Postverbal	Based on L1 Postverbal
Anaphoric one-word negation	I	I	I	I
Anaphoric two-word negation	II			+
Nonanaphoric neg X ∼ X neg	III	II	II	+
Internal negation	IV			
Internal *be*-negation		III	III	
X (be) neg Y		+	+	+
X neg (be) Y		+	−	−
Internal V-negation		IV	IV	
Subj neg V		+	+	+
Subj V neg		−	+	+
Bound negators	V	V	V	II

* Roman numerals indicate stages; +/− indicates presence/absence of structural
type.

TABLE 5

INDIVIDUAL VARIATION IN SOME DEVELOPMENTAL STRUCTURES FOR FOUR GERMAN
CHILDREN ACQUIRING ENGLISH AS L2 *

| | | Date of First Occurrence/ Productivity | | | |
Structural Type	Illustrative Example	Hei	Bi	La	Ig
Subj V neg X					
. . . V no X	everybody catch no the fish	1;24	3;29	1;23	3;18
. . . V not X	John go not to the school	1;13	2;5	1;26	4;6
Subj V Pron neg (X)					
. . . V Pron not	I catch that not	2;7	3;22	—	4;1
. . . V Pron not X	you got me not out	—	1;24	—	5;19
Subj neg VP					
. . . no VP	me no close the window	—	—	—	3;16
. . . not VP	you not shup up	1;13	3;1	1;18	4;20

* From Reference 46.

as to whether the negative is *no* or *not* and as to whether the negative occurs before or after the verb. Consider, first, the type *Subj V neg X*. Both *no* and *not* occur with each child, but not in the same chronological order. Two children use *not* before *no;* the other two have the reverse, i.e., *no* before *not*. This looks like a straightforward case of individual variation. Consider, next, the type *Subj V Pron neg (X)*. There is one child for whom this type was not observed at all. Why? A gap in the data? Or is this child, in principle, unable to produce it? Now consider the type *Subj neg VP*. Three children have only *not;* one child has *no* and *not,* with *no* preceding *not* developmentally. Again the same questions: An incidental gap in the data? Or language learning or processing inability or difference? The answer is clear for one child, Lars. He was given a translation test, after he was already well beyond the stage of *pre-V negation* and while he was already confidently employing *don't, didn't, can't,* and other enclitic negatives. The test was intended as a checkup on negated indefinites. Lars is asked to translate the German phrase *ich kann nichts sehen* (I can't see anything). His first attempt: *I can't see.* He is then asked in German, how about *nichts* (nothing). He ponders for a while and then says in German that it must be something involving *no.* He goes on to say with several hesitations, *I eh I no eh I eh I eh I no can't see.* This shows that he is quite capable of producing *Subj no VP* utterances. Furthermore, there is no reason to assume that the child should have learned this use of *no* since the time when he employed *not.* Rather, he probably could do it all along, except that for reasons we do not know he chose *not* instead of *no.*

There is additional evidence to support this conclusion. Lars is one of the children in our study on relearning L2 English (L1, German). He had forgotten (most of) his English in the course of two years. When he relearned English, his preference was *Subj no VP,* with *Subj not VP* being extremely rare. It seems, then, that in terms of language acquisitional regularities, such cases are instances of individual variation. The problem is to determine its nature in terms of linguocognitive functioning.

To conclude the review of the data, it should be noted that, although the acquisition data presented above concern negation, comparable material could have been cited for phonology, interrogation, or inflections.[39,41,44,46] The general impact would have been the same. There are numerous parallels across the acquisitional types in spite of the external learning situations, the respective cognitive maturity, etc. What do we make of this?

On the Nature of Linguocognitive Functioning: Language-Learning Strategies

Obviously, researchers of language learning have to inspect learner utterances. However, the ultimate interest is not in the utterances themselves, but in what they are the product of. That is, learner data must be inspected for what they reveal about the nature of the underlying language-learning and language-processing mechanisms. In this respect, the notion of decomposition probably is the most immediate reflex of how the formal properties of the linguistic devices used in natural languages are processed by the brain or mind. If we can generalize on the observed learner data as to which property crucially led to a given learner structure, then we should at least come close to characterizing the respective linguocognitive correlates. I assume, therefore, that the global notion of decomposition reflects linguocognitive strategies minutely geared to handle the formal properties of the linguistic devices. They are structure specific because it should take different strategies to cope with, say, phonology, word order, embeddings, or bound forms. Moreover, depending on whether these generalizations hold for all acquisitional types or whether they are more restricted, the corresponding linguocognitive strategies can be inferred to be either universal or limited to specific types.

An Illustrative Example: The Free-Form Strategy

One such truly universal strategy can be inferred from the negation data of the preceding section, in particular from the anaphoric one- and two-word stages, as well as from the negation types *neg X* and *Subj neg VP*. What needs to be explained is the word-order patterns and the fact that only specific negators of the target language(s) are used in these types.

As for the two word-order patterns, it is unlikely that they reflect any target word order at all. They seem to be provided by the learners.

As for the choice of the negatives, they are, clearly, reflexes of the respective target negatives. But why these, and why not, for example, English *-n't?* What is the crucial property that makes learners select *no* or *not* rather than other negatives? It seems that learners are operating according to a strategy that leads them to pick out free forms, i.e., forms capable of occurring in isolation, for example, in answer to questions, as one-word commands, or in other situations. These forms are used in the early stages of a learner's development, even in places not permitted by the grammar of the target, as in the two developmental structures *neg X ~ X neg* and *Subj neg VP*.

The free-form strategy not only accounts for the negation data, but it also applies to other structural areas provided that the formal property of being a free form is involved. For example, in Finnish, the affixal *yes* or *no* questions involving the bound form $-ko \sim -k\ddot{o}$ are learned later than the pronominal questions that involve free forms.[9] Similarly, in L1 English, the free form *will* is learned before the bound form *-'ll,* although the latter occurs much more frequently in the speech of mothers.[5] More evidence of this sort is available elsewhere (details in References 45 and 46). It clearly indicates that the acquisitional strategy is not limited to L1 acquisition or negation, but that it applies to other structural areas and other acquisitional types. In fact, it seems that the same linguocognitive strategy also accounts for individual variation.

As for the latter, recall, first, the variation between *no* and *not* as displayed in TABLE 5. Clearly both are free forms. There is no reason why a learner should use both forms if one will do just as well. Similarly, during their early stages of development, L2 learners of German may have *nein* (no), *nix* (nothing), *nie* (never).[17,26] In L1 English and L1 Russian, children generally start with *no* and *njet* (no), respectively. However, one English-speaking child is on record who first used *nomore*.[8] Gvozdev reported that his son started with [nada].[21] The forms *nomore* and [nada] were reflexes of polymorphemic forms of the target, i.e., *no more* and *ne nado*. Both target strings may occur in isolation, hence as free forms. The two children used their forms as monomorphemic items. In this respect, the most telling evidence is provided by Finnish. In Finnish the negator is inflected. This yields a good number of phonologically different negatives. In fact, Toivainen, in a longitudinal study of 25 children, found their first negatives to vary considerably.[38] Some children's first negative was *ei,* others first had *eikä,* still others *eu, euka,* or *eio.* It seems, then, that this acquisitional strategy generates and determines the range that the individual variation can take among learners, i.e., with respect to this strategy.

The Nature of Language-Acquisitional Strategies

The observations on the free-form strategy can be generalized. First, the concept seems to fit other structural areas as well. L1 phonological processes [as reviewed in the papers by Macken and Ferguson or Ingram (this volume)] can be reinterpreted as linguocognitive strategies directed at phonology. Bever's noun-verb-noun strategy, such peculiarities as reported by Carol Chomsky, and many others along such lines point into the same direction.[6,14] (See survey in Reference 15.) Likewise, Slobin's notion of operating principles comes close to my notion of acquisitional strategies,[36] although I insist on more precision as regards the linguistic domain of a given strategy.[45] Second, the notion also seems to apply to other acquisitional types, as illustrated by the developmental parallels across different acquisitional types. Third, even the regularities of interference can be described in terms of acquisitional strategies.[43]

Universals

It is with reference to the general nature of the linguocognitive strategies that the issue of acquisitional universals has to be posed. If one looks at the product level, i.e., at the linguistic structure of learner utterances, then, obviously, certain regularities are restricted to L1, others to L2, etc. For example, interference is restricted to the non-L1 types. However, if one looks at this issue in terms of the underlying processing abilities, of which interference is the product, namely, the linguocognitive strategies, then the issue appears in a different light. It still may make sense to maintain that some regularities and abilities are restricted to L2. This, however, should not be interpreted such that the ability itself is learned or developed in the course of learning an L2. The ability to rely on prior language knowledge is very likely just as much a part of man's built-in language-learning system as the non-L1-transfer acquisitional abilities. The difference is that the transfer strategies do not apply in L1 acquisition because their domain of applicability is void, because there is no prior language knowledge to fall back on.

Conclusion: Some Implications

Only a few implications of the approach presented above can be hinted at. Developmental psycholinguists must adopt a more unified approach. What used to be thought of as L1 child peculiarities, e.g., $neg\ X \sim X\ neg$,[35] now turn out to have a totally different status. In general, claims about what is, or is not, peculiar to a given acquisitional type require that it be shown that the respective peculiarity was, or was not, observed elsewhere.

The study of language acquisition needs to be related to language typology. Dahl, in a survey of the negation systems of some 240 languages, reported that $neg\ X$ and $Subj\ neg\ VP$ are well attested.[16] This supports speculation to the effect that both learner languages and the typology of fully developed languages are constrained by the processing abilities of the human brain or mind.

This unified approach has important implications for foreign-language teaching. If there are such truly universal universals, then the question arises of to what extent they can be influenced or manipulated by teaching. No teacher would want his students to say *no play baseball, I no want envelope.* In our investigation of German students who were taught English, we found many utterances like *doesn't John go to school.* Such utterances occurred in exercises to teach students to use *do*-support in negating declarative sentences. Such utterances are intended as negated declarative sentences, not as questions.[18] Apparently students rely on their linguocognitive strategy to prepose the negative, in this case *doesn't,* to what is to be negated.† Similarly, Hyltenstam found many errors like *Subj neg VP* among 160 adult L2 students of Swedish from more than 30 different L1 backgrounds.[23] Teachers, therefore, should not devise their teaching materials and teaching procedures to go counter to these natural learner abilities.

Lastly, attempts to explain language acquisition, even child acquisition, require certain reorientations. Appeals to interactional, pragmatic, or cognitive immaturity, even along Piagetian lines, simply fail to explain

---

† The developmental type with negative preposed to a whole sentence has been observed only rarely, at least in the major studies on L1 English. However, such structures have been found more frequently in the L1 acquisition of other languages (see summary in Reference 42). I suspect that the situation concerning English may be due to gaps in the presently available data.

the parallels in the data in view of the enormous differences in age and in the external settings. We must look for a more autonomous language-learning theory, integrated but not identical with the learning of these domains.

Summary

In this paper I argue for a unified approach to the study of language acquisition. It is suggested that exploring the relationships between, and the implications of, for example, L1 research for L2 acquisition or vice versa requires that reference be made to people's overall capacity for language learning. This capacity is species specific, it is part of any human being's biological endowment, and it is not limited to L1 or L2 acquisition. This approach not only has important implications for issues concerning language learning and language teaching, but it also relates language acquisition or learning, among other things, to linguistic theory, language typology, cognitive development, and the language-processing abilities of the human brain or mind.

In this paper my particular interest is in language-acquisitional universals and their relationship to typological universals. I summarize data on the acquisition of negation that indicate that certain developmental learner structures and errors occur in all nonpathological types of language acquisition or learning. These learner structures conform to structures well attested in a typological survey of the negation systems of natural languages across the world, including pidgins and creole languages. It is concluded that these error types result from underlying processing abilities that are universally available to any human being throughout his lifetime. It is these processing abilities that constrain both the linguistic structure that learner errors can take as well as the range of structural diversity among natural languages in terms of language typology.

REFERENCES

1. ADAMS, M. S. 1974. Second language acquisition in children. A study in experimental methods: observation of spontaneous speech and controlled production tests. Master's Thesis. University of California. Los Angeles, Calif.
2. ALLENDORF, S. 1980. Wiedererwerb einer Zweitsprache, dargestellt am Beispiel der englischen Negation. Doctoral Thesis. University of Kiel. Kiel, Federal Republic of Germany.
3. BAILEY, B. L. 1966. Jamaican creole syntax. A transformational approach. Cambridge University Press. Cambridge, England.
4. BAUER, A. 1974. Das melanesische und chinesische Pidginenglisch. Linguistische Kriterien und Probleme. Hans Carl. Regensburg, Federal Republic of Germany.
5. BELLUGI, U. 1967. The acquisition of negation. Doctoral Dissertation. Harvard University. Cambridge, Mass.
6. BEVER, T. G. 1970. On the cognitive basis for linguistic structures. *In* Cogni-

tion and the Development of Language. J. R. Hayes, Ed.: 279–362. Wiley. New York & London.

7. BICKERTON, D. 1975. Dynamics of a Creole System. Cambridge University Press. Cambridge, England.
8. BLOOM, L. 1970. Language Development: Form and Function in Emerging Grammars. MIT Press. Cambridge, Mass.
9. BOWERMAN, M. 1973. Early Syntactic Development. A Cross-Linguistic Study with Special Reference to Finnish. Cambridge University Press. Cambridge, England.
10. BROWN, R. 1973. A First Language: The Early Stages. Harvard University Press. Cambridge, Mass.
11. BURGSCHMIDT, E. & P. GÖTZ. 1974. Kontrastive Linguistik. Deutsch/Englisch. Theorie und Anwendung. Hueber. Munich, Federal Republic of Germany.
12. BUTTERWORTH, G. A. 1972. A Spanish-speaking adolescent's acquisition of English syntax. Master's Thesis. University of California. Los Angeles, Calif.
13. CARR, E. B. 1972. Da Kine Talk. From Pidgin to Standard English in Hawaii. University of Hawaii Press. Honolulu, Hawaii.
14. CHOMSKY, C. 1969. The Acquisition of Syntax in Children from 5–10. MIT Press. Cambridge, Mass.
15. CROMER, R. F. 1976. Developmental strategies for language. In Development of Cognitive Processes. R. Hamilton & M. Vernon. Eds.: 305–358. Academic Press. London, New York & San Francisco.
16. DAHL, Ö. 1979. Typology of sentence negation. Linguistics 17: 79–106.
17. FELIX, S. 1978. Linguistische Untersuchungen zum natürlichen Zweitsprachenerwerb. Fink. Munich, Federal Republic of Germany.
18. FELIX, S. Psycholinguistische Aspekte des Zweitsprachenerwerbs. Gunter Narr. Tübingen, Federal Republic of Germany. (In press.)
19. FERGUSON, C. A. & D. I. SLOBIN, Eds. 1973. Studies of Child Language Development. Holt, Rinehart & Winston. New York, N.Y.
20. FILLMORE, L. W. 1976. The second time around: cognitive and social strategies in second language acquisition. Doctoral Thesis. Stanford University. Stanford, Calif.
21. GVOZDEV, A. N. 1949. Formirovaniye u rebenka grammaticheskogo stroya russkogo yazyka. Akad. Pedag. Nauk RSFSR. Moscow, Russia.
22. HALL, R. A. 1966. Pidgin and Creole Languages. Cornell University Press. Ithaca, N.Y.
23. HYLTENSTAM, K. 1977. Implicational patterns in interlanguage syntax variation. Lang. Learn. 27: 383–411.
24. JAKOBSON, R. 1941. Kindersprache, Aphasie und allgemeine Lautgesetze. Uppsala, Sweden. (Reprinted 1969. Suhrkamp. Frankfurt, Federal Republic of Germany.)
25. LANE, H. 1962. Some differences between first and second language learning. Lang. Learn. 12: 1–14.
26. LANGE, D. 1979. Negation im natürlichen englisch-deutschen Zweitsprachenerwerb. Eine Fallstudie. Int. Rev. Appl. Linguistics 17: 331–348.
27. LANGE, S. & K. LARSSON. 1973. Syntactical Development of a Swedish Girl Embla, between 20 and 42 Months of Age. I. Age 20 to 25 Months. Project Child Language Syntax, Report No. 1. Stockholm University. Stockholm, Sweden.
28. McLAUGHLIN, B. 1978. Second Language Acquisition in Childhood. Erlbaum. Hillsdale, N.J.
29. McNEILL, D. 1966. Developmental psycholinguistics. In The Genesis of Language. F. Smith & G. A. Miller. Eds.: 15–84. MIT Press. Cambridge, Mass.
30. MILON, J. 1974. The development of negation in English by a second language learner. TESOL Q. 8: 137–143.

31. PREYER, W. 1912. Die Seele des Kindes: Beobachtungen über die geistige Entwicklung der Kindes in den ersten Lebensjahren. Grieben. Leipzig, Germany.
32. RAVEM, R. 1974. Second language acquisition. A study of two Norwegian children's acquisition of English syntax in a naturalistic setting. Doctoral Dissertation. University of Essex. Essex, England.
33. SCHAERLAEKENS, A. M. 1973. The Two-Word Sentence in Child Language Development. A Study Based on Evidence Provided by Dutch-Speaking Triplets. Mouton. The Hague, the Netherlands.
34. SCHUMANN, J. H. 1975. Second language acquisition: the pidginization hypothesis. Doctoral Dissertation. Harvard University. Cambridge, Mass.
35. SLOBIN, D. I. 1970. Universals of grammatical development in children. In Advances in Psycholinguistics. G. Flores d'Arcais & W. J. M. Levelt, Eds.: 174–186. Amsterdam, the Netherlands.
36. SLOBIN, D. I. 1973. Cognitive prerequisites for the development of grammar. In Studies of Child Language Development. C. A. Ferguson & D. I. Slobin, Eds.: 175–208. Holt, Rinehart & Winston. New York, N.Y.
37. TODD, L. 1974. Pidgins and Creoles. Routledge & Kegan Paul. London & Boston.
38. TOIVAINEN, J. 1980. Inflectional Affixes Used by Finnish-Speaking Children Aged 1 to 3 Years. Suomalaisen Kirjallisunden Sawa. Helsinki, Finland.
39. UFERT, D. 1980. Der natürliche Zweitsprachenerwerb des Englischen: Die Entwicklung des Interrogationssystems. Doctoral Dissertation. University of Kiel. Kiel, Federal Republic of Germany.
40. WODE, H. 1974. Natürliche Zweitsprachigkeit: Probleme, Aufgaben, Perspektiven. Linguistische Ber. 32: 15–36.
41. WODE, H. 1976. Some stages in the acquisition of questions by monolingual children. In Child Language 1975. Word 27 (Special Issue). W. von Raffler-Engel, Ed.: 261–310.
42. WODE, H. 1977. Four early stages in the development of L1 negation. J. Child Lang. 4: 87–102.
43. WODE, H. 1978. The beginnings of non-schoolroom L2 phonological acquisition. Int. Rev. Appl. Linguistics 16: 109–125.
44. WODE, H. 1978. The L1 vs. L2 acquisition of English interrogation. Working Pap. Bilingualism 15: 37–57. (Revised version in Indian J. Appl. Linguistics 4: 31–46.)
45. WODE, H. 1979. Operating principles and 'universals' in L1, L2, and FLT. Int. Rev. Appl. Linguistics 17: 217–231.
46. WODE, H. 1981. Learning a Second Language. An Integrated View of Language Acquisition. Gunter Narr. Tübingen, Federal Republic of Germany.
47. WODE, H. & V. RUKE-DRAVINA. 1967. Why 'Kathryn no like celery'? Folia Linguistica 10(1977): 361–367.

ENGLISH SPEAKERS' ACQUISITION OF DUTCH SYNTAX *

Catherine E. Snow

Graduate School of Education
Harvard University
Cambridge, Massachusetts 02138

A major source of research designs in the field of second-language acquisition during the last decade or so has been the question of similarity between first- and second-language acquisition. Ervin-Tripp's formulation of the question "Is Second Language Learning Like the First?" and the data she presented to support her affirmative answer were extremely valuable in stimulating new ways of thinking about second-language acquisition, and in helping researchers break out of the paradigms of contrastive analysis and interference theory.[1] Unfortunately, however, the question in my opinion is formulated poorly, and failure to identify the exact nature of the question being asked has prevented researchers from maximally illuminating the similarities or differences between first- and second-language acquisition.

The problem is simple: comparison of first- and second-language acquisition constitutes comparison of two processes that differ in many ways, so observations of differences between the two processes leave unanswered the question of what to attribute the differences to. What are the differences between the processes of first- and second-language acquisition, in addition to the fact that one involves a first and the other a second language? At least the following may differ grossly:

1. Age of learner.
2. Cognitive stage of learner.
3. Learner's need for the language as a communicative tool.
4. Learner's metalinguistic knowledge.
5. Learner's attitude toward and relationship with the native speakers.
6. Learner's access to contact with native speakers.
7. The nature of the speech that learners hear from native speakers.

Because all these sources of difference are interrelated in complex ways, it would involve several studies to assess their contribution to the differences between first- and second-language acquisition. Perhaps the single most important confounding variable is age, since it can be seen as the source of many of the other confounds. Almost inevitably, second-language acquisition occurs in older learners than does first-language acquisition, at least if the first-language acquisition is in any sense normal. The contribu-

* Supported by the Netherlands Foundation for the Advancement of Pure Research (Z.W.O.).

0077-8923/81/0379-0235 $01.75/2 © 1981, NYAS

tion of greater age (and thus of higher levels of cognitive accomplishment, of greater metalinguistic knowledge, etc.) to the process of language acquisition really can be assessed only by looking at age and at order of acquisition separately, i.e., by looking at age differences in second-language acquisition, and by looking at the difference between first- and second-language acquisition in same-aged learners. Comparing child first-language learners with adult second-language learners, or even with elementary-school-aged second-language learners, as generally has been done, contributes very little clarity to the issue of the differences between first- and second-language acquisition.

In the present paper I will use the following approach to the problem of analyzing the differences between first- and second-language acquisition: I will present an analysis of the similarities and differences between older and younger second-language learners as a basis for discussing the effects of age on language acquisition. The second-language learners in all the age groups were the same on two major factors of importance: all spoke English as a first language, and all were learning their second language, Dutch, without access to significant amounts of formal tutoring.

Given the many sources of difference between first- and second-language acquisition enumerated above, in a sense interpretable findings emerge only if there are *no* differences between first- and second-language acquisition. If striking similarities between the processes of first- and second-language acquisition are found, then one must conclude that some determinant of the course of acquisition overrides the many sources of difference between first- and second-language acquisition. One might want to conclude, for instance, that the most important determinants of the course of language learning are the nature of the language being learned and the nature of the learning strategies available to the learners, and that, furthermore, there is no evidence for age or other sources of variation in those learning strategies.

THE STUDY

The data I will discuss here were collected in the course of a large-scale study of age difference in second-language-acquisition ability. The major results of that larger study have been reported.[2] However, the published data have been limited to relatively global measures of ability, and all have been directed to the question of age differences in speed of second-language acquisition. In the present paper I will look at the data from a few of the administered tests in a more detailed way, analyzing the order of acquisition of various structures for evidence of strategies of acquisition that might be similar or different across different groups of learners.

To place the present results in the context of the larger study, I will summarize those findings briefly. The age of the second-language learners was correlated highly *positively* with speed of acquisition for all components of second-language ability tested except pronunciation, for which there was no lasting age effect. In the course of approximately one year of second-language learning, which was all we could follow for the majority of the subjects, the youngest subjects approached, but often did not attain, the levels of second-language skill achieved within a few months by the older learners. The conclusion that older learners are more efficient and faster than younger ones at second-language acquisition (as at most other learning tasks) has been confirmed by a large number of studies of age differences in second-language acquisition (see Reference 2 for a review of these studies).

The Subjects

Two groups of English-speaking subjects were included in the study: monolingual English speakers who were just starting to learn Dutch (beginners), and English speakers who had been living in Holland and speaking Dutch for at least 18 months (advanced). The beginners were tested three times at four- to five-month intervals. The first session was held within six months of their arrival in Holland and within six weeks of their starting at school or work in a Dutch-language environment. The advanced subjects were tested only once. The beginners were distributed in the following way over the age groups: 10, age 3–5; 8, age 6–7; 13, age 8–10; 9, age 12–15; and 11 adults. There was some attrition in the course of the year, and a few subjects did not complete all the tests, leading to slight variability in the numbers actually reported on for the various tests.

For ease of comparison, the advanced subjects' scores will be presented in the results section as representing time 4, whereas the beginners' scores are presented for times 1, 2, and 3. The statistical comparisons across times all have been carried out using an independent groups design, since there was some attrition even in the beginners groups. All subjects were learning Dutch without significant amounts of formal training, from attending Dutch schools or working in Dutch-language environments.

The General Test Procedure

The subjects were tested individually, at home or at school, in a relaxed session lasting about 1½ hours. The test sessions were tape recorded for later checking or scoring. Both testers could speak both Dutch and English; one was a native Dutch speaker, the other a native English speaker.

The Translation Test

This was designed to tap English speakers' productive knowledge of Dutch syntax and morphology. It consisted of 60 sentences, given to the subjects in English with the instruction to translate them into Dutch. The sentences were chosen to tap Dutch structures that were intrinsically complex, or that differed from English in ways that could be expected to potentiate the occurrence of interference errors. As the test was not intended to assess vocabulary knowledge, subjects were given help with any Dutch lexical item they did not know. Subjects' knowledge of the correctly translated lexical item figured in the scoring only for pronouns, prepositions, conjunctions, and articles.

The sentences in the test ranged in length from 2 to 11 words; examples

TABLE 1

EXAMPLES OF SENTENCES AND THEIR SCORING
FROM THE TRANSLATION TEST

English Sentence	Dutch Translation	Examples of Categories Scored
We're going away	Wij gaan weg	word order, s-v-x
	* * * *	*
I'm going to Amsterdam tomorrow	Ik ga morgen naar Amsterdam	time-place word order
Lies put the cup down	Lies heeft het kopje neergezet	word order, s-aux-x-v article *het*
	* * * *	*
Lies gives bread to the ducks who are swimming in the canal	Lies geeft brood aan de eenden die in de gracht zwemmen	article *de* 2× relative pronoun *die* word order, main clause s-v-x word order, subordinate clause
Jan doesn't know if he wants to go	Jan weet niet of hij wil gaan	negation word order, main clause s-v-x word order, subordinate clause
I was bicycling to school when I saw him	Ik fietste naar school toen ik hem zag	article ϕ conjunction *toen* word order, main clause s-v-x word order, subordinate clause

of sentences of low-, intermediate-, and high-difficulty level are given in TABLE 1, along with correct translations into Dutch and indications of how they would have been scored. The sentences were administered individually by the native English-speaking tester, who gave as much help and encouragement as possible. The sentences were presented in ascending order of difficulty, so that testing could be stopped within a few sentences after those with which the subjects had great difficulty. Thus, at the initial test sessions, especially with the younger subjects, many sentences were not even attempted.

Scoring was carried out by assessing each occurrence of a set of 23 target structures as correct $(+)$, absent (0), or incorrect $(-)$. The most common alternative forms also were tabulated, to see if there was some pattern of errors. Clearly, some structures (such as person marking on verbs) occurred much more frequently than others, such as modals or adjective agreement.

The structures that were tested for are listed in TABLE 2, together with some information about the grammar of these structures in Dutch. Since this was an initial study of English speakers' acquisition of Dutch, the selection of Dutch structure was less than perfectly systematic.

RESULTS

Complementizers, Conjunctions, and Relative Pronouns

The first set of structures we will consider consists of the mechanisms for linking clauses, complementizers, conjunctions, and relative pronouns, the most common of which were tapped by items in the translation test. Medians of total scores for the subjects in the five age groups at the four test sessions are given in TABLE 3. It can be seen that this category reflects the findings from the entire test in that older subjects generally performed better and age differences tended to decrease with greater exposure to the second language, as the youngest subjects caught up with the older ones.

Despite differences in speed of acquisition, an impression of great similarity among the learners of different ages is obtained from looking at the nature of the errors made in the different groups. Consider, for instance, the opposition toen/wanneer (past vs. present or future tense), which is relatively difficult for English speakers to learn, though its basis in Dutch grammar is quite regular (see TABLE 2). The first stage in the acquisition of these forms for our subjects (see TABLE 4) consisted of finding some way of expressing temporal conjunction in Dutch—often, using a phonologically adapted form borrowed from English, such as */vɛn/, */van/, or */If/ in all cases. Acquisition of the correct form wanneer or als ("if," in free variation with wanneer in many temporal contexts) usually supplanted the quasi-Dutch form, both in contexts where wanneer was correct and in contexts where toen was required. Some subjects, however, persisted in using */vɛn/ or other forms in the contexts requiring toen, thus making the required distinction before knowing the correct marking for it (see Reference 3 for examples of a similar phenomenon in morphological acquisition). Lack of insight into the grammatical basis for the toen/wanneer distinction is revealed by the persistence of occasional errors substituting wanneer for toen even in the more advanced subjects who usually used toen correctly. Age comparisons in TABLE 4 reveal the following:

TABLE 2

STRUCTURES ANALYZED

Dutch Form	English Translation	Description of Use
dat	"that"	Complementizer. Obligatorily present
of	"if," "whether"	Introducing indirect questions; Note that the conditional conjunction "if" is *als,* not *of*
wanneer	"when," "whenever"	Temporal conjunction, introduces clauses in present or future tense only
toen	"when"	Temporal conjunction, introduces clauses in past tenses only
omdat	"because"	Causal conjunction; alternate form *want* with same meaning is less frequent, introduces clauses with main-clause verb-2 rather than subordinate-clause verb-final word order
dat	"who" or "which"	Relative pronoun, subject or direct object form refers to singular neuter nouns only. Obligatorily present
die	"who" or "which"	Relative pronoun, subject or direct object form; refers to singular masculine/ feminine or any plural nouns. Obligatorily present. Note that no case distinctions are made and no animacy distinction for subject or direct object
een	"a"	Indefinite singular article
het	"the"	Definite singular article, used only with neuter nouns
de	"the"	Definite article used with singular masculine/ feminine and all plural nouns

1. Subjects in all age groups used the (seemingly childlike) strategy of producing a quasi form, though some subjects in all groups never used this strategy.

2. Most subjects in all age groups learned the toen/wanneer distinction eventually, though in all age groups a minority continued to neutralize this distinction.

3. The neutralization of toen/wanneer persisted longest for the adults.

4. The maintenance of the toen/wanneer distinction in the absence of knowledge of the lexical item *toen* was most marked and persistent for the youngest age group.

A further point of interest in the data emerges from subjects' translation of "because": two six- to seven-year-olds used */vɛn/ at the first test session, and a few subjects in all groups used *als* or *wanneer* to translate "because." *Als, wanneer,* and to a lesser extent the quasi-form */vɛn/ seem to function as "imperial conjunctions" for English speakers learning Dutch. Subjects in all age groups, furthermore, used *als* incorrectly for *of,*

TABLE 3

MEDIANS ON CONJUNCTIONS, COMPLEMENTIZERS, AND RELATIVE
PRONOUNS FOR THE FIVE AGE GROUPS (MAXIMUM = 14)

Age Group	Time			
	I	II	III	IV
3–5	0.0	0.3	3.0	
6–7	0.1	2.0	4.0	11.0
8–10	3.0	4.0	9.0	10.0
12–15	6.0	9.6	12.0	10.8
adult	4.5	5.9	5.0	10.7

introducing indirect questions. This was one of the most persistent errors; at time 4, only 8 of the 23 subjects consistently were using *of,* and 12 substituted *als* for all cases where *of* was required.

Two problems arise in mastering the complementizers and relative pronouns: learning that they must be supplied (unlike English, where they can be deleted), and learning the correct forms. TABLE 5 shows that subjects were much less likely to delete relative pronouns incorrectly, but that accuracy in supplying the obligatory complementizers took many months of learning.

The form of the complementizer *dat* offered no problem to English speakers, understandably. If supplied, it was correct. The relative pronouns, on the other hand, caused considerable confusion. The Dutch system is relatively simple: subject and object relative pronouns agree with singular antecedent nouns in gender, *dat* for neuter and *die* for masculine/

TABLE 4

STAGES OF ACQUISITION OF TEMPORAL CONJUNCTIONS *

Time	Group	n	I — No Attempt	II — /If/, /ven/, /van/ in All Contexts	III — Wanneer Correct, Other Form or ø for toen	IV — Als/ Wanneer in All Contexts	V — Wanneer Correct, Toen > 60% Correct	VI — All Correct
I	3–5	7	100.0					
	6–7	8	62.5	25.0	12.5			
	8–10	9	44.5	55.5				
	12–15	8	12.5	25.0		25.0	12.5	25.0
	adult	11	18.0	36.0		45.4		
II	3–5	7	57.1	28.6	14.2			
	6–7	5	40.0		40.0	20.0		
	8–10	8	25.0	12.5	12.5	50.0		
	12–15	6		16.7		16.7	16.7	50.0
	adult	11		18.2	18.2	63.6		
III	3–5	6	50.0		33.3			16.7
	6–7	4	25.0	25.0		25.0		25.0
	8–10	6		16.7	16.7	33.3		33.3
	12–15	6				16.7	16.7	66.7
	adult	11		9.1		72.7	9.1	9.1
IV	6–7	4			25.0			75.0
	8–10	5				20.0		80.0
	12–15	5				20.0		80.0
	adult	9				22.2		77.8

* Entries in the table represent percentages of subjects within each group.

feminine nouns. The gender of the noun is identifiable from the definite article. Plural antecedents take *die.* The English-speaking subjects tended to take one of two approaches to finding a relative: using *dat,* a choice presumably supported by the presence of *dat* as complementizer and deictic in Dutch as well as by its use as a relative in some contexts, or using *wie* (who), the interrogative pronoun that can be used as a relative pronoun only for animate objects of prepositions. TABLE 6 gives more specific data on strategies of acquisition of relative pronouns; these are arranged roughly from less to more sophisticated, but many were relatively idiosyn-

TABLE 5

PERCENTAGE OF SUBJECTS IN EACH AGE GROUP WHO CONSISTENTLY SUPPLIED OR OMITTED THE COMPLEMENTIZER AND THE RELATIVE PRONOUN

		Complementizer *dat*		Relative Pronouns	
	n	Consistently Omitted	Consistently Supplied	Consistently Omitted	Consistently Supplied
3–5	7	—	—	—	—
6–7	8	12.5	—	25.0	—
8–10	9	0.0	33.3	0.0	33.3
12–15	8	0.0	87.5	0.0	87.5
adult	11	36.4	54.5	9.1	63.6
3–5	7	14.3	28.6	0.0	0.0
6–7	5	40.0	0.0	0.0	40.0
8–10	8	25.0	25.0	0.0	62.5
12–15	6	16.7	83.3	0.0	83.3
adult	11	36.4	63.6	0.0	90.9
3–5	6	16.7	33.3	16.7	16.7
6–7	4	25.0	50.0	0.0	50.0
8–10	6	0.0	83.3	0.0	67.7
12–15	6	16.7	83.3	0.0	83.3
adult	11	27.3	63.6	0.0	72.7
6–7	4	0.0	75.0	0.0	25.0
8–10	5	0.0	100.0	0.0	100.0
12–15	5	0.0	80.0	0.0	100.0
adult	9	0.0	66.7	0.0	100.0

cratic and infrequent. It is striking here that subjects in all age groups used *wie* as their only relative pronoun; this clear example of an interference error (the sentences offered all had animate antecedents, so *who* would have been the correct English relative pronoun) did not seem to be more frequent among older subjects. Given the relative infrequency of neuter singular nouns, the "relative pronoun=*die*" strategy would be quite effective in producing correct sentences, and indeed many subjects in all age groups persisted in this strategy throughout the period examined.

TABLE 6

STRATEGIES OF ACQUISITION OF RELATIVE PRONOUNS *

Time	Group	No Interpretable Pattern	wie Everywhere	dat Everywhere	wat Everywhere	dat = Singular	wie & die	die = Singular	die Everywhere	die & dat	All Correct
I	3–5	100.0									
	6–7	87.5	12.5								
	8–10	44.4		11.1		44.4					
	12–15	12.5	37.5	25.0					12.5	12.5	
	adult	36.4		18.2			27.3			18.2	
II	3–5	57.1	14.3		14.3					14.3	
	6–7	40.0	60.0								
	8–10	25.0	25.0					37.5			12.5
	12–15	16.7	16.7	33.3					33.3		
	adult	0.0	36.4	18.2			9.1	9.1	18.2		9.1
III	3–5	66.7	16.7						16.7		
	6–7	25.0	25.0						50.0		
	8–10		16.7	16.7					50.0		
	12–15		16.7				33.3		33.3	16.7	16.7
	adult		54.5	27.3			9.1		9.1		
IV	6–7	25.0		25.0					50.0		
	8–10						20.0		80.0		
	12–15						20.0		80.0		20.0
	adult		11.1	22.2					66.7		

* Entries in the table represent percentages of subjects within each group.

The Determiner System

The major problems for English speakers in learning the Dutch determiner system are the following: (1) Learning that no article is used in Dutch in several contexts where one is required in English. These contexts include a number of common idiomatic expressions (e.g., *op ø tafel* for "on the table") and some plural indefinite cases (*Heb jij ø zusters* for "Do you have any sisters?"). (2) Learning to mark gender on definite articles preceding singular nouns. This involves two steps—learning that gender must be marked and learning which nouns are neuter (for which the definite article is *het*) and which are masculine/feminine (for which the definite article is *de*). A majority of nouns are masculine/feminine; the neuter nouns used in the translation test were selected to be identifiable morphologically as neuter, so that correct use of the determiner *het* would not depend solely on subjects' vocabulary knowledge.

The subjects acquired correct use of the indefinite article *een* quite easily, as would be predicted from its simplicity and similarity to English (see TABLE 7). All but the youngest used *een* as soon as they used any

TABLE 7

MEDIANS ON THE CATEGORY DETERMINERS FOR
THE FIVE AGE GROUPS AT FOUR TIMES
(MAXIMUM = 37)

Age Group	Time			
	I	II	III	IV
3–5	0.0	9.5	14.0	
6–7	8.0	12.0	17.5	23.5
8–10	9.0	15.0	21.0	23.0
12–15	21.0	22.0	21.5	28.0
adult	14.0	21.0	21.0	26.0

nouns. Similarly, acquisition of the plural definite *de* was quite fast, except for a few subjects who persisted in using the deictic *die* for plural (as well as for singular) definite.

In acquiring the singular definite article, the most popular first strategy adopted (see TABLE 8) was universal use of *de*. This strategy, which does in fact produce a fairly low level of errors, still was used by some of the most advanced subjects. Other subjects moved on to a seemingly random use of both *de* and *het,* whereas others started to identify words that required *het* but still made errors of using *de* with some *het* words. A few subjects used the opposite strategy, of using *het* too widely but never making a false positive *de* error. Only in the highest age groups did any subjects attain even 90% accuracy on the *de/het* distinction. No strategy of acquisition was exclusive to any particular age group; the only differences among

TABLE 8

STRATEGIES IN THE ACQUISITION OF THE DETERMINER SYSTEM *

Time	Group	Not Scorable	de = Definite Singular	die for de	het & de Mixed	het correct, de Mixed	de Correct, het Mixed	de & het Largely Correct
I	3–5	83.3	16.7					
	6–7	60.0	40.0					
	8–10	33.3	66.7	33.3				
	12–15	12.5	37.5				50.0	
	adult	0.0	36.4		27.3		27.3	9.1
II	3–5	42.9	57.1					
	6–7	0.0	60.0					
	8–10		57.1		40.0			
	12–15		83.3		42.9			
	adult		45.4		18.2		27.3	16.7
III	3–5	50.0	50.0					
	6–7	25.0	75.0					
	8–10		16.7				83.3	16.7
	12–15		50.0				33.3	
	adult		18.2		18.2	9.1	36.4	18.2
IV	6–7						100.0	
	8–10		40.0		20.0		40.0	
	12–15		40.0		40.0		20.0	
	adult		22.2		22.2	22.2	22.2	11.1

* Entries in the table represent percentages of each age group.

the age groups were those related to the faster acquisition by the older groups.

Word Order

A final analysis of age differences in strategies of acquisition looks at acquisition of word order in Dutch sentences (see TABLE 9). Dutch word order has been identified as basically subject-object-verb (S-O-V),[4] with an obligatory movement of the inflected verb to second position in main clauses. The preverbal position in main clauses normally is filled by the subject, though any focused constituent can take that position and adverbials quite commonly do so. In this case, the subject takes the position to the right of the verb. Children acquiring Dutch as a first language typically adopt a verb-final order in early utterances; this has been explained by the prevalence in speech to children of utterances containing modals or other auxiliaries, in which the stressed, main verb is sentence final.[5]

TABLE 9

MEDIAN SCORES ON WORD ORDER FOR THE FIVE AGE
GROUPS AT THE FOUR TIMES (MAXIMUM = 49)

Age Group	Time			
	I	II	III	IV
3–5	0.0	10.0	26.0	
6–7	5.0	9.0	33.0	43.5
8–10	18.0	32.0	45.5	41.0
12–15	35.0	44.0	47.0	47.0
adult	29.0	34.0	37.0	42.0

Another difficulty for English speakers acquiring Dutch has to do with the relative order of place and time adverbials; though these are typically ordered place-time in English ("I'm going to Amsterdam tomorrow"), in Dutch the order is reversed ("Ik ga morgen naar Amsterdam"). A special problem is posed by the existence of a number of postpositions, typically expressing direction and identical in form to prepositions of place (e.g., *Hij loopt in het park* "He's walking in the park" vs. *Hij loopt het park in* "He walks into the park").

The categories of word order scored included the following: (1) subject-verb inversion in interrogatives (V-S-X); (2) word order in S-V main clauses with only one other constituent; (3) word order in S-V main clauses with more than one adverbial or noun phrase following the verb; (4) word order in main clauses with an auxiliary verb, forcing sentence final position for the main verb, and an additional constituent; (5) word order in main clauses with a preposed adverbial; (6) relative order of time and place; (7) placement of negation markers relative to the verb; (8) verb-final order in subordinate clauses; and (9) postpositions. The percentage of subjects in each group who achieved mastery of each of these categories of word-order rules is given in TABLE 10. Questions were the easiest category, followed by the S-V-X main clause type, which matches English word order. The greater difficulty of the S-V-X-X category arises from errors in ordering the two postverbal constituents. Surprisingly for those who expect word order to be influenced primarily by the first language, both the verb-final rule in sentences with auxiliaries and the S-V inversion rule following preposing of an adverbial were acquired relatively easily. The time-place order for adverbials, on the other hand, was acquired by only a minority of subjects; most persisted in using the English place-time order. This was even harder than the late-acquired postpositions, perhaps because a mistake in time-place does not change meaning, whereas a mistake in placement of postposition alters a directional to a locative meaning. Verb-final order in subordinate clauses generally was acquired somewhat later than verb-final main clauses with auxiliaries. Interestingly, some subjects in all age groups simplified the problems of word order for themselves either by reformulating many sentences so as to insert auxiliaries, thus enforcing on many clauses an S-aux-X-V order, or by preposing a constituent, giving many main clauses the X-V-S-X form. Using an idiosyncratic canonical order for main clauses was a strategy adopted by a minority of subjects in all age groups.

DISCUSSION

This comparison of older and younger learners on strategies for acquiring specific features of Dutch syntax reveals more similarities than differences across age. The major age differences are quantitative: older learners were much faster, and therefore skipped (or seemed to skip) some of the very early stages of acquisition. However, the majority of hypotheses adopted and errors made were found for subjects in all age groups.

The one possible exception to this conclusion emerges from the results on the *toen/wanneer* distinction. The youngest subjects marked subordinate clauses in the past tense differently from those in present or future much earlier in their course of acquisition than did older subjects. This finding suggests that the younger subjects may have been more open to the possibility that this distinction is marked grammatically than were the older subjects, who perhaps had acquired more convincing information from English that this distinction need not be marked.

Comparison of older and younger learners reveals a general pattern of similarity. Comparison of any of these age groups to native Dutch children probably would reveal a much greater disparity. Some of the errors found in the English speakers of all age groups—e.g., use of *wie* as a relative pronoun, reversal of order of time and place adverbials, and the use of verb-second order in subordinate clauses—have never been noted in native speakers. Other errors, however, such as overgeneralization of *de*

TABLE 10

PERCENTAGES OF SUBJECTS IN DIFFERENT GROUPS WHO HAD ACHIEVED 75%
OR BETTER SCORES ON THE VARIOUS WORD ORDERS

Time	Group	Questions	S-V-X	S-V-Adv	S-Aux-X-V	Adv-V-S	Time-Place	Negation	Subordinate Clause	Post-position
I	3–5	20.0								
	6–7	25.0				25.0		12.5		
	8–10	66.7	44.4	22.2	22.2			11.1		
	12–15	87.5	87.5	22.2	87.5	55.6		44.4	33.3	9.1
	adult	100.0	63.6	55.6	54.5	45.4		27.3	18.1	
				9.1						
II	3–5	42.9	42.9					14.3		
	6–7	40.0	60.0		28.6	20.0		20.0		16.7
	8–10	100.0	80.0	12.5	40.0	50.0	20.0	50.0	12.5	
	12–15	100.0	100.0	50.0	66.7	83.3		66.7	83.3	9.1
	adult	100.0	91.9	27.3	54.5	78.8		27.3	36.4	
III	3–5	50.0	50.0	16.7	50.0	33.3		16.7		
	6–7	75.0	75.0	75.0	75.0	50.0	25.0	75.0	50.0	
	8–10	100.0	100.0	50.0	100.0	83.3		100.0	83.3	
	12–15	100.0	100.0	66.7	100.0	83.3		100.0	83.3	
	adult	100.0	81.8	45.4	81.8	72.7	45.4	27.3	9.1	
IV	6–7	100.0	100.0	75.0	75.0	100.0		50.0	100.0	25.0
	8–10	100.0	100.0	100.0	100.0	100.0	20.0	80.0	80.0	60.0
	12–15	100.0	100.0	80.0	100.0	100.0	40.0	100.0	80.0	40.0
	adult	88.9	88.9	88.9	100.0	88.9	33.3	88.8	55.5	0.0

to *het* words as singular definite article, overgeneralization of *die* as relative pronoun, and overuse of verb-final order in main clauses, are quite typical of young native Dutch speakers. The similarity in these errors across first- and second-language learners does not prove, however, that the two groups of learners are following similar courses of acquisition. A given error can be produced as the result of very different hypotheses or failures of knowledge. Similarity in forms produced cannot in itself be taken as proof of identity in underlying systems.

ACKNOWLEDGMENT

The author would like to express her appreciation to Marian Hoefnagel-Höhle, who collaborated in the collection of the data discussed here.

REFERENCES

1. ERVIN-TRIPP, S. 1974. Is second language learning like the first? TESOL Q. **8:** 111–127.
2. SNOW, C. & M. HOEFNAGEL-HÖHLE. 1978. The critical period for language acquisition: evidence from second language learning. Child Dev. **49:** 1114–1128.
3. SNOW, C., N. S. SMITH & M. HOEFNAGEL-HÖHLE. 1980. The acquisition of some Dutch morphological rules. J. Child Lang. **7:** 539–554.
4. KOSTER, J. 1975. Dutch as a SOV language. *In* Linguistics in the Netherlands 1972–1973. A. Kraak, Ed.: 165–177. Van Gorcum. Assen & Amsterdam, the Netherlands.
5. KLEIN, R. 1974. Word Order: Dutch Children and Their Mothers. Publication No. 9. Institute for General Linguistics. University of Amsterdam. Amsterdam, the Netherlands.)

SOME USES FOR SECOND-LANGUAGE-LEARNING RESEARCH

Vivian J. Cook

Department of Language and Linguistics
University of Essex
Colchester CO4 3SQ, England

To many people the uses of second-language-learning research are beside the point; they feel it is an area that can stand on its own feet as an academic subject with its own internal rationale unsupported by other disciplines. To others, however, the interest in second-language-learning research is chiefly in its potential for application. This paper adopts the latter of these two positions and looks at two pieces of research with possible relevance outside second-language (L2) learning itself in the fields of second-language teaching and developmental psychology.

Let us start by looking at the relationship between L2 research and language teaching. There seem to be three main periods in the development of L2 research, each of which has had a slightly different relationship to language teaching. The first period ran from the the 1950s to the mid-60s and was dominated by the ideas of language-teaching theorists such as Robert Lado and Nelson Brooks.[1,2] Because of this, the ideas found a ready application in the classroom and were responsible for the flowering of the audiolingual method, many of whose techniques such as pattern practice still are found in language teaching today. The second period covered the mid-60s to the mid-70s. During this time, L2 learning began to be investigated directly but still was interpreted in terms of a methodology and conceptual apparatus drawn from first-language (L1) acquisition, such as the importance of syntax and the concept of the systematic nature of learner languages, expressed for example by McNeill for L1 acquisition,[3] and utilized in L2 learning most importantly by Selinker as "interlanguage." [4] This period had a predominantly negative effect on language teaching. Teachers were told that their ideas of language learning were inadequate, but they were not given any coherent methodology to put in the place of their audiolingual techniques—unless it were to abandon their students to unedited spontaneous language so that their natural learning abilities could operate effectively, a view associated with Newmark and Reibel; [5] few, however, accepted this alternative. The third period runs from about 1975 and is called the period of "models," even if few of the proposals that have been made are models in a scientific sense. While proposals such as the monitor model have stimulated considerable discussion among researchers,[6] in Europe at any rate, they still have had little impact on the average language teacher, nor have they led to a coherent overall theory of teaching. Occasionally the research can be used to justify

251

0077-8923/81/0379-0251 $01.75/2 © 1981, NYAS

existing teaching techniques: grammatical explanation now can be justified in some sense as exploiting the student's monitor; communication games can be claimed to help the students' communicative strategies. But this largely is *post hoc* justification of standard techniques, not the discovery of new ones. Indeed the major innovations in techniques have come from the wave of alternative methods based on a quite different humanistic tradition, such as the "silent way" suggested by Gattegno or "confluent language teaching" described by Galyean.[7,8]

Why is this so? One reason may be the emphasis that L2 learning still places on syntax. Undoubtedly the main movement in language teaching in Europe has been toward a specification of the learner's communicative needs: the syllabus no longer is specified in terms of grammatical rules and lists of vocabulary and situations but in terms of the functions for which the learners need to use language, the notions they wish to express, the topics about which they want to talk, and so on, best exemplified in the work of the Council of Europe.[9] Most of the current models of L2 learning have little to say about this. Partly this is because they mostly accept the centrality of syntax; the monitor model for instance only seems meaningful in terms of syntax. But however sophisticated our discussions of syntax may be, the language teacher may dismiss them as irrelevant; it simply doesn't matter how the learners acquire syntax, as their main task is learning to communicate. To a great extent, L2 research has not caught up with the change in the paradigm from syntax toward language as a system of communication, found in present-day L1 research and L2 teaching. It might seem perhaps that the strategy model or the conversational analysis model has more to say to the teacher, because they seem to deal with wider aspects than syntax. At a general level this must be true, and the idea of a communicative strategy goes some way toward justifying such techniques as communication games and role play. But more specific guidance is still lacking. This may be because of a certain incompatibility between the two approaches. Language teachers talk of "language functions," L2 researchers of "language strategies." This goes deeper than just terminology. To the teacher, a language function often is something that can be isolated and taught separately; it is an item like a word or a grammatical structure. To the L2 researcher, the function exists within the negotiation of conversation; each participant has certain strategies for conducting the conversation and these have to be modified continually by the interaction with the other person's strategies. The L2 strategies research has a dynamic concept of conversation as a process of give and take; L2 teaching has a static structural approach.

How can these two be brought together? One possible point of contact is the idea of speech acts. Communicative syllabi make extensive use of this idea in one shape or another but usually do not attempt to link speech acts to the negotiation of conversation. Strategy models of L2 learning also require some idea of the purpose of the participants in a conversation. It seems that it might be fruitful to attempt to reconcile these two approaches.

There are, however, grave problems. The initial problem is that the basis for considering speech acts within conversation has been ignored within linguistics until recently and only now are we starting to see discussions by such linguists as Levinson and Ferrara as to the feasibility of using the idea of speech acts in the analysis of conversation.[10,11] Nor have speech acts been studied very extensively in the psychological work on the comprehension of speech, apart from the handful of pioneering experiments by Jarvella and Collas and by Clark and his associates.[12,13] The literature devoted to speech acts in L2 learning is equally sparse and largely consists of a general article by Schmidt and Richards and some experiments with Spanish-speaking learners of English by Rintell and by Walters.[14–16] It seems time then to try out some basic work in this area and to report on work in progress with speech acts in L2 learning.

The first simple point to be established was that speech acts did have some psychological reality to L2 learners. This was tested with a small-scale experiment in which 16 Spanish speakers who had been learning English for four months had to distinguish between two different speech acts for the same syntactic structure. They heard declarative sentences, such as "the floor's dirty," and interrogative sentences, such as "Have you got a hankie?," embedded in dialogues and were given a choice of paraphrases expressing the speech act meaning; for declaratives, they chose between a request and a statement; for interrogatives, between a request and a question. They heard two dialogues, each of which had two versions in which four test sentences had particular illocutionary force. The dialogues were rotated so that each version was heard the same number of times; thus each student gave 8 responses. The results were that the students were correct in assigning speech acts to the sentences 73% of the time, i.e., 93 correct responses out of 128. Even at this low level of English, learners have some idea of speech acts. This hardly goes very far, and it was decided to investigate one aspect of speech acts in more detail—how the learners knew that one speech act was intended rather than another. Clark has described six of the factors involved.[17] In the present research, it was decided to look at the linguistic context. For the only reason that listeners know that "Have you got a hankie?" is a request or a question is the context in dialogues such as those used in the preceding experiment. One aspect of linguistic context is the idea of adjacency pairs developed by Harvey Sacks and his associates.[18] An adjacency pair consists of two linked turns in conversation, usually occurring consecutively but sometimes separated. One example is question and answer, "What's the capital of France?"—"Paris," or request and acknowledgment, "A ticket to London please"—"Okay." Looked at in terms of speech-act assignment, the adjacency pair ties down some of the possible assignments: we know that a turn that follows a question is likely to be an answer. So adjacency pairs are one of the contextual factors that help us to assign a speech act to a sentence.

How can this be linked to L2 learning? The first need was to establish that these pairs have some reality to the learner. The same test group was used, who had now been studying for five months and numbered 17. The method consisted of written dialogues in which the subjects had to fill in halves of adjacency pairs, the other halves being supplied. One dialogue supplied first halves—three statements such as "This soup isn't very nice" and three questions such as "Do you know John?"—and the subjects had to fill in the second halves. The other dialogue supplied second halves—three reactions such as "Really?" and three responses such as "a medium size"—and the subjects had to give the first halves. The results were that 90% of the subject's sentences formed possible adjacency pairs in English: only 16 out of 204 answers were impossible, 4 answers being blank (a possible adjacency pair was defined as one that could occur in English even if it was not the one that had been anticipated). First halves were slightly more difficult for the learners to devise; 13 out of the 16 mistakes were first halves. These results suggest that the learners even at this stage had a well-developed awareness of adjacency-pair relationships in English. A second experiment went on to test the hypothesis that adjacency pairs affect long-term memory; in other words, the listener may store not just the meaning of the sentence, as Sacks suggests,[19] but also some record of the environment in which it occurred. The same learners were given a cued recall task in which they first heard short dialogues and then were given cue sentences and asked to supply the next sentence after each cue. Half the time the cue sentence was the first part of an adjacency pair and the subjects had to supply the second part; the rest of the time, the cue sentence was the second part of the pair and so the subjects had to supply the opening part of the next pair. There were two dialogues, each with four test items, making eight for each subject. This time the results were scored slightly differently since the learners could be divided into two subgroups, one of which—the "higher" group—had been studying in England for an average of six months, the other, "lower" group having been there for four months (there were nine in the higher and eight in the lower group). The overall results were that the subjects remembered 44% of the sentences within adjacency pairs (30 out of 68) and only 24% across adjacency pairs (16 out of 68); the lower group scored 25% within pairs (9 out of 32) and 16% across pairs (5 out of 32); the higher group scored 58% within pairs (21 out of 36) and 31% across pairs (11 out of 36). The numbers involved are too small to regard the result as significant, but it does suggest that a more elaborate experiment may succeed in proving the implication not only that adjacency pairs are stored together in memory but also that the capacity for this improves very rapidly in the early stages of learning a second language.

So it seems that there may be useful results to be gained by pursuing this line of research integrating speech acts with L2 learning in specific ways. One now can say at least that it is not an entirely arbitrary whim to use speech acts and adjacency pairs in second-language-teaching methodology since they appear to have some reality to the learner. Supposing this can be established more positively, the next stages of application are to establish which speech acts and which adjacency pairs are important and to examine the tricky problem of whether these are transferred from one language to another. This type of work can form the basis for syllabi based on actual information about the use of language in conversation; it can define the speech acts and adjacency pairs that are needed and suggest which of them have to be stressed. Another level of application is through teaching techniques. The recognition of speech acts as important to learning means that we need to examine the demands of the classroom and the techniques through which speech acts can be taught. It may be, for instance, that the virtue of pattern practice is not the learning of grammatical structures, as its advocates supposed, but the learning of an adjacency-pair relationship between the input the student hears and the output he or she has to produce.[20] Indeed this line of thinking has already led to two textbooks for teaching English as a foreign language: one, *Using Intonation,* teaches intonation as a part of conversational interaction and relates the choice of tone to the speech function of the sentence; [21] the other, *People and Places,* uses a syllabus expressed in interactional categories and relies on a teaching technique called a conversation exchange in which the students build up chains of adjacency pairs in the classroom.[22] Thus, even if the applications are broad and general, this type of research is already yielding fruit.

Let us now turn to the other area of potential application of L2 research—developmental psychology. Here L2 research can make a distinctive contribution to one or two areas. Take the example of cognitive development. Here it is notoriously difficult to separate the effects of language and cognition: the phenomenon that we are explaining as language development may in fact be due to cognitive development, and vice versa. It would be highly useful if we could, so to speak, disengage the two processes of language and cognitive development and look at people whose level of thinking is out of step with their level of language. One way of doing this is by hypnotic age regression, but this has a number of methodological problems. A more practical way of disengaging the two processes is in L2 learning, where one can study people whose cognitive processes usually are at a higher level of operation than their language. One instance is syntactic acquisition: some point of syntactic development might require that the child first acquire a certain cognitive level; the adult L2 learner is already there. For example, there is a stage in the order of acquisition of "before" and "after" where the child uses a strategy that the order of events in the sentence must mirror the order of events in the real world, the order of mention strategy described by Clark.[23] The child can learn to use these properly only when he can disconnect linguistic from real-world order. Is this then a stage of cognitive development or of language development? This has been tested with adult second-language learners, and the results were that they interpreted "before" correctly but used an order-of-mention strategy for "after," the equivalent to Clark's B1 stage.[24] It may be that L2 learners also start with an order-of-mention strategy, which they gradually overcome. So it is not linked to cognitive development but to language development. However, not too much weight should be attached to this because, like morpheme acquisition studies, it may be simply an idiosyncrasy of some grammatical items in English rather than any general principle.

However, let us look at a more precise point of cognitive development that can be tested through L2 research. This is the development of memory in the child. Though much remains controversial, two broad statements can be made about memory development; one is that the capacity of the child's memory increases with age; the other is that the child only gradually acquires adult memory strategies.[25] One question is the extent to which memory is transferred to a new language. So far as short-term memory is concerned, it seems that not only is a large part of the capacity transferred but also the adult use of encoding through sounds. With long-term memory, there seems less transfer, and even learners at an advanced stage do not show clustering effects of vocabulary.[24] Let us take one particular memory strategy, namely, rehearsal, and see if this is transferred from one language to another. The earlier research with native children suggested that rehearsal developed rather late in the child;[26] children will rehearse if they are instructed to but will not do so spontaneously.[27] However, attention now is focused more on the different ways of rehearsal; Craik and Watkins suggest within a levels-of-processing model that "maintenance" rehearsal is less effective than "elaborative" rehearsal.[28] The child therefore may not be learning how to rehearse so to speak but learning different ways of rehearsing. Ornstein and Naus have shown in several experiments that younger children rehearse by repeating each item they hear several times, a repeating strategy;[30] older children rehearse by combining several of the items they have heard together, a combining strategy. The main developmental shift therefore is from a repeating strategy to a combining strategy.

But is this a question of cognitive or of language development? It might be that you need a certain cognitive level before you can use a combining strategy effectively, or it might be that you need a certain amount of language development in a particular language, as for instance Stolz and Tiffany found occurs with the syntagmatic paradigmatic shift in word associations.[30] Since adult L2 learners are cognitively mature but at a low level of language, here again L2 research may provide the crucial test. An experiment therefore was carried out to see if rehearsal strategies are transferred to a memory task in a new language rather than relearned from the beginning. Nine Spanish-speaking learners of English were used, who had been in England for six months. The task was modeled on that used by Orstein, Naus, and Liberty.[31] The materials were four lists of 12 monosyllabic high-frequency English nouns, recorded with a five-second pause after each item. At the end of each list, the students had two minutes to write down as many words as they could remember. But they were also asked to rehearse aloud as they listened, and this was recorded. The subjects were given examples of repeating and combining strategies but were not told which to use. The results were that the students on average repeated an item 6 times per list and combined an item 18 times. Taken individually, only one of the nine students used the repeating strategy more often than the combining strategy. Put another way, out of the 36 sets of rehearsal recorded, 33 had more combining responses than repeating responses, 3 had more repeating responses ($p < 0.05$, sign test). This suggests that the combining strategy is indeed transferred to a new language, that it is part of cognitive rather than language development. The loophole that is left unfilled is whether these subjects used combining in Spanish, since it is possible, even if highly implausible, that Spanish speakers do not use combining strategies in Spanish and learn it specifically for using English. But putting aside this faint possibility, we do seem to have shown that the development of rehearsal strategies is indeed dependent on cognitive development; adults learning a second language rehearse in an adult way, not a childlike way. In this case, as with "before" and "after," L2 research can be used as a kind of touchstone to test ideas in developmental psychology.

To conclude, this paper has traced some of the links between L2 research and the areas of language teaching and developmental psychology. Whatever the faults of earlier researchers in second-language learning, they saw themselves in a broader context. In the present period of L2 research, we are in danger of isolating ourselves from our neighbors and of underestimating the importance of our potential contribution outside our own area. We should not forget that our research can have at least two far-ranging consequences. One is as a contribution to the study of the human mind, because of the unique nature of L2 learning. The other is as a contribution to the learning and teaching of languages; language teaching is a worldwide enterprise. Let us not forget that the insights from our field of inquiry can influence for better or worse the lives of vast numbers of people.

ACKNOWLEDGMENT

I am grateful to Paul Meara and Fred Chambers for substantial comments on this paper, many of which have been incorporated.

REFERENCES

1. LADO, R. 1964. Language Teaching: A Scientific Approach. McGraw Hill Book Company. New York, N.Y.
2. BROOKS, N. 1960. Language and Language Learning: Theory and Practice. Harcourt Brace Jovanovich, Inc. New York, N.Y.
3. McNEILL, D. 1966. Developmental linguistics. In The Genesis of Language. F. Smith & G. A. Miller, Eds.: 19–84. MIT Press. Cambridge, Mass.
4. SELINKER, L. 1972. Interlanguage. IRAL 10: 139–152.
5. NEWMARK, L. & D. REIBEL. 1968. Necessity and sufficiency in language learning. IRAL 6: 145–161.
6. KRASHEN, S. D. 1977. The monitor model for adult second language per-

formance. *In* Viewpoints on English as a Second Language. M. Burt, H. Dulay & M. Finocchario, Eds.: 152–161. Regents. New York, N.Y.

7. GATTEGNO, C. 1972. Teaching Foreign Languages in School: The Silent Way. Educational Solutions. New York, N.Y.

8. GALYEAN, B. 1976. Gestalt theory: new wine in old skins. *In* The Live Classroom. G. I. Brown, Ed.: 206–220. Penguin Books. Harmondsworth, England.

9. TRIM, J. L. M., R. RICHTERICH, J. A. VAN EK & D. A. WILKINS. 1980. Systems Development in Adult Language Learning. Pergamon Press. Oxford, England.

10. LEVINSON, S. C. The essential inadequacies of speech act models of dialogue. *In* Possibilities and Limitations of Pragmatics. H. Parret, M. Sbisa & J. Verscheuren, Eds. John Benjamins B.V. Amsterdam, the Netherlands. (In press.)

11. FERRARA, J. 1980. Appropriateness conditions for entire sequences of speech acts. J. Pragmatics **4:** 321–340.

12. JARVELLA, R. J. & J. G. COLLAS. 1974. Memory for the intentions of sentences. Mem. Cognit. **2:** 185–188.

13. CLARK, H. H. & P. LUCY. 1975. Understanding what is meant from what is said: a study in conversationally conveyed requests. J. Verbal Learn. Verbal Behav. **14:** 56–72.

14. SCHMIDT, R. W. & J. RICHARDS. 1980. Speech acts and second language learning. Appl. Linguistics **1**(2): 129–157.

15. RINTELL, E. 1979. Getting your speech act together. Work. Pap. Bilingualism **17:** 97–106.

16. WALTERS, J. 1979. Language variation in assessing bilingual children's communicative competence. Bilingual Educ. Pap. Ser. **3**(3): 1–23.

17. CLARK, H. H. 1979. Responding to indirect speech acts. Cognit. Psychol. **11:** 430–477.

18. SACKS, H., E. A. SCHEGLOFF & G. JEFFERSON. 1974. A simplest systematics for the organisation of turn-taking for conversation. Language **50**(4): 696–735.

19. SACHS, J. 1967. Recognition memory for syntactic and semantic aspects of connected discourse. Percept. Psychophys. **2:** 437–442.

20. COOK, V. J. Structure drills and the learner. Can. Mod. Lang. Rev. (In press.)

21. COOK, V. J. 1979. Using Intonation. Longman. Harlow, England.

22. COOK, V. J. 1980. People and Places. Pergamon Press. Oxford, England.

23. CLARK, E. 1971. On the acquisition of the meaning of "before" and "after." J. Verbal Learn. Verbal Behav. **10:** 266–275.

24. COOK, V. J. 1977. Cognitive processes in second language learning. IRAL **15**(1): 1–20.

25. HAGEN, J. W. 1971. Some thoughts on how children learn to remember. Human Dev. **14:** 262–271.

26. DAEHLER, M. W., A. B. HOROWITZ, F. C. WYNNES & J. H. FLAVELL. 1974. Verbal and nonverbal rehearsal in children's recall. Child Dev. **40:** 443–452.

27. BERNBACH, H. A. 1967. The effects of labels on short-term memory for colours with nursery school children. Psychonomic Sci. **7:** 149–150.

28. CRAIK, F. I. M. & M. J. WATKINS. 1973. The role of rehearsal in short-term memory. J. Verbal Learn. Verbal Behav. **12:** 599–607.

29. ORNSTEIN, P. A. & M. J. NAUS. 1978. Rehearsal processes in children's memory. *In* Memory Development in Children. P. Ornstein, Ed.: 69–99. Lawrence Erlbaum Associates. Hillsdale, N.J.

30. STOLZ, W. & J. TIFFANY. 1972. The production of "childlike" word associations by adults to unfamiliar adjectives. J. Verbal Learn. Verbal Behav. **11:** 38–46.

31. ORNSTEIN, P. A., M. J. NAUS & C. LIBERTY. 1975. Rehearsal and organisational processes in children's memory. Child Dev. **46:** 818–830.

INPUT, INTERACTION, AND
SECOND-LANGUAGE ACQUISITION

Michael H. Long

Department of Educational Linguistics
Graduate School of Education
University of Pennsylvania
Philadelphia, Pennsylvania 19104

INTRODUCTION

It is now well established that, under as yet little understood conditions, native speakers modify their speech when addressing non-native speakers. Discussion of native speaker–non-native speaker (NS-NNS) conversation, however, often conflates two related but distinguishable phenomena, input to and interaction with the NNS. *Input* refers to the linguistic forms used; by *interaction* is meant the functions served by those forms, such as expansion, repetition, and clarification. This paper explores the possibility that a distinction between these two facets of NS-NNS conversation is important both theoretically, in order better to understand the second-language-acquisition (SLA) process, and in practice, when considering what is necessary and efficient in SL instruction.

INPUT

Following pioneering research by Ferguson,[14] considerable attention has been focused on the linguistic attributes of speech addressed by NS to NNS of a language. In some ways analogous to talk to young children ("baby talk"), "foreigner talk" has been defined as

> a register of simplified speech . . . used by speakers of a language to outsiders who are felt to have very limited command of the language or no knowledge of it at all.[13]

There now have been at least 30 studies of foreigner talk (FT). Some investigations have been indirect, using elicited written or spoken data, others have looked at NS-NNS conversation in natural settings, a third group has involved arranged conversations in quasi-laboratory conditions, and a fourth has dealt with the classroom speech of teachers instructing students in a second language. TABLE 1 lists the studies grouped according to the kind of data treated.

Certain patterns have emerged in the findings of these studies. Most obvious among them is the NS's tendency to "simplify" their speech in various ways. Ferguson, for example, reported an indirect study of FT conducted in a sociolinguistics class at Stanford.[14] Students were asked

0077–8923/81/0379–0259 $01.75/2 © 1981, NYAS

TABLE 1

STUDIES OF LINGUISTIC INPUT TO NON-NATIVE SPEAKERS, 1975–1981

Study	Language(s)	Age of Speaker-Hearer *	Ungrammatical Input (x)
1. Indirect Elicited			
Andersen [1]	English	C-C	x
Ferguson [14]	English	A-A	x
McCurdy [33]	English	A-A	x
Meisel [34]	German, French, Finnish	A-A	x
2. Observational, Naturalistic			
Clyne [10, 11]	English	A-A	x
Dutch Workgroup [12]	Dutch	A-A	x
Fillmore [15]	English	C-C	(almost none)
Freed [16]	English	A-A	x
Hatch et al. [21]	English	A-A	x
Heidelberg [22]	German	A-A	x
Katz [27]	English	C-C	x
Ramamurti [38]	English	A-A	x
Snow et al. [45]	Dutch	A-A	x
Valdman [50]	Tai Boy	A-A	x

3. Quasi Experimental

Study	Language		Relationship
Arthur et al.[2]	English		A-A
Campbell et al.[5]	English		A-A
Chan & Choy[6]	Mandarin		A-A
Chickinsky[9]	English		A-A
Hatch et al.[21]	English		A-A
Long[29]	English		A-A
Long[30]	English		A-A
Long[31]	English		A-A
Scarcella & Higa[41]	English		A-T, A-C

4. Classroom

Study	Language		Relationship
Chaudron[7]	English		A-A
Chaudron[8]	English		A-A
Gaies[17]	English		A-A
Hatch et al.[21]	English	x	A-A
Henzl[23]	Czech		A-A
Henzl[24, 25]	Czech, German, English		A-A
Long & Sato[32]	English		A-A
Steyaert[46]	English		A-A
Trager[49]	English		A-A

* A is adult, C is child, and T is adolescent.

to rewrite 10 English sentences as they would use them in addressing a group of illiterate non-Europeans who spoke a language other than English. Based on his analysis of this corpus, together with some literary fiction, Ferguson produced a list of features he suggested were characteristic of English FT.

Ferguson specified three areas of difference between standard English and FT. In phonology, FT was characterized by a slow rate of delivery, loudness, clear articulation, pauses, emphatic stress, exaggerated pronunciation, occasional (although infrequent) addition of a vowel after a word-final consonant, and a few reduplicated forms. In lexis, he found occasional use of words from other languages, substitutions of items by synonyms or paraphrases and analytic paraphrases (*which place* for *where*). In syntax, there was evidence of three kinds of modification, omission, expansion, and replacement or rearrangement. Omission was exemplified by deletion of articles, copula, inflectional morphology, conjunctions, and subject pronouns. Expansion was illustrated by the addition of unanalyzed tags to questions (*okay? yes? no?*) and insertion of subject pronoun *you* before imperatives. Replacement and rearrangement included such features as forming negatives with *no* plus the negated item (*no like*), replacing subject with object pronouns (*him go*), converting possessive pronoun-plus-noun constructions to noun-plus-object pronoun (for *my sister, sister me*), and preference for uninverted question forms (with deletion of the *do* auxiliary).[14]

Very similar findings to Ferguson's have been obtained since in replication studies in German, French, and Finnish and in English.[33,34] Cued by doll puppets, young children also have been found capable of similar speech modifications.[1] Most important, the results have been confirmed in studies of spontaneous NS-NNS communication in natural settings, such as in a department store, in factories, between young children at play, and in service encounters.[10,11,27,38,45] Thus, Snow *et al.* recorded 28 conversations between five Dutch NS and 28 foreigners in two government offices in Holland.[45] FT features observed included a very high frequency of possessive pronoun and determiner deletion (partly attributable to the specialized nature of some of the questions asked in filling out forms), deletion of auxiliaries, copulas, and subject pronouns, nonstandard word order in main and subordinate clauses, substitutions of infinitival for tensed verb forms, and lexical substitutions. Ungrammatical utterances in individual conversations ranged from 0 to 37.8%, with a mean of 10.5%. The five NS varied considerably in their use of ungrammatical speech, ranging from a mean of 2.2% to 20.1%.[45]

While the studies cited thus far have been consistent in their findings of simplified and often ungrammatical speech to NNS, and thereby present a clear pattern, there has been considerable variability, too, in this line of research. Some individual differences among speakers already have been mentioned, and more will emerge later. Of greater significance at this point, however, is the disparity between these studies and some others in their findings at the level of groups. For example, not all studies have found the kinds of simplification that result in ungrammaticality. This is obvious in the case of the quasi-laboratory and classroom studies in sections 3 and 4 of TABLE 1, but also holds for two studies in natural settings. Thus, Fillmore reports that there were *very* few instances of ungrammatical speech by young children observed over a period of months interacting with NNS age peers in school.[15] Freed found not a single ungrammatical utterance in another study, which involved 11 adult NS and their NNS partners in meetings over time at a conversation club for foreign students in Philadelphia.[16]

Freed's study included comparisons of the American NS's speech with that they addressed to the investigator,[16] and with naturalistic data on 15 mothers' speech to children from a previous study.[35] Freed found that speech to NNS shared many of the formal properties of linguistic input to children. It was articulated clearly, utterances were shorter and less complex syntactically, and there were higher proportions of questions than statements in the NS-NS interaction than in the NS's speech to the investigator. Utterances to linguistically more proficient NNS also were longer and more complex propositionally. Similar findings have been obtained in several of the studies listed in sections 3 and 4 of Table 1 (e.g., References 7, 17, and 41). Here again, however, there has been some lack of consistency in the findings. Both Chaudron and Trager report considerable variability at the level of individual teachers,[7,49] and Steyaert found no statistically significant differences in syntactic complexity between the speech of English-as-a-second-language (ESL) teachers retelling stories to ESL students and to NS.[46] Steyaert's teachers, unlike those in the Gaies study,[17] received no verbal feedback from the listeners, however. This suggests, as shown by Snow for speech to children,[43] that verbal feedback must be present to trigger some of the modifications normally found in the linguistic input to SL acquirers.

A possible explanation for the variability in these findings may lie in the nature of the comparisons made. In some studies, NS-NS baseline data have been derived from different speech situations from those in which the NS-NNS data were obtained. Corpora have differed along one or more of the following sociolinguistic parameters : speech event, setting, task, and kind of interlocutor. Thus, some studies have been of teachers talking during lessons in classrooms while giving instruction to a large group of NNS, and so may be providing as much description of a variety of teacher talk as of FT. Control data usually have consisted of speech by these or other individuals in some other role (e.g., student, research subject, or friend), interacting during less formal classroom discussions or completely informal conversations outside classrooms with a small group or a single interlocutor, sometimes the researcher. Prior to the study to be reported shortly, the only investigation to have avoided all of these problems was that by Arthur *et al.*[2] This, however, was of partly scripted telephone conversations and, hence, perhaps of lesser generalizability.

The other obvious inconsistency in findings so far concerns the grammaticality of linguistic input. Limitations of space prevent a detailed discussion of possible causes of these results. (See Reference 29 for a review.) However, it would appear that ungrammatical FT is more probable if the following conditions are met:

1. The NNS has very limited command of the language of communication.
2. The NS is, or thinks he or she is, of higher social status than the NNS.
3. The NS has considerable FT experience.
4. The conversation occurs spontaneously.

There exist counterexamples to each of these conditions, and possible additional variables. The lack of any clear design in many studies, with a consequent confounding of variables, makes any more precise definition of conditions currently impossible.

INTERACTION

Those studies that have looked at interactional features of NS-NNS conversation have found several of the same processes observed in conversations between young children and their older caretakers, but also some differences. NS use a variety of devices presumably intended to facilitate comprehension and participation by the NNS. Conversational topics are dealt with simply and briefly compared with those in NS-NS interaction, as indicated by the number of information bits exchanged or the ratio of topic-initiating to topic-continuing moves.[2,30] Topics will also often be dropped altogether during informal chat if a communication breakdown occurs, as when the NNS unintentionally switches topic and the NS repairs the discourse by treating the inappropriate response as a topic nomination:

> NS: Are you going to visit San Francisco? Or Las Vegas?
> NNS: Yes I went to Disneyland and to Knottsberry Farm.
> →NS: Oh yeah? [31]

NS seem to try to allow the NNS to determine what is talked about, as indicated above, for example, and through the use of "or-choice" questions,[19,20] such as the following:

> NS: Aha Do you study?
> → Or
> 　　do you work?
> NNS: No.[30]

If they introduce a new topic, NS often seem to attempt to make it transparent through additional stress and left dislocation,[19-21] intrasentential pauses before topic words, the use of question forms for topic-nominating moves,[30,31] and the use of frames (*okay, now, well*) as utterance boundary markers and to signal topic change.[31,41]

NS also use a variety of techniques to help sustain conversation and to lighten other aspects of the NNS's interactional burden. At least with child and adolescent interlocutors, they engage in cooperative dialogue, the NS supplying utterances that, taken with those of the NNS, help the latter to communicate an idea *across* utterances:

NS: Okay and then another square.
NNS: like that.
NS: goes there.[41]

In this process, Scarcella and Higa point out, NS introduce a new topic and allow the NNS to comment, adding new and relevant information.[41] NS ask rhetorical questions, answer their own questions, and often use a generally "interrogative" style.[5,19,31,37,41] As found with adult-child first-language interaction, English-speaking NS, at least, tend to favor statistically significantly higher proportions of questions to statements when conversing with NNS.[30,41] This may be due to the fact that in English-speaking cultures, most types of questions usually "compel" answers,[18] and so are more likely to produce one from the NNS, thereby sustaining the interaction. Also, the marking that questions receive in English (wh-morphology, subject-auxiliary inversion, or rising intonation) may make it easier for the NS to signal, and for the NNS to recognize, a conversational turn for the NNS. Imperatives, also relatively more frequent in adult-child conversations, are not so in NS-NS interaction between adults.[16,30] Freed argues that this is due to an important functional difference between baby talk and FT. The former, she points out, usually is more concerned with shaping and adapting behavior; the latter usually concerns the exchange of information.[16]

NS do a lot of work to avoid conversational trouble, and to fix up the interaction when it does occur. Many of the "clarification" devices mentioned are examples of this. Hatch also has drawn attention to the way in which questions are recoded in alternative interrogative forms.[19,20] The recasting of questions often involves substitution of yes-no for wh-questions,[19,21] but changes of other kinds, including many in the opposite direction, also are frequent.[33] Several researchers (e.g., References 7, 21, and 23) have noted many examples of lexical substitution by NS that appear to be similarly motivated. A great many confirmation checks and clarification requests, too, are employed to help ensure that the NS have understood what the NNS have said. Scarcella and Higa found statistically significantly more of them being employed by adult NS with child NNS than with adolescent NNS, and with both non-native groups than with adult NS controls.[41]

Apparently for similar reasons, NS repeat both their own and the NNS's previous utterances, either wholly or in part.[2,8,21,38] Repetition is pervasive whether the NS or NNS is an adult or a child.[5,15,27,37,41] Campbell *et al.* found expansions to occur more frequently than reductions in repetitions, often with an increase in redundancy.[5] They also found restatements to be frequent, often involving substitution of apparently problematic lexical items with definitions and synonyms, findings confirmed in other studies.[8,21,24,25]

Another more complex repair device is "decomposition." [29,31] Decomposition refers to exchanges such as the following:

a.
    NS: When do you go to the uh Santa Monica? (2) You say you go fishing in Santa Monica, right?
    NNS: Yeah.
    NS: When? [29]

b.
    NS: Uh what does uh what does your father do in uh you're from Kyoto, right?
    NNS: Yeah.
    NS: Yeah What does your father do in Kyoto? [29]

In each case, the NNS is asked to comment on a new conversational topic or subtopic introduced by a wh-question. When this task proves or (as in b) is believed likely to prove too difficult, the task is broken down (decomposed) into two parts. First, the (sub)topic is established by its repetition in isolation from the request for commentary, often accompanied by rising (question) intonation, and often with a tag (*right?*) asking for confirmation that the topic has been established (cf. the "try-marking" intonation noted in Reference 40). Then, if the requested confirmation is forthcoming, the comment, in the form of a question about the new topic, is restated.

Almost no work has been done on variables related to characteristics of NS-NNS interaction, but two studies suggest that this may be a profitable area for future investigation. As reported earlier, Scarcella and Higa found several of the devices described used more frequently with child than with adolescent NNS,[41] which may imply that some features are related to communication with children rather than (or as well as) with NNS. Another study found that it was relative frequency of use of some of the devices illustrated for conversational management that distinguished NS with and without previous experience in conversation with NNS.[31]

While several studies have described features of NS-NNS interaction, very few have quantified their data or compared findings with baseline data on NS-NS conversation. Consequently, little is known about the commonality of the processes and features noted or about whether they occur only in NS-NNS interaction or only more frequently so. Further, as with studies of linguistic input, almost no studies among those with control data have had NS-NS conversation deriving from comparable tasks or settings. In an attempt to avoid potentially confounding factors of these kinds, a recent study looked at various features of input and interaction in NS-NNS conversation when tasks were the same in both NS-NS and NS-NNS conditions.[29] It was felt that this kind of study could test the robustness of previous findings on input and interaction.

A Study of NS-NS and NS-NNS Conversation

Modified Input and Modified Interaction

Controlling for sex and prior FT experience, 48 adult NS and 16 adult NNS from a variety of first-language backgrounds were assigned randomly to form 32 dyads, 16 NS-NS and 16 NS-NNS, in a matched-pairs design. Each dyad performed the same six tasks in the same order. These were (1) informal conversation, (2) vicarious narrative, (3) giving instructions for two communication games, (4) playing the first game, (5) playing the second game, and (6) discussing the supposed purpose of the research. About 25 minutes of conversation from each dyad were transcribed for analysis. Some 16 features of input and interaction were examined and formed the study's dependent variables.*

The main findings relevant to the present discussion are presented in TABLES 2 and 3. TABLE 2 shows differences between NS-NS and NS-NNS performance across all tasks on 16 measures, and levels of statistical significance for these differences $(\alpha = 0.005)$.† The most striking feature of these results is the fact that 10 out of 11 interaction variables attained significance, while 4 out of 5 input variables did not, although the direction of such differences as did obtain on the nonsignificant items was as predicted.

Another part of the study sought to test whether the *degree* of modification of input and interaction features was related to the nature of the tasks involved. It was hypothesized that tasks making genuine communicative demands on participants, here defined as those tasks whose successful completion required a two-way exchange of information, would elicit more modifications of both kinds from the NS, and might in some cases result in ungrammatical input. TABLE 3 presents findings for 11 measures when the six tasks were grouped into two sets of three, one group containing three tasks (1, 4, and 5) requiring a two-way information exchange, the other group involving tasks (2, 3, and 6) that did not. It can be seen that on measures of interactional features, differences between NS-NS and NS-NNS conversation were greater on tasks in group 1 than on tasks in group 2 in seven out of nine cases. The same division of tasks showed differences in the same direction for the two input variables treated, but did not yield differences that were statistically significant at the required level on either set of tasks. There were no ill-formed sentences in the NS's speech.

Caution always must be exercised when generalizing from the results of studies conducted in controlled, quasi-laboratory conditions. By the

---

* The full study considered additional morphology variables, input-output relationships, and results by individual tasks.

† The unusually high α level of 0.005 was established in order to minimize the likelihood of chance findings of significance when so many variables were examined on the same data set. This procedure, of course, also increases the likelihood of a type 2 error, i.e., of not finding significant differences when differences in fact obtain.

TABLE 2

DIFFERENCES BETWEEN NS-NS AND NS-NNS CONVERSATION ACROSS SIX TASKS *

In NS-NNS conversation, there were:	p level
INPUT	
1. shorter average length of T-units ‡	0.005
2. lower number of S-nodes per T-unit §	†
3. lower type-token ratio	†
4. higher average lexical frequency of nouns and verbs	†
5. higher proportion of copulas in total verbs	†
INTERACTION	
6. more present (versus nonpresent) temporal marking of verbs	0.001
7. different distribution of questions, statements, and imperatives in T-units (more questions)	0.001
8. different distribution of question-types in T-units (more wh-questions)	0.001
9. more conversational frames	†
10. more confirmation checks	0.005
11. more comprehension checks	0.005
12. more clarification requests	0.005
13. more self-repetitions	0.005
14. more other repetitions	0.005
15. more expansions	0.005
16. more of 9 through 15 combined	0.005

* Data from Reference 29.
† Not significant.
‡ A T-unit is defined as "a main clause plus all subordinate clauses and nonclausal structures attached to or embedded in it." (HUNT, K. W. 1970. Monogr. Soc. Res. Child Dev. No. 35, Serial No. 134.)
§ The number of underlying sentences per T-unit, e.g., *I wonder if he went* = 2.

same token, however, this is the first study to have used comparable NS-NS baseline data, attained by virtue of that control, in investigating face-to-face NS-NNS conversation. Its findings, therefore, may be considered to strengthen confidence in previous claims as to interactional rather than input differences between NS-NS and NS-NNS conversation. It is not being suggested that NS speech to NNS is unmodified under certain conditions, or that some input differences may not on occasion be great. From the findings of this study,[29] however, it does seem that there is better evidence for modifications in features of NS-NNS interaction than input, and that interaction features are more sensitive to the communicative demands of a conversation.

INPUT, INTERACTION, AND SECOND-LANGUAGE ACQUISITION

Clearly, input and interaction often are related, but equally clearly, modification in one is possible without modification in the other. The study just reported provides evidence for this, but two hypothetical examples may help clarify the distinction:

1. NS: You come.
   NNS: OK.

2. NS: Do you wanna hamburger?
   NNS: Uh?
   NS: What do you wanna eat?
   NNS: Oh! Yeah, hamburger.

Example 1 is typical of the kind of exchange found in some observational studies where the NS uses an FT command (with addition of the usually deleted subject pronoun) in what is otherwise a normal two-part exchange. The input, that is, is modified, but the interaction is not. Example 2 illustrates just the reverse, and is typical of NS-NNS conversation found in the quasi-experimental studies. After the initial failure to communicate, the NS repairs with a semantic repetition, thereby modifying the interaction. Note, however, that the rerun sentence (*What do you wanna eat?*) is syntactically more complex than the utterance that caused the breakdown in communication (*Do you want a hamburger?*). That it successfully

TABLE 3

RELATIONSHIP BETWEEN TASK TYPE AND NS-NS AND NS-NNS CONVERSATION *

	The degree of difference between NS-NS and NS-NNS conversation in performance on:	
	Tasks 1, 4 & 5 (+ information exchange)	Tasks 2, 3 & 6 (− information exchange)
INPUT		
1. average length of T-units	$p < 0.025$ †	$p > 0.025$ †
2. number of S-nodes per T-unit	$p < 0.01$ †	$p < 0.025$ †
INTERACTION		
3. distribution of questions, statements, and imperatives in T-units	$p < 0.001$	$p < 0.005$
4. number of conversational frames	$p > 0.025$ †	$p > 0.025$ †
5. number of confirmation checks	$p < 0.005$	$p < 0.01$ †
6. number of comprehension checks	$p < 0.005$	$p > 0.025$ †
7. number of clarification requests	$p < 0.005$	$p > 0.025$ †
8. number of self-repetitions	$p < 0.005$	$p < 0.005$
9. number of other repetitions	$p < 0.005$	$p > 0.025$ †
10. number of expansions	$p < 0.005$	− †‡
11. number of 4 through 10 combined	$p < 0.005$	$p < 0.025$ †

* Data from Reference 29.
† Not significant.
‡ There were no instances of expansions on these tasks.

communicates the original message probably is due to the lexical changes, one of which introduces a word (*eat*) that, with the accompanying intonation and contextual clues, is sufficient to enable the whole message to be decoded.‡

Facts like these prompt consideration of whether modified input, modified interaction, or a combination is necessary for or facilitates SLA in a natural or a classroom setting. There are eight logical possibilities, as shown in TABLE 4, where a plus sign indicates modification, and a minus sign means no modification. The remainder of this paper considers those eight propositions concerning the roles of modified input and interaction in SLA.

TABLE 4

POSSIBLE RELATIONSHIPS BETWEEN MODIFIED INPUT, MODIFIED INTERACTION, AND SECOND-LANGUAGE ACQUISITION

Input *	Interaction *	SLA Possible †	SLA Facilitated †
−	−	P1 (F)	P2 (F)
+	−	P3 (F)	P4 (F)
−	+	P5 (T)	P6 (T)
+	+	P7 (T)	P8 (T)

* Minus signs mean unmodified. Plus signs mean modified.
† Letters in parenthesis indicate projected status (true or false) of proposition.

PROPOSITION 1

SLA is Possible with neither Modified Input nor Modified Interaction

P1 is, first of all, counterintuitive. For it to be true, it would be necessary to show that an SL (as distinct from a few isolated words and conversational formulae) could be acquired by a novice when the *only* samples of the target language (TL) available consisted of NS-NS conversation, TV and radio broadcasts, movies, newspapers, etc. On the basis of personal experience, it seems clear that the most acquired from exposure of this sort is a "feel" for the SL phonology, some isolated lexical items, and some frequently heard chunks (typically greetings and leave takings). The problem is, however, that few experiences with this sort of exposure last long enough to test P1, or if they do, they are "contaminated" by SL instruction or some other form of modified input or interaction. Further,

‡ A clarification is in order here. The example does show input modifications, lexical and syntactic. The point is, however, that on another occasion, a wh-question will be changed to a yes-no question, and so on, with the net result that overall input frequencies of different lexical items and syntactic constructions will be the same, i.e., not statistically significantly different from those occurring in NS-NS conversation, as shown in the study just reported.

the individuals undergoing such exposure rarely are motivated to learn the new language, knowing their contact with it will be short.

Two cases of longer exposure have been reported, however. Larsen-Freeman noted the case of a German adult who claimed to have acquired Dutch by listening to Dutch radio broadcasts.[51] Snow *et al.* observed that Dutch children who watched German television did *not* acquire German.[44] There are several obvious problems with the first case. First, Dutch and German are closely related, and knowledge of one might substitute for a basic competence in the other, a competence sufficient to allow use to be made of unmodified TL samples. Second, the claim is based on self-report, and no Dutch proficiency test data are available. It is in any case a matter of one individual. The present writer had the opportunity, while on a recent visit to the People's Republic of China, to observe another case of prolonged exposure to an unknown language by three adult NS of English, which had resulted only in some 50 vocabulary items and a few stock expressions. The individuals concerned had spent seven months in the country, and knew they would be staying for a total of one or two years. Two were sophisticated linguistically; all were psychologically and socially well disposed toward speakers of the TL. They heard Chinese (both Mandarin and Cantonese) all around them every day, but rarely had occasion to speak it, as most of their contacts were with proficient English speakers. They could get by in shops by pointing, by skillful use of context, through the handful of vocabulary items and expressions they knew, and by relying on translations by their two young children (three and six years of age), who already were quite proficient after spending seven months in Chinese schools. While there clearly is a need for properly documented studies in this area, it seems reasonable on the data currently available to reject P1.

PROPOSITION 2

Unmodified Input and Unmodified Interaction Facilitate SLA

P2 can be falsified in two different SLA settings. First, there is the case where unmodified TL samples constitute the *only* form of exposure to the SL, illustrated by the situation of the three English speakers in China described above. Second, there is the situation in which unmodified TL samples are available to SL acquirers who *also* are obtaining samples modified in some way. The latter circumstances pertain, for example, in the case of French-immersion children in Montreal, where roughly 65% of the language heard on the streets is French.

If, as has been argued, P1 is false, then it follows that in situations of the first type P2 must be false too. That P2 probably also is false in the second type of situation is suggested by the results of a recent study of French immersion in Canada. Swain compared the performance on various tests of listening, reading, and writing skills of French-immersion students across Canada living in communities where use of French ranged from 0 to about 65%.[47] Contrary to Swain's predictions, she found performance generally to be unaffected by amount of French in the out-of-school environment, although there was an initial but temporary tendency for improved performance on listening comprehension tests by those exposed to more French outside the classroom. While the types of tests (mostly discrete point, pencil and paper) employed in the study may not be those most likely to tap the effects of wider exposure, these findings certainly are not consistent with P2. Instead, they may be argued to show that either input or interaction, or both, must be modified before TL samples become usable for SLA.

PROPOSITION 3

SLA is Possible with Modified Input but Unmodified Interaction

Discussion of P3 through P8 is limited by the failure of most studies to distinguish modified input and modified interaction, although it is clear that the two phenomena often cooccur. However, it can be argued that modification in the input alone is unlikely to make possible the acquisition of anything but a marked variety of a standard language. This is because there seem to be no cases recorded of modified input but unmodified interaction other than the kind of task-oriented communication sometimes found in work settings, such as when an NS foreman addresses a migrant worker on the factory floor using ungrammatical FT of the sort described by Ferguson. While no causal relationship has been established, it is just these types of SL environments that also have been found to be associated with the acquisition of a very restricted "pidginized" variety of an SL (see, e.g., References 11 and 42). It must be recognized, however, that in situations like these, there often is the possibility of insufficient as well as inadequate input.

There is an alternative, stronger motivation for rejecting P3, however. This is very simply that, other than in the kind of work-oriented communication just referred to, there appear to be no examples of the study of NS-NNS conversation that have found sustained conversation without modified interaction. Given a speaker of limited SL proficiency, it seems impossible for an NS to converse for any length of time without recourse to at least some of the devices described earlier in this paper. Given the additional (surely reasonable) assumption that there must be a lot of input for SLA to occur, it follows that P3 is false; the necessary quantity of input could be obtained only through modified interaction.

PROPOSITION 4

Modified Input but Unmodified Interaction Facilitates SLA

P4 can be rejected for two reasons. First, it must be false because P3 is false. Second, as argued above with respect to P3, modified input probably never occurs for more than very brief periods (and then only in certain SLA settings) without modified interaction.

PROPOSITION 5

SLA is Possible with Unmodified Input but Modified Interaction

P5 would seem to be true. Consistent with the idea is all the evidence that shows modified interaction, but not modified input, in NS-NNS conversation. The only assumption being made here is that conversation is an important arena for successful SLA.

There are three potential problems with accepting P5. First, it may be argued that just as there is rarely, if ever, modified input without modified interaction, so the reverse. It is hoped that the literature reviewed earlier and the recent study reported in this paper will be accepted as dealing with this issue. Second, it might be claimed that there exist reports of successful first-language acquisition without the blessing of modified interaction. Ochs, for example, has claimed that adults in Western Samoa do not indulge in the kind caretaker-child interaction so pervasive in western societies, and address children, when they do so at all, in an unmodified form of the adult language.[36] As pointed out in the same paper, however, older children, not adults, are the primary care givers, and their speech may well turn out to show the usual modifications. Further, judging from the illustrative fragments quoted by Ochs, adults do modify the *interactional* features of their conversations in the normal way. Third, some may question the implied linkage between conversation and SLA made in the assumption. For the great majority of uninstructed SL acquirers, however, conversation is the only experience they receive of the TL, which they proceed to master, and so must provide sufficient data for successful SLA, whether or not it presents them in the most efficient form.

PROPOSITION 6

Modified Interaction with Unmodified Input Facilitates SLA

That P6 is true follows from acceptance of P5 coupled with rejection of P1 through P4.

PROPOSITION 7

SLA is Possible with Modified Input and Modified Interaction

Given prior acceptance of P5, P7 again must be true, as it contains the element, modified interaction, that is claimed to be the necessary and sufficient characteristic of TL samples for SLA to occur. It is, however, possible to imagine certain kinds of (ungrammatical) input that, although embedded in conversation marked by the necessary interactional changes, might lead to the same kind of limited SL competence referred to earlier in the discussion of P3. More important from a theoretical perspective, P7 is much more powerful than P5 and, it is hypothesized, unnecessarily so. It is accepted here only because logically it must be, given the claimed status of P5, and because there are as yet no empirical studies that have tested the *sufficiency* of P5.

PROPOSITION 8

Modified Input and Modified Interaction Together Facilitate SLA

Proposition 8 again must be accepted currently for the same reasons that force acceptance of P7. (And the same caveats apply.) In addition, there are what appear to be independent supporting data from two sources. First, several cases of abnormal language exposure during first-language acquisition seem to suggest that modified speech is helpful. Thus, Sachs and Johnson report the case of Jim, a hearing child of deaf parents.[39] At age three, the boy had only a limited vocabulary, probably acquired from playmates and television, and language generally far behind children of that age. Although Jim had heard adult-adult speech on television, he had had no direct interaction with caretakers or input modified for his benefit. When he began to receive this, his language improved rapidly. Similar findings exist for other hearing children of deaf parents, unless alternate sources of interaction exist for the child,[4,26] and for institutionalized children. Second, several researchers have reported success for what might be called "input methods" of SL instruction, e.g., Asher for total physical response [3] and Terrell for the natural approach [48] (see Reference 28 for a review). Basically, there is some evidence from these studies that teaching methods that do not insist on early production, but instead provide students with plenty of comprehensible "input," do better than traditional methods. As should be clear by now, however, it is not at all certain in either the first-language or second-language teaching studies just what aspect of the "treatment" is bringing about these results. None of the studies report the kind of data necessary to determine this. However, from published descriptions of the teaching methods, at least, it is the interaction rather than the input itself that is modified. Indeed, some published materials associated with the methods clearly use polished, nativelike sentences from the earliest stages, making them comprehensible through skillful use of real-life and picture contexts.

CONCLUSION

A review of the literature on modified input and modified interaction in NS-NNS conversation, together with the results of an empirical study described here, suggests that while input to NNS unquestionably is modified on occasion in various ways, it is modifications in interaction that are observed more consistently. In fact, current knowledge suggests that they are found in all cases of the successful acquisition of a full version of an SL. While there as yet is insufficient evidence to justify rejection of modified input as a necessary or facilitative condition for SLA, there is no evidence for its supposed role that cannot be explained more parsimoniously by modifications in interaction. A host of additional variables no doubt affect the course and rate of naturalistic and instructed SLA. However, research is needed that tests the current hypothesis: participation in conversation with NS, made possible through the modification of interaction, is the necessary and sufficient condition for SLA.

SUMMARY

There have been over 30 studies of the speech addressed to second-language learners by native speakers of the language they are learning. A smaller body of research exists on the nature of conversation between native and non-native speakers. Findings in these areas are summarized briefly, and methodological problems noted. A recent study then is reported that attempted to avoid the problems indicated. The paper concludes with a discussion of the roles of modified input and modified interaction in second-language acquisition.

REFERENCES

1. ANDERSEN, E. 1977. Learning to speak with style: a study of the sociolinguistic skills of children. Doctoral dissertation. Stanford University Department of Linguistics. Stanford, Calif.
2. ARTHUR, B., R. WEINER, M. CULVER, Y. LEE & D. THOMAS. 1980. The register of impersonal discourse to foreigners: verbal adjustments to foreign accent. *In* Discourse Analysis in Second Language Research. D. Larsen-Freeman, Ed.: 111–124. Newbury House. Rowley, Mass.
3. ASHER, J. 1969. The total physical response approach to second language learning. Mod. Lang. J. **53:** 3–17.
4. BARD, B. & J. SACHS. 1977. Language acquisition in two normal children of deaf parents. Paper presented to the Second Annual Boston Conference on Language Development, Boston, Mass. (ERIC #150 868.)
5. CAMPBELL, C., W. GASKILL & S. VANDER BROOK. 1977. Some aspects of foreigner talk. *In* Proceedings of the First Los Angeles Second Language Research Forum. C. R. Henning, Ed.: 94–106. University of California. Los Angeles, Calif.
6. CHAN, B. L. & C. CHOY. 1980. Foreigner talk in Chinese. University of Pennsylvania. Philadelphia, Pa. (Unpublished.)
7. CHAUDRON, C. 1978. English as the medium of instruction in ESL classes: an initial report of a pilot study of the complexity of teachers' speech. Modern Language Center, OISE. University of Toronto. Toronto, Ontario, Canada.
8. CHAUDRON, C. 1979. Complexity of teacher speech and vocabulary explana-

tion/elaboration. Paper presented at the Thirteenth Annual TESOL Convention, Boston, Mass., March 2.

9. CHICKINSKY, I. 1980. Foreigner talk or foreigner register: a matter of time, place, speaker or listener? University of Pennsylvania. Philadelphia, Pa. (Unpublished.)

10. CLYNE, M. 1977. Multilingualism and pidginization in Australian industry. Ethnic Stud. **1:** 40–55.

11. CLYNE, M. 1978. Some remarks on foreigner talk. *In* Papers from the First Scandinavian German Symposium on the Language of Immigrant Workers and Their Children. N. Dittmar, H. Haberland, T. Skutnabbkangas & U. Teleman, Eds.: 155–162. Roskilde Universitetscenter, Linguistgrupper. Roskilde, Denmark.

12. Dutch Workgroup on Foreign Workers' Language. 1978. Nederlands tegen Buitenlanders. (Dutch addressed to foreigners.) Publication No. 18. Institute for General Linguistics. University of Amsterdam. Amsterdam, the Netherlands.

13. FERGUSON, C. A. 1971. Absence of copula and the notion of simplicity. *In* Pidginization and Creolization of Language. D. Hymes, Ed.: 141–150. Cambridge University Press. London, England.

14. FERGUSON, C. A. 1975. Towards a characterization of English foreigner talk. Anthropol. Linguistics **17:** 1–14.

15. FILLMORE, L. WONG. 1976. The second time around. Doctoral Dissertation. Stanford University. Stanford, Calif.

16. FREED, B. F. 1978. Foreigner talk: a study of speech adjustments made by native speakers of English in conversation with non-native speakers. Doctoral Dissertation. University of Pennsylvania. Philadelphia, Pa.

17. GAIES, S. 1977. The nature of linguistic input in formal second language learning: linguistic and communicative strategies in teachers' classroom language. *In* On TESOL '77. Teaching and Learning English as a Second Language: Trends in Research and Practice. H. D. Brown, C. A. Yorio & R. H. Crymes, Eds.: 204–212. TESOL. Washington, D.C.

18. GOODY, E. N. 1978. Towards a theory of questions. *In* Questions and Politeness: Strategies in Social Interaction. E. N. Goody, Ed.: 17–43. Cambridge University Press. London, England.

19. HATCH, E. M. 1978. Discourse analysis and second language acquisition. *In* Second Language Acquisition: A Book of Readings. E. M. Hatch, Ed.: 401–435. Newbury House. Rowley, Mass.

20. HATCH, E. M. 1978. Discourse analysis, speech acts, and second language acquisition. *In* Second Language Acquisition Research. W. Ritchie, Ed.: 137–156. Academic Press, Inc. New York, N.Y.

21. HATCH, E. M., R. SHAPIRA & J. GOUGH. 1975. Foreigner talk discourse. Paper presented at the Second Language Acquisition Forum, University of California, Los Angeles, Calif. (Also 1978. Int. Rev. Appl. Linguistics: 39–60.)

22. Heidelberger Forschungsprojekt "Pidgin Deutsch." 1978. The Unguided Learning of German by Spanish and Italian Workers. A Sociolinguistic Study. UNESCO. Paris, France.

23. HENZL, V. M. 1974. Linguistic register of foreign language instruction. Lang. Learn. **23**(2): 207–222.

24. HENZL, V. M. 1975. Speech of foreign language teachers: a sociolinguistic register analysis. Paper presented at the Fourth International AILA Conference, Stuttgart, Federal Republic of Germany, August.

25. HENZL, V. M. 1979. Foreigner talk in the classroom. Int. Rev. Appl. Linguistics **17**(2): 159–167.

26. JONES, M. & S. QUIGLEY. 1979. The acquisition of question formation in

spoken Spanish and American sign language by two hearing children of deaf parents. J. Speech Hear. Dis. **44:** 196–208.

27. KATZ, J. T. 1977. Foreigner talk input in child second language acquisition: its form and function over time. *In* Proceedings of the First Los Angeles Second Language Research Forum. C. A. Henning, Ed.: 61–75. University of California. Los Angeles, Calif.

28. KRASHEN, S. 1980. The input hypothesis. *In* Current Issues in Bilingual Education. J. E. Alatis, Ed. Georgetown University Press. Washington, D.C.

29. LONG, M. H. 1980. Input, interaction, and second language acquisition. Ph.D. Dissertation. University of California. Los Angeles, Calif.

30. LONG, M. H. 1981. Questions in foreigner talk discourse. Lang. Learn. **31:** 135–157.

31. LONG, M. H. 1982. Prior foreigner talk experience and the negotiation of conversation with non-native speakers. Stud. Second Lang. Acquisition **5:** 2. (In press.)

32. LONG, M. H. & C. J. SATO. Classroom foreigner talk discourse: forms and functions of teachers' questions. *In* Classroom Language Acquisition and Use: New Perspectives. H. Seliger & M. H. Long, Eds. Rowley, Mass. (In press.)

33. McCURDY, P. 1980. Talking to foreigners: the role of rapport. Doctoral Dissertation. University of California. Berkeley, Calif.

34. MEISEL, J. M. 1977. Linguistic simplification: a study of immigrant workers' speech and foreigner talk. *In* Actes du 5eme Colloque de Linguistique Appliquee de Neuchatel. S. P. Corder & E. Roulet, Eds.: 88–113. AIMAV Didier. Paris, France.

35. NEWPORT, E. 1976. Motherese: the speech of mothers to young children. *In* Cognitive Theory. N. Castellan, D. Pisoni & G. Potts, Eds. **2.** Lawrence Erlbaum Associates. Hillsdale, N.J.

36. OCHS, E. 1980. Talking to children in Western Samoa. University of Southern California. Los Angeles, Calif. (Unpublished.)

37. PECK, S. 1978. Child-child discourse in second language acquisition. *In* Second Language Acquisition: A Book of Readings. E. M. Hatch, Ed.: 383–400. Newbury House. Rowley, Mass.

38. RAMAMURTI, R. 1977. How do Americans talk to me? University of Pennsylvania. Philadelphia, Pa. (Unpublished.)

39. SACHS, J. & M. JOHNSON. 1976. Language development in a hearing child of deaf parents. *In* Baby Talk and Infant Speech. W. von Raffler-Engel & Y. Lebrun, Eds. Swets and Zeitlinger. Lisse, the Netherlands.

40. SACKS, H. & D. E. SCHEGLOFF. 1974. Two preferences in the organization of reference to persons in conversation and their interactions. *In* Ethnomethodology, Labeling Theory and Deviant Behavior. N. H. Avison & R. J. Wilson, Eds. Routledge and Kegan Paul. London, England.

41. SCARCELLA, R. & C. HIGA. Input and age differences in second language acquisition. *In* Child-Adult Differences in Second Language Acquisition. S. Krashen, R. Scarcella & M. H. Long, Eds. Newbury House. Rowley, Mass. (In press.)

42. SCHUMANN, J. H. 1978. The Pidginization Process. A Model for Second Language Acquisition. Newbury House. Rowley, Mass.

43. SNOW, C. E. 1972. Mothers' speech to children learning language. Child Dev. **43:** 549–565.

44. SNOW, C. E., A. ARLMAN-RUPP, Y. HASSING, J. JOBSE, J. JOOSTEN & J. VORSTER. 1976. Mothers' speech in three social classes. J. Psycholinguistic Res. **5:** 1–20.

45. SNOW, C. E., R. VAN EEDEN & P. MUYSKEN. The interactional origins of FT: municipal employees and foreign workers. Int. J. Sociol. Lang. (In press.)

46. STEYAERT, M. 1977. A comparison of the speech of ESL teachers to native

and non-native speakers of English. Paper presented at the winter meeting of the Linguistic Society of America, Chicago, Ill.

47. SWAIN, M. 1981. Target language use in the wider environment as a factor in its acquisition. *In* New Dimensions in Second Language Acquisition Research. R. W. Andersen, Ed.: 109–122. Newbury House. Rowley, Mass.

48. TERRELL, T. D. 1977. A natural approach to second language acquisition and learning. Mod. Lang. J. **61:** 325–337.

49. TRAGER, S. 1978. The language of teaching: discourse analysis in beginning, intermediate and advanced ESL students. M.A. Thesis. University of Southern California. Los Angeles, Calif.

50. VALDMAN, A. 1976. L'effet de modeles culturels sur l'elaboration du language simplifie (Foreigner Talk). Paper presented at Colloque "Theoretical Models in Applied Linguistics" V. Université de Neuchatel, Neuchatel, France, May 19–22.

51. LARSEN-FREEMAN, D. 1979. The importance of input in second language acquisition. Paper presented at the LSA winter meeting, Los Angeles, Calif., December.

SOCIAL CONSTRAINTS ON ADULT LANGUAGE LEARNING

Robbins Burling

Department of Anthropology
University of Michigan
Ann Arbor, Michigan 48109

INTRODUCTION

No doubt we all can agree that adults and children tend to cope with language in rather different ways, but we do not seem to agree on the causes for the differences. At least since Penfield,[1] and more strongly since Lenneberg,[2] many students have found it attractive to suggest that neurofunctional maturation governs a "critical period," during which time language is learned most readily or most "naturally." There has been debate on just how critical and just how narrow this period is,[3] and Lamendella even has offered the term "sensitive period" as a more suitable way of expressing the concept;[4] but a number of workers, including Lamendella, have pointed to specific aspects of neurological maturation as possible explanations for the apparent decline in the adult's ability to acquire language.

In a somewhat different vein, Krashen has suggested that the close of the critical period may be related to Inhelder and Piaget's stage of formal operations, which is believed to begin at about the time of puberty.[3,5] It is claimed that this is the period when the child begins to formulate abstract hypotheses in order to explain phenomena and the time when he wants general solutions to problems rather than merely *ad hoc* solutions. The tendency of adolescents to construct theories may inhibit "natural" language acquisition, with the result that adolescents and adults no longer are able to avoid constructing a conscious theory of the language they are learning.

Whether the emphasis is placed upon neurofunctional maturation or upon Piagetian stages of mental operation, these arguments point to maturational changes that turn the postadolescent into a different kind of learner than the younger child, but others have been more impressed with the social and psychological factors that hamper adult learning. In his book *The Pidginization Process,* John Schumann offers us a case study of an adult Costa Rican worker in the United States who made very little progress in English.[6] Schumann attributes the worker's low achievement to what he calls the "social and psychological distance" of the learner from speakers of English.[6] As factors of social distance that can affect the rate of learning, Schumann cites the political, cultural, technical, and economic dominance relationships between the two language groups; the degree of assimilation desired; the cohesiveness of the groups; relative size of the

279

0077–8923/81/0379–0279 $01.75/2 © 1981, NYAS

groups; the congruence of the cultures; the attitudes of the people toward each other; and the expected period of residence of language learners in the area of the target language. As factors of psychological distance, he considers language and culture shock, motivation, and ego permeability.[6]

Maturational factors are, presumably, universal and can be cited as explanations for the difficulties that all adults seem to face. Schumann's factors of social and psychological distance, however, are variable, so the implication would seem to be that an adult learner who is not burdened by these factors would learn a language quite easily. A few other observers have pointed to more general social factors that put barriers in the way of most or all adults. Wagner-Gough and Hatch, for instance, point to the different kinds of language input received by adults and children as governing, in important ways, their differential success.[7] Neufeld even suggests that the most parsimonious hypothesis is to assume that adults retain the language-acquisition abilities of children and that "the disparity between child and adult performance can be explained primarily by social and psychological factors which are independent of psycholinguistic abilities." [8]

As a way of agreeing with those who have emphasized the importance of social and psychological factors, I want to summarize some observations of another adult foreign-language learner. My subject was a native speaker of English who spent a year in Sweden, and he lacked most of the social and psychological characteristics that limited Schumann's subject, Alberto. Unlike Alberto, my subject had high status; he dealt constantly, and as an equal, with speakers of the target language; his culture and the culture of his friends and fellow workers in Sweden were neatly congruent and entirely receptive to each other; attitudes on all sides were open and accepting. My subject's motivation also was very high, language and culture shock were minimal, and ego permeability seemed fully adequate to the task at hand. In spite of all the vital advantages that my subject had over Alberto, however, he judged his own progress to be distinctly unsatisfactory. He was in his mid-50s and thus safely past any conceivable critical age for language learning, but he—and I—were loath to admit that the problem was simply that neurological maturation had carried him beyond the age when he could hope to learn a language. On the other hand, the kinds of social and psychological factors that Schumann considers hardly seem to provide an adequate explanation for my subject's difficulties. I want, therefore, to summarize the somewhat different set of social factors that put barriers in the way of my subject's acquisition of Swedish.

I was, of course, my own subject, and what I have to say in the remainder of this paper is the result of my own experience with language acquisition during 1979 and 1980. I spent the year as a "guest professor" at the University of Göteborg, and since I had grown interested in language acquisition, I decided to keep track of what was happening to me. I not only peered into my own head and listened to what came out of my mouth, but I watched what my students, colleagues, and friends did for me—and to me—and I was endlessly impressed by the social barriers that were placed in my way. I was, in fact, continually frustrated by my inability to gain access to the kinds of language and to the kinds of situations that I thought would help me most. I want to outline the frustrations of one high-status, reasonably well-educated, and certainly highly motivated adult learner, hoping that I can offer a small corrective for what has struck me as excessive emphasis on narrow maturational factors as the explanation for adult disabilities.

The difficulties I faced were many and varied, but in a rough way they can be categorized under three headings: difficulties brought about by the characteristics of the language to which I was exposed; difficulties brought about by my own adult attitudes and behavior; and difficulties brought about by the attitudes and actions of the native speakers with whom I dealt. Each of these calls for comment.

THE LANGUAGE

First, I had to cope with a more complex language and with a language that was both dialectally and stylistically more heterogeneous than the language with which a child deals. Even the linguistic environment of a high-school student is considerably less varied than was mine. A community of preadolescents, or even of high-school-aged students, probably speaks in a more repetitive way, on a narrower range of topics, with less extreme style shifting, a narrower dialectal range, and a less extensive active vocabulary than did the adults with whom I dealt in Sweden. I wanted to understand the news on the radio, drama on television, lectures at the university, to engage in serious conversations on a wide range of topics, and to join in the banter around the lunch table. I wanted to read newspapers, novels, instructions in the telephone book, and directions on soup cans as well as scholarly books and articles in my specialty. In every respect in which the range of topics, styles, and dialects is narrowed, the task of the child or the teenaged learner is made easier.

One dimension of variability, the difference between formal and informal Swedish, was particularly troublesome to me. My problem, common to many adult learners, was in finding my way into the informal and colloquial styles of the language. Rapid colloquial Swedish differs in many ways from formal Swedish. I could work on formal styles by reading, by listening to the radio, and even by consulting grammar books, but fast speech was an unending problem. People spoke so rapidly that words were clipped beyond ready recognition. Many things were left out, and yet people seemed hardly aware of their omissions. The most common Swedish pronunciation of *något* ("some, any") is *nåt,* but a high-school girl denied to me, at first, that people really said anything except *något.* Perhaps she thought that, as an educated adult, I should speak "properly" and put in all the sounds. I learned to read, and to understand the formal spoken language of lectures and the radio news, more readily than I learned to understand rapid conversation. A child begins with rapid colloquial speech and moves only gradually to the more formal levels. I moved into the language backward, and never found an easy way to find the connections between the two varieties of the language.

As one example of the kind of difficulty I repeatedly faced, I can cite the example of *hur står det till*. I was quite baffled the first time I heard this expression. It was said very rapidly, as Swedes usually say it, and I could not make out the individual words or distinguish the sounds that formed them. I had to have the phrase explained carefully and repeated several times before I could understand that its words meant literally "How stands it also?" and more loosely "How is everything?" It was only later, and through a deliberate experiment, that I found an appropriate reply. I tried the phrase on a friend, and I must have said it reasonably well for I evoked a similarly slurred response—a rapid burst of sound that, once again, I had to have repeated several times. When I sorted through to the phrase *bara bra* ("just fine"), I had one formulaic answer to one formulaic question. Now I could participate in one small Swedish conversational ritual, but in order to do so, I had had to stop people and insist that they explain. A learner less stubborn than I would have let it go.

Another Swedish formula, *Det är så att,* almost always appears at the beginning of a sentence, usually at the beginning of an utterance. It means, literally, "it is so that" or more loosely "it is the case that," but it is used more frequently than any corresponding phrase in English. It also tends to be mumbled so softly and rapidly that its individual parts fade into a slur that the foreign learner has trouble sorting through. Moreover, it adds little to the meaning of a sentence, and a speaker who is asked to slow down and speak more deliberately is likely to leave it out altogether. Sometimes Swedes even seem slightly embarrassed to realize that they have used it, and this may make them reluctant to repeat it. The phrase, nevertheless, is not completely redundant, and the learner makes progress when he can understand it, and he exhibits fluency when he can use it. It is, in part, a breath catcher, a wind up, a pause to let the speaker collect his thoughts. In this capacity it hardly is needed in print, so it is not likely to be learned by reading or even by listening to formal spoken styles. When spoken, however, it also is an announcement that what follows is a statement rather than a question or an exclamation or even a complaint. It sets the stage, and the listener will understand more easily if he catches the stage setting.

In addition to coping with a more varied language, an adult also must cope with a different language than that of a child and a language that is, in some respects, less suitable for early practice. The vocabulary to which an adult has ready access, for instance, is remarkably different from that of a child. A first-language learner begins with concrete words, not always nouns by any means, but with words that he can learn in the context of events that surround him and that are in no way dependent upon other aspects of the language. I am indebted to Staffan Hellberg for the following list of verbs that formed about one-third of the vocabulary of his daughter

Tina when she was 16 months old: *titta* "look at," *tappa* "loose," *hoppa* "jump," *kasta* "throw," *ramla* "fall down," *ligga* "lie down," *lägga* "put," "place," *slänga* "throw," "throw away," *sjunga* "sing," *släcka* "put out," *gunga* "swing," *öppna* "open," *hänga* "hang," *leka* "play," *sitta* "sit," *dricka* "drink," *åka* "go," *stänga* "shut," *ringa* "ring," "telephone," *äta* "eat." [9]

At a stage when I had a far more extensive vocabulary than did Tina, I still lacked some of these most fundamental of all words. I was, for instance, not even aware of the word *ramla,* the everyday word for "fall down" that every young Swede masters in the course of gaining stability on his legs. Instead of Tina's concrete verbs, I was using the Swedish equivalents of can, need, use, want, try, speak, talk, remember, begin, and finish as well as verbs for a good many more concrete activities.

Most of my words could not be learned by direct association with events in the world around me, but required a complex linguistic context. I usually learned them, of course, with the help of English translations. I was fighting my way into relatively abstract levels of the vocabulary without having laid the concrete foundation. Even in my first two months in Sweden I needed ways to be polite, to ask questions, to express doubt. I needed to say "Ten minutes to four," "Five crowns 25 öre," and "Do you have a danish pastry?" and I even would have liked to be able to say such things as "I wonder if you would be good enough to get me another glass of water?" On the other hand, I felt no need for "fall down," and I would have been regarded as quite eccentric had I gone about falling down and muttering *ramla,* even though it is through exactly such physical acts that a small child first builds up the tight associations between words and events that will last him throughout a lifetime.

A child's first words must be learned in a context that is not dependent upon the rest of the language. Tina's first verbs needed the context of actions, rather than other words, to give them meaning; and of course, this also is true of words like "hot" and "bye-bye," which are so common among English-speaking children, as well as of names for concrete objects. None of these words need other words for their interpretation. All can be learned in total isolation from the rest of a language. The words that I wanted, however, usually needed the support of other words. I had to extract most of my words from a complex linguistic environment, and, from the beginning, I had to use words as mere pieces of larger wholes.

In a few cases, however, I could learn words in clearly defined contexts without the support of other words. Greetings and courtesy phrases are the most obvious example, and a few of them were among my earliest acquisitions. After a few hundred Swedes said *hej* to me, I could hardly escape learning, deeply and unforgettably, that *hej* is used sometimes where Americans say "hi" and sometimes where we say "bye-bye." In this case, I could learn a word in the same manner as a child learns it. Even an adult is given the privilege of hearing this word repeatedly, in linguistic isolation but in a social context where its meaning is unmistakable.

I was surprised to discover one other extensive set of words that I could learn in isolation from much other linguistic context. Adults, or at least Swedish adults, use and accept isolated adjectives more readily than they accept isolated nouns or verbs. Upon hearing of a pleasant situation, people sometimes said *trevligt,* and after hearing it a few times alone, stressed, and clearly articulated, I grasped the idea that the word conveys a sense of "pleasant" or "nice," although, since I learned the word without the prop of an English translation, I now find the precise English equivalent less obvious than for many other words. People said *konstigt* in situations where something was just a bit peculiar, and I soon grasped the idea that it means something like "strange" or "odd" or "funny." Someone would look out the window, shake his head, and say *dåligt väder.* From the speaker's dour expression and from the clouds and drizzle outside, I soon associated *dåligt* with unpleasant events. Only later did I learn that it is simply the ordinary word for "bad."

The ease and clarity with which the meanings of these adjectives percolated into my awareness made me realize how much help is provided by the nonverbal context and, in particular, how much it can help the learner to escape his own language. At the same time, I realized how restricted were my own opportunities to learn in this direct way. For most of language, isolated words simply are not enough for an adult. He wants whole phrases and sentences. He wants his essential words to have grammatical decoration; he wants his verbs to have subjects and objects. Naming things and events in isolation is a reasonable activity for a small child, but only rarely is it a reasonable activity for an adult.

Fluent adult use of a language also presumes an enormous range of background knowledge. If it is not quite insulting to spell out this knowledge in detail for an adult, it certainly is tedious. Children, of course, must have these things spelled out. Through all of childhood, we gradually assimilate the basic knowledge and the background assumptions that we need if we are to use a language fluently. To speak a language like a native requires a knowledge of all the assumptions that a fluent native speaker can be expected to make. With the first language, this process takes well over a decade for every human being. Long before a decade has elapsed, an adult is likely to give up and conclude that he has lost the capacity to learn a language.

THE LEARNER

In addition to the difficulties posed by the nature of the language he faces, an adult learner also is burdened by certain inevitable characteristics of being an adult. The relative complexity of the language he faces indeed is a reflection of the complexity of his adult interests, and an adult who is limited to childish speech must be frustrated constantly by the immature level of his conversation. Even if he is willing to subject himself to simplistic and childish conversation, other adults, from whom the foreigner might hope to learn, often are unwilling to do so.

One way in which an adult must, from the very beginning, act differently from a child is in the use of courtesy phrases. Small children are given clear and careful instructions on how to be courteous (Say "excuse me" to the nice man, darling.) and even a high-school child might be advised about linguistic etiquette. An adult, however, somehow is expected to know already. If he is not polite enough to say "excuse me," it certainly would be impolite to tell him to do so. An adult with even the most minimal desire to learn Swedish will want, from his very first day in the country, not only to say *ursäkta mig* ("excuse me"), but to express politeness in many other, more subtle ways as well. He needs these to show the world that he is a civilized and mature adult. But no Swede ever said gently to me, *Sag "ursäkta mig" till farbron*. Without such guidance, *ursäkta mig* was not at all easy to master. Its sounds seemed totally arbitrary, and when I heard it at all, it was mumbled so quickly that I could hardly make it out. Still, in its range of use, *ursäkta mig* is enough like "excuse me" to be relatively easy, but this is not the case with another ubiquitous courtesy phrase, *var så god*. This is used when offering someone something—money, an object, the chance to come in or sit down—a range of circumstances that is quite peculiar to English habits. I needed this phrase, along with *ursäkta mig* and *tack* ("thank you"), during my first days in Sweden—far earlier than a child would need them—but I was given much less help with them than Swedish children must get. It simply would not have been polite to tell me how to be polite.

Being interested in a wider range of activities than a child is, an adult always is tempted to use his language in a more elaborate way than his limited resources allow. In particular, he is likely to attempt syntactic acrobatics while his morphology remains rudimentary. I felt pressed from early in my stay to construct the complex sentences that fitted my complex needs and interests. I managed to learn a good deal of general vocabulary, and I got hold of enough signs of subordination, relativization, and conjunction to allow me to combine my words into rather elaborate sentences at a time when my word- and phrase-level morphology still was a disaster. Signs of gender distinction, the morphology of irregular verbs, the suffixed definite article, even the marking of the plural, were a shambles. I knew, as abstract rules, how to form some plurals, how to attach some definite article suffixes, and how to make the past tense of some verbs, but in the heat of conversation I was quite unable to use these rules. I could produce relatively complex syntax on a poorly developed morphological foundation. I was, in a sense, inventing my own pidgin Swedish, and I was approaching the language along a path quite different from that taken by a small child who masters morphology relatively early, or from that followed in older traditional foreign-language courses, where morphological details were given so much early weight. (For the analogy of pidginization and foreign-language learning, see References 10 and 11.)

My language was too flimsy to support my heroic efforts, but my choice was between speaking with garbled morphology and not speaking at all, and

I was not content to remain silent. An adult wants to talk about complex things, and unless he is content to limit his language to carefully prepared drills, he cannot avoid copious mistakes. To the extent that he acts like an adult by reaching for adult topics and adult complexity, his language is bound to be distorted.

Simply by already knowing one language, moreover, we raise the standards by which we judge our progress in a new language. A child may recognize many words without being at all clear about their exact meaning. The adult's standard of comprehension, however, is likely to be his ability to translate what he hears into his own language—a very high standard, indeed. If a child has no other language, he lacks that external standard of judgment. He may recognize many words and know that they sound right in the context, but fail to know their full meaning. A child may not realize how much he does not know. An adult recognizes his own limitations more clearly and is in danger of being correspondingly discouraged.

An adult who works on a second language and who is unwilling to restrict himself to childish matters always has goals that are beyond his ability, and the variables that determine the success of a particular linguistic encounter are legion: the willingness of the other person to go slowly, to simplify his language, and to avoid exotic vocabulary; the familiarity of his dialect, his voice quality, and the habitual volume at which he speaks; the ambient noise and the acoustic characteristics of the setting; and, of course, the familiarity of the learner with the topic, his interest in the subject, the strength of his determination to try, and, profoundly important, his state of fatigue. Occasionally a learner can take pleasure in a triumph, but each new triumph tends to set a new level of expectation: "But I did so well when I talked to that lady yesterday! Why am I having so much trouble talking to this man now?" Inevitably the precious moments of triumph are few; the moments of frustration are many.

THE NATIVES

The special characteristics of the adult learner are, of course, mirrored by the way in which the adult is treated by those who already speak the language. (The special registers used with children and with foreigners recently have received increasing attention.)[12,13] With children, we guide, we coax, we repeat, we simplify our language in ways that we are reluctant to do with adults. Even a high-school teacher, even fellow high-school students, probably are more willing to instruct, to suggest, to lead, to take by the hand, and, when necessary, to push and to demonstrate physically so that the learner will understand.

We are also much less upset by breakdowns in understanding with children. We want to understand children and to make ourselves understood, and when we do not understand, we may ask for a repetition, or we may test a guess by asking a question. Too much effort of this sort with an adult becomes embarrassing. Before asking a fourth time, we smile and pretend that all is clear. Except when we guide children about the avoidance of stigmatized forms, however, instruction in grammar is rare. What we want is the message, and the way he says it is not so important. With an adult, it always is a temptation to give explicit and fussy grammatical advice. At a time when I still was groping desperately for a few simple Swedish words, people insisted upon correcting my genders. I simply could not afford to be distracted with such details so soon.

Many adults also must contend with the experience of earlier failure. If other foreign visitors have failed to learn the language, the natives will not expect much more success from the next visitor. Living among people who are skeptical about one's ability to learn can qiuckly dampen initiative. When adults are burdened with so many other difficulties, the suspicion soon grows that the task is impossible.

There remains, of course, one final barrier that faces an American professor who tries to learn Swedish: the high standard of English of the Swedes whom he meets. When everyone speaks such excellent English, playing with pidgin Swedish becomes an embarrassing game. How much does one dare burden one's colleagues? One can try an occasional word or phrase. Here and there a knowledge of some language fragments slowly becomes modestly useful, but for many long months, when the crunch finally comes and one really wants to talk or to understand, when one really wants to pass some important information, the temptation to resort to English is irresistible. There is an iron law of ordinary bilingualism: when two bilinguals of unequal ability meet, they avoid the worst speaker's worst language. To speak poor Swedish to someone who speaks excellent English is an insult, an embarrassment, a waste of time, and a strain upon good will. One needs an extraordinarily high level of Swedish before it becomes a serious candidate in a conversation with Swedish academics.

My colleagues read English easily, and they did most of their writing in English. They expected foreign visitors—from France, Russia, and Japan as well as from England and America—to hold conversations and give lectures in English. There were occasions when even Swedes with distinctly limited ability in English could hardly be persuaded that I could manage in Swedish. They acted as if broken English were an acceptable and reasonable medium of communication, but they hardly knew how to cope with someone who spoke broken Swedish. An English-speaking visitor can hardly resist the expectations of the natives, but these expectations do limit any opportunity to be immersed in Swedish. Escape from English is impossible. I passed many days, sometimes several days in succession, with only marginally more Swedish in my environment than I would have had at home in the United States. The occasions when I really needed Swedish were almost nonexistent.

The ease of resorting to one's native language does more than simply stretch out acquisition time. It erodes motivation. If one can get along so easily with English, why bother with Swedish? But reliance upon

English probably has still another effect. It has been suggested that the more hours spent per day in the study of a language, the more will be learned in each hour.[14,15] That is to say, eight hours spent in a single day will achieve more than eight hours spread out across eight days. When working on Swedish, I had the feeling that it was helpful to cram just as much as possible into my short-term memory. I felt as if this increased the pressure there, and that this higher pressure then would force a part of the Swedish deeper into my long-term memory. The only way to keep the pressure high and to keep a steady flow moving into long-term memory was to spend several hours a day working on Swedish. As soon as other work intervened and as soon as the hours spent on Swedish dropped, I began to feel that my rate of forgetting climbed to compete with my rate of learning. What little got placed in short-term memory escaped before it could be consolidated into a longer-term memory. I then would have to learn the same things all over again.

My subjective feelings about short- and long-term memory may be quite fanciful, but during periods when I spent relatively little time with Swedish, I did feel that my rate of acquisition dropped even more rapidly than the number of hours devoted to study. A child who is immersed in a situation where he is exposed to the language for many hours every day would have a better chance than I of consolidating things into long-term memory before they escaped in forgetfulness.

CONCLUSIONS

In the face of the many difficulties with which an adult must cope, one strategy remains open to anyone who is sufficiently stubborn to keep trying—a concentration upon comprehension. A learner can read, listen to the radio, and watch TV. He can attend lectures. He can try to understand whatever Swedish swirls around him. Even here, of course, he meets barriers. Standards of courtesy may make it seem rude to speak a language in the presence of an adult who does not understand it. When in my presence, Swedes often shifted to English, even when speaking to each other. Even when people did speak Swedish, they sometimes courteously dropped their voices, as if to apologize for lapsing into a language that I could not be expected to understand. In this way, they acknowledged that I could not be included in that part of the conversation and they demonstrated that I did not need to feel responsible for understanding it. By speaking quietly, people were both apologizing to me and absolving me of responsibility, but at the same time they were depriving me of an opportunity to practice.

When Swedes did speak to me, they showed little skill in simplifying their speech to a level that I could more easily understand. Perhaps it would have seemed insulting to speak to me in the same simple terms that they would use with a child. I tried to ask them to speak more slowly, but they found it difficult to maintain a slow pace, and they soon would speed up again. Often it was easier to switch to English than to produce an artificially simple Swedish. As a result, my opportunities even to listen to Swedish were severely restricted.

First-language learners are immersed in language from the time they are born. For thousands of hours, through month after month and year after year, they are bathed by it. Even a high-school student who attends school for several hours every day, and who associates with contemporaries after school, has far longer hours of intensive foreign-language exposure than I could have, or than most adults ever can have. If the language of children, even the language of teenagers, is a bit simpler and a bit less varied than the language I needed, then young people have both less ambitious goals and a greater opportunity to work toward their goals than I did. To the extent that their teachers and contemporaries are less able, or less willing, to resort to English than were my Swedish colleagues, children get far more chance to hear and to use the new language. We should not be so surprised if children seem to learn languages more quickly than adults. They often have far more opportunity, and the standards by which we judge them are much lower.

The factors that slowed my acquisition of Swedish are in no way mysterious. They strike me, in fact, as quite obvious. They are the kinds of problems that any adult who has tried to learn a foreign language must have experienced. But they are not the factors that seem to be considered under the label of the "critical period" for language acquisition, nor do they reflect the problems of having reached a Piagetian stage of formal operations. They do not even seem to reflect the kinds of generalized social and psychological factors that Schumann cites to explain his subject's poor performance. My problems were simpler and more obvious than any of these, but I think that we ought to take them into account more adequately before we resort to neurological or Piagetian factors, or to social and psychological circumstances that affect only a limited number of learners. I faced so many obvious barriers that I feel no urge to blame some cellular or neurofunctional disability with which I have been burdened since puberty.

At a more generalized level, however, one can hardly rule out maturational changes. Perhaps children are, by nature, more talkative human beings than adults. Perhaps they are more inclined to play. A small human being with a strong impulse both to talk and to play who is surrounded by similar small human beings may venture more vigorously and less fearfully into a new language than would his less talkative and less playful parent. Perhaps we are by "nature"—by genetic endowment—prone to regard the baby talk of our children as cute but to regard the equally broken speech of the foreigner as annoying. Perhaps we more "naturally" reach out to help the child than to help the foreigner. Conceivably, we are also, by nature, the kind of animals that become burdened, as adults, with a consciousness of status and dignity that is incompatible with the childish activity of learning a language. In these very general senses, one hardly can reject the suggestion that children find it more "natural" to learn a language than adults do. But these are far more generalized abilities than those sought under the rubric of a "critical period" for language learning. Instead of searching for neurological changes at puberty, I would emphasize the more generalized social changes that give an adult a different status among his fellows.

ACKNOWLEDGMENTS

I would like to thank Staffan Hellberg, Anders-Börje Andersson, Alvar Ellegård, Jens Allwood, A. L. Becker, and Larry Selinker for their careful and thought-provoking comments on an earlier version of this paper.

REFERENCES

1. PENFIELD, W. & L. ROBERTS. 1959. Speech and Brain Mechanisms. Princeton University Press. Princeton, N.J.
2. LENNEBERG, E. H. 1967. Biological Foundations of Language. John Wiley & Sons, Inc. New York, N.Y.
3. KRASHEN, S. D. 1975. The critical period for language acquisition and its possible bases. Ann. N.Y. Acad. Sci. 263: 211–224.
4. LAMENDELLA, J. T. 1977. General principles of neurofunctional organization and their manifestation in primary and non-primary language acquisition. Lang. Learn. 27: 155–196.
5. INHELDER, B. & J. PIAGET. 1958. The Growth of Logical Thinking from Childhood to Adolescence. Basic Books. New York, N.Y.
6. SCHUMANN, J. H. 1978. The Pidginization Process. Newbury House. Rowley, Mass.
7. WAGNER-GOUGH, J. & E. HATCH. 1975. The importance of input data in second language acquisition studies. Lang. Learn. 25: 297–309.
8. NEUFELD, G. G. 1979. Toward a theory of language learning ability. Lang. Learn. 29: 227–241.
9. HELLBERG, S. (Personal communication.)
10. SCHUMANN, J. H. 1978. The relationship of pidginization, creolization, and decreolization to second language acquisition. Lang. Learn. 28: 367–379.
11. ANDERSEN, R. W. 1979. Expanding Schumann's pidginization hypothesis. Lang. Learn. 29: 105–119.
12. SNOW, C. E. & C. A. FERGUSON. 1977. Talking to Children. Cambridge University Press. Cambridge, England.
13. FERGUSON, C. A. 1972. Toward a characterization of English foreigner talk. Anthropol. Linguistics 17: 1–14.
14. STREVENS, P. 1977. New Orientations in the Teaching of English: 28 ff. Oxford University Press. Oxford, England.
15. DEVENY, J. J., JR. & J. C. BOOKOUT. 1976. The intensive language course: toward a successful approach. Foreign Lang. Ann.: 58–63.

SYNTAX, SEMANTICS, AND PRAGMATICS—SECOND LANGUAGE: GENERAL DISCUSSION

Moderator: Karl Diller

Department of English
University of New Hampshire
Durham, New Hampshire 03824

L. BLOOM (*Teachers College, Columbia University, New York, N.Y.*): Dr. Wode, you talked about two different ways in which the negative marker occurs first in the sentence. Your presentation included examples of preposed negative markers, which occur first in a sentence when the subject is omitted. However, at the end of your presentation, you provided an example of a negative marker preposed in front of a sentence subject. Your example was "Doesn't John go to school." An example of this kind does not represent the negation types that were summarized in your paper.

H. WODE (*University of Kiel, Kiel, Federal Republic of Germany*): In your 1970 book, you said somebody else found examples of that sort, and you suspected that this was not really nonanaphoric negation, but something else. You found only one example, a doubtful one, of this sort in your data.

L. BLOOM: I am not sure that I follow you because I understand that "no," preposed in front of the sentence subject, occurs in a situation in which the sentence subject is indeed the subject of an affirmative sentence. When a child says "No, Kathryn play self," she means "No, I don't want to play with you, I want to play by myself." Your summary data indicate that when "no" is the first item in the sentence, the sentence subject does not occur except for your reference to negative declarative sentences in the concluding part of your paper.

H. WODE: We are talking about the same thing. Your impression is due to the way I have summarized my data. The kind of utterance that we have here—negative item preposed to a sentence including subject plus predicate—has been observed, although only rarely. There are a few such utterances in the Brown corpus, and there was one such utterance in your 1970 book, although it was a doubtful one. Such utterances are reported for L1 [first-language] acquisition in other languages (German, Bulgarian, Finnish, etc.). However, my overall impression is that this elaborate structure—the placement of negative before a whole sentence—is rare, but not impossible. For L2 [second-language] acquisition, the situation is quite comparable.

P. M. LIGHTBOWN (*Concordia University, Montreal, Quebec, Canada*): Dr. Wode, I would like to know whether your example of a negative declarative sentence was said within the context of a classroom language exercise in which the teacher might have requested a response to the question "Does John go to school?"

291

0077–8923/81/0379–0291 $01.75/2 © 1981, NYAS

H. WODE: Yes. Such examples occur in exercises in which declarative sentences are to be negated.

P. M. LIGHTBOWN: I have seen this construction also. For the situation where the teacher says "Does John go to school?" the child will negate the auxiliary by saying "Doesn't John go to school" because he knows that he is supposed to generate a negative sentence. In this case it is the result of a classroom exercise, but I can't imagine seeing students use sentences such as this in other contexts.

H. WODE: Next time you come to Germany, Dr. Lightbown, make sure you visit me. I shall take you through some classes, and you can witness this structure for yourself. Everybody thinks this sentence to be an interrogative, but it is not. Such examples are quite frequent, and they come from teaching situations where students are taught to negate declaratives.

UNIDENTIFIED SPEAKER: Dr. Snow, first, about your translation test—was that given in written form and did the students have a limited time to respond or did they have as much time as they wanted? Second, the adult age group included subjects who ranged up to 60 years of age. Were you to classify the adults into discrete age levels, you might have had a better basis for assessing the effect of age.

C. E. SNOW (*Harvard University Graduate School of Education, Cambridge, Mass.*): With regard to your first question, the test was given orally and there was no limit at all on time. Furthermore, the students received as much help as they needed with lexical items. Clearly the ability to translate is independent of knowledge of a language. The translation task by itself is not a good basis for concluding that older subjects learn Dutch faster than younger subjects do. I drew this conclusion from the larger study, in which all of the language tests revealed the same age patterning.

With respect to your question about age groupings, my reasons for establishing the different age groups involved pragmatic considerations, but also reflected important differences in the language-learning situations of the subjects. The 5-year-olds were preschoolers. Everybody above that age was learning Dutch, in part, through formal training. Additionally, those age 3 to 15 were all school-going whereas the subjects above that age were non-school-going learners. Learning language in a classroom situation where individuals function as pupils would appear to be an important consideration, and one that was reflected by the age groupings in my investigation.

M. PATKOWSKI (*Hostos Community College, Bronx, N.Y.*): Mr. Cook, you mentioned the difference between psycholinguistic processes, which you regard as dynamic, and most teaching methodologies, which are thought to be static. You offered your own methodology as being more dynamic. Can you elaborate on this difference?

V. J. COOK (*University of Essex, Colchester, England*): The point I was making was in reference to syllabus design and the work done by the

Council of Europe at the threshold level. Communicative syllabuses in the past few years have included precise specification of the language functions that people use and that the learner needs to acquire, to the point that vast lists are provided and minute specifications of functions are presented. This approach is reflected in textbooks and in teaching methods. For example, teachers will say, "Today we are going to do complaining; tomorrow we are going to do requesting." These functions, as they are currently being taught, are not meaningfully integrated or of communicative value. For example, a request is meaningless without a following acknowledgment or compliance or whatever. If we are going to use syllabuses based on communicative descriptions, as people have been trying to do for the past few years, then we have to consider the total communicative situation and not just denote items as grammatical or functional.

S. ERVIN-TRIPP (*University of California, Berkeley, Calif.*): Dr. Long, I would like to mention a study by Lily Wong-Fillmore, to be included in Louise Cherry Wilkinson's *Communicating in the Classroom* [Wiley]. Wong-Fillmore has been observing the rate of English acquisition in classrooms differing both in composition and structure. She found an interaction between classroom linguistic homogeneity and whether the structure was teacher or activity centered. If half the children were native speakers of English and half native speakers of Spanish, the activity-centered classroom had two advantages. The children split into groups and learned from each other in face-to-face interaction. The teacher also organized groups that were linguistically homogeneous, allowing her to adapt her English to the learners' level. The teacher-centered classroom as a whole was too heterogeneous for adaptation. In mixed classrooms, activity-centered instruction led to the most rapid learning of English.

In contrast, where all the students are at the same level of foreigner's English, appropriate accommodation isn't a problem. In homogeneous classes, the teacher-centered approach produced the most rapid learning of English. The teacher made the modified interaction with each child that was necessary and that could be heard and understood by the rest of the children. Here the best results were in teacher- rather than activity-centered classrooms because the children heard English from its best speaker. This result fits with Postovsky's proposal that starting with comprehension methods avoids learning from poor models. But of course the results depend on what the teacher does. With appropriate interactive methods by the teacher, the teacher-centered method was more effective than the activity-centered method in all foreign-student classes.

F. STEVENS (*Concordia University, Montreal, Quebec, Canada*): I have a comment about the activity-centered method about which Dr. Ervin-Tripp spoke. In my research, 12-year-old youngsters in activity-centered second-language-immersion classes in Montreal learned as much in about two-thirds of the time as did students in teacher-centered programs.

M. H. LONG (*University of Pennsylvania Graduate School of Education, Philadelphia, Pa.*): Thank you for the information. One of the probable pedagogical implications of this research is that any classroom technique, no matter what "method" it is taken from, that will boost the *quantity* of modified interaction opportunities would be likely to produce either faster or ultimately superior second-language acquisition or both. Where there is a teacher-centered class, this could by definition involve a group of 30 people with different levels of interlanguage development. That is obviously an inefficient setting in which to learn a language because of the evidence, from Snow's [1972] work and others, that you only get the kind of speech modification needed when there is feedback. Here we have a similar and parallel finding in that we observe increased modification on tasks requiring information exchange. When the task is not one that forces the native speaker to *exchange* information, you find far fewer modifications.

C. A. FERGUSON (*Stanford University, Stanford, Calif.*): Dr. Long, I just have three brief comments. The first is to welcome wholeheartedly the look at interaction patterns as well as all the grammatical features and so on. The second is about the four criteria, the conditions that you set up as likely to involve a greater degree of ungrammaticality and foreigner talk. I would suggest at least two others. One is the degree of conventionalization of a foreigner-talk register in particular speech communities. The other is the nature of the occasion, a criterion that you yourself used, as when you talked about changing information. The third comment is about your assumption that this kind of modified input is necessary for first-language acquisition. Although such phenomena are widespread in the world, and we can find them in many different societies and cultures, there seem to be some speech communities in which there is little or no modification of the type we are familiar with but where the children manage to learn the language anyway. I was thinking of Elinor Ochs' work on Samoan, Bambi Schiefflin's on the Kaluli, or Shirley Heath's on the Trackton community in South Carolina.

M. H. LONG: Thank you for your valuable comments. I am aware of that work. There are cross-cultural studies in L1 that show different *sources* of that input, for example, in Samoa and so on. I am not aware of any cases where the input is not modified by another *child* or primary caretaker.

A. J. BRONSTEIN (*Lehman College, Bronx, N.Y.*): I share with you, Professor Burling, a very similar experience. I find your remarks fascinating, having spent a year in the Scandinavian country of Norway last year.

I found that if a critical period meant anything at all, it was that I had to behave like a child. In this sense, every time I sat down at the luncheon table in the faculty hall, I asked a question in Norwegian and was answered in English. When I went to the supermarket after having practiced at great length on how to order bread and cheese and what not, and asked a question like "Can we have half a pound of cheese?" the person always seemed competent in English for some cockeyed reason and would answer, "Yes, you may have half a pound of cheese."

I noticed that the children of visiting professors weren't having the same difficulty. They would go out on the ice-skating rink and skate, and if they fell down, they would say, "Somebody help me up." Although they were not understood, people helped them up while talking to them in Norwegian. When they slid down the snowbank and were in the way of the next person coming, the next kid yelled "Get out of the way" in Norwegian. The youngsters did not understand what was being said, but they got out of the way after the first time to avoid getting hurt. So, the critical period meant "Either you understand what is being said to you in Norwegian or you are going to be in tremendous trouble."

I found out that the best way to learn Norwegian was to relate to people who knew no English. We skated and skied with people who spoke only Norwegian.

I think there must be something to the critical period. It pays to be a child sometimes!

J. P. MOOIJMAN (*St. Ignatius College, Amsterdam, the Netherlands*): Dr. Burling, I am sure that if you had concentrated almost exclusively on learning to understand the language and paid hardly any attention to the skills of speaking and writing, your progress would have been very rapid, indeed even more so if you had taught yourself the recognition of about 25 to 30 words every day as well. May I talk briefly about the experience of one of my English friends in London, England. He used to suffer from two apprehensions. First, if a friend rang him from Paris, he would think: "Oh, my God, how am I going to understand all this French? He speaks much too fast for me." His second apprehension was even worse: "How am I going to answer him in French the moment he stops talking?"

The problem was solved when he had learned to understand French fluently and his French friend had no difficulty in understanding English, allowing each to communicate in his native language. From then on, both apprehensions had disappeared and communication between them was perfect!

The problem of perfect communication between the 12 member states of the European Economic Community can be solved in the same way. It is not only the most efficient, but also the most democratic approach.

R. BURLING (*University of Michigan, Ann Arbor, Mich.*): If I may make a comment, I did concentrate on comprehension, and in spite of all the problems that I mentioned, I did learn to understand quite a bit of Swedish. I gave a three-hour seminar in Stockholm one afternoon. I started off in Swedish but admitted that I did not think I could make it all the way in Swedish. I did encourage them to ask questions in Swedish, and if I couldn't understand, I knew somebody would help me. We went back and forth for three hours. They spoke only Swedish, and I spoke almost entirely in English. We had hardly any trouble whatsoever. I would never have believed that such a thing would be possible had I not actually experienced it. Nobody can tell me that comprehension does not advance far more rapidly than production.

INPUT CONSIDERATIONS IN THE COMPREHENSION
OF FIRST AND SECOND LANGUAGE *

Harris Winitz

Department of Psychology
University of Missouri–Kansas City
Kansas City, Missouri 64110

For more than a decade the factor of language input has been the topic of concern in child language research.[1] Recently there has been interest in the study of input to the second-language learner largely because of the current belief that simplification of style and structural form, recognized as an important factor in the acquisition of children's first language (L1), is a potentially important condition for the adult learner of a second language (L2).[2] Yet, as I soon will describe, there appears to be a significant restriction on this generalization that makes its application to adult language learning less than satisfactory unless adequately controlled for.

The concept of simplification has not been ignored by writers of language manuals and texts. Almost all texts begin with material that is regarded as easy by the community of language teachers. The putatively complex structures, including the frequently feared subjunctives and conditionals, are presented relatively late in the course of study.

In this paper, input will be considered relative to differences observed between adults and children in the acquisition of L2. In particular, the "crossover" effect, observed by Snow and Hoefnagel-Höhle,[3] is a significant consideration. Snow and Hoefnagel-Höhle found that adult speakers of English who acquire Dutch are initially superior to children, but in time the children overtake and surpass the adults. We have termed this change in the language performance of children and adults the "crossover" effect.

The initial superiority of adults learning a second language has been reported previously. For example, Asher and Price found that adults acquired Russian faster than did children in a relatively short training session.[4] This initial superiority of adults in language learning may continue for a relatively long period of time, perhaps up to a year, according to the findings of Snow and Hoefnagel-Höhle.[3]

In the Snow and Hoefnagel-Höhle investigation, adults and children of several ages were compared on a battery of tests that assessed competency in the phonology, syntax, and vocabulary of Dutch.[3] Prior to their acquisition of Dutch, all subjects had been monolingual speakers of English. One group of subjects, designated as beginners, consisted of recent arrivals to Holland. They were tested three times at four- to five-month intervals, with the first testing administered shortly after their arrival. A second group

* Supported by the National Institute of Neurological and Communicative Disorders and Stroke, No. 16161.

0077–8923/81/0379–0296 $01.75/2 © 1981, NYAS

of subjects, who had been living in Holland and speaking Dutch for at least 18 months, also was studied. Data from this advanced group of speakers were used to make the fourth and final assessment. The adults generally were superior to the children in the first two testing sessions, and the adults generally were behind the children in the final two testing sessions. There was one exception to this generalization regarding age and language achievement. A 12- to 15-year age group consistently was superior to the adults and children in all four testing sessions.

These results are not easily reconcilable with the critical-period hypothesis of language acquisition, which specifies that nativelike competency only can be acquired prior to puberty.[5] First, this theory contains no provision for the initial superiority of adults in language achievement. Second, it cannot explain the superior performance of the 12–15 age group, which no doubt included subjects several years postpuberty.

In this paper the language learning of children and adults will be examined further to determine whether adults differ from children on phonetic distinctions with which they are unfamiliar. New phonetic responses are said to be particularly difficult for adults.[5,6] This difficulty may stem from an inability to distinguish between unfamiliar phonetic units or from an inability to articulate new sounds and sound sequences.

Another reason for the focus on discrimination (or comprehension) rather than production was because of the strong possibility that adults structure input differently from children. These differences and their implications also will be considered.

EXPERIMENT ON THE PERCEPTION OF MANDARIN CHINESE TONES AND SOUNDS

Snow and Hoefnagel-Höhle compared the discrimination of children and adults on a test of Dutch phonological distinctions.[3] The adult group was marginally superior to an 8- to 10-year age group in the first session (Figure 2, Reference 3). In the subsequent testing sessions, the adults fell behind the children of 8–10 years of age by about four percentage points. Of additional interest is that the adults in the first two test sessions made fewer discrimination errors than did two other groups of children, aged 3–5 years and 6–7 years, but fell behind these young children on the last two test sessions. In contrast, the performance of the 12- to 15-year age group consistently was superior to the adults and the other children, with the exception that the 6- to 7-year age group performed as well as the 12- to 15-year age group in the final testing session. Overall, however, the percentage differences were not large.

The subjects in the Snow and Hoefnagel-Höhle study also were judged on pronunciation. In the first test session, the adults performed slightly better than did the 8- to 10-year group. However, in the final testing session, the pronunciation of Dutch by the 8- to 10-year age group was rated as better than that of the adults. Surprisingly, the pronunciation of the

12–15 age group fell slightly behind the 8–10 age group. There always is the possibility that young children will be rated higher in pronunciation, other things equal, than will adults because listeners do not expect children's speech to be perfect. Without a control group of native Dutch speakers, it is difficult to conclude that young children achieve best in pronunciation.

Cochrane compared native Japanese children and adults residing in the United States on the perception and production of English /r/-/l/.[7] Exposure to English ranged from 1–12 years for the children and 18–43 years for the adults. The performance of the adults and children did not differ on discrimination. On production, however, the children were found to be clearly superior. In summary, the findings of Snow and Hoefnagel-Höhle indicate that adults and children 12–15 years of age perform best on auditory discrimination in the early stages of language learning. However in the later stages of language achievement, the adults fall behind the 12- to 15-year age group and also fall behind children much younger in age who do as well as the 12- to 15-year age group. Cochrane's findings suggest that for long periods of exposure to L2, adults and children perform similarly on speech-sound discrimination. The difference between these two studies may well reflect the differences and similarities in the phonology of the first and second languages as well as the time period over which the comparisons were made. In this present investigation, phonetic elements from Mandarin Chinese were selected because this language is unrelated to English and because the discrimination of its tones and sounds is regarded as difficult for English speakers.

Materials

Two sets of tapes were prepared. One set contained the four tones of Mandarin Chinese, and the other set the five Chinese obstruents /dz/, /tʃ/, /ʒ/, /dʒ/, and /ts/. These elements were selected because they are regarded as particularly difficult for English speakers to distinguish.

The tone tapes were prepared as follows. Recordings were made of one male and one female Taiwanese speaker of Mandarin Chinese uttering appropriate tokens of each element in isolation, in a Chinese disyllable, and in a short Chinese sentence. The syllable [ma] was the segmental frame for all tone tokens. Each tone was recorded in the following three contexts:

    a. Isolation: ma.
    b. Disyllable: swayma.
    c. Sentence: shou ma-idza zi fung lee (the small ma-chair is in the room).

The average intensity of the tone syllable was equivalent to or greater than the other syllables in the disyllable and sentence contexts, as measured by amplitude displays (voice identification spectrograph 700 series).

Each listening tape contained tokens of either the male or female speaker for each one of the above three contexts. A total of six tapes was prepared. There was one male-speaker isolation, disyllable, and sentence tape and one female-speaker isolation, disyllable, and sentence tape respectively.

The total number of item pairs for each tone tape was 48. Half of the 48 pairs (24 items) contained identical tokens, and half (24 items) different tokens. Each of the four tones appeared equally often in the same pairs and different pairs. Item order for tones within pairs appeared equally often in the first and second position. The order of the 48 item pairs was random with the restriction that each pair, regardless of the order of items within a pair, appeared no more than two times in succession. The interitem stimulus was 10 seconds, and the interval between items for each pair was 1 second.

The sound tapes were prepared similarly. Each obstruent appeared in a consonant-vowel syllable in which the vowel was [a] and the tone contour was tone 1. The number of item pairs for each sound tape was 80. There were 40 same-item pairs and 40 different-item pairs. Each of the five consonants appeared equally often in the same-item and different-item pairs. Six separate tapes were prepared. There was one male-speaker and one female-speaker tape for the isolation, disyllable, and sentence contexts respectively. In all other respects, the procedures were similar to those used for the tones.

Subjects

The subjects were monolingual English-speaking Americans attending third-grade classes (mean age, 8.8 years; standard deviation, 0.4 years; $n = 24$ males, 24 females) in Kansas City, and monolingual English-speaking college students (mean age, 21.7 years; SD, 4.8 years; $n = 24$ males, 24 females) from the University of Missouri at Kansas City. Each subject took only two tapes, a tone tape first and a sound tape second. Of the 24 subjects of each sex within each age group, 8 were randomly assigned an isolation tape, 8 a disyllable tape, and 8 a sentence tape. Male- and female-speaker tapes were assigned randomly to subjects with the restriction that an equal number of subjects of both sexes took each of the six tapes.

Adults were administered both tapes in one session. Only one tape was administered to each child in each listening session; the second tape was completed within a week. All testing was conducted under free-field conditions at a comfortable listening level in a quiet room at the university for the college students and in a testing room at the school for the children.

In all cases the subjects were to indicate whether the items of each pair were the same or different. The subjects received appropriate instructions, which included a small number of examples taken from the listening tapes. In addition, the children were preinstructed thoroughly on the concept of same and different by receiving pretraining with visual forms and English sounds. They were required to pass a preliminary test containing same-different visual symbols and English sounds in order to qualify for the experiment. Two children were excluded because they failed to pass this preliminary test. Adults recorded their answers by circling *s* for same and *d* for different on their test sheets. Children were prompted by the examiner who said "same or different" after each item pair and recorded the oral responses of the children.

Results

Means and standard deviations for the tone scores are presented in TABLE 1. For all three contexts, the adults achieved higher scores than did the children [F = (1,90) 56.2; p < 0.0001]. Context is significant [F = (2,90) 70.0; p < 0.0001], indicating that the tasks increased in difficulty from isolation to disyllable to sentence. The interaction effect also was significant [F = (2,90) 9.8; p < 0.001], indicating that the difference between the

TABLE 1

MEANS AND STANDARD DEVIATIONS FOR TONES AND SOUNDS FOR CHILDREN AND ADULTS

		Isolation	Disyllable	Sentence
Tones				
	Children	44.56	42.06	32.00
		(3.99)	(4.16)	(4.77)
	Adults	47.69	46.56	42.50
		(0.77)	(2.06)	(3.08)
Sounds				
	Children	71.88	65.63	53.13
		(4.20)	(7.59)	(9.50)
	Adults	76.25	71.25	72.56
		(2.14)	(4.98)	(3.30)

adults and the children increases as a function of an increase in contextual complexity.

Means and standard deviations for the sounds also are displayed in TABLE 1. The adults achieved higher scores than did the children [F = (1,90) 63.2; p < 0.0001]. Context was significant [F = (2,90) 27.5; p < 0.001], indicating that scores decrease as structural complexity increases. However, the adults showed no decrease between the disyllable and sentence contexts. The interaction effect was significant [F = (2,90) 15.3; p < 0.001], signifying that as structural complexity increases, the difference between the children and the adults increases.

Discussion

Our findings are in agreement in direction but not in magnitude of difference with those obtained by Snow and Hoefnagel-Höhle for the first testing session of beginning speakers of Dutch.[3] The differences reported by Snow and Hoefnagel-Höhle for the speech-sound discrimination test were small, favoring adults; whereas in the present investigation, a large difference favoring the adults was found. As yet, we have not tested children of 12–15 years of age, but we plan to do so shortly.

The findings of the present study are different from those obtained by Snow and Hoefnagel-Höhle and Cochrane when late stages of language acquisition are considered. Snow and Hoefnagel-Höhle found adults to be inferior to children,[3] and Cochrane found no difference between adults and children,[7] for advanced speakers of L2.

In each of these three studies, sounds from different languages were examined. This difference does not obscure the one consistent finding: adults perform better than prepubescent children on the discrimination of L2 speech sounds when the language experience of subjects in L2 is limited, but do not perform as well after a significant amount of the language has been acquired. This interpretation, we are reminded, does not take into account Snow and Hoefnagel-Höhle's 12–15 age group, which performed better than the adults both as beginners and advanced speakers.[3]

Our next problem is to try to account for the initial superiority of adults and the later superiority of children. There is the possibility that superior intelligence, memory, and social experience give adults an advantage. In time, however, the constraints of learning a language after the critical period surface.

Another interpretation of the crossover effect is to acknowledge that speech-sound discrimination tasks can be used to assess two levels of perceptual processing, a psychophysical level and a phonological level. Prior to any significant acquisition of L2, a speech-sound discrimination task, such as that used in this experiment, can be regarded as a psychophysical task because it involves the discrimination of speech sounds in a language for which linguistic functions have not been acquired. However, the Mandarin-Chinese sounds in this study are phonetic units that are somewhat contrastive in English, although /ts/ and /ʒ/ are not realized in the initial word position. No doubt there was some generalization from English for the speech sounds. The tones, on the other hand, would appear to test discrimination primarily at a psychophysical level for English speakers.

The findings of this study may be interpreted as supportive of advanced psychophysical skills on the part of adults, and in this regard they do not disconfirm the critical-period hypothesis, which implicates children as more skilled in making linguistic judgments and adults as more skilled in making nonlinguistic judgments.

There are two reasons why the psychophysical explanation cannot be used generally to explain the initial superiority of adults in speech-sound discrimination or in any of the other language functions. In the Snow and Hoefnagel-Höhle investigation, the beginners had a certain degree of sophistication in Dutch.[3] They performed acceptably on measures of linguistic knowledge encompassing morphology, syntax, and vocabulary. For example, when scores on a Dutch-language version of the Peabody picture vocabulary test for the first testing session were reported as a percentage of the average native-speaker performance (extrapolating across age levels from Reference 3, Figure 7), subjects in all but the two younger age groups scored 75% or better. This percentage value suggests considerable knowledge of Dutch for the beginners at the time of the first testing, even when similarities between Dutch and English are taken into consideration.

The results of other investigations indicate that adults perform better than children early in training, and continue to perform well when the language training involves almost exclusively the discrimination of sounds and/or the comprehension of meaning. For example, in a short training session involving the understanding of Russian commands, Asher and Price found that college adults performed better in acquisition and retention than did 8-, 10-, and 14-year-old children.[4] Snow and Hoefnagel-Höhle found that English-speaking adults produced Dutch words more accurately than did children who ranged in age from 5 through adolescence.[8] Furthermore, Postovsky found that the performance of adults in comprehension improves rather than declines as language lessons increase in complexity.[9]

The fact that adults perform better than children in short-term experimental studies and in the early stages of language acquisition when acquired under natural circumstances can be explained in terms of adults' superior ability to process phonetic and linguistic structures. What defies explanation at this point is why the L2 performance of adults later falls behind that of children.[3,5,10]

COMPREHENSION AND SIMPLIFICATION

Recognition that simplification of style and structural form contributes importantly to the acquisition of L1 is the reason for the recent attention given to the study of input to L2 learners.[2,11] I will try to show briefly that a significant restriction often is placed on L2 learning that makes the application of principles of simplification to the adult second-language learner less than satisfactory unless another condition is met.

In L1 acquisition, the construction and internalization of grammatical principles is an implicit learning process. The L1 learner is not aware consciously of grammatical principles, utterance meaning, discourse properties, or performance processing strategies. On the other hand, the adult L2 learner, and to some degree the child L2 learner, is provided with experiences that emphasize explicit learning of language principles. This difference, I believe, significantly distinguishes between the L1 and the L2 learner.†

---

† Krashen's use of the terms "acquisition" and "learning" is similar in meaning respectively to the terms "implicit" and "explicit" learning, used by Winitz and Bialystok.[12-14] I prefer the latter usage because it does not distort the meaning of the term learning as it is used in theoretical psychology.

An explicit learning experience is the result of formal classroom instruction, which emphasizes the learning of grammatical rules and patterns as a strategy for language acquisition. Adults with little or no classroom instruction also may apply explicit learning strategies, based on their knowledge of form and content of L1, if they believe that it is a useful strategy for language learning and especially if they have found it to be moderately efficient for acquiring limited but functionally communicative skills in L2. The extent to which explicit processing influences language acquisition will depend, of course, on a number of social and educational factors of which the primary ones probably are the need to communicate when acquiring a language in an L2 environment and the perceived value of correction or conscious monitoring after the student has gained considerable facility with a language.

LANGUAGE
LEVEL

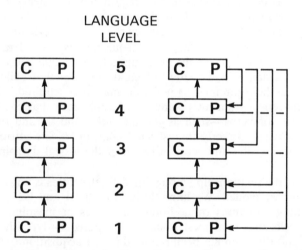

FIGURE 1. An illustration of the linear (left panel) and nonlinear (right panel) models of learning.

Explicit processing is a component of the linear model of language instruction, illustrated on the left side of FIGURE 1. According to this model of instruction, the student begins at the first-language level and is taught or acquires comprehension (C) and production (P) of language according to a series of predetermined steps. This manner of learning is termed linear learning because the acquisition (or elaboration) of grammatical structures within a language level is dependent only upon knowledge acquired at a previous language level.

The linear model of language teaching is common in L2 teaching. It also is a widely advocated model for teaching language to language-retarded children.[15,16] When the linear model is used to teach language-delayed children, the goal, according to Prutting, "is to move the child beyond the existing stage to the next stage."[16] The goal at each stage of training is to teach oral mastery before moving on to the next stage.

Stages usually are defined according to observations made from normally developing children.

In the linear model, the stages of language growth are regarded as reflecting underlying processes of development in that each successive stage is an enlargement upon a previous stage of development. In contrast, in the nonlinear model of language acquisition, to be described below, developmental language stages are not equated with learning stages. According to the nonlinear model, a language stage indicates a stage of development, but it does not indicate how and in what sequence the knowledge for a particular stage was obtained. The right side of FIGURE 1 contains a representation of the nonlinear model of language acquisition. As illustrated here, the learning of grammatical structures depends upon C and P within each level, as well as on C and P from structures much more complex and later appearing. In this regard the nonlinear model is not unlike the Piagetian concept of equilibration, which describes the process of learning as an oscillatory cycle between the states of certainty and doubt.

In the nonlinear model, language acquisition is viewed as involving continuous reorganization of the rules underlying language use. There is considerable evidence in the study of child language that children revise and reorganize their grammar as new information is acquired.[17-20] Bowerman recently reported an interesting set of confusions that children make among a series of verbs—such as *put* and *take,* and *let* and *make*—that initially were used correctly in restricted contexts.[20] She attributes these later errors to revision and reorganization of the lexical domains of these words.

Currently the relationship among linguistic structures is not well defined for the nonlinear model. We know little in both L1 and L2 about which later-appearing structures or additions in shades of meaning of learned structures have an effect upon structures acquired early, although some research in this direction has been reported for L1 acquisition.[17,18,20,21]

When developmental stages or textbook steps are used as reference guides for teaching language, there is the ever present danger that at each point in training, too much will be required from the student. The reason is that simplification does not define a correspondingly appropriate range of linguistic information that specifies what is to be learned. That is, it cannot be assumed that because language input is simplified, students will acquire facility with a certain restricted set of structures corresponding to the input that they receive. According to the nonlinear model of language learning, the input should be rich, varied, and more complex than the student's level of output so as to assure an appropriate range of linguistic information.

Explicit instruction usually means the teaching of grammatical rules. Often the rules that are taught are incomplete and yet so detailed that non-native speakers (and most native speakers) cannot appreciate their complexity. Furthermore, students often are taught to apply these rules according to the prescribed sequences that are used to generate linguistic derivations. This practice is not in accord with current psycholinguistic interpretations of sentence processing. It is not believed that the application of transformational rules, for example, defines the psychological routines (executive functions) involved in producing or comprehending sentences. The practice of teaching rules also is not in accord with the strategy of nonlinear teaching because an essential component of this model is the interrelationships of rules rather than emphasis on the study of isolated rules. The nonlinear model considers implicit rule learning to take place by exposure to sentences that reflect a wide range of different but interrelated rules. For this reason the application of nonlinear learning principles to the teaching of L2 primarily has stressed comprehension rather than production training.[22]

The term fossilization refers to a cessation of further development in L2.[23,24] This rigidity on the part of L2 acquirers in accepting new grammatical knowledge is well known, although its cause largely is unknown. Possibly fossilization is a consequence of having been taught, directly and indirectly, that knowledge is determinate at each language stage.

Linear teaching largely is a rejection of the principle that linguistic information is continuously reformulated and reorganized. It is this aspect of language learning that probably led Valdman to insist that rigorously specified step-by-step criterial behavior, a concept of programmed instruction, is not a useful construct in foreign-language teaching.[25]

Linear learning may be an effective acquisition strategy in the early stages of language instruction. Adults are particularly skillful in acquiring a minimal degree of competency in a foreign language through linear learning. They can memorize vocabulary items and surface grammatical rules fairly easily, enabling them to generate simple and functionally useful sentences. Furthermore, almost their entire educational experience has stressed this method of instruction. It is not unlikely, then, that they will apply the linear approach to L2 learning and because of it fail to acquire grammatical knowledge beyond a certain point.

In the monitor hypothesis of Krashen, it is proposed that language knowledge that is acquired implicitly can be modified by the use of a monitor that utilizes conscious (explicit) understanding of linguistic rules.[12] Krashen further suggests that individuals will vary in their use of this monitor. Some seem to edit their output a lot, while others correct occasionally or not at all. The monitor is a component of linear learning. It plays no substantive role in nonlinear learning. In fact every effort is made to suppress it in those language approaches that teach L2 learners to acquire L2 through implicit understanding.[26-28] Of course, a monitor whose rules contain prescriptive and stylistic devices of usage would be introduced when advanced reading and writing skills are taught.

Subsequent research should address the issue of the "crossover" effect and different strategies of learning. Is the "crossover" effect the result of a failure on the part of adults to utilize fully a nonlinear learning strategy or do other factors contribute to it?

The nonlinear strategy of language teaching now is recommended by a number of investigators who insist that input should be controlled carefully in the early stages of language instruction.[26-28] As soon as the student demonstrates an elementary understanding of the language, these investigators recommend that the input should be as free and natural as possible. According to this approach, no demands are placed on the L2 learner to speak grammatically correct sentences. The L2 learner is provided with as much comprehensible input as possible without the artificial forcing of oral and written production. In this way the L2 learner is placed into an environment similar to that of the L1 learner whose level of oral language competency is not pushed beyond his level of language comprehension by the creation of artificial or real circumstances that demand adultlike and grammatically correct oral production. It is this artificial demand on oral production that largely is thought to encourage linear processing and, again, may be responsible for the "crossover" effect.

SUMMARY

I began by considering the initial superiority of the adult over the child in the early stages of language acquisition, and the subsequent relinquishing of this dominance as L2 is acquired (termed the crossover effect in this paper). An experiment was presented that demonstrated that adults were significantly better than children in distinguishing among Mandarin tones and sounds respectively. This finding confirmed earlier reports that adults perform better than children in the early phases of L2 learning. Next I proposed that nonlinear learning typifies the L1 learner and that, in contrast, the experiences of the L2 learner often are significantly different. The several implications of the nonlinear model of language acquisition are that it provides an approach for studying and comparing the acquisition of L1 and L2 and perhaps may account for the crossover effect in L2 learning.

REFERENCES

1. SNOW, C. A. & C. A. FERGUSON. 1977. Talking to Children, Language Input and Acquisition. Cambridge University Press. New York, N.Y.
2. KRASHEN, S. D. 1980. The theoretical and practical relevance of simple codes in second language acquisition. In Research in Second Language Acquisition. R. C. Scarcella & S. D. Krashen, Eds.: 7–18. Newbury House. Rowley, Mass.
3. SNOW, C. A. & M. HOEFNAGEL-HÖHLE. 1978. The critical period for language acquisition: evidence from second language learning. Child Dev. 49: 1114–1128.
4. ASHER, J. J. & B. S. PRICE. 1967. The learning strategy of the total physical response: some age differences. Child Dev. 38: 1219–1227.
5. LENNEBERG, E. 1967. Biological Foundations of Language. John Wiley & Sons, Inc. New York, N.Y.

6. CARROLL, J. 1961. The Study of Language. Harvard University Press. Cambridge, Mass.
7. COCHRANE, R. M. The acquisition of /r/ and /l/ by Japanese children and adults learning English as a second language. J. Multilingual Multicultural Dev. (In press.)
8. SNOW, C. E. & M. HOEFNAGEL-HÖHLE. 1977. Age differences in the pronunciation of foreign sounds. Lang. Speech 4: 357–365.
9. POSTOVSKY, V. A. 1981. The priority of aural comprehension in the language acquisition process. In The Comprehension Approach to Foreign Language Instruction. H. Winitz, Ed.: 170–186. Newbury House, Rowley, Mass.
10. KRASHEN, S. D., M. A. LONG & R. C. SCARCELLA. 1979. Age, rate and eventual attainment in second language acquisition. TESOL Q. 13: 573–582.
11. HAMAYAN, E. V. & G. R. TUCKER. 1980. Language input in the bilingual classroom and its relation to second language achievement. TESOL Q. 14: 453–468.
12. KRASHEN, S. 1978. The monitor model for second-language acquisition. In Second-Language Acquisition and Foreign Language Teaching. R. C. Gingras, Ed. Center for Applied Linguistics. Arlington, Va.
13. WINITZ, H. 1978. Comprehension and language learning. In On TESOL '78. C. H. Blatchford & J. Schacter, Eds.: 49–56. Teachers of English to Speakers of Other Languages. Washington, D.C.
14. BIALYSTOK, E. 1978. A theoretical model of second language learning. Lang. Learn. 28: 69–83.
15. MILLER, J. F. & D. E. YODER. 1974. An ontogenetic language teaching strategy for retarded children. In Language Perspectives—Acquisition, Retardation, and Intervention. R. L. Schiefelbusch, Ed.: 505–528. University Park Press. Baltimore, Md.
16. PRUTTING, C. A. 1979. Process: the action of moving forward progressively from one point to another on the way to completion. J. Speech Hearing Dis. 44: 3–30.
17. SLOBIN, D. I. 1971. On the learning of morphological rules: a reply to Palermo and Eberhart. In The Ontogenesis of Grammar, a Theoretical Symposium. D. L. Slobin, Ed.: 215–223. Academic Press, Inc. New York, N.Y.
18. CHOMSKY, C. 1969. The Acquisition of Syntax in Children from 5 to 10. MIT Press. Cambridge, Mass.
19. ANISFELD, M. & G. R. TUCKER. 1967. English pluralization rules of six-year-old children. Child Dev. 38: 1201–1217.
20. BOWERMAN, M. 1978. Systematizing semantic knowledge: changes over time in the child's organization of word meaning. Child Dev. 49: 977–987.
21. JOHNSON, C. N. & H. M. WELLMAN. 1980. Children's developing understanding of mental verbs: remember, know and guess. Child Dev. 51: 1095–1102.
22. WINITZ, H. & J. REEDS. 1975. Comprehension and Problem Solving as Strategies for Language Training. Mouton. The Hague, the Netherlands.
23. SELINKER, L. 1972. Interlanguage. Int. Rev. Appl. Linguistics 10: 209–231.
24. SELINKER, L. & J. T. LAMENDELLA. 1978. Fossilization in interlanguage learning. In On TESOL '78. C. H. Blatchford & J. Schacter, Eds.: 240–249. Teachers of English to Speakers of Other Languages. Washington, D.C.
25. VALDMAN, A. 1968. Problems in the definition of learning steps in programmed foreign language materials. In Proceedings of the Seminar on Programmed Learning. The University of Kentucky Twentieth Foreign Language Conference, Lexington, Kentucky, April 29, 1967. T. H. Mueller, Ed.: 50–62. Appleton-Century-Crofts. New York, N.Y.

26. WINITZ, H. 1981. The Comprehension Approach to Foreign Language In-
    struction. Newbury House. Rowley, Mass.
27. DULAY, H. C. & M. K. BURT. 1973. Should we teach children syntax?
    Lang. Learn. 23: 245–258.
28. GARY, J. O. 1978. Why speak if you don't need to? The case for a listening
    approach to beginning foreign language learning. *In* Second Language Ac-
    quisition Research, Issues and Implications. W. C. Ritchie, Ed.: 185–199.
    Academic Press, Inc. New York, N.Y.

TOWARD THE ACQUISITION OF A SECOND LANGUAGE: NUCLEATION REVISITED

Simon Belasco

Department of Foreign Languages
University of South Carolina
Columbia, South Carolina 29208

An examination of investigation in second-language acquisition over the past 10 years reveals a plethora of methodological studies devoted to the analysis of errors.[1] One may wonder why the foreign-language-teaching profession today is so preoccupied with an orientation that is basically negative. It is true that none of the approaches that preceded error analysis—the grammar-translation method, the direct method, the audio-lingual method, or contrastive analysis—had much success in helping the learner to acquire a second language in a unicultural, artificial situation exemplified by the average classroom. Nonetheless, all of these approaches shared a constructive orientation. They made a deliberate effort *to teach* language. There is reason to believe that the potential of much of the recently discarded methodology was not understood or appreciated very well by the teacher or the methodologist.

If one takes the trouble to consider the grammatical principles contained in foreign-language textbooks during the past 40 years, it becomes understandable why language learners make so many errors. For the most part, the texts contain the same principles: use of the indicative and subjunctive moods, sequence of tenses in complex clauses, regular and irregular verbs, comparisons of adjectives and adverbs, and so forth. Some 50-odd principles are treated, all of which are supposed to be internalized by the language learner after one or two years of study.

What is particularly curious is that native speakers of any given language often can communicate effectively with each other without utilizing many of these principles. Most surprisingly, there is little experimental evidence indicating that these or any other principles *must be* acquired before a language can be learned. One thing is certain. There are foreign-language teachers who have internalized thoroughly all 50 principles and still cannot understand the language when overhearing a conversation conducted by native speakers. This is distressingly more evident when non-native teachers watch a foreign film spoken in the language they teach.

It is not being suggested that emphasis be shifted from analyzing learners' errors to analyzing grammatical principles. Statistically, the number of errors that students may commit—and often do—is astronomical. The number and kind of linguistic elements that must be internalized in order to insure second-language acquisition have yet to be determined. Given a normal social context, an individual with normal hearing and vocal

0077–8923/81/0379–0309 $01.75/2 © 1981, NYAS

apparatus cannot prevent himself from learning a first language. Under these conditions, even a moron learns his native tongue. Given the conditions presented by the average classroom, few learners—if any—really acquire a second language.

We have examined elsewhere the conditions under which foreign-language acquisition is expected to take place [2]—conditions involving present foreign-language goals, learning materials, the role of the teacher, the role of the learner, the physical make-up of the learning situation, and especially the time needed to get a student to nucleate.[3] Suffice it to say that they are wanting. What we should like to suggest here is a way of minimizing errors and internalizing linguistic principles whether they have, or have not, been understood cognitively.

The term "nucleation" as applied to language learning first was introduced by Kenneth L. Pike.[4] Pike compared language learning to the crystalization process in chemistry, pointing out how difficult it is for the first small clustering of atoms or molecules to clump together in a structural pattern that, once effected, rapidly repeats the process to form a crystal. This is nucleation. Few students of a foreign language are exposed to learning conditions that will insure nucleation. They never internalize the long chain of "abstract interpretive rules" that determine the form of sentences, i.e., the rules that convert underlying structure to surface structure.[5] In a system where such "composing" skills as speaking and writing are emphasized over the "receiving" skills, listening and reading, it is unreasonable to assume that nucleation can be achieved for any of these skills after two years of study. Existing foreign-language materials are not structured to accomplish such goals. The teacher functions as a purveyor of information rather than as a trained guide. The learner plays the role of observer rather than that of principal participant, and the ordinary classroom is set up to teach facts not skills.

At least three factors are shared by speaker and hearer in a basic model of verbal communication: a body of knowledge (a grammar), a body of nonlinguistic knowledge and beliefs (an encyclopedia), and a set of inference rules (a logic).[6] Add to this the important role played by judgments of relevance when utterances are combined—i.e., the yielding of new information—as well as the function of statements implying commands, warnings, threats, insults, etc.—i.e., illocutionary acts—then the principles underlying actual conversational exchanges begin to shape up as multiple and complex.

If we accept the premise that in acquiring linguistic knowledge (a grammar), the learner constructs a system that correlates meaning with sound over a nonfinite domain of sentences, then he must control the sound system. This implies that listening comprehension must precede speaking. Control of the system that pairs meaning with writing sequences similarly implies precedence of reading comprehension over writing. Speaking and writing are not to be discouraged, but early training in these skills should be designed to aid comprehension. Any early success in developing speaking and writing will be the result of "concomitant fallout."

Listening comprehension and reading comprehension are not unreasonable goals after two years of training in a foreign language—even at the
college level. There are some pertinent features of surface grammar that
relate syntax and the sound system—the morphophonemic structure—
which may be taught effectively by pattern practice. Through training by
properly structured drills, it is possible to learn how to recognize and to
pronounce fairly well all sounds and combinations of sounds in a foreign
language, in isolation and in basic structures, that a native speaker encounters in conducting his daily affairs. The acquisition of this ability—
this kind of nucleation in second-language learning—is prerequisite to
developing the creative aspect of language use. More so than syntax, the
sound system is a closed system that may be internalized from a relatively
restricted number of utterances occurring in a basic model of verbal
communication. Communication implies *receiving* as well as *sending*. In
the absence of comprehension, there can be no communication. The
grammatical principles underlying the pattern drills of the average commercial audiolingual textbook do little more than put the language learner
on top of a plateau.[7] These principles are geared to "composing" and
underestimate to a considerable degree the barrier of "inhibition" set up by
first-language acquisition.

By the time the second-language learner is exposed to a foreign language, he is well along the way to developing a state of "language inhibition." The more language uninhibited the learner is, the better are his
chances for acquiring a second language. Unlike any other creature, the
human being is able to engage in a certain amount of symbol switching without having to undergo an extensive period of retraining. He can be instructed to "lie down" when commanded to "sit," or "sit" when commanded
to "lie down" with a fair measure of success. Or he can be told to "lie
down" when he hears *couchez-vous* or "sit" when he hears *asseyez-vous*
and be able to execute both commands on short notice. In other words, an
animal is inhibited to the degree that he cannot "symbol switch" on short
notice, but a human being is far less—but not totally—uninhibited. He
can do some "symbol switching," and unfortunately for him it is this ability
to "partially inhibit" that educators, teachers, and methodologists have been
exploiting ever since the idea of teaching someone a second language was
conceived!

Techniques misusing the symbol-switching approach will do little to
raise the second-language learner from the prenucleation plateau. He has
learned his first language only too well.

Techniques garnered from all the aforementioned methods—grammar-
translation, direct, audiolingual, contrastive analysis—may be utilized in a
foreign-language program to internalize traditional and nontraditional
grammatical principles, including the morphophonemic system. We will
illustrate this by a somewhat lengthy example from teaching French as a
second language to native speakers of American English.

A most difficult and frustrating principle of French grammar for

American second-language learners to internalize is the use of the partitive. Stated traditionally, the rules go something like this:

1. The form *de* plus the definite article is used after transitive verbs.

2. When the verb is used in the negative, the definite article is omitted, i.e., only *de* is used.

3. Before a plural prenominal adjective, the definite article likewise is omitted; again only *de* is used.

Now learners have no great problem understanding the principle involved. They may successfully manipulate forms involving the partitive as part of pattern-drill exercises. A relatively short time after the drill experience, however, they make all kinds of errors when trying to use the partitive in conversation, in question-answer-type oral exchange, in English-to-French oral or written exercises, and even in the same or similar pattern-drill exercises they successfully practiced before. This comedy of errors persists, and even worsens, as new and different grammatical principles are introduced day by day. Moreover, if the students are told that they will be given a short quiz on the partitive every day, their performance does not improve measurably. In other words, their ability to "compose" does not improve despite persistent warning and testing.

On the other hand, if they are presented with utterances or written sentences containing examples of the use of the partitive, they can justify each use readily in terms of the three partitive rules cited above. This indicates that under normal classroom conditions, second-language learners can understand spoken and written utterances in the foreign language—and even grasp cognitively certain grammatical principles—*long before* they can use them actively in contrived utterances or in actual conversation. And as new grammatical principles are introduced, it takes no great stretch of the imagination to see why learners may improve in their ability to understand spoken and written foreign language and may cognitively grasp grammatical principles that are structurally related, yet persist in their inability to use them actively.

A course of action seems to suggest itself. Over a two-year period, one might begin by attempting to concentrate on a small number of structurally related grammatical principles for cognition and production, at the same time emphasizing the acquisition of the listening and reading of materials that may or may not contain these principles. The related grammatical principles would concentrate on the function of nouns, verbs, adjectives, and adverbs in basic grammatical sentences including specifiers and other modifiers, i.e., noun phrases, verb phrases, adjectival phrases, adverbial phrases, and prepositional phrases implicit in both tagmemic analysis and the X-bar convention.[8,9] The morphophonemic system would be programmed structurally within this framework. Pattern-practice exercises would be designed for "active" and "passive" internalization of the basic grammar by step-by-step assimilation and correlation procedures.[10] Later, more complex constructions and functions might be introduced via embeddings involving conjunction, subordination, and relativization. Where pertinent, transformation exercises could be employed involving noun-phrase-movement and certain aspects of trace theory.

The listening-comprehension exercises at first would consist of "contrived" passages illustrating the structurally programmed grammatical principles and then would be extended to cover "live" materials. The cognitive appreciation of new and different grammatical principles would be suggested by the live materials, thereby extending knowledge of the traditional principles and even replacing them where necessary.[11]

The reading-comprehension materials would follow much the same format, with the addition of side-by-side bilingual materials written in the source and target languages.[12] Subsequent materials would employ actual news items, plays, and short stories in which the source language would be eliminated asymptotically to effect a smooth transition from "crutch" comprehension to natural reading comprehension.

FIGURE 1 contains sentences that represent the basic linguistic structures. The type A basic sentence consists of a noun (N) and a verb (V) followed by no complement. Type B contains the same categories but—as indicated by the "inclusive or" left-to-right slanted line—the verb is followed by a noun functioning as a direct object complement or an indirect object complement, or both. Type C has a subjective complement made up of an adjective, a noun, an adverb, or preposition plus noun. The verb functions as a copula—a link verb. Corresponding sentences in English for type A would be "John speaks"; for Type B, "John speaks French \ to Mary"; and for Type C, "John is French," "president," "far," and "on land." The noun, verb, adjective, or adverb in the three sentences may be replaced by other nouns, verbs, adjectives, and adverbs—each of which in turn may be modified by a specifier. For example, for "John speaks" we might have "The boy can speak" *Le garçon peut parler.* For "John speaks French \ to Mary," we might have "the boy can speak the language \ to the girl" *Le garçon peut parler la langue à la fille.* And for "John is French," "president," "far," "on land (earth)," we might have "The boy can be quite French," "our president," "very far," "on the earth" *Le garçon peut être très français, notre président, très loin, sur la Terre.* Of course, such substitution procedures provide the basis for audiolingual pattern practice. It can be seen that the French and English sentences are very similar in form and meaning. This resemblance is only superficial however. As such, the sentences serve as a basis for contrastive analysis. For example, consider the following three basic type B English sentences:

1. John spoke the words to Mary.
2. John said the words to Mary.
3. John told the words to Mary.

Sentence 3 may undergo "dative movement," but sentences 1 and 2 may not. In other words, one may say "John told Mary the words," but not "*John spoke Mary the words" or "*John said Mary the words." The

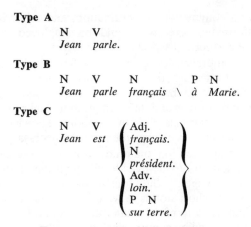

FIGURE 1. Basic linguistic structures.

English verbs "spoke" and "said" may not be followed immediately by a noun containing the feature [+animate] in the same simplex sentence. This constraint does not hold true for verbs such as "tell," "send," and "give." A native speaker of English who is learning French constantly will have to be reminded not to use dative movement in French, to prevent him from rendering such ungrammatical sentences in French as *Jean a dit Marie la fable, *Jean a envoyé Marie la fable, *Jean a donné Marie la fable for the grammatical English sentences "John told Mary the fable," "John sent Mary the fable," "John gave Mary the fable." The learner knows which verbs of communication and transfer are "marked" for dative movement in English, and must be constrained by "brute force" techniques from changing the basic word order: subject, verb, direct object, indirect object in French.

The basic word order also may be used to point up constraints on the passive-voice transformation in both languages. For example, the basic word order in English for "John sent the package to Mary" is the same in French—Jean a envoyé le paquet à Marie. In English, either the direct object or the indirect object may be moved to the subject position in the passive voice: "The package was sent to Mary by John" or "Mary was sent the package by John." In French, only the direct object may be so moved: Le paquet a été envoyé à Marie par Jean but not *Marie a été envoyé le paquet par Jean.

Let us now consider how a three-avenued approach using (1) structurally related basic materials, (2) listening-comprehension materials, and (3) reading materials might be implemented in the first year of a beginning course in college French. Following a treatment of basic word order and a limited number of transformations, the French partitive would be analyzed as part of a holistic approach that considers articles as functional determiners of nouns in basic grammatical structures.

In part a of FIGURE 2, each of the three sentences in French and English contains a mass noun. The nouns are written in capital letters, and their function is indicated at the extreme left as generic, specific, or partitive. It will be noted that the definite article is used in both French and English when the noun is specific; the definite article is used in French but no article is used in English when the noun is generic; and the partitive article is used in French and partitive "some" is used optionally in English when the noun functions partitively.

. In part b of FIGURE 2, each of the six sentences has a count noun written in capital letters. Accordingly, three sentences contain singular nouns and three contain plural nouns, functioning generically, specifically, and partitively. It will be noted that the articles modifying the plural French and English count nouns exhibit the same formal differences as the articles modifying the essentially singular French and English mass nouns. On the other hand, the formal distribution of the articles of the singular count nouns is identical in English and French. Where French has the definite or indefinite article, so does English. Now, charts a and b may be used not only to point up contrastive functional differences between French and English noun phrases, but also to isolate the aforementioned partitive *de* rules, used after transitive verbs in negative sentences and before plural prenominal adjectives. These rules never involve noun phrases used generically or specifically—only partitively. Traditional grammars rarely emphasize this constraint, which accounts for repeated errors wherein learners continuously use partitive *de* with specific and generic noun phrases.

It will be observed that the sentences in charts a and b represent basic type B and C sentences. As such, they may serve as a framework for drilling (1) morphophonemic structure: sandhi variation forms involving

(a) Mass Nouns

	French	English
generic	LE PORC est une viande.	PORK is a meat.
specific	LE PORC est dans la marmite.	THE PORK is in the pot.
partitive	Le cannible cuit DU PORC.	The cannibal is cooking (SOME) PORK.

(b) Count Nouns

generic

	French	English
s	${UN \brace LE}$ COCHON est un animal.	${A \brace THE}$ PIG is an animal.
p	LES COCHONS sont des animaux.	PIGS are animals.

specific

s	Le cannibale cuit LE COCHON.	The cannibal is cooking THE PIG.
p	Le cannibale cuit LES COCHONS.	The cannibal is cooking THE PIGS.

partitive

s	Le cannibale cuit UN MISSIONNAIRE.	The cannibal is cooking A MISSIONARY.
p	Le cannibale cuit DES MISSIONNAIRES.	The cannibal is cooking (SOME) MISSIONARIES.

FIGURE 2. Articles as functional determiners of nouns.

liaison obligatoire, facultative, interdite; mute and pronounced unstable *e*; etc.; (2) morphological structure: variation in form of specifiers, nouns, verbs, adjectives, adverbs, etc.; (3) syntactic structure: transitive, intransitive, link verbs; reflexive verbs; movement transformations in simplex sentences, etc. In short, the learner may be trained to recognize and to pronounce reasonably well all sounds and combinations of sounds not only in isolation but in the context of natural speech, which pairs meaning with sound sequences.

FIGURE 3 is a sandhi variation drill that is designed to help the learner to use the partitive article before count nouns beginning with a vowel or semivowel sound. Part a is an assimilation drill, since it already provides the correct forms for the learner to manipulate in alternate slots. Part b

(a) **Mixed Assimilation Drill.** Progressive Substitution in Verb Slot and Direct Object Slot Only.

Le cannibale cherche un homme.

cue: *trouve, des hommes, frappe, une anguille, tue, des anguilles, cuit, un oiseau, mange, des oiseaux*

Le cannibale *trouve* un homme.
                        des hommes.
            frappe
                        une anguille.

etc.

(b) **Mixed Testing Drill.** Progressive Correlation in Direct Object Slot Only.

Le cannibale mange un homme.

cue: *des, oiseaux, un, anguille, des, oeufs, un, orange, des*

Le cannibale mange *des* hommes.

                        des *oiseaux.*
                        un oiseau.
                        une *anguille.*
                        des anguilles.
                        des *oeufs.*

etc.

FIGURE 3. Sandhi variation in partitive count nouns.

is a testing drill, since the learner is required to make a change in—or an addition to—the cue provided by the drill. These sample exercises are to be used in conjunction with similar step-by-step drills designed to internalize selected basic grammatical principles. The structures in FIGURES 2 and 3 presumably are based on sentences occurring in a cohesive, coherent piece of discourse as found in a news item, story, etc.

FIGURE 4 may be considered a set of basic propositions or possible semantic entailments to be inferred from the content of any type A, B, or C syntactic structure treated above. The verbs written in capital letters represent "neutral" proforms, and the nouns, adjectives, and adverbs likewise have been replaced by "indefinite" proforms. Borrowed in some measure from functional grammar,[13] the basic propositions may be said to

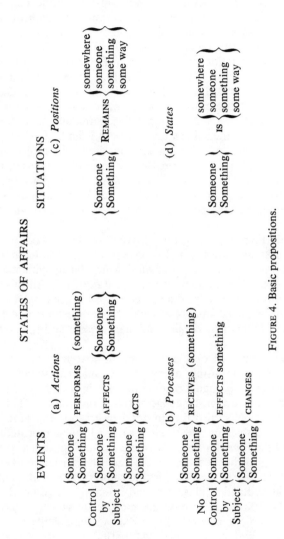

FIGURE 4. Basic propositions.

represent STATES OF AFFAIRS that occur either as EVENTS or SITUATIONS. SITUATIONS are propositions that contain link verbs and represent either *positions* over which the subject exercises some control or *states* over which the subject exercises no control. EVENTS are propositions that contain non-link verbs and represent either *actions* over which the subject exercises some control or *processes* over which the subject exercises no control. Depending on the role of the subject, a nonlink verb may function as an *action* or a *process,* and a link verb as a *position* or a *state.* For example, the French causative verb *cuit* functions as an *action* in *Le cannibale cuit un mission-naire* "The cannibal is cooking a missionary," since the subject exercises control over the EVENT. But in *Un missionnaire cuit* "A missionary is cooking," the subject exercises no such control and the verb is a *process.* Again in *Le cannibale embellit la hutte* "The cannibal embellishes the hut," control is exercised by the subject and the verb is an *action*; whereas in *Un enfant embellit la vie* "A child embellishes life," the subject only has a passive function and the verb represents a *process.* Similarly, the subject controls the SITUATION in *Le cochon reste dans la boue* "The pig stays in the mud," the verb thereby being a *position;* but in *Le cochon est dans la marmite* "The pig is in the pot," the subject has no control and the verb is a *state.*

Accordingly then, type C syntactic structures have SITUATIONS as their semantic reflexes, and types A and B have EVENTS. The learner conceives of FIGURE 4 as a semantic skeleton onto which basic syntactic structures may be fitted, depending on their semantic entailments. All this constitutes part of the linguistic knowledge that a student of French may acquire during the first year of language study—provided of course he is not beleaguered by traditional grammatical details and has these notions crystallized by frequent reentry.

Almost any contrived or live passage or text may be used to teach reading comprehension using modified grammar-translation techniques. FIGURE 5 represents a bilingual reading passage in which the English text is on the left and the foreign-language text on the right.[14] The beginning student reads the English text first in order to grasp the meaning. He then shifts back and forth from the English to the French repeatedly until he can understand the French passage with the entire English text covered, that is, without having further recourse to the English translation. He then goes on to the next passage, proceeding in the same fashion. Idiomatic expressions as well as syntactic differences and semantic correspondences stand out in bold relief. Subsequent passages may delete selected portions of the English text. The dictionary may be used as a supplementary tool to check certain meanings and expressions. At periodic points, French reading passages occur without any equivalent English translation.

The same or different selections are used to teach listening comprehension. All selections are recorded on tape and are available to the student in the language laboratory before class time. In class, the sentences or selected portions thereof are read aloud by the teacher in a fairly rapid conversational style. Students translate these utterances orally into English.

In the early stages, the students may keep the French written text before them for quick consultation. By the second semester, all written "crutches" have been eliminated from the oral-translation sessions. The teacher first reads the sentences in the order in which they occur and then rereads the selection by skipping to different parts of the text. Prior to—and even after—the oral translation practice, students are requested to read portions of the text for practice in pronunciation. Grades in pronunciation are given after each reading. Time is allocated for practicing the conjugation of regular verbs and certain key irregular verbs in isolation, as is done frequently in the grammar-translation approach. After a few sessions, passages may be contrived to contain short statements having illocutionary force, i.e., assertions, commissives, directives, expressives, declarations.[15]

"A woman, Austin. A couple is always less suspect. Yes, I've already found her. The more I think of it, the more convinced I am that my choice is a good one. With her, I'm pretty sure he'll toe the line. Furthermore, she knows every inch of the region to which I want to send him. It's where she comes from; she's a Breton. But of course, you know her—she's mentioned in our man's file. She already belongs to the service. Don't you think it's a first-rate idea?"	—Une femme, Austin. Un couple est toujours moins suspect . . . Oui, je l'ai déjà trouvée. Plus j'y réfléchis, plus je pense que mon choix est bon. Avec elle, je suis certain qu'il marchera droit. De plus, elle connaît fort bien la region où je veux l'envoyer. C'est son pays; elle est bretonne. Mais vous la connaissez; elle est mentionnée dans le dossier de notre homme. Vous ne devinez pas? Voyons, il s'agit de Claire. —La soeur de Morvan! —Sa soeur, précisément. Elle travaille dans le service. Elle est un excellent opérateur de radio . . . et elle est volontaire, elle aussi. Vous ne trouvez pas que c'est une excellente idée? —Je trouve. Sir, que c'est . . . que c'est un abus de confiance. —Rassurez-vous. Elle sait. —Elle sait? —Elle avait déjà entendu parler de l'affaire dans le service, et je ne lui en ai presque rien caché.

FIGURE 5. Bilingual text as aid in reading comprehension.

Since native speakers of English share much nonlinguistic knowledge with native speakers of French, it is easy to design paired statements in French that permit learners to infer pragmatic implications.

The technique employed here involves what is aptly called the "brute force" approach. For 30 minutes of each 50-minute period, the classroom atmosphere is "electrified" by rapid-fire exchange between teacher and students. The students are required to repeat parts of sentences and whole sentences, first in unison and then individually, after which the sentence is translated orally from French into English. By the middle of the second semester, the students are translating orally from English into French. Much of what is said is written as a dictation and recurs as part of a question-answer exchange during the last 20 minutes of the period. It is during this period that the direct method can be used to give directions, have students correct spelling mistakes in French, and engage in short dialogues with the teacher. No English is spoken during the entire 20 minutes.

Throughout the 50-minute period, the teacher is expected to provide immediate constraints. When a mistake is made, the student is stopped and corrected. If he still is unable to perform, one or more students are called on to provide the correct answer. The original student then is asked to repeat the answer. The pace often is hectic. Slow students respond slowly at first but do much better after a few sessions.

The following is the actual fall term 1980 final examination given to 19 students in a beginning French class (French 101, section 06) at the University of South Carolina. The students spent one semester working with the method just described. The test is based on materials provided by a very fine commercial textbook, which was adapted for the purpose.[16] Except for part F, which is a reading selection, the entire examination was administered orally. Students wrote all answers using complete sentences. Part A was presented as a connected discourse *dictée* recombined from sentences in several dialogues of the textbook. Part B is an English-to-French connected discourse translation, also taken from recombined dialogues of the text. Part C is a contrived listening-comprehension exercise utilizing the vocabulary and sentence structure—but not the original sentences—from reading selections in the book. In part D, students are required to translate from oral English into written French a passage of connected discourse based on selected basic grammatical principles treated in the text. The present, *passé composé,* and immediate future are the only tenses covered during the first semester. Part E contains a series of questions that have to do with the learner's activities and personal life. The final section, part F, is a contrived reading selection containing facts found in the text as well as facts introduced for the first time. Students answer in French but are required to translate their answers into English to verify comprehension of certain passages and lexical items.

FRENCH 101—FINAL EXAM—FALL 1980

All parts of the examination are administered *orally* except part F, which is in written form and read by the students.

A. *Dictée* based on recombined dialogues.
— Vous revenez de France, n'est-ce pas?
— C'est ça. Moi, je viens de passer une année à Montpellier.
   C'est mon premier voyage depuis 1945.
— Mon amie Barbara a l'occasion de passer plusieurs mois à Grenoble.
   Elle a un oncle qui habite là-bas.

B. Translation based on recombined *dialogues.*
1. I have just spent 6 months in France.

2. Where did you go?
3. I went to Provence. In fact, I traveled a lot.
4. A few months abroad isn't much.
5. Yes, but I met French people, and at least I spoke some French.

C. Auditory comprehension exercise based on the *renseignements culturels* and *instantanés*.
Ecoutez, puis répondez en français avec une phrase complète.

Jacques: — Tout le monde a envie d'aller en France.
Robert: — Mais, dis-moi pourquoi.
  J.: — Pour visiter la ville de plaisirs, la ville où l'on s'amuse.
  R.: — Oui, c'est ça. J'ai passé trois semaines dans la capitale de la gaieté l'année dernière.
  J.: — Ecoute, Robert. J'ai l'intention de retourner là-bas avec un voyage organisé. Tu veux aller avec nous?
  R.: — Non, Jacques, mon cher ami. Si je fais un voyage à la capitale de l'élégance, je vais aller tout seul.

1. Pourquoi est-ce que tout le monde veut aller en France?
2. Combien de temps Robert a-t-il passé dans la capitale de la gaieté?
3. Avec qui est-ce que Jacques a l'intention de retourner là-bas?
4. Si Robert a l'occasion de retourner à la capitale, il va faire le voyage avec Jacques, n'est-ce pas?

D. Free translation of connected discourse containing numbers and the *passé composé*.
1. Have you ever been to France?
2. Certainly. I landed in Normandy on June 6, 1944.
3. Did you spend a lot of time in Paris?
4. I never went to Paris, but I spent 45 days in Alsace.
5. Did you drink a lot of wine?
6. No, not too much, but I ate my first meal with wine there.
7. When did you return to the United States?
8. Two years later, on the 26th of August.
9. That's my birthday. I was born in Montpellier in 1962.

E. Questions personnelles.
1. Que faites-vous pendant le week-end?
2. A quelle heure quittez-vous l'université le vendredi?
3. En quelle année êtes-vous né(e)?
4. Quel âge avez-vous?
5. Où allez-vous passer vos vacances?
6. Quand allez-vous rentrer à l'université?

F. Lecture. Lisez le passage suivant. Puis, répondez aux questions avec une phrase complète. Ensuite, traduisez vos réponses en anglais.
    Mon ami Jacques a un oncle qui habite à Montpellier. Son oncle nous a invités à passer deux semaines chez lui. La région où est situé Montpellier est une zone de transition entre deux dialectes de la langue occitane: *le*

provençal et *le languedocien.* La région sud de la France actuelle s'appelle souvent *l'Occitanie.* En réalité, les voisins de l'oncle de Jacques parlent deux langues: *le français* et *l'occitan.* On dit qu'il y a douze millions de Français dans le sud qui parlent ou qui comprennent *l'occitan.*

L'identité occitane n'a pas disparu. Nous avons passé deux semaines dans une famille de fermiers. On a bien mangé et bien bu. On a tendance à considérer les Provençaux et les Languedociens comme des gens sympathiques mais un peu vantards. En fait, nous avons gardé un très bon souvenir de ces gens heureux qui aiment discuter, plaisanter et échanger des idées.

1. Où habite l'oncle de Jacques?
2. Quelle est cette région où son oncle habite?
3. Les habitants de Montpellier comprennent uniquement le français, n'est-ce pas?
4. Combien de Français ont connaissance de la langue *occitane?*
5. Les Français du sud qui parlent *occitan* ont perdu leur identité, n'est-ce pas?
6. Où est-ce que Jacques et son copain ont bien mangé et bien bu?
7. Comment considère-t-on les gens qui habitent la zone de transition entre les deux dialectes de *l'occitan?*
8. Quel souvenir les deux amis ont-ils gardé des voisins de l'oncle de Jacques?
9. Qu'est-ce que les habitants de Montpellier aiment faire?

With practice, it is possible for the teacher to adapt listening and reading materials from any commercial textbook with just those phonological, syntactic, and semantic basic data that are necessary to raise the student from "the plateau" to the necessary level of nucleated learning.

REFERENCES

1. CHUN, J. 1980. A survey of research in second language acquisition. Mod. Lang. J. **64**(3): 287–296.
2. BELASCO, S. 1981. Aital cal aprene las lengas estrangièras, comprehension: the key to second language acquisition. *In* The Comprehension Approach to Foreign Language Instruction. H. Winitz, Ed. Newbury House. Rowley, Mass.
3. BELASCO, S. 1965. Nucleation and the audio-lingual approach. Mod. Lang. J. **49**(8): 483–491.
4. PIKE, K. L. 1960. Nucleation. Mod. Lang. J. **44**: 291–295.
5. CHOMSKY, N. 1977. Essays on Form and Interpretation: 1–21. Elsevier/North-Holland. New York, N.Y.
6. SMITH, N. & D. WILSON. 1979. Modern Linguistics. The Results of the Chomsky Revolution: 173–174. Indiana University Press. Bloomington, Ind.
7. BELASCO, S. 1967. The plateau; or the case for comprehension: the "concept" approach. Mod. Lang. J. **51**(2): 82–88.
8. BELASCO, S. 1971. Les structures grammaticales orales. *In* Les exercices structuraux pour quoi faire? P. Delattre, Ed.: 69–90. Hachette. Paris, France.

9. JACKENDOFF, R. 1977. X̄ Syntax. Linguistic Inquiry Monograph No. 2. MIT Press. Cambridge, Mass.
10. BELASCO, S. & A. VALDMAN. 1968. Applied Linguistics and the Teaching of French: 18–63. Nittany Press. University Park, Pa.
11. BELASCO, S. 1969. Toward the acquisition of linguistic competence: from contrived to controlled materials. Mod. Lang. J. 53(3): 185–205.
12. BELASCO, S. 1971. C'est la guerre? or can cognition and verbal behavior co-exist in second language learning? *In* Toward a Cognitive Approach to Second Language Acquisition. R. C. Lugton & C. H. Heinle, Eds.: 191–230. Center for Curriculum Development. Philadelphia, Pa.
13. DIK, S. C. 1978. Functional Grammar. Elsevier/North-Holland. New York, N.Y.
14. BELASCO, S. 1975. Reading College French: A Bilingual Functional Approach. Harper and Row. New York, N.Y.
15. SEARLE, J. R. 1979. Expression and Meaning. Cambridge University Press. New York, N.Y.
16. VALETTE, J. P. & R. VALETTE. 1976. Contacts. Langue et Culture Françaises. Houghton Mifflin. Boston, Mass.

THE TOTAL PHYSICAL RESPONSE: THEORY AND PRACTICE

James J. Asher

Department of Psychology
San José State University
San Jose, California 95192

Acquiring another language—any language, including the sign language of the deaf [1]—can be accelerated, stress free, and have long-term retention. That is our fundamental discovery, which has held for children or adults learning a second language such as English,[2-5] French,[6-10] German,[11-14] Japanese,[15,16] Russian,[17-23] or Spanish.[24-27]

The stress-free feature of our approach is especially important because of all American students who begin the study of a second language, we can expect 96% to give up.[28] People quit because they have experienced a level of stress that they could not cope with.[29]

The consequences of this stress are evident in the declining enrollment of high-school students in foreign languages. It is now less than 15%. According to Congressman Paul Simon, "the U.S. Foreign Service no longer requires any foreign language background before you can enter . . . State Department Officials say they want people with language skills, but because so few Americans have studied foreign languages, they had to drop the requirement." [30]

The paradox is that most people express an interest in learning another language. The intrinsic motivation seems to be there, but apparently something in the instructional format has inflicted an experience of failure for most people.[28-30]

We do not believe it is the fault of instructors. They seem to be more dedicated than ever to helping students achieve skill in another language.

Then what is the problem? My hypothesis is that the unbearable stress experienced by children or adults who attempt the study of another language is a function of left-brain instructional strategies.[31,38]

For example, "teaching people to talk" is a left-brain instructional strategy. Exercises designed to "teach talking" would be "listen and repeat after me," "memorize this dialogue," and "pronounce these words." All of those exercises are valuable instructional activities, but only at more advanced stages of language training.

An Instructional Model Based on Children Acquiring Their First Language

Clues for solving this difficult instructional problem may be detected in children acquiring their first language. Linguists and psycholinguists

324

0077-8923/81/0379-0324 $01.75/2 © 1981, NYAS

have studied children's first-language development for years, but most researchers started to investigate at the point in development when the child begins to talk. But when the child talks, most of the clues have vanished.

The critical period to investigate is the period of silence from birth to the appearance of talk. Silence is difficult to study because most linguistic techniques are focused upon the analysis of talk. "Talk" is the primary subject matter of linguistics.

During the silent period in infant development, there are three important clues. The first is that *we cannot teach an infant to talk.*[2,31-33,38] Children will speak when they are *ready*.

Secondly, children become ready to talk only after they have acquired a rather intricate map of how the language works.[2,34] This cognitive map is not internalized through conscious rule learning, since children—as Krashen has observed—"may self-correct on the basis of a 'feel' for grammaticality." [35] Once children are producing language, perhaps they can be fine tuned, but even this is yet to be established firmly.[36-38]

The unconscious cognitive map probably is acquired through the right hemisphere of the brain,[39] when caretakers gently direct the child with utterances such as:

Let's wash your hands.
Pick up your teddy bear and come with me.
Give Daddy a kiss.

The home is an "acquisition-enriched environment" in which there is maximum understanding of spoken language in transactions between the caretakers and the child. Notice that these transactions do *not* demand speech from children. The child responds exclusively with a physical action initially and later in development with simple one-word utterances such as yes or no.[2,31,39,40] Examples would be:

Where is your teddy bear? Go find your teddy bear!
Do you want more orange juice?
Do you want to go for a walk?

The infant can give a nonverbal response, such as a nod, or a simple yes or no.

In the "acquisition-enriched environment" of the home there is maximum intake by the infant, in contrast with input but minimal intake in the usual classroom. The reason for minimal linguistic intake by students is that utterances from teachers favor declarative sentences.[41] Since there is abundant input from teachers but little intake by students, school is an "acquisition-impoverished environment." [2,31,42,43]

The Declarative Sentence

The declarative sentence is fascinating because on the surface it would seem to be ideal for communicating meaning in the target language. And, in fact, it does. But it communicates meaning *without believability*.

For example, if I say in Arabic:

Haatha kitaab. (This is a book.)
Haathii sabuura(t). (This is a blackboard.)
Haathii *t*aawla(t). (This is a table.)

For a moment the student will understand what I said, especially if I point to objects or translate, but this is short-term memory. There will be no long-term memory for most people because the utterances were understood momentarily but were not believable. The critical thinking of the left hemisphere will automatically evaluate those utterances as noises that have no validity.[39] Therefore there is no reason to store them in long-term memory.

How can this object, which the student knows through thousands of transactions as "table," be called a "*t*aawla(t)"? How can this "chair" be called a "kursii"? It must not be true, especially since the instructor is the only person in the room to assert this idea. Everyone else in the room believes that this object is called a "table" and that that object is called a "chair."

Of course, this is not conscious resistance by the student. The students consciously want to internalize the utterances they are hearing, but unconsciously the utterances are rejected as noise. This hypothesis is not Freudian speculation, but it is a heuristic extension of the classic research in "yielding" by the psychologist Solomon Asch of Swarthmore College.[44] In a forthcoming book, I discuss in detail how Asch's work relates to student resistance in foreign-language classes.[39]

Application to Second-Language Acquisition

With children acquiring their first language used as a heuristic model, we have discovered a format for second-language instruction that accelerates learning, is stress free, and produces long-term retention.

Features of the Instruction

One can acquire a second language faster than an infant can acquire a first language because the student can (a) follow directions and (b) easily generate a network of physical responses that is vastly more varied and intricate than the infant's primitive repertoire, which consists, for instance, of looking, touching, grasping, laughing, crying, eating, and eliminating.

The result is that within minutes, a skillful instructor can achieve near-perfect long-term comprehension for utterances in the target language such as:

Stand, walk to the chalkboard, and write your name.
Walk to me; give me the chalk; then return to your seat and sit down.

Further, we have discovered that the most grammatical features of the target language can be nested in the imperative. As an example, for the *future tense,* utter directions such as "When Luke walks to the window, Marie *will* write Luke's name on the chalkboard." For the *past tense,* say "Abner, run to the chalkboard." After Abner has completed the action, say "Josephine, if Abner *ran* to the chalkboard, run after him and hit him with your book." The *present tense* can be nested in the imperative as follows: "When Ezra *walks* to the window, Dolores will write Ezra's name on the chalkboard."

Since the imperative makes second-language acquisition accessible and enjoyable for both children and adults, we call it the "golden tense."

Second-language development can be compressed into a fraction of the time necessary for the child to achieve a sophisticated understanding and then speaking skill in a first language. Notice that in the child's development, speaking always shadows comprehension. Notice also that speech cannot be forced or coaxed to appear before the child is ready. And when speech appears, it will *not* be perfect. But gradually, in time, the individual's production will approximate that of the mature native speaker.

We have observed that an analogous development occurs in second-language acquisition when the scenario is a choreography in which language guides movements of the student's body.[2] Physical responses from students enable immediate understanding of what the instructor is saying. Even more important, the student not only understands, but believes that the noises coming from the instructor's mouth are authentic information. This belief reduces resistance to assimilation, and therefore there is long-term retention.

This belief that the noises coming from the instructor carry information may be conceptualized as analogous to a type of James-Lange theory of emotion.[45] One does not run because one has experienced fear; rather, fear follows the response of running. First comes the body response, then the emotional reaction.

If the utterance of "tate" coming from the instructor's mouth does not mean "stand up," why did my body respond by standing? If "suwara" does not mean to "sit down," why did my body sit? An utterance in the target language followed immediately by a physical action is a cause-effect relationship that the mind must cope with as a fact. These facts are primary experiences that are difficult for the student to dismiss as assertions of dubious validity, which probably would be the case in situations where the instructor makes a declarative statement that "tate" means to stand and "suware" means to sit.[39]

Pronunciation

It has been demonstrated by Asher and Price that there is an inverse relationship between intake of the target language and age of the student.[20] That is, when our body-oriented instructional model was applied, adults achieved the most accelerated comprehension in Russian followed by eighth graders and then first graders. When the instructor played the role of a caretaker who utters directions in the target language to guide the physical actions of students, adults vastly outperformed the children.

For pronunciation, however, we would expect children to have the advantage. For example, Asher and García have shown that Cubans who immigrated to the United States *before* puberty had an extremely high probability of eventually acquiring a near-native pronunciation. If the Cubans entered the United States *after* puberty, there was only a rare probability of a near-native pronunciation no matter how many years they lived in the U.S.

Adults acquiring a second language can realistically expect to understand and communicate in the target language, but with a noticeable foreign accent.

Abstractions

Most books written for students learning another language enter the target language at a rather high level of abstraction. For example: "Good morning. It's a beautiful day today. How are you feeling?" seems to be transparent and simple to the native speaker, but the learner has difficulty with comprehension because the utterances are abstract.

Abstractions, as is the case with infants taking in their first language, are delayed until a more advanced stage of training. The phonology and morphology of the target language can be internalized without stress using semantic content that is related to physical reality. After this, the student has "many hooks" for incorporating abstractions, either vocabulary items or idioms.

Future Research

There is an urgent national need for longitudinal studies that follow children from kindergarten through the eighth grade with our stress-free instructional model.[30] My hypothesis is that American and Canadian children can easily acquire basic listening fluency in *several languages* before they complete elementary school.

Just as children acquired fluency in their first language, they will achieve, with pleasure, understanding of several spoken languages. This comprehension skill will have positive transfer of learning to such skills as speaking, reading, and writing.

Junior and senior high school then would build upon the comprehension skills to fine tune for near-native pronunciation and excellence in grammatical usage.

All of our experiments in the past 20 years indicate that a goal of a multilingual American and Canadian child is a realistic expectation—and perhaps the most important educational contribution to our cultural, economic, and military survival in the 21st century, the century of the international community.

Summary

From a 20-year program of experimental research, an instructional format has been developed for acquiring another language. The format is a model based on infants acquiring their first language.

For children and adults learning such languages as English, German, French, Japanese, Russian, or Spanish, the results were accelerated stress-free acquisition that had long-term retention. These gains also seemed to hold for people acquiring the sign language of the deaf.

Specific features of the stress-free instruction are first, to delay production until students spontaneously demonstrate a readiness to speak; second, to maximize student intake of the target language by nesting all grammatical features in the "golden tense," the imperative; and third, to postpone abstractions until a more advanced stage of training, when meaning is transparent from the context of the situation.

REFERENCES

1. MURPHY, H. J. 1979. Am. Ann. Deaf **124**(3). (Book review of Reference 2.)
2. ASHER, J. J. 1982. Learning Another Language through Actions: The Complete Teacher's Guidebook. 2nd edit. Sky Oaks Productions. Los Gatos, Calif.
3. JACKSON, P. 1979. Final Report on Quick-Start in English. Whisman School District. Mountain View, Calif.
4. SUTHERLAND, K. Accuracy vs. fluency in the foreign language classroom. CATESOL Occasional Pap. (In press.)
5. NORD, J. R. 1980. Shut Up and Listen: An Alternative Approach. Michigan State University. East Lansing, Mich. (Prepublication paper.)
6. MEAR, A. 1969. Experimental investigation of receptive language. Paper presented at the Second International Congress of Applied Linguistics, Cambridge University, Cambridge, England, September 8–12.
7. DAVIES, N. F. 1976. Receptive versus productive skills in foreign language learning. Mod. Lang. J. **60**(8): 440–443.
8. DAVIES, N. F. 1977. Ett realistiskt mal för skilans sprakundervisning [A realistic goal for school language teaching]. Skolvärlden (Stockholm): 3.
9. DAVIES, N. F. 1978. Putting Receptive Skills First: An Investigation into Sequencing in Modern Language Learning. Department of Language and Literature. University of Linköping. Linköping, Sweden.
10. DAVIES, N. F. 1978. Putting receptive skills first: an experiment in sequencing. In Proceedings of the Fifth International Congress of Applied Linguistics, Montreal, Quebec, Canada.
11. ASHER, J. J. 1972. Children's first language as a model for second language learning. Mod. Lang. J. **56**: 133–139.
12. REEDS, J. A., H. WINITZ & P. A. GARCÍA. 1977. A test of reading following comprehension training. Int. Rev. Appl. Linguistics **14**(4): 308–319.
13. WINITZ, H. & J. A. REEDS. 1973. Rapid acquisition of a foreign language

(German) by the avoidance of speaking. Int. Rev. Appl. Linguistics **11**(4): 295–317.

14. SWAFFAR, J. K. & M. S. WOODRUFF. 1978. Language for comprehension: focus on reading, a report on the University of Texas German program. Mod. Lang. J. **62**: 27–32.

15. KUNIHIRA, S. & J. J. ASHER. 1965. The strategy of the total physical response: an application to learning Japanese. Int. Rev. Appl. Linguistics **4**: 277–289.

16. KANOI, N. 1970. The Strategy of the Total Physical Response for Foreign Language Learning. Hanover College. Hanover, Ind. (Unpublished student research project.)

17. ASHER, J. J. 1965. The strategy of the total physical response: an application to learning Russian. Int. Rev. Appl. Linguistics **3**: 291–300.

18. ASHER, J. J. 1969. The total physical response approach to second language learning. Mod. Lang. J. **53**: 3–17.

19. ASHER, J. J. 1969. The total physical response technique of learning. J. Special Educ. **3**: 253–262.

20. ASHER, J. J. & B. S. PRICE. 1967. The learning strategy of the total physical response: some age differences. Child Dev. **38**: 1219–1227.

21. NORD, J. R. 1975. A case for listening comprehension. Philologia **7**: 1–25.

22. INGRAM, F., J. NORD & D. DRAGT. 1975. A program for learning comprehension. Slavic and East Eur. J. **9**(1): 1–10.

23. POSTOVSKY, V. 1974. Effects of delay on oral practice at the beginning of second language learning. Mod. Lang. J. **58**: 229–239.

24. KALIVODA, T. B., G. MORAIN & R. J. ELKINS. 1971. The audio-motor unit: a listening comprehension strategy that works. For. Lang. Ann. **4**: 392–400.

25. ASHER, J. J., J. KUSUDO & R. DE LA TORRE. 1974. Learning a second language through commands: the second field test. Mod. Lang. J. **58**: 24–32.

26. ASHER, J. J. 1977. Children learning another language: a developmental hypothesis. Child Dev. **48**: 1040–1048.

27. GARY, J. O. 1975. Delayed oral practice in initial stages of second language learning. *In* New Direction in Second Language Teaching, Teaching and Bilingual Education. M. K. Burt & H. C. Dulay, Eds.: 89–95. TESOL. Washington, D.C.

28. LAWSON, J. H. 1971. Should foreign language be eliminated from the curriculum? *In* The Case for Foreign Language Study. J. W. Dodge, Ed.: 3–7. Modern Language Association Materials Center. New York, N.Y.

29. JAKOBOVITS, L. 1969. Research findings and foreign language requirements in colleges and universities. For. Lang. Ann. **4**: 448.

30. THIMMESCH, N. 1977. American spoken here, and nothing else. San Francisco Examiner (December 25).

31. ASHER, J. J. 1979. Motivating children and adults to acquire another language. SPEAQ J. **3**: 87–99.

32. GESELL, A. & H. THOMPSON. 1929. Learning and growth in identical twins: an experimental study by the method of co-twins control. Genet. Psychol. Monogr. **6**: 1–124.

33. BÜHLER, C. & H. HETZER. 1935. Testing Children's Development from Birth to School Age. Farrer & Rinehart. New York, N.Y.

34. KRASHEN, S. D. Adult Second Language Acquisition and Learning: A Review of Theory and Application. Center for Applied Linguistics. Arlington, Va. (In press.)

35. KRASHEN, S. D. 1979. The monitor model for second-language acquisition. *In* Second Language Acquisition and Foreign Language Teaching. R. Gingras, Ed.: 1–26. Center for Applied Linguistics. Arlington, Va.

36. KRASHEN, S. D. 1979. Adult second language acquisition as post-critical

period learning. Paper presented at the MEXTESOL conference in Guadalajara, Mexico, October 10, 1976. (For reprints, write to the author at the Department of Linguistics, University of Southern California, Los Angeles, Calif.)

37. BELASCO, S. 1965. Nucleation and the audio-lingual approach. Mod. Lang. J. **49:** 482.

38. CONDER, S. P. 1967. The significance of learner's errors. Int. Rev. Appl. Linguistics **5:** 161–170.

39. ASHER, J. J. 1981. *In* The Comprehension Approach to Foreign Language Instruction. H. Winitz, Ed. Newbury House Publishers. Rowley, Mass.

40. ERVIN-TRIPP, S. 1973. Some strategies for the first two years. *In* Language Acquisition and Communicative Choice. A. Dil, Ed.: 204–238. Stanford University Press. Stanford, Calif.

41. TRAGER, S. 1978. The language of teaching: discourse analysis in beginning, intermediate, and advanced ESL classrooms. MA Paper. University of Southern California. Los Angeles, Calif.

42. SCARCELLA, R. & S. KRASHEN. 1981. The theoretical and practical relevance of simple codes in second language acquisition. *In* Research in Second Language Acquisition. R. Scarcella & S. Krashen, Eds. Newbury House Publishers. Rowley, Mass.

43. NEWPORT, E., H. GLEITMAN & L. GLEITMAN. 1977. Mother, I'd rather do it myself: some effects and non-effects of maternal speech style. *In* Talking to Children. C. Snow & C. Ferguson, Eds.: 109–149. University Press. Cambridge, England.

44. ASCH, S. E. 1956. Studies of independence and submission to group pressure. I. A minority of one against a unanimous majority. Psychol. Monogr. **70**(416).

45. JAMES, W. 1890. Principles of Psychology. Holt, Rinehart & Winston. New York, N.Y.

46. ASHER, J. J. & R. GARCÍA. 1969. The optimal age to learn a foreign language. Mod. Lang. J. **53:** 334–341.

COMPREHENSION-BASED LANGUAGE
INSTRUCTION: THEORY

Judith Olmsted Gary and Norman Gary *

Department of English and
English Language Center
Cairo University
Cairo, Egypt

Introduction

This conference is concerned with native- and foreign-language acquisition. The main point of our paper is that foreign-language learners—like first-language learners—need an extended period of receptive learning to comprehend the language they are learning before they begin producing in that language. In this paper we will discuss and summarize both recent and past theoretical arguments supporting this claim. These arguments are an expansion of arguments discussed in J. Gary and described in more detail than time and space permits here in J. Gary and N. Gary.[1,2] In the final section of the paper, we discuss consequences for curriculum organization of the arguments presented here.

Specifically, we would like to argue that foreign-language instruction should give primary emphasis to the comprehension skills of listening and reading, and should relegate the productive skill of speaking to a later and less conspicuous role in the typical classroom, especially in the early stages of language teaching. We arbitrarily limit our discussion to foreign-language instruction for linguistically mature learners who are already literate in another language.

Over the past 15 years or so, there has been an accumulation of research that strongly suggests that there should be more emphasis on the comprehension aspects of language in foreign-language teaching than usually is the case. The most important notion to emerge from this research is that emphasizing speaking in the early stages of language instruction actually retards language acquisition (see, e.g., References 3–5). This has led to the conclusion that practice in oral production should be delayed and that early language instruction should emphasize developing substantial competence in comprehension before requiring learners to talk in the new language.

This conclusion may not seem startling. However, if one examines recently published language-teaching materials, it is clear that this research is having very little impact on textbook preparation and, consequently,

* Please address all correspondence to Dr. Norman Gary. From the United States: c/o Fulbright/CAIRO, Department of State, Washington, D.C. 20520. From outside the U.S.: P.O. Box 2098, Cairo, Egypt.

0077–8923/81/0379–0332 $01.75/2 © 1981, NYAS

very little effect in the average language classroom. For example, most mainstream English-language texts—both American and British—provide for massive amounts of oral practice and pronunciation correction through a variety of oral drills. Listening per se is usually relegated to only a small amount of practice minimally necessary for participation in the oral drills; or there may be an isolated section of the lesson in which some listening tasks are done, such as recognition of numbers, times, words, evaluation of sentences as *true* or *false,* etc. However, in terms of total instructional time devoted to *systematic* listening—that is, listening that is carefully structured from task to task and from lesson to lesson—listening is relegated to a relatively minor role in the total instruction, and primary emphasis is given to speech. As Postovsky pointed out,[3] most current language-teaching methodologies and practices—both *audiolingual* and *cognitive-code*—view language learning primarily as *learning to talk.*

Usually, listening comprehension is taken most seriously at more advanced levels, as for example in books prepared for students taking various British or American proficiency tests used for screening academic candidates. Such materials typically concentrate on presenting fairly long narrative passages or dialogues for comprehension and then having students answer comprehension questions over the aural material, often from notes taken during the listening. There is nothing wrong with this type of procedure per se, but linguistically and pedagogically, it seems exactly backwards. We think that concentration on listening comprehension should be most massive at the earlier stages of language learning. And it should begin with shorter, contextualized utterances more closely approximating the kind of communicative interaction that the learner is likely to meet in everyday language use, rather than concentrating on discourse types that are mostly limited to such things as lectures and radio broadcasts.

It is clear that many language-teaching theorists and methodologists have a fuller appreciation of the role of comprehension in language learning than perhaps was the case 10 or 15 years ago, due to the work of such people as Asher, Davies, Newmark and Diller, Ingram, Nord, and Dragt, Postovsky, and Winitz and Reeds,[6-11] to name a few of the people who have made substantial contributions to our understanding of the role of comprehension in language learning and suggestions for how comprehension might be approached methodologically.

However, despite this increased awareness, there does seem to be a significant gap between theory and practice. After all, Newmark and Diller said many of the things we are saying here more than 15 years ago.[8] Asher has been reporting his very convincing research since 1964. Intensive listening comprehension and delay of oral practice are among the best documented notions in language-teaching research. Yet, one is hard pressed to find significant changes in the relative status of *listening* versus *speaking* in classroom practice, at least as it is embodied in the most widely used materials. We would like to think that this gap between theory and practice is at least partially a result of confusion about what listening comprehension entails and a lack of methodological guidelines and techniques for incorporating listening comprehension into instructional procedures that can be used effectively and efficiently in the average classroom.

In this paper we first of all would like to review and expand the arguments for delaying oral production and reducing the role of oral practice, while providing for increased listening practice. Then we will illustrate how this might be translated into curriculum organization.

RATIONALE FOR DELAYING ORAL PRACTICE
AND INCREASING LISTENING

First of all, we need to consider the relationship between listening and speaking. In terms of linguistic competence, listening and speaking require the same kind of language knowledge, not two different kinds. The same set of rules (or perhaps a subset) is used in language comprehension as in language production. When we comprehend something—decoding spoken or written symbols into meaning—we arrive at the meaning by the rules of the grammar that in normal human language relates meaning and sound or graphic sequences. Similarly, when we encode a meaning, we do so by utilizing the same rules that we use in decoding. The major differences between the encoding and decoding tasks—aside from the motor movements required for speech or writing—have to do with processing: information retrieval, short- and long-term memory processes, control of speed of processing, etc. Also there are different strategies required in processing for comprehension and production. In production the speaker controls the structures and vocabulary used; thus a foreign-language learner can use various paraphrastic devices when he is producing language, avoiding problematic lexical and grammatical structures. But when he is comprehending, he does not have this control; he must deal with an essentially open grammatical and lexical system.[10] But these differences aside, the underlying system of the language is the same for both comprehension and production.

However, there are crucial differences between comprehension and production. In both first- and second-language acquisition, *comprehension is prior to production.* Knowing a language does not necessarily entail the ability to speak it. For example, a mute who can comprehend what is said to him but who cannot speak certainly possesses language.[12] However, consider the reverse. Imagine a person who can produce the sounds and sentences of a language, perhaps impeccably, but who cannot comprehend either what he says or what is said to him; clearly he does not possess the language.

Communicative speech requires comprehension, but *comprehension does not require speech.* To speak communicatively, one must comprehend incoming messages and then organize appropriate responses for production.

Finally, *speech requires linguistically more complex tasks than does comprehension.* Comprehension—at least at all but the most advanced levels—allows many linguistic signals to be ignored, e.g., redundant grammatical and semantic functions such as concord, definite-indefinite distinctions, and singular-plural distinctions very often can be ignored without seriously distorting the message being comprehended. However, all of these nonfunctional signals need to be controlled in order for fluent speech to result. Thus speech requires much more complex behavior than does comprehension.[3]

If comprehension is prior to production, what should we say about the sequencing of the two in teaching or learning? Since the same set of rules underlies both speech and listening, any instructional methodology that teaches the system will of necessity have effects on the total language competence. The question then is, What methodology teaches the system most effectively and efficiently? It is clear that we cannot teach speech first and then listening later. Obviously, you cannot say what you do not know. We then come to the crucial methodological question. Why not teach listening comprehension and speaking together, as in the usual oral-emphasis approach? Why teach listening comprehension first and insist on delaying speaking? There are several strong arguments for this position. These arguments are related to the affective and cognitive dimensions of language acquisition, and to pedagogical considerations.

The Cognitive Advantage

Postovsky argues convincingly that requiring learners to produce material that they have not yet stored in their memory will lead to language interference and overload of short-term memory.[3] Experimental studies, including Postovsky's own, support his premise, showing a high degree of transfer between a listening-only focus and other language skills, with lower scores in the four language skills reported when students were required to develop speaking and listening skills simultaneously (see, e.g., References 4, 5, 13, and 14).

According to Krashen's *monitor* hypothesis, oral production tends to lead to monitoring, that is, the use of conscious knowledge of the rules of the language to "monitor" the output.[15] On the other hand,

> the success of "input methods" that require basically active listening . . .
> is quite consistent [with the idea that too early production may cause
> first-language substitution for the second]. . . . It is meaningful intake
> that allows acquisition to occur. Speaking comes with time. Too early
> production before sufficient acquisition is built up results in the use of
> the surface structure of the first language.[15]

Thus it can be argued that a comprehension emphasis leads most naturally to language acquisition, in the sense that Krashen uses the term *acquisition*.

From a neurofunctional point of view, Lamendella argues that oral practice not serving any communicative functions can be carried out by an automated speech sequence that can be disassociated functionally from higher-level language systems that depend on cognition, intellectual functions, and creative aspects of language: "Pattern practice drills (and oral approaches in general) prompt the learner to engage in Foreign Language Learning . . . rather than Second Language Acquisition." [16] Lamendella's distinction is basically the same as Krashen's distinction between "conscious learning" and "acquisition learning." Since we believe (and argue below) that comprehension is inherently communicative, Lamendella's arguments against an oral approach support our arguments for intensive listening comprehension and delay of oral practice.

The Affective Advantage

For many learners, trying to produce language before they are cognitively and emotionally ready is traumatic. Both first- and second-language learners generally prefer not to speak a language that they perceive only imperfectly (see, e.g., References 6, 17, and 18).

In a comprehension approach, the learners can make their mistakes privately, and privately make the corrections. Everyone who has worked with comprehension-oriented language instruction has reported very favorably on the affective side of the instruction. Swaffer and Woodruff report quite dramatic reductions in student attrition from first-semester university beginning-German courses after a change from a more traditional German program to one that emphasized comprehension. [19]

The Efficiency Advantage

Comprehension-oriented instruction uses classroom time more efficiently than does production-oriented instruction. In a listening-oriented class, all of the students can be listening and responding individually, e.g., in workbooks, at the same time. They can respond and get feedback from the teacher at the same time without the necessity of individual public response. This way they can be exposed to much more of the target language in less time than if they were required to respond orally.

The Communicative Advantage

Comprehension is inherently communicative, and comprehension-oriented classroom techniques are always potentially communicative in nature. As long as a message is being sent that the learner cannot predict and the learner is attempting to comprehend it, there is a potentially communicative act. If the message is structured pragmatically and linguistically so that the learner has a reasonable chance of understanding it, based on previous knowledge of and exposure to the language, then there is a high potential for communication to take place. Of course, the greater the interest the learner has in the content of the message, the more potential communicative value it will have for him.

On the other hand, much oral practice—at least as commonly used in the classroom—is manipulative rather than communicative.

The Media Compatibility Advantage

Listening-oriented foreign-language materials are the most appropriate materials for use with aural media, such as audio- and videotape. Aural media have very limited and questionable usefulness in speaking-oriented instruction. Language laboratories using aural media have relied heavily on materials designed to facilitate practice in speech production, usually in the form of various kinds of oral drills for the students to perform. Indeed, the repetitive-oral-drill possibility of the laboratory was what originally made it such an attractive tool. However, the results of such laboratory uses have been disappointing (see, e.g., References 20 and 21).

This has led a number of foreign-language teachers to begin using taped materials for active listening-comprehension purposes rather than for oral drills (e.g., References 22–25). It seems clear that listening comprehension is the ideal companion for use with taped media. As Dakin indicated,

> it is the fields that have been least exploited commercially that I have suggested laboratory work is most promising. . . . A teacher who invests his time and tapes in designing listening materials and comprehension activities is most likely to reap the benefits of the special facilities afforded by the laboratory.[21]

Language programs that are listening intensive are in the position of being able to use language laboratories much more effectively than they have been typically used in the past. The authors have worked with and seen programs using active listening-comprehension exercises in the language laboratory in which one of the favorite classes was the laboratory—a radically different situation from the laboratory classes that use oral drills.

The Utility Advantage

Language learners who have been taught to capitalize on the advantages of a receptive approach to language learning are more likely to be inclined to continue their language study alone, independently of a particular language program. This can be carried out, for example, by their listening to the radio, watching TV, or going to foreign-language films.

Many of the above arguments have been supported by extensive research in teaching various foreign languages to both adults and children. The most important finding is that language learners *not required* to speak immediately—though they are allowed to if they wish—make more significant gains in reading, writing, and *speaking,* as well as in listening comprehension, than do learners required to speak right away. We do not have enough space to discuss this research. The reader is referred to J. Gary, N. Davies, or J. Asher for a review of some of the empirical support for these arguments.[4,6,7] There probably is more empirical support for the notion of delayed oral practice and intensive listening comprehension in early language teaching than for any other methodological issue that has been investigated.

Consequences for Curriculum Organization

If we accept the theoretical position that speaking should be delayed and comprehension should be given priority in the instructional program, how would this affect the organization of a foreign-language curriculum? In FIGURE 1 we attempt to schematize what we think should be the overall organization of a comprehension-based curriculum. The vertical dimension represents the percentage of daily instructional time devoted to each of the skills, and the horizontal dimension represents the sequencing of the four skills in a beginning foreign-language program for adults who already are literate in another language. Time differences are intentionally not specified fully here; we intend only to indicate basic relationships in the sequencing of skills and proportioning of time allotted. This sequence turns the usual *listening-speaking-reading-writing* sequencing of skills on its head.

In this diagram, *comprehension* refers to the decoding of grammatically structured messages of unspecified length. Under comprehension, we probably would want to include recognition of basic morphophonological distinctions in listening and graphological distinctions in reading. In reading, in particular, we would want to include decoding at the word level as well as at the longer, grammatically organized levels.

The terms *writing* and *speaking* refer to the encoding of grammatically organized messages—they do not refer to writing or saying things that have little or no grammatical organization, as for example writing or saying single words or formulaic combinations such as greetings, or copying or mimicking something read or said. We would like to leave the door open for allowing very simple written and spoken responses during the early stages of instruction, mainly for reasons of classroom efficiency.

Looking at the chart, we see that comprehension would take all of the instructional time for some (indeterminate) time before the productive tasks are introduced into instruction. Listening comprehension would precede reading by some relatively short period, and generally we think it advisable that reading initially be limited lexically and structurally to what learners have already shown that they comprehend aurally. That is, they would read only what they have already heard. The reason for having aural comprehension precede visual comprehension is to prevent internalizations of incorrect representations through faulty sound-graphic correspondences. This would be especially important where sound-graphic correspondences are fairly deviant, as in English.

One could argue that reading should be postponed until a very substantial base of listening comprehension is built up, paralleling more closely the usual time difference in listening and reading in first-language acquisition. While this may or may not be sound psycholinguistically, it is our experience working with literate adults that they much prefer having access to the visual representation very quickly. Having the written form available gives the learners a chance to deal with the language presented aurally in the more temporal-free form of writing. If they have missed something, or misunderstood something, later access to the written form of what they have listened to gives them a chance to check their prior aural comprehension. We are not aware of any research that shows that the presence

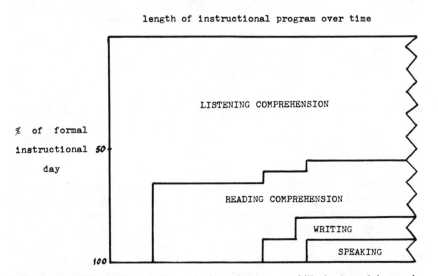

FIGURE 1. Relationships and sequencing of language skills in formal instruction for literate adults.

of reading enhances the acquisition of listening ability, but we think that it is very likely to be the case.

One thing that does seem sure is the effect of listening on reading ability. There appears to be a very high transfer from listening to reading. The most dramatic support for this is found in the work of Reeds, Winitz, and Garcia, which demonstrated significant ability for learners to translate from written German to English after only eight hours of listening and *no* practice in reading German.[26] In a recent study done in Egypt with the materials we have been developing, Nermine Fahmy demonstrated that English reading comprehension is improved significantly in the presence of aural accompaniment compared with reading without aural accompaniment.[27] Her research suggests that even if you are concerned only with teaching reading, you may be able to do it best by also teaching listening. Methodologically, this suggests that reading—especially in fairly early stages—should be accompanied by aural input, as for example by having a teacher read the material aloud while the students are attempting to read it silently. This might be continued until students reach the stage when they can read silently faster than a fluent teacher can read the same material aloud to them.

This brings us to the productive skills. The chart indicates that *writing* will be introduced before *speaking* and that speaking will be the last of the skills introduced. The reason for this has to do with the fact that speech requires the user to operate under time constraints, while writing allows the user to control the rate of encoding. Thus writing allows the learner to match the rate of production with his competence. Speech, on the other hand, forces the learner into a more rapid organization of linguistic material and may fail to give him time to use fully what competence he has.

Norman Davies has suggested for instruction in third languages (i.e., where two or more foreign languages are studied) that the study of the productive skills be eliminated altogether.[7] He argues that having to attain proficiency in the productive side is so difficult that it seriously discourages language students and should be eliminated in favor of concentrating on attaining greater proficiency in the comprehension skills. And, of course, it could be argued that attaining proficiency in the receptive skills might very well lead to a greater willingness and ability to become more proficient in the productive skills.

In our chart we have been deliberately vague about when the productive skills should be introduced. We have indicated only the relative sequence and overall priority of the sequencing. In programs in the past, speaking has been delayed from a few weeks to months, even in intensive programs. The timing of when to begin providing formal oral practice in instruction often will depend on the circumstances of the learners: their immediate needs for the language, their potential jobs, the instructional setting, etc.

We have little to say here about how writing and speaking should be introduced or about the most effective type of instructional tasks and techniques. However, we do think that such traditional language-teaching practices as *dictation,* which provide for both comprehension and production, may well provide very natural transitions into writing; similarly, the reading aloud of dictated material might provide a good transitional device into speech.

Finally, we would like to emphasize that the sequence and time illustrated in this diagram refer only to *formal* instructional situations. There will of course be many informal situations arising in classes where teacher and students are interacting informally, and it is entirely possible that these informal situations may be as valuable for language acquisition as the formal instruction. Communication needs in these informal situations rightly will override all other considerations.

By emphasizing comprehension in the instruction, we are not advocating preventing students from speaking when they want to, but rather we are trying to organize the instruction so that they also will have other ways of responding, ways that will be more effective in providing for language acquisition and more efficient in use of instructional time.

REFERENCES

1. GARY, J. 1978. Why speak if you don't need to? The case for a listening approach to beginning foreign language learning. *In* Second Language Acquisition Research: Issues and Implications. W. Ritchie, Ed.: 185–199. Academic Press, Inc. New York, N.Y.
2. GARY, J. & N. GARY. 1981. Caution: talking may be dangerous to your linguistic health. Int. Rev. Appl. Linguistics **19:** 1–14.
3. POSTOVSKY, V. 1975. On paradoxes in foreign language teaching. Mod. Lang. J. **59:** 1–2, 18–21.
4. GARY, J. 1975. Delayed oral practice in initial stages of second language learning. *In* New Directions in Second Language Teaching, Learning and Bilingual Education. M. Burt & H. Dulay, Eds.: 89–95. TESOL. Washington, D.C.
5. ASHER, J. 1969. The total physical response approach to second language learning. Mod. Lang. J. **53:** 3–17.
6. ASHER, J. 1979. Learning Another Language through Actions: The Complete Teacher's Guidebook. Sky Oaks Productions. Los Gatos, Calif.
7. DAVIES, N. 1978. Putting Receptive Skills First. Department of Language and Literature. Linköping University. Linköping, Sweden.
8. NEWMARK, G. & E. DILLER. 1964. Emphasizing the audio in the audio-lingual approach. Mod. Lang. J. **48:** 18–20.
9. INGRAM, F., J. NORD & D. DRAGT. 1974. Developing a programmed workbook for listening comprehension in Russian. Paper read at the Soviet-American Conference on the Russian Language, Amherst, Mass., October.
10. POSTOVSKY, V. 1976. The priority of aural comprehension in the language acquisition process. Paper read at the Fourth Association Internationale Linguistique Appliquée World Congress, Stuttgart, Federal Republic of Germany, August 25–30.
11. WINITZ, H. & J. REEDS. 1973. Rapid acquisition of a foreign language (German) by the avoidance of speaking. Int. Rev. Appl. Linguistics **11:** 295–317.
12. LENNEBERG, E. 1962. Understanding language without ability to speak: a case report. J. Abnorm. Soc. Psychol. **65:** 419–425.
13. POSTOVSKY, V. 1970. The effects of delay in oral practice at the beginning of second language learning. Ph.D. Dissertation. University of California. Berkeley, Calif. (Available from University Microfilms, Ann Arbor, Mich.)
14. POSTOVSKY, V. 1974. Effects of delay in oral practice at the beginning of second language learning. Mod. Lang. J. **58:** 229–239.
15. KRASHEN, S. 1978. The monitor model for second language acquisition. *In* Second Language Acquisition and Foreign Language Teaching. R. Gingras, Ed.: 1–26. Center for Applied Linguistics. Washington, D.C.
16. LAMENDELLA, J. 1979. The neurofunctional basis of pattern practice. TESOL Q. **13:** 5–20.
17. ERVIN-TRIPP, S. 1974. Is second language learning like the first? TESOL Q. **8:** 111–128.
18. SORENSON, A. 1967. Multilingualism in the northwest Amazon. Am. Anthropol. **69:** 674–684.
19. SWAFFER, J. & M. WOODRUFF. 1978. Language for comprehension: focus on

reading. A report on the University of Texas German program. Mod. Lang. J. **62:** 27–32.

20. EPTING, J. & J. BOWEN. 1979. Resurrecting the language lab for teaching listening comprehension and related skills. *In* Teaching English as a Second or Foreign Language. M. Celce-Muria & L. McIntosh, Eds. Newbury House Publishers. Rowley, Mass.

21. DAKIN, J. 1973. The Language Laboratory and Language Learning. Longman. London, England.

22. SWALES, J. 1968. Language laboratory materials and service courses: problems of tape course design for science students. J. Appl. Linguistics Lang. Teach. Technol. **6:** 17–22.

23. DICKINSON, L. 1970. The language laboratory and advanced teaching. English Lang. Teach. **21:** 32–47.

24. BOWEN, J. 1972. Materials designs for intermediate and advanced second language classes. UCLA Workpapers in Teaching English as a Second Language **6:** 1–10.

25. GARY, N. & J. GARY. 1978. A report on an experimental ESP curriculum research report. UCLA Workpapers in Teaching English as a Second Language **12:** 113–132.

26. REEDS, J., H. WINITZ & P. GARCIA. 1977. A test of reading following comprehension training. Int. Rev. Appl. Linguistics **15**(4): 307–319.

27. FAHMY, N. 1979. An investigation of the effectiveness of extensive listening and reading practice on students' ability to read English. M.A. Thesis. American University in Cairo. Cairo, Egypt.

COMPREHENSION-BASED LANGUAGE INSTRUCTION: PRACTICE

Norman Gary * and Judith Olmsted Gary

*Department of English and
English Language Center
Cairo University
Cairo, Egypt*

INTRODUCTION

In the preceding paper, we presented a number of arguments for the theoretical position that formal language instruction should begin with comprehension—both listening and reading—and that the teaching of the productive skills should be delayed for some unspecified time until a substantial base of competence in comprehension has been established. At this point, the productive skills of writing and speaking would find their way into the formal instructional program. We suggested that the skills be sequenced for instruction as follows: *listening, reading, writing,* and finally *speaking.* And even after required speaking is introduced, comprehension activities still should make up the bulk of the instructional program, perhaps as much as 80%.

If we accept this theoretical position in some form or another, how do we translate it into actual classroom practice? The following discussion is an attempt to provide some guidelines for preparing comprehension lessons and some concrete suggestions about classroom activities and procedures. We will illustrate by discussing part by part one lesson from a series we have developed. The particular lesson is not discussed as a model for all lessons, but simply as an illustration of one way in which the theory can be translated into classroom reality.

CRITERIA FOR EFFECTIVE COMPREHENSION LESSONS

We would like to list what we think are the main criteria for effective comprehension lessons. These criteria are drawn from our observations of the most effective comprehension lessons we have seen or read about being used in the classroom.

Comprehension Should Focus on Messages

By this we mean that the main concern of comprehension should be on understanding grammatically structured meanings. Initially, the messages

---

* Please address all correspondence to Dr. Norman Gary. From the United States: c/o Fulbright/CAIRO, Department of State, Washington, D.C. 20520. From outside the U.S.: P.O. Box 2098, Cairo, Egypt.

0077–8923/81/0379–0343 $01.75/2 © 1981, NYAS

might be quite short utterances, gradually becoming longer and more complex as proficiency is gained. This also means that comprehension should be concerned more with content than with form.

The Messages Should Be Presented Systematically

Any time the learner is given a task, it should be built on his prior experience with the language up to that point. The actual organizational principles behind the sequencing of materials for comprehension might be grammatical, notional, lexical, or something else. But the learner should be able to perceive the steps he is asked to take in relationship to previous steps he has taken. This sounds very commonsensical, but it is one of the major weaknesses of almost all listening-comprehension materials produced commercially. Most speaking-oriented materials are well sequenced, moving from simple structures and situations to increasingly more complex ones. In contrast, activities labeled "listening" usually begin at a much more advanced level than they should, and the progression of material presented often is not very systematic.

The Message Should Be Understandable

The learner should be able to comprehend all of the meaningful parts of the messages presented, given the explanation, demonstration, and practice received during the instructional period. This means that ways have to be found to explain or demonstrate the meanings of the lexical and grammatical structures of which the messages are composed.

Initially, there is no need to focus on the nonmeaningful parts of the message; it probably is counterproductive, distracting the learner from his central concern—comprehending meaning. This is another way of saying that great care should be taken to assure that input data become intake on the part of the learner. Again, this sounds only commonsensical, but this probably is the weakest point of most of the "listening-comprehension" materials we are acquainted with, especially materials that depend on relatively long passages of narration or conversation as the matter for comprehension.

The criterion of making sure that the messages are understandable raises the question of using various kinds of simplifying devices, such as found in caretaker speech—repetition, slower speed of delivery, grammatical simplifications, etc. It is our position that these kinds of devices are useful and probably necessary to meet the criterion of making the message understandable.

The Message Should Be Contextualized

Most of the language we use is context rich. Comprehension will be enhanced and learning more assured if there is a rich context for the language used in the message. Wherever possible, this context should be extralinguistic, that is, it should be provided through classroom realia or visual media rather than through language itself. Providing a context for language use allows the learner to narrow down the universe of discourse and limit the number of hypotheses needed to account for the meaning being presented in the messages.

Of course the competent language user has the ability to use language in relatively context-impoverished situations, as in the beginnings of a telephone conversation or radio broadcast, where there are only linguistic cues to guide the comprehension. And ultimately this is a skill a learner will have to acquire. However, the early stages of listening comprehension probably is not the best place for it.

The Message Should Be Communicative

Here we use the word "communicative" in its narrowest sense: the matter for comprehension should be structured meanings that are not fully predictable from the context. Learners should be forced to deal with new combinations of learned items; this means that they always must be listening *actively,* not simply hearing the sounds.

The Learner Should Make Some Overt Response

This perhaps is more a matter of sound pedagogy than psycholinguistics. Theoretically, one should be able to learn by making only a mental response to a message. However, human attention being what it is, and perhaps human cognition being what it is, it seems likely that making an overt response—moving or gesturing, choosing a written answer, writing a short response, saying a word or phrase—will enhance the learning, if for no other reason than that it will demand attention from the learner.

These then are what we think are the essential elements in comprehension-oriented language lessons. There are of course other desirable qualities: materials should be interesting; they should be perceived as relevant by the learners; they should be attractive, etc. But it is our experience that students, properly presented with comprehension materials meeting the above criteria, will tend to view them as challenging and interesting tasks in and of themselves, and will tolerate a lack of other qualities that they might otherwise insist on.

Many, if not most, of the widely used, commercially produced texts for comprehension do not meet these criteria. However, there are materials that do. The comprehension lessons designed by James Asher and others using the *total physical response* (TPR) meet all the above criteria.[1] And we think that this is why they have been so successful. We remain somewhat skeptical of the argument that their success is due mainly to the physical actions underlying the TPR mode.[1] We see some potential drawbacks in TPR-type lessons, mostly having to do with practicality. When the lessons get to the place where individuals, rather than groups, are carrying out the commands, many of the learners are not making any overt response; they are watching the person following the command. Second, in very large classes like the ones we have encountered in Egypt (as many as 60 students in a single classroom), the use of TPR might well produce chaos. For these reasons, we have relied more on paper-and-pen responses in designing our comprehension-based lessons.

A number of other researchers have produced language-teaching materials that also meet the criteria we have listed, notably Winitz and Reeds' German materials,[2] Ingram, Nord, and Dragt's Russian materials,[3] and especially the late Valerian Postovsky's Russian materials at the Defense Language Institute in Monterey, California.[4] However, in many cases, these materials require fairly elaborate equipment and facilities.

We would like to discuss a sample lesson from a set of materials we have developed for use in teaching English to hotel personnel in Egypt, built on the theoretical and methodological criteria discussed above. The materials are designed to be used in an ordinary classroom. They use a cassette tape player of sufficient power and quality to be heard clearly in the classroom and an overhead projector. The listening part of the lesson uses what we call the *interactive tape and teacher (ITT) technique,* which involves a taped narrator interacting with the teacher and classroom learners through accompanying visual materials. The ITT technique has been used with over 2,000 adult students in large class situations under widely varying conditions for more than three years in Egypt. Two sets of specialized materials have been developed using the technique. To the best of our knowledge, this is a methodological innovation in language teaching. However, it should be emphasized that this particular technique is only one of several modes of presentation possible; it is the comprehension-based approach that is important and critical, not the technical means of presentation. The tape player and overhead projector could be eliminated, and the materials used by the teacher acting alone with a script, using only the students' printed materials, and the blackboard or a previously prepared flip chart. In fact, an earlier set of scientific materials with a similar format was used in this way. Shaker Rizk compared the materials taught with a teacher using a script versus a teacher using the accompanying tapes; students fared about the same either way.[5] If possible, we retain the tape because it provides for much greater flexibility in the classroom, while at the same time providing a variety of voices for the learners to listen to.

The specific lesson illustrated here is given at approximately the 80th hour of instruction to students who began the program with a very small amount of English. The minimum requirement for entrance to the program is a working knowledge of the English alphabet and some very basic lexical and grammatical knowledge. The students mostly are nonacademic, young adults in relatively lower ranks of hotel employment: housekeeping, security, physical and technical maintenance, cook's assistants, etc.

We will discuss only the listening and reading parts of this lesson; there are other parts, including practice listening to and using number combinations, extensive vocabulary building with pictures and worksheet activities, and practice in following and giving directions on a city map. Comprehension activities make up more than 80% of the lesson.

ANALYSIS OF A COMPREHENSION-BASED LESSON

Here we will discuss part of one lesson from a set of materials called *More English Now!,* which provide the second half of approximately 150 hours of instruction in English for hotel personnel. The lesson will be examined in light of the six criteria developed above.

The lesson parts to be discussed are *Listen Now!* and *Let's Read!,* listening and reading respectively. Actually both parts involve listening and reading activities, but the emphasis is different in each part. The reading is sequenced after listening for reasons discussed above.

Listen Now! takes approximately 30 minutes of tape time and should not take more than 35 or 40 minutes to present completely, assuming the teacher stops the tape occasionally to do some task specified in the lesson or to clarify something. *Let's Read!* should take about 15 minutes; there is little vocabulary preparation required, and the grammatical and lexical items should be familiar from the listening part and from previous lessons.

The student work-sheet materials for this lesson are given in the Appendix to this paper (*More English Now!,* pages 23–27). The reader may find it useful to look through them before reading further.

The basic approach of this lesson (and four other lessons forming an instructional unit) centers around the use of hotel-reservations charts. After studying the vocabulary for the lesson, via Arabic glosses and a short exercise, the students watch a demonstration in which the teacher listens to instructions given by the tape narrator about filling out reservations, such as:

> Please reserve room 104 for the Stones from Sunday through Wednesday, next week.
> You spell Stones as S-T-O-N-E-S, Stones. Write it in the chart.

After sufficient demonstration, the students listen to the narrator and follow similar instructions, completing the chart. They have completed the chart for *last week* in the previous lesson, and it is printed above the *next week* chart for them to refer to.

Next the narrator and teacher demonstrate new language structures in the lesson by the narrator asking questions about the reservations and the teacher answering the questions on the overhead projector. Again, after sufficient demonstration, the narrator begins asking the students questions about the reservations, such as:

> Who was in room 101?
> Who is going to be in 101?

When are they going to check out?
How many days are they going to be there?
Is the person in 102 going to check out on Tuesday?

The students respond on their work sheets, referring to the two charts. The narrator provides the students with correct answers after each question, so they can check themselves. At this point in the lesson, the teacher is free to observe the students individually as they respond to the narrator's questions. If any problems become apparent, the teacher stops the tape and deals with the problem. This gives the teacher enormous flexibility in monitoring student understanding and progress.

The objective of this lesson is twofold. It provides learners with language centered around common hotel topics and procedures, allowing previously introduced structures such as *when* and *how many* questions to be used in a new context, and it provides a natural way of contrasting use of the simple past tense with the *going to* and *will* futures. Before this lesson the learners always have had access to adverbs like *last week* and *next week* in comprehending time relationships; in this lesson, they have to comprehend using only the auxiliary and verb forms.

In this lesson, the device of the reservations chart provides for both *communication* and *contextualization*. There is enough information in the charts to provide for many novel utterances, using the grammatical and lexical structures available. And the charts provide in a natural way for an appropriate context for language use.

Let's look at the lesson in some detail now.

Listen Now! consists of six steps divided into three main divisions: *Preview, Let's Listen,* and *Review.*

Preview
   1. statement of objectives for lesson
   2. vocabulary preparation (Arabic glosses and exercise)
Let's Listen
   3. a. following instructions about reservations
       b. answering questions about reservations
          i. from tape narrator
          ii. from teacher
   4. Listen and Write (sentence cloze dictation)
   5. Test over objectives presented in the lesson
Review
   6. List of sentences used in 3.

The Preview section prepares the students for the lesson. In *Step 1* they listen to and read sample sentences they will be expected to understand fully at the end of the lesson (the objectives), and in *Step 2* they are presented with critical vocabulary and asked to demonstrate their understanding of the meaning by completing a short cloze-type exercise, requiring them to choose words from the vocabulary list to fill in the missing words.

The Preview section thus prepares the students by showing them the structures they will be expected to learn, and providing them with vocabulary preparation to help ensure their *understanding* of the lexical matter to be presented. Vocabulary items often are given redundantly from lesson to lesson because we are interested only in making the input *understandable,* not in testing vocabulary retention.

The second section, Let's Listen, provides the actual instruction, through demonstration and practice. In *Step 3,* any new language or actions needed are demonstrated by the tape narrator and teacher. Then students are given similar tasks to carry out, and they receive feedback on their performance either by watching the teacher carry out the same task or by receiving a direct response from the tape narrator. This is best illustrated by looking at a partial script. In the following, the students have just finished filling out the reservation chart for next week and have corrected themselves by comparing their reservations with the teacher's. Then the lesson moves to questions about the reservations.

> Narrator: Now, watch the teacher again. At number 1. Teacher, look at last week's reservations. Answer this question: Who was in room 101?
> Teacher: (writes in *Abdullah* at space 1a on the overhead projector)
> Narrator: That's right. Mr. Abdullah was in room 101. Now teacher, at b. How many days was he there?
> Teacher: (writes 4)
> Narrator: That's right, Mr. Abdullah was in 101 for 4 days last week.
>
> . . . .
>
> Narrator: Now students, look at last week's reservations. At number 3, answer this question: Who was in room 103?
> Students: (write their answers)
> Narrator: OK. The question was: Who was in room 103? And the answer is: the Porters. Now students, at b. What day did they check in?
> Students: (write their answers)
> Narrator: The question was: What day did they check in? And the answer is: Sunday, the 18th. The Porters checked in on Sunday, the 18th.
> *and so on.*

The students continue answering novel questions about the two charts, each using different grammatical and lexical structures, including the appropriate pronoun forms. The narrator provides them with feedback after each response in the form of a repetition of the question and the correct answer.

In this particular lesson, the students are presented with some 45 different questions to answer, and it takes approximately 15 minutes of time. While the students are responding to the narrator, the teacher is free to move around and watch the students' responses and to spot any potential problems. If there are problems, the teacher can stop the tape and give any explanation or further practice that might be needed. Also at the end of *Step 3,* provision is made on the tape for the teacher to continue asking more questions if it is thought useful or necessary, and the teacher may provide additional practice if it seems needed.

In the next step, *Step 4,* the students are provided with cloze versions of some of the questions they have been listening to. They listen to the narrator read the question, and they fill in the missing words by choosing from a group of words provided. This is intended to do two things. First, it gives the learners visual access to the material they have been listening to. Also, by careful use of the cloze procedure, we can systematically call attention to various lexical and grammatical items presented. For example, in this lesson these two sentences are given:

1. —— —— in room 103 all last week?
2. —— is —— —— —— in it next week?

As the students listen to the sentences and attempt to fill in the missing words, their attention is called to the different auxiliaries and verb forms that are contrasted in this lesson. Notice that they are not being asked to produce the forms, only to show that they have comprehended what is said and then copy the correct responses.

The last activity in this section is in *Step 5*, where there is a short test over the structures demonstrated and practiced. It allows both teacher and students to evaluate the learning.

Review is the third section of *Listen Now!*. It simply provides a list of the questions the students listened to in *Step 3*. It gives the learners full access to all of the utterances they have practiced earlier in the lesson for use in checking their own perceptions and for possible review outside of the classroom. This list was added in the current revision of the materials at the learners' request. And that is the end of *Listen Now!*, the listening part of this particular lesson.

Let's Read! is the reading part of this lesson, and it is a direct follow-up of the language and situation used in the listening. It requires the learners to follow commands given in writing and fill in a reservations chart appropriately, and then answer written questions about the reservations. Instructions to the teacher specify that the written material should be read aloud with the students following in their work sheets. This is to provide the aural accompaniment that we have found to be useful in early reading.

These two parts of one lesson, *Listen Now!* and *Let's Read!*, illustrate what we mean by comprehension-based language instruction. The learners have been presented *systematically* and *communicatively* with a wide range of *messages* with appropriate extralinguistic *context* and with suitable preparation to assure *understanding;* they in turn will have made a number of *overt responses* to the messages presented. The only production required of the students is short written or spoken answers with very little grammatical structuring; they will have been able to devote all of their attention to trying to comprehend the messages and building up their receptive competence.

Students who took the first 70 hours of this program showed consistent mean scores of approximately 85% in four periodic, cumulative achievement tests. Students who were in the program from the very beginning showed gain scores from pretest to posttest of over two and one-half standard deviations in two different types of proficiency tests of comprehension skills—very substantial gains, indeed. These results are shown in TABLE 1. Test 1, "Listening Multiple Choice," requires the learners to look at a picture, listen to a short description of the picture, then listen to and answer 20 multiple-choice questions about the picture, using a wide range of language. Test 2, "Listening Recall," is a type of listening cloze test, where learners are given a short written passage to read that has 15 content words deleted, and these words cannot be replaced from the written version alone. The students then listen to the passage read aloud to them and try to replace the missing words from their aural memory. One of the problems we faced in devising proficiency tests for this program was a consistent underestimation of the kind of progress that the students would make in the comprehension skills, as can be seen in the results of the "Listening Multiple Choice" measure, where students clearly are showing a ceiling effect in the test by the time of the third administration.

TABLE 1

COMPREHENSION-PROFICIENCY SCORES *

	First (zero hours)	Second (at 40 hours)	Third (at 70 hours)
Test 1. Listening Multiple Choice (20 points)	9.84 (3.12)	15.97 (2.36)	17.56 (1.34)
Test 2. Listening Recall (15 points)	2.96 (2.39)	6.67 (3.13)	9.59 (2.85)

* Means and standard deviations of scores of two comprehension-proficiency tests over three administrations: first at zero hours of instruction, second at approximately 40 hours of instruction, and third at approximately 70 hours of instruction. $n = 27$.

Students who took the program showed very favorable attitudes toward the materials. For example, they were asked the following question near the end of the program: "Would you recommend this course to a friend?" Fifty-three of the 54 respondents answered positively, and 1 did not respond to the question.

Our less formal observations confirm also that the learners using the materials are making substantial progress in learning English, even in *speaking* it, and are thriving in the tension-free atmosphere provided by comprehension-based language instruction.

CONCLUSION

We have tried to indicate what we think are the major theoretical and methodological considerations in trying to provide effective language instruction through comprehension-based materials. And we have tried to demonstrate concretely how these considerations can be applied in an individual lesson. We have discussed this lesson in detail solely to illustrate one way we have found to translate the theory into effective classroom materials. We do not present the lesson as a model for all lessons. No doubt creative curriculum writers can construct better, more interesting, more effective lessons, while building on a sound theoretical base, which we have tried to define.

We hope we have been able to suggest some things that might contribute toward the development of sound comprehension-based language materials.

REFERENCES

1. ASHER, J. 1979. Learning Another Language through Actions: The Complete Teacher's Guidebook. Sky Oaks Productions. Los Gatos, Calif.
2. WINITZ, H. & J. REEDS. 1973. Rapid acquisition of a foreign language (German) by the avoidance of speaking. Int. Rev. Appl. Linguistics **11:** 295–317.
3. INGRAM, F., J. NORD & D. DRAGT. 1974. Developing a programmed workbook for listening comprehension in Russian. Paper read at the Soviet-American Conference on the Russian Language, Amherst, Mass., October.
4. POSTOVSKY, V. 1976. The priority of aural comprehension in the language acquisition process. Paper read at Fourth Association Internationale Linguistique Appliquée World Congress, Stuttgart, Federal Republic of Germany, August 25–30.
5. RIZK, S. 1980. The effectiveness of native ESL cassette supplemental instruction with a decoding-based methodology compared with the same methodology used without the supplemental cassette instruction. M.A. Thesis. American University in Cairo. Cairo, Egypt.

MORE ENGLISH NOW !

Lesson 3

Listen Now !

PREVIEW (Study this before class begins. Write the answers in 2)

1. **"What are we going to learn?"**

   a. We are going to listen to and follow commands like:

      1. Please reserve room 104 for Mr and Mrs Stone
          from Sunday through Wednesday next week.
      2. Let's put Miss Jones in room 102 from Wednesday
          through Friday.
      3. You spell Jones as J-o-n-e-s, Jones. Write it out.

   b. We are going to answer questions like:

      1. Is the person in room 102 going to check out on Tuesday?
      2. Did the people in room 105 check in on Thursday?
      3. Who was in room 101?
      4. Who is going to be in room 101?
      5. When did he check in?
      6. When are they going to check out?
      7. Who checked out of that room?
      8. How many days were they there?

2. Important Words

   a. is, are   present tense of (to) be   يكون

   b. was, were   past tense of (to) be   كان

   c. last week   الاسبوع الماضي

   d. next week   الاسبوع القادم

   e. (to) check in to someplace   يسجل نفسه في مكان ما

      checked in (past tense)   سجل نفسه

   f. (to) check out of someplace   يسجل نفسه للخروج من مكان ما

   g. checked out   (past tense)   (في الماضي)

   Write one of the words above in each blank in these. sentences:

   a. Mr and Mrs Porter _____ here last week.

   b. Mr Latrec _____ in room 104 last week.

   c. When you go to a hotel, you must _____ _____ .

   d. When you leave a hotel, you must _____ _____ .

   e. Yesterday, the guests _____ ____ to their hotel

      before dinner.

   f. They _____ _____ of their rooms in the morning just

      before they left the hotel.

(continued on next page)

page 23

Lesson 3

Listen Now !

LET'S LISTEN

3. a. Listen and write in the reservations for next week.

RESERVATIONS
last week

Room No.:	Sun 18	Mon 19	Tue 20	Wed 21	Thur 22	Fri 23	Sat 24
101	Abdullah	~~~	~~~	~~~			
102			Laura Arthur	~~~	~~~	~~~	~~~
103	Porters	~~~	~~~		~~~	~~~	~~~
104			Latrec	~~~	~~~	~~~	
105		Bullocks	~~~	~~~	~~~	~~~	~~~
106					Sami Aziz	~~~	~~~

RESERVATIONS
next week

Room No.:	Sun 1	Mon 2	Tue 3	Wed 4	Thur 5	Fri 6	Sat 7
101							
102							
103							
104							
105							
106							

b. Answer these questions

1. a. _____   2. a. _____   3. a. _____

    b. _____   b. _____   b. _____

    c. _____   c. _____   c. _____

4. a. _____   5. a. _____   6. a. _____

    b. _____   b. _____   b. _____

    c. _____   c. _____   c. _____

(continued on next page)

Lesson 3

Listen Now!

7.	a. _____	8. a. _____		9. a. _____	
	b. _____	b. _____		b. _____	
	c. _____	c. _____		c. _____	
10.	a. _____	11. a. _____		12. a. _____	
	b. _____	b. _____		b. _____	
	c. _____	c. _____		c. _____	
13.	a. _____	14. a. _____		15. a. _____	
	b. _____	b. _____		b. _____	
	c. _____	c. _____		c. _____	

4. <u>"Let's Listen and Write!"</u>

Listen to each sentence and then write in the missing words.
Choose the words from the list provided. Then answer the
questions.

<u>Words:</u> who   is / are   check in / checked in
         what   was / were   check out/ checked out
         which day   going to be

1. _____ _____ in room 103 all last week?   _____

2. _____ is _____ ___ ___ in it next week?_____

3. What day is she going to _____ ___?   _____

4. Who _____ _____ of room 104 on the 24th?_____

5. Who _____ _____ to room 105 on the 19th?_____

5. <u>"What have we learned?"</u>

1. _____
2. _____
3. _____
4. _____
5. _____

(continued on next page)

Listen Now!   **Lesson 3**

REVIEW. Here are the questions you listened to in Step 3.

1.   Teacher, look at last week's reservations.
    a. Who was in room 101? ?
    b. How many days was he there?
    c. What day did he check in?
2.   Teacher, look at next week's reservations.
    a. Who is going to be in room 106?
    b. How many days is he going to be there?
    c. What day is he going to check out?
3. Students, look at last week's reservations.
    a. Who was in room 103?
    b. What day did they check in?
    c. What day did they check out?
4. Students, look at next week's reservations.
    a. Who's going to be in room 101 from Sunday to Wednesday?
    b. What day are they going to check in?
    c. What day are they going to check out?
5. Teacher,
    a. Who was in room 104?
    b. When did he check in?
    c. When did he check out?
6. Teacher,
    a. Who is going to be in room 104?
    b. When is he going to check in?
    c. How many days is he going to be there?
7. Students,
    a. Who was in room 106?
    b. When did he check out?
    c. How many days was he there?
8. a. Who is going to be in room 106?
    b. How many days is he going to be there?
    c. What day is he going to check out?
9. a. Did the people in room 105 check in on Tuesday
    b. When did they check in?
    c. How many days were they there?
10. a. Is the person in room 102 going to check in on Tuesday?
    b. When is she going to check in?
    c. When is she going to check out?
11. a. Who is going to check in to room 106?
    b. When is he going to check out?
    c. Who checked out of that room?
12. a. What's the name of the person who was in room 101?
    b. What day did he check out?
    c. Who is going to check in there on next Thursday?
13. a. Which room was free from Sunday through Wednesday?
    b. Was anyone in that room on Thursday?
    c. Who was in it?
14. a. Which room was reserved all week?
    b. Who was in it?
    c. Is it going to be reserved all week next week?
15. a. Which room is going to be reserved all week?
    b. Who is going to be in it?
    c. Who was in it?

page 26

Lesson 3

Let's Read !

1. Important Words:

    a. client = customer

    b. employee, employees = workers

2. Reading Passage

    a. Read this message and complete the reservations chart.

    We have a letter from the ABC Tourist Office. They want us to make the following reservations for their clients:

    a) reserve two rooms for Mr and Mrs Johnson and children from Sunday through Saturday,
    b) reserve one room for Dr and Mrs Yousiri from the tenth through the fourteenth,
    c) reserve three rooms for employees of The Atlas Company from the ninth through the thirteenth.

    Please put the Johnson family in rooms 101 and 102. Put the Yousiris in room 103. And put the Atlas people in rooms 104 through 106.

RESERVATIONS
Week of *Sept. 8*

Room No.:	Sun 8	Mon 9	Tue 10	Wed 11	Thur 12	Fri 13	Sat 14
101							
102							
103							
104							
105							
106							

    b. Answer these questions:

    1. How many days do the Johnsons have reservations for? _____
    2. What day are they going to check in? _____
    3. How many rooms do they need? _____
    4. How many rooms does the ABC office want for the Atlas Company? _____
    5. How long will they need the rooms? _____
    6. What day are they going to check out? _____
    7. Can anyone be put in room 101 from the 12th to the 14th? _____
    8. Why not?
    9. Is room 104 reserved all week? _____
    10. Which room is free Sunday and Monday? _____

page 27

IMPLICATIONS FOR LEARNING A SECOND LANGUAGE: GENERAL DISCUSSION

Moderator: Robbins Burling

Department of Anthropology
University of Michigan
Ann Arbor, Michigan 48109

UNIDENTIFIED SPEAKER: How do you know that the Chinese tones weren't perceived as nonlinguistic units, such as musical tones, especially if the subjects did not know Chinese?

H. WINITZ (*University of Missouri, Kansas City, Mo.*): I did speak to that issue in the paper, indicating that in Snow's paper the same general findings with regard to age and acquisition were obtained for linguistically meaningful elements. Furthermore, I referred to studies in which comprehension of language was taught and in which adult subjects performed at a high level, as did the adults in my study. Therefore, I believe that the listening capabilities of adults are generally superior to children in the early stage of language acquisition. Although the discriminations I was testing may not be regarded as linguistic events, it is of interest to observe that they are skills that are essential if oral language is to be acquired, and in that regard, adults seem initially to have more advanced abilities than children have.

C. YORIO (*University of Toronto, Toronto, Ontario, Canada*): Dr. Belasco, many of the examples that we have heard are fairly traditional, in the sense that you are presenting what one could call a structural syllabus. The point is, what is your feeling about the application of this approach to a functional syllabus?

S. BELASCO (*University of South Carolina, Columbia, S.C.*): My remarks pertain to the first semester only. I outlined what the students are able to do in the first semester. Teaching speech acts, illocutionary acts, takes place in the second semester. In the first semester, the emphasis is placed on interpretation and not on production. The goal of these procedures is to improve comprehension and to reinforce comprehension.

The purpose of the translation exercises is to teach the student to concentrate on the perception and interpretation of utterances. Exposure to "illocutionary acts" in the form of readings and comprehension exercises must precede the actual teaching of the use of illocutionary acts in conversational situations.

C. YORIO: One more quick question about correction and accuracy. You talked in particular about stopping the student when he makes a mistake. If your concern is with comprehension, during the first semester, why stop him if he has communicated? Finally, when you have a translation test for them to write out, do you correct for errors in spelling, accent marks, etc.?

S. BELASCO: What I want the student to do is approximate the pronunciation. I am interested in his knowing sandhi variation, when to make liaison, when not to make liaison, about dropping final consonants, and so forth. If the student doesn't repeat correctly, I call on another student. Most importantly, content is stressed. Later I correct for errors.

R. BLAKE (*Dartmouth College, Hanover, N.H.*): Dr. Asher, my question relates to your remarks regarding caretakers. Not all caretakers provide a warm and supportive environment for the child. Children who come from the most abusive and deprived home conditions learn to talk. I would like to hear you comment about that.

J. J. ASHER (*San José State University, San Jose, Calif.*): The clinical literature suggests that there is a relationship between the quality of caretaking and impairments in child development. For example, neglect of infants can slow the rate of language acquisition, and even produce aberrations in understanding and production.

UNIDENTIFIED SPEAKER: Dr. Asher, how does your total-physical-response approach compare with other ways of achieving comprehension?

J. J. ASHER: Most approaches for comprehension training, such as the ones developed by Asher, Winitz, Nord, the Garys, Postovsky, and others, are in harmony because they play to the right hemisphere of the brain—which is the kind of stimulation that infants experience especially in the pretalking period of language development.

UNIDENTIFIED SPEAKER: I have a question, Dr. Gary. After some 80 hours of training, what can we expect from the students? Can they write or answer in English? And furthermore, how many lexical items do they know?

N. GARY (*English Language Center, Cairo University, Cairo, Egypt*): At the end of the 80 hours of instruction, the students average 85% proficiency in comprehension and reading on the structures they have been studying. The tests are not simple repetitions of items. They include new combinations. We do not emphasize writing, and so we do get terrible spelling. However, the students are able to write out appropriate messages in accord with their level of training. Speaking could not be fairly assessed given the constraints of our program. However, speaking has been assessed under controlled conditions in other studies. Finally, the students learn 1,000 to 1,200 lexical items during this period of instruction.

CONCLUDING REMARKS AND SUMMARY

Harris Winitz

Department of Psychology
University of Missouri–Kansas City
Kansas City, Missouri 64110

This conference was convened for the purposes of exploring relationships between first-language (L1) and second-language (L2) acquisition, and for determining whether research in L1 and L2 acquisition can be appropriately utilized to teach L2. The focus on theoretical as well as practical interests resulted in a set of papers that covers a broad spectrum of issues in language acquisition and language teaching.

It would be unrealistic to expect that the topics presented and discussed at this conference represent a set of ideas that departs significantly from the current mainstream of thought. Nonetheless, the issues that are presented are timely, well conceived, and challenging. Additionally, there is the strong suggestion that research in the acquisition of L1 and L2 may assist language teachers in forging new methodologies of teaching or enable them to choose among competing contemporary methodologies.

In the opening paper, Alatis and De Marco present major issues of concern in the teaching of foreign languages. They firmly focus on methodological and sociological problems associated with the teaching of foreign languages to native English speakers, and the teaching of English to non-native speakers living in the United States. They emphasize the importance of utilization and preservation of existing resources, such as encouraging adults whose native language is not English to enter professions for which a second language is in demand, and providing opportunities for children who have native competency in a foreign language to increase and develop this skill by receiving some of their education in the foreign language. Unfortunately, there are sociological forces, as Alatis and De Marco remark, that militate against such innovative programs, of which the usual concern is the unfounded belief that teaching in languages other than English will cause children to have a poor command of English.

The absence of effective foreign-language teaching in this country is given careful consideration by Alatis and De Marco, who recommend resourceful application of research findings. Here the focus, they advise, should be multivaried and should take into account language methodology, motivation, curriculum design, and implementation of bilingual instruction.

Support for the importance of bilingual education is summarized by Lambert, who contends that the bilingual student's competencies extend beyond mastery of non-native languages to include advantages in cognitive and social development. According to Lambert, bilingualism develops insights about the use, form, and vocabulary of language, which in turn will

0077–8923/81/0379–0360 $01.75/2 © 1981, NYAS

broaden an individual's cognitive perspective and increase the potential for creativity and problem solving. Bilingual education is most effective when the second or third language has social value and respect. Lambert calls this condition "additive" bilingualism in contrast to "subtractive" bilingualism, which takes place when a native or ethnic language is forced aside through social pressures and replaced by a prestigious or majority language. Lambert recommends that bilingualism be encouraged in the home and school whenever possible.

Foreign-language education in North America typically begins in high school or college, and as Lambert notes, "the majority seem to just get started as the training ends." In this regard, Lambert cites the success achieved in L2 competency from immersion programs beginning in kindergarten. No concurrent impairment in L1 is observed to occur.

Lambert concludes his paper with an important review of recent research on differences in neurological functioning among monolinguals, and among bilinguals who are distinguished by the age at which their second language was acquired. Psycholinguistic study suggests that late bilinguals retain greater functional independence of the two languages than do early bilinguals. Furthermore, late bilinguals appear to utilize the right hemisphere more than do early bilinguals and monolinguals, although this interpretation is not shared by Kinsbourne. As Lambert points out, these neurological and linguistic differences among early and late bilinguals and monolinguals suggest important components for future study in the acquisition and storage of language, in the instructional methodologies used to teach language, and in the role of age and hemispheric involvement in language learning.

One condition that may determine variation in acquisition between early and late bilinguals is classroom language experience. This is a topic of considerable interest today, and McLaughlin provides some important insights here. As he suggests, the formal study of language may encourage students to construct "tactics" that can improve learning efficiency and increase linguistic awareness and understanding. On the other hand, as McLaughlin points out, formal classroom instruction in language can exaggerate the differences between L1 and L2 acquisition, because students simultaneously are applying universal strategies of acquisition and developing tactics to handle material that is inappropriately sequenced or beyond their ability to learn.

The question of differences and similarities between L1 and L2 language learning is carefully examined in McLaughlin's paper. He notes that many considerations need to be taken into account when addressing this topic. When young children learn languages simultaneously (simultaneous bilingual acquisition), the emphasis given to each language may not be equivalent. A difference in balance between the two languages may determine, in part, the magnitude of transfer from the dominant language.

In his discussion of sequential bilingual acquisition in children, McLaughlin, along with other investigators, concludes that there is, for the most part, uniformity in the acquisition of language forms for a target language, an observation that suggests that children apply universal language-acquisition strategies in acquiring L1 and L2. However, he further notes that there is individual variation in the development of language among L2 acquirers. An explanation for this finding is that children additionally use particular or idiosyncratic learning strategies that reflect their cognitive maturity and L1 experience, and other situational considerations. However, diversity in acquisition does not seem to alter substantially developmental regularities.

The term used by McLaughlin to designate universal processes is "acquisition heuristics," whereas Seliger employs the term "strategies." Idiosyncratic processes are referred to as "operating procedures" and "tactics" by McLaughlin and Seliger respectively. As defined by McLaughlin, strategies are "superordinate, abstract, constant, and long-term cognitive [or language-acquisition] processes," which both L1 and L2 learners use, and which account for similarity in acquisition of L1 and L2. Specific acquisition strategies or tactics are utilized to achieve "temporary or immediate goals" and may account for diversity in the acquisition of language for L1 and L2 learners.

Ervin-Tripp's paper focuses on transfer functions in second-language learning and, in particular, semantic usage and conversational routines. She provides illustrations from transcripts of young children whose contact with the second language was relatively minimal.

In the second language, the children quickly acquired skill in using (a) discourse functions, such as repairs, adjacency pairs (e.g., question and answer, summons and reply), local discourse (e.g., calls, attention getters), speech acts (e.g., persuasion, joking, indirect asking of permission, contradiction, explanation), and (b) semantic categories and relationships that affect the way in which words are used in a language to describe objects, events, abstractions, attributes, etc.

Differences between second-language learners and first-language learners are indicated by Ervin-Tripp. She cogently points out that the older children (and adults) know how to impose structure on their environment in the beginning phases of language acquisition, as evidenced by the way they are able to organize play, to pretend an activity, to teach a lesson, to argue, and so forth. In some cases their vocabulary and linguistic competence had not achieved a similar level of development, although their conversational skills were remarkably advanced relative to the performance of first-language learners for the same period of language contact and experience.

Ervin-Tripp clearly illustrates that second-language learners have advanced knowledge of discourse rules, semantic properties, human interaction, and other concepts. Yet, as she points out, they often have limited linguistic skills that must be taken into consideration.

Ervin-Tripp's method of analysis provides an inviting framework for further research along several dimensions. Of particular interest is whether some of the advantages that L2 learners show in the functional use of language later turn out to be deficits as the second language becomes more fully acquired and subtle differences in fit surface. Thus, it is important to know how and in what way adults and children differ in learning to transfer previously acquired discourse functions from L1 to L2, whether the transfer of these functions follows universal principles of language acquisition, and how cultural differences and linguistic skills affect this process.

There were three papers in the session on neurophysiological processes in language acquisition. The first presenter was Kinsbourne, who provided a critique of a number of investigations on brain functioning and bilingualism. He began by succinctly listing a series of hypotheses that have been offered by investigators. They are (1) L1 and L2 use the same area of the brain, which may or may not be greater than that used by monolinguals; (2) L1 and L2 utilize overlapping cerebral areas, for which the area for L2 is equal to or more extensive than that for L1; and (3) the cerebral areas for L1 and L2 are separate, and this separation may or may not be a function of the age at which L2 was acquired.

Kinsbourne does not believe there is evidence to support the position that there are different cerebral territories for L1 and L2. He notes, however, that within a relevant part of the brain there may be differences in hemispheric activation for L1 and L2 that may represent different skill levels for L1 and L2. With regard to the differential role of the hemispheres in L1 and L2, Kinsbourne contends that the well-done laterality studies and clinical studies do not show hemispheric asymmetry for L1 and L2. Additionally, he indicates that the well-recognized ability of the immature brain to compensate for damage of brain tissue does not provide evidence for the claim that L1 and L2 are processed in different cerebral areas or are differentially lateralized.

Whitaker, Bub, and Leventer's paper provides recent information and analysis that calls into question previously held concepts about the physical maturation of the brain and its relationship to the development of language. They also summarize current research endeavors on differential localization in the brain for verbal naming of objects by bilinguals.

The first part of Whitaker, Bub, and Leventer's paper contains an extensive analysis of the physical maturation of the brain, work that reflects significantly on Lenneberg's critical-period hypothesis. Lenneberg's position was that there was a single pattern of structural change in the brain for the neurological correlates of language, and that the growth rate of the neurons (cell-body volume and neurodensity) in the cerebral cortex is largely complete by puberty. Whitaker and his colleagues have shown that the neuronal growth rate varies in the different language areas and within the same area for different types of cell structures. Furthermore, they point out that it is difficult to draw a correlation between the growth of language and maturation of the brain because, according to current indices of neural maturation, the brain is at about 90% of adult values by five to six years of age. The remaining 10% occurs slowly and into middle adulthood. It is of interest to point out that L1 acquisition continues many years beyond the five- to six-year point and also, in most instances, individuals who have acquired a second language between five years and puberty in almost all cases demonstrate nativelike competency.

Whitaker, Bub, and Leventer conclude their paper with a summary of their research on intrahemispheric localization of language for bilingual subjects. They had subjects name objects while certain points in and neighboring the principle language areas of the brain received electrical stimulation. The individual placement sites for which speech arrest occurred were not always the same for the naming responses in the two languages, a finding that might suggest that the neural substrate is not exactly the same for L1 and L2 within a circumscribed area.

Diller begins his paper with a discussion of neurological components of the critical-period hypothesis. Initially he notes that adults are faster than children in learning a second language even though they are generally unable to acquire nativelike competency in pronunciation. The stellate cells, which are associated with higher order cortical functions, and which continue to mature beyond puberty, he contends, provide the adult with sufficient neuroplasticity to learn a second language. In contrast, the pyramidal cells, through their long descending tracts, are responsible for establishing relations between neural control centers and for the control of motor functioning. According to Diller, after left-hemisphere injury, the formation of language centers in the right hemisphere and the development of authentic L1 pronunciation patterns only can take place prior to maturation of the pyramidal cells in childhood.

Diller then addresses the issue of hemispheric activity and language acquisition. He argues that different language-teaching methods activate different cortical areas and pathways. Certain traditional methods fail to utilize appropriately Wernicke's area and the semantic areas of the supramarginal gyrus. The position that Diller holds is that language-teaching methodologies should make proper use of the various cortical centers important for speech and language.

The session on phonology and phonetics began with a paper by Cole on the perceptual identification of elements in fluent speech by children and adults. The perception of phonetic entities in fluent speech is, of course, a major consideration in the acquisition of L1 and L2. Cole focuses on mispronunciations to draw inferences about underlying processes in speech perception.

Cole found that mispronunciations are detected more often by children and adults when the sounds are stop consonants and when the sounds appear in word-initial position. Further study of children's identification of mispronunciations showed that sounds that appeared in isolated words, in contrast to fluent speech, and sounds that violate English phonotactic rules were more easily detected. Cole infers that one language-processing strategy, and by generalization a language-acquisition strategy, is that sounds in word-initial position are used to generate candidate words prior to receiving sounds in word-final position. Support for this inference comes from his research findings that detection of mispronunciations in word-final position is less than in word-initial position. No doubt a constraint on this strategy is that a word be fairly short and somewhat predictable from context.

Little is known of the phonetic acquisition strategies that L1 and L2 learners use. Cole's paper is a step in this direction, as he cites a number of potentially important factors (meaning, word position, feature difference, speech style or rate, etc.) that merit further investigation.

The Macken and Ferguson paper on phonological development is a valuable contribution in two ways. First, the authors provide an insightful review of contemporary issues in the study of developmental phonological universals, and second, they present an interpretative model for studying phonological acquisition within a universalist framework. Here they touch on considerations that are of general concern not only for phonology, but for other linguistic branches as well. Also they provide an illuminating discussion of phonological processes in young children. Of those described are substitution, syllable structure, reduplication, and various assimilatory processes.

Their discussion of phonological universals in acquisition is illustrated by a thoughtful account of the development of voicing in stops. Here they indicate that there is support for the phonological universal: voiceless unaspirated stops are acquired before there is development of a phonological voicing contrast for stops in a particular language. They note, however, that procedural points of difference among investigations may have confounded prior attempts to arrive at uniformity in the assessment of voicing in stops. Additionally they acknowledge that variation in phonological development may reflect language-specific differences in the utilization and distribution of sounds across languages, and the particular input that a child receives.

Macken and Ferguson indicate that diversity in phonological acquisition does not destroy the concept of language universals in acquisition. They note, in particular, that phonological universals can be viewed as probable outcomes (statistical universals) of universal processing strategies. Universal processing strategies (acquisition strategies) are applied by the child to construct theories about the patterned input of a language. There is continual revision and reorganization throughout the learning process, of which the end result is a comprehensive, systematic, and thus mature phonological system. Within this perspective, variation in phonological development is accommodated by consideration of universal forces that are applied to individual circumstances. This approach is more complex than early universal theories of acquisition, in which language development was viewed as the linear unfolding of innate universal abilities.

The approach offered by Macken and Ferguson is particularly appealing for the study of phonological acquisition in L2 (and, of course, L1) because due consideration is given to universal acquisition strategies, the relationship between L1 and L2, the cognitive maturity and prior linguistic knowledge of the individual learner, and the language input to the learner. In this regard, variation in development may reflect differences in the target language, the linguistic experiences of a child, and the psychological and physiological capabilities of a child at a particular point in development.

Menn's paper complements the position taken by Macken and Ferguson. She introduces the term "problem solving" to describe the process of phonological development as one in which the child is actively involved in the application of language-acquisition strategies in order to solve articulatory and phonological problems posed by a particular language. As Menn indicates, the child's implicit goals are to sound like adults and to communicate to them.

Menn describes well factors that may contribute to the variation observed in phonological development. She does not, of course, discount the operation of innate universal processes in language acquisition, but recognizes that input factors and individual differences in addressing solutions will introduce a certain degree of diversity in language acquisition. Under these circumstances, variation in development is an expected consequence of a more general cognitive strategy called problem solving.

That children apply cognitive strategies, Menn points out, can be inferred from the fact that overgeneralization is common in phonological acquisition. Words that are initially produced in a certain way—in some cases, correctly—are often produced in an almost entirely different way at later points in development. A change in pronunciation implies a restructuring or reorganization of the underlying representation of phonological segments. Early proposals, as mentioned above, countenanced a different view of universals in language acquisition. Universal acquisition was viewed as a linear unfolding of events, for example, in the case of Jakobson's theory, a systematic unraveling of phonological contrasts. This approach largely ignores the active and dynamic participation of the child in formulating theoretical constructs about the language he or she is learning.

In Ingram's paper, focus is given to the phonological development of children whose phonology is delayed and to bilingual influences in development within a universalist framework. One metric that he analyzes is the well-known phonological process called reduplication, which is evident from early infancy. He reports that reduplication during the early period of language acquisition is the result of a child's attempt to reproduce the nonreduplicated multisyllabic words of the adult language.

Ingram reports that reduplication is equally common in older phonologically delayed children and in young children whose phonological development is considered normal. Furthermore, in his study of a two-year-old child acquiring Italian and English simultaneously, there were differences in the frequency of reduplicated and checked syllables. Words in English are primarily monosyllabic, in Italian polysyllabic. Furthermore, syllables in English are predominantly closed syllables and in Italian the tendency is toward unchecked syllables. In Italian, the child's use of multisyllabic words was high and her use of syllable-final consonants was low. In English the reverse took place. Furthermore, reduplication was more than three times as great in Italian. Ingram concludes that at the early age of two, separate phonological systems were evident that preserved the form of the input languages.

This investigation by Ingram shows the importance and early effect of input in language acquisition. Universal processes of acquisition, such as reduplication, may be constrained by the input language and by the way in which the input language is represented to the child. Ingram's method of study, like that of Wode and Snow, illustrates that the study of L2 acquisition can enhance our understanding of language-acquisition universals.

The fourth session focused on syntax, semantics, and pragmatics in first-language learning. Nelson began the session with a paper on word learning that has important implications for first- and second-language learning. She commented that the acquisition of words in L1 relates to the child's conceptual development, whereas in L2 learning conceptual development is more highly advanced or largely complete, depending, of course, on the age of the L2 learner.

Word acquisition, according to Nelson, involves several different processes of conceptual inference. Initially children learn words from their use in situational contexts. Later they learn words through various types of linguistic contexts, such as through explicit definition, or inferred from an explanation or instruction that requires a preestablished conceptual space. Furthermore, two considerations emerge. First, word learning involves both processes throughout life, but the order of mention above suggests a rough correlation with age in that situational learning is early and linguistic learning relatively late. Second, word learning is easier and faster when the child possesses the concept that is to be associated with the new word.

The spurt in vocabulary development observed in some children after they have been speaking for a few months suggests to Nelson that conceptual development may have advanced sufficiently to accommodate a large number of words through the mechanisms described above. Furthermore, overextensions in word usage (using the wrong class word to signify the meaning of an object, such as calling a horse "dog"), fairly common in children's speech, reflect the development of concepts and their interrelationships. Formulaic expressions or unanalyzed wholes (e.g., strings of words used in greetings or expressions) are characteristic of both L1 and L2 learners. They seem to develop from situational contexts in which the words themselves have no conceptual basis.

All of these considerations—vocabulary spurt, overextensions, and formulaic expressions—suggest areas of study and comparison between L1 and L2 acquisition. For example, Diller in his paper indicated that under certain circumstances adults acquire rapidly large amounts of new vocabulary items in L2. Presumably these L2 learners are making use of a highly developed conceptual system. However, as Nelson and others have observed, the lexical system of the second language may provide interference in that the new terms are associated differently across categories (for example, in German, *Student* refers only to a university student and *Schüler* to a student elsewhere).

The centrality of verbs in the early stages of language development is explored by Bloom. She provides a convincing argument to assign to the verb system, through its growth and coextensive relationship with other grammatical units, a significant function in determining the growth of a large number of different grammatical categories and structures.

Verbs begin to appear in the language of children when multiword expressions are acquired. Here the distinction between transitive and intransitive verbs is useful in showing the differential growth of syntax. The appearance of grammatical categories, such as verb suffixes, *wh*-question words, and conjunctions, reflects the influence of the development and use of specific verbs. For example, -*ing* was appended to verbs that entailed duration and noncompletion, such as *playing, reading,* and *swinging.* A past-tense marker was added to verb stems that signified both nonduration and completion, such as *broke, found,* and *pushed.* Differential use of *wh*-question words reflected semantic and syntactic development in verb usage. In short, as Bloom expresses it, there is an interaction between the verb system and the development of complexity in children's language.

The interrelationship between verbs and other grammatical units is a consideration of general importance for L1 and L2 learning. It demonstrates that studies that are designed to chart the development of isolated units can provide only a limited understanding of child language development. The paper by Bowerman, which follows Bloom's, indicates that there are changing and dynamic relationships in the semantic lexicon of children that reinforce Bloom's position on the need to study interrelationships among grammatical units in the acquisition of language. Also, communicative considerations, as presented by Ervin-Tripp, Cook, Bates and MacWhinney, Long, and others at this conference, relate importantly to the grammatical growth of the child and, within Bloom's perspective, may potentially provide the underlying focus for verb usage and growth.

Relationships in development between component parts of a grammar and the encoding of meaning were considered by Bowerman in her paper on the acquisition of lexicalization patterns. She began by providing an interesting discussion of how alternative linguistic devices are used to represent a given semantic content. She raises the question as to how children acquire alternate grammatical encoding devices, often considerably different in form, to express the same or nearly the same meaning. Her research leads her to the position that children acquire a fundamental semantic understanding of how language is used to express meaning, from which they develop certain expectations about the form of language.

Particular attention is given to causative verbs and to verbs that express directed motion and manner. An example of an error of the latter group is "OK, then I'm *frowning* out the door," meaning "I'm moving out the door in a frowning manner." Bowerman observes that errors in verb usage are "preceded by months or in some cases even years, during which usage is syntactically impeccable." She concludes that the appearance of these errors reflects not confusion, but rather an increased understanding of how these forms function in the English lexical system.

Next, Bowerman turns to the issue of the role of verbs in imposing syntactic arrangements on nouns. Whereas younger children may make errors coordinating verb choice with nouns on the basis of a frequently stored syntactic distribution or semantic relatedness, older children, Bowerman speculates, may commit errors because of the personal perspective of the event they wish to describe. In one example, a child used the verb *pour* in the sentence, "Look, Mom, I'm gonna pour it with water, my belly" (pour water into my belly button), in order, so it seemed, to utilize the perspective of the verb pour with the container (it=belly button) as direct object. The verb *fill,* which the child knew, was apparently not appropriate from the child's perspective.

A consideration in the study of child language acquisition is how conflicts between expression and grammaticality become resolved. For the second-language learner, differences in perspective must also be resolved, but here the grammar of L1 may serve as a point of conflict. Snow's paper, summarized below, suggests that in the early stages of language learning, adults do better than children in L2 acquisition, but later fall behind. Possibly, the reason adults have difficulty in the later stages of language acquisition stems from the fact that the grammar of L1 appears to provide the L2 learner with a more apt way to express perspective, even when the L2 grammar is almost fully acquired. As suggested by some of the presenters at this conference (see below), comprehension training might reduce this problem somewhat for L2 learners.

The concluding paper of this section, by Bates and MacWhinney, serves as an important theoretical transition between the study of L1 and L2 acquisition. As Bates and MacWhinney point out, grammatical processing involves rapid integration of information from every level of discourse. Furthermore, their contention is that the surface forms of natural languages are conventions that are used in "the service of communicative functions." A grammatical theory that makes use of the multidimensional components of competence and performance to orchestrate communication is called a functionalist grammar. They add that L2 language learners begin their process of learning by discerning those forms that are to service the same communicative functions in L2 as in L1. In this sense L2 learners are different from L1 learners, who must learn both form and function.

A major portion of Bates and MacWhinney's paper contains a description of a model, called *the competition model,* that provides an accounting of how various language functions compete for surface grammatical representation. Certain surface forms are regarded as more salient or information bearing than others, causing underlying functional forms to compete for their use. Presumably, functional categories that are of high value have a greater claim on surface grammatical resources. There will, of course, be doubling up of functional categories (e.g., agent and topic expressed as a grammatical subject and, perhaps, additionally marked by gender and number). The authors refer to such situations as coalitions because joint functional categories utilize joint surface categories. The end result of all this is a proposal for a functionalist grammar that assigns functions to surface positions or roles depending on how well an utterance element represents a coalition of functional categories, in addition to a number of other considerations.

The experiments reported by Bates and MacWhinney were directed to ascertain the strength of association between form and function in order to compare the processing strategies of bilinguals and monolinguals from diverse language backgrounds. One finding they obtained was that Italian speakers and English speakers demonstrated opposite processing strategies. The Italians were more likely to use the feature of animate to interpret the meaning of short sentences containing two nouns and a verb, whereas the Americans almost always used word order. That is, when these two cues are set into competition, the two languages differ as to which one is regarded as dominant.

Their results indicated also that some bilinguals interpret sentences in L2 according to L1 processing strategies, a finding that might not be revealed by other commonly used descriptive approaches. In particular, two native speakers of German who had been speaking English for a long period of time in professional capacities showed marked differences on the Bates-MacWhinney test of processing strategies. One person who had a marked German accent in English reflected German strategies, while the performance of the other, whose accent was "barely detectable," was identical to that of native English speakers. These results on the processing strategies of monolinguals and bilinguals suggest interesting relationships for further study that might include such factors as age, method of instruction, and attitudinal considerations.

In the session on syntax, semantics, and pragmatics in L2, Wode forcefully punctuated a significant reason for studying L2 acquisition. This research, he stated, is another way to approach the problem of universal language-acquisitional regularities. The study of L2 acquisition will help us to understand whether there are parallel language-acquisition processes in L1 and L2. Wode states that all types of language learning, including classroom language learning, should be studied if we are to achieve an "integrated theory of language acquisition."

Wode discusses his findings in terms of three premises: decomposition of target structure, developmental sequence, and individual variation. He notes that the acquisition of target structures is not acquired "all at once."

Initially there is decomposition of complex structures into elements that are later reintegrated step by step into the target structure. This process of decomposition is reflected in the errors that are made by the acquirers of L1 and L2. Additionally, there will be a developmental sequence for each structure. Finally there is always individual variation, which, according to Wode, may reflect preferences in learning style (tactics) and not necessarily a lack of knowledge.

Wode provides a detailed analysis of the acquisition of negation in L1 and L2 (including pidgins and creoles) in which he demonstrates that the occurrence of errors and the sequence of development for negative constructions reflect universal processes of acquisition. For example, there are many negative constructions (e.g., *no-VP* and *Subj no VP*) that are common to L1 English, and to L2 English for speakers from different L1 backgrounds, such as German, Norwegian, and Spanish. On the other hand some negative constructions (e.g., *pre-Aux no* as in *Subj no Aux VP*) have been observed only for L2 English. Still other negative constructions reflect the form of negative structures of L1. Also provided by Wode is an account of the sequence of development for negative constructions in L1 and L2, in which certain parallels are identified. Wode makes a significant point when he proposes that there may be general or universal acquisitional principles that systematically accommodate the several types of language acquisition. Although diversity in language acquisition occurs, it may, according to Wode, reflect general acquisitional principles. Wode's work, presented here and elsewhere, illustrates well that the formulation of universal principles in language acquisition cannot reasonably be made without taking into account L1 and L2 acquisition, and the correlation between the two. His approach adds a degree of complexity to investigative research on developmental language universals, but nonetheless, it appears worthwhile and necessary if acquisitional universals are to be identified.

The effect of age on L2 language-learning strategies is considered by Snow in her paper on English-speaking monolinguals acquiring Dutch. Snow remarks that age is a macrovariable that interacts in a confounding way with other variables. In particular, age seems to have an influence on the choice and sequencing of acquisition strategies. Older individuals may reason differently than younger subjects partly because their educational background encourages the conscious development of the L2 grammar and/or because, by virtue of their adulthood, they use formal analytic processes to solve grammatical problems.

Snow's investigation involved comparisons between monolingual English-speaking children of several age levels, and adults acquiring Dutch in Holland. Both beginners and advanced speakers of Dutch were studied. Essentially the findings are that children start off more slowly, but in most cases outpace adults after a little more than a year of learning Dutch. However, there are some inconsistencies across age levels that are discussed in Snow's paper, and later in Winitz' paper.

A thorough and provocative analysis of the learners' errors for a variety of structures is provided. Snow relates the findings to grammatical properties of the two languages as well as to the development of Dutch by native speakers. Strategies of acquisition are presented to account for the errors that were observed. For example, a strategy of acquisition that a large proportion of all age groups initially applied to the learning of the Dutch singular definite articles *de* and *het* was to use *de* for both forms. Of interest is that some of the advanced speakers, children and adults, continued to use this strategy after a year and a half of contact with the Dutch language. This finding would seem to suggest that factors other than cognitive skill level accounted for the use of this strategy. Of importance is that Snow's investigative approach provides a way to study the effect of cognitive skill level and language-learning strategies.

Snow concludes that there is considerable similarity among the learners of the different age levels in the errors that they make and in the strategies that they apparently use. She remarks, however, that an error pattern and an underlying hypothesis of grammar construction are not necessarily the same. Conceivably, a child might select *de* on the basis of phonological reasons and an adult might select *de* on the basis of frequency of usage. Snow reminds us to be cautious when constructing theories on the basis of error data alone.

In the following paper Cook suggests that the study of second-language acquisition can provide substantial understanding of a number of important issues that involve not only L2 acquisition, but language learning and use, cognition, and memory. The heart of L2 acquisition, Cook contends, is communication. He points to several studies that suggest that interpersonal functions expressed through speech acts and adjacency pairs have psychological reality for beginning L2 acquirers, and yet the analysis and application of the theory of discourse analysis has not become a substantive issue for L2 investigators and teachers except in isolated cases.

Cook contributes a significant point when he indicates that L2 research need not be restricted to problems of L2 learning. He provides examples of research designs that might be used to separate cognitive development from language development and that at the same time might show relationships between strategies of language acquisition and cognitive development. On the other hand, Cook points to beneficial derivatives of L2 research, such as the study of memory and memory strategies and their impact on language development. He reports research that seems to show that L2 learners will apply strategies of rehearsal commensurate with their age and cognitive development. In this regard, adult L2 learners may be different from L1 learners and child L2 learners. These areas of study are potentially useful for understanding L1 acquisition, and for teaching L2.

Long distinguishes between two kinds of modification in the speech of native speakers when talking to non-native speakers, of which one pertains to input and the other to interaction. Input refers to linguistic structures that are modified, for example, by altering the length and complexity of sentences. Interaction is defined as those communicative functions that are used by native speakers to facilitate comprehension of language and participation in discourse by non-native speakers. Examples are asking for clarification, repairing the non-native speaker's utterances, maintaining the topic, clarifying requests, confirming what was said, repeating, expanding, and asking questions.

Long provides an extensive and insightful review of research on the modification of input and interactional features. One topic that he discusses concerns the use of ungrammatical utterances in the speech addressed to non-native speakers. Apparently, this type of simplification is not frequent, and occurs only under certain circumstances.

An interesting form of interaction is the repair device called decomposition, in which the non-native speaker is requested, usually by a tag question (e.g., right?), to comment on a topic imbedded within a wh-question. After confirmation by the non-native speaker, the wh-question is presented in a simpler form.

Modifications are more frequent when native speakers talk to non-native speakers than when native speakers talk to each other. This result was especially true for interactional features in a study conducted by Long. He also found that tasks that require communication and transfer of information elicited significantly greater modification of language from native speakers. Long speculates that modification of input and interaction work synchronously to facilitate second-language acquisition. It is an area of study that will continue, no doubt, to provide a rich source of data for understanding L2 acquisition and child language acquisition.

It is of interest to note that the two types of modification studied by Long are not easily executed within the constraints imposed by the standard foreign-language classroom setting. Changes in the speech addressed to non-native speakers, as Long indicates, primarily occur when information is exchanged between individuals who are engaged in natural conversation, a situation that departs significantly from traditional methods of instruction in grammar and dialogue.

In the final paper of this session, Burling provides a sophisticated introspective analysis of second-language learning by an American professor of linguistics and anthropology learning Swedish. "I was . . . my own subject," relates Burling, who spent a year as a visiting professor at the University of Göteborg.

Of the many interesting aspects of Burling's personal account were those pertaining to language input. The language addressed to an adult contained elliptic forms that the native-speaking Swede often denied producing. Additionally the sentence structure and vocabulary addressed to Burling were often too complex to be understood from the context. These observations by Burling indicate that adults, like children, require simplified auditory input and interactional modification in order to decode conversational speech in a second language, and ultimately to speak it.

Furthermore, as Burling points out, rules that are explicitly acquired are difficult to utilize in the context of a conversation. His personal experience in this regard seems to confirm the importance of emphasizing listening in language acquisition, a point that was made in the papers by Belasco, Asher, and the Garys. Burling's willingness to retain a flexible attitude by not necessarily seeking definitive and explicit grammatical solutions no doubt contributed to his success in learning Swedish.

Burling notes that in learning Swedish, his development of syntax was in advance of morphology, a finding that is in general agreement with observations obtained from quantitative studies of L1 and L2 acquisition. Students of a second language are hesitant to use that language until most of the morphology has been acquired, because they do not wish to appear ignorant. Native-speaking adults regard non-native-speaking adults whose language shows such weaknesses as incapable of mature or meaningful dialogue, whereas native-speaking children whose language shows the typical morphological errors of development are not regarded in this way.

When there is a common language that both adults speak well, such as English in Burling's case, there is less opportunity to have experience in the second language because there is usually an unwillingness on the part of the individual who knows both languages well to use the less-developed language. Burling concludes that differences in attitude toward children and adult language learners can be a significant consideration in language development.

In the final session of this conference, the investigators directed their attention to learning strategies in L2 that may have a direct impact on L2 teaching. The first paper by Winitz discusses research in L2 acquisition that shows adults have greater success in language acquisition than children have in the early phases of language learning, although in the later stages children catch up and eventually outperform adults. He further compares the abilities of adults and children in language learning by focusing on auditory discrimination. He presents the findings of an investigation in which monolingual English-speaking adults showed higher levels of performance than did children in discriminating among obstruents and among the four tones of Mandarin Chinese. These results support previous findings that the language capability of adults is not inferior to that of children in the early stages of language learning. He speculates that because adults are often trained to acquire a set of formal, prescriptive rules of grammar, and additionally are forced to show evidence of this learning through production, they will stop processing linguistic information at the point at which they believe they have sufficient knowledge to use L2 effectively.

In this regard, Winitz distinguishes between two language-learning strategies, denoted linear and nonlinear learning. Linear learning involves a step-by-step progression of language learning in that at each level the student is required to master a corpus of information. Nonlinear learning contains a sequential component, as does linear learning, but, in addition, includes provision for restructuring and reformulation of early acquired knowledge. Nonlinear learning, Winitz believes, more closely reflects L1 learning and also, in part, L2 learning, especially when L2 learning is not constrained by formal teaching procedures.

The next series of papers was primarily concerned with theoretical and practical aspects of L2 teaching. All of the investigators focused on comprehension, but their approaches show wide variations in actual practice.

Belasco's paper is a description of a methodology he has devised to teach French at the college level in the United States. He remarks that internalization of grammatical structures is not directly achievable in two years of college study when the "composing" skills of speaking and writing are emphasized over the "receiving skills" listening and reading. He holds to the belief that listening and reading comprehension are reasonable goals after two years of training in a foreign language at the college level. Furthermore, he comments that teaching these skills well will insure the development of nucleation, which is defined as a level of learning in which there is systematic understanding on which all further development can easily and rapidly build. Nucleation can be thought of as that point in development at which the student's level of knowledge adds new information to an underlying integrated system of knowledge. Until this point, the student of L2 has acquired only unrelated bits and pieces.

The remainder of Belasco's paper is concerned with procedures that are to take a student from "prenucleation" to nucleation. He recommends using simultaneous translations to teach listening and reading of the target language. With the transcripts in hand, grammatical differences between the two languages and constructions particular to the target language are explained. Belasco's use of simultaneous translations is for the purpose of bringing the student to the level of learning at which nucleation takes place, and not simply to teach mastery of specific grammatical structures. Although procedures recommended by Belasco appear to be traditional in format, they differ fundamentally from current teaching methods.

Largely influenced by research in child language and neurology, Asher has proposed two primary and interlocking components for a successful foreign-language program. They are (1) talking is not taught, it is the result of the child's achievement in understanding language; and (2) the right hemisphere acquires concepts through an enriched environment. Asher actualizes these premises by recommending that comprehension of language be taught through the understanding of physical activity.

Language and activity, according to Asher, are linked together in providing an unconscious cognitive map of the world for the child. Adults acquiring a second language are largely subject to this same principle of language acquisition, he concludes, even though they have already acquired a first language and a cognitive map of the world. Asher has gathered considerable evidence to support his position on language teaching by showing the effectiveness of teaching L2 through comprehension.

In the two concluding papers of this conference, the Garys, Judith and

Norman, provide the theoretical background for the comprehension approach to foreign-language instruction, and additionally clearly illustrate its application.

The Garys note that comprehension of speech is essential for communication, but that comprehension does not require speech. They further remark that although the same set of rules underlies both speech and comprehension, the acquisition of speech is linguistically more complex than the acquisition of comprehension, for which context and linguistic redundancy are available to the listener.

The major reasons they give for teaching language through comprehension are (1) speaking requires that language information be stored in memory, a process that is best achieved through comprehension training; (2) when production is difficult, it is often associated with emotional trauma; (3) comprehension instruction is an efficient method of instruction in that all students of a class simultaneously participate in listening; (4) comprehension is potentially a communicative act, whereas classroom language-production exercises are not; (5) aural media instruction is most appropriate for comprehension training and not for production training, to which it has been applied in the past; and (6) students are more likely to continue study of L2 when a receptive approach is used.

An outline of the Garys' instructional program, including the sequencing of language skills, is provided. Furthermore, they include guidelines for effective use of comprehension lessons.

All presenters, directly or indirectly, addressed the issue of language-acquisition strategies. In this regard, a theoretical framework was presented that is certain to continue to prevail throughout the decade of the 1980s. This position, most generally stated, is that a host of complex factors—including universal tendencies, presentation and form of the input language, communicative or functionalist considerations, cognitive and social development, and, in the case of L2, previous language experience—contribute to the formulation of language-acquisition strategies.

An investigative approach of this type is more comprehensive and of greater intrinsic value than universalist theories, in which only innate "tendencies" or linguistic constraints are considered. The language learner, as Macken and Ferguson point out, is regarded as an active participant who seeks to establish underlying regularity in the language system, and who is influenced by the input language and a great number of other factors. Wode adds that all aspects of language learning should be considered, including differences between L1 and L2, in order to develop a comprehensive theory of our capacity as human beings to acquire language. Statistical exceptions do not necessarily provide counterevidence to this claim because the processes that are employed are not limited to innate tendencies, but include many interacting factors.

That there can be modification of universal tendencies was reported in several papers. One interesting example is that provided by Ingram's study of a bilingual child. Ingram found that L1 and L2 can differentially affect the frequency of reduplication in the same child. Furthermore,

Macken and Ferguson note that reduplication is age dependent in that it is not reported to occur in L2 classroom learning, although as they indicate it would be of value to examine for the presence of this behavior in young children learning a second language and perhaps in adults in the early phase of second-language learning in nonclassroom settings.

A challenge to investigators is to account for diverse sets of data within a universalist framework, suggest Macken and Ferguson, Menn, and Wode. Investigators, then, will seek to explain both variation and central tendency by examining all possible contributing factors.

In L2 acquisition there are circumstances in which the first language appears to influence the formulation of language-acquisition strategies, as Wode, Snow, and McLaughlin cite. Additionally, Macken and Ferguson comment that transfer from L1 and L2 may involve only certain components of a grammar; other components may be governed more directly by developmental processes. For example, as Nelson suggests in her paper on word acquisition, older children, and by generalization L2 learners, may make greater use of linguistic context than situational context to learn words. In addition the adult's advanced conceptual knowledge can affect the way in which words are acquired, as Nelson, Cook, and others noted. Similarly, the second-language learner's advanced understanding of discourse rules, as Ervin-Tripp suggests, may provide a certain selectivity in the choice of communicative functions. Cook adds that children and adults may apply different strategies of rehearsal to the language material they are learning. The advanced cognitive skill level of adults may account for Snow's finding that adults are initially superior to children in L2 learning. Also, according to Cole and Winitz, adults may be superior to children in applying perceptual processing skills.

L2 learning may differ from L1 learning because of biological conditions or constraints, but the contributing factors are not well known, according to the review by Kinsbourne. On the other hand, Whitaker, Bub, and Leventer report differences in intrahemispheric localization for naming responses in the first and second language by bilinguals. Lambert cites other research findings that seem to suggest differences in biological functioning between L1 and L2 users. Finally Diller suggests that different language-training approaches emphasize different language centers, a possible consideration in the differences that one observes between native-language learning and L2 acquired in the classroom. Possibly, social factors—influenced and constrained by developmental, cognitive, biological, and environmental considerations, as discussed by Alatis and De Marco, and Burling—are responsible for some of the differences between L1 and L2 acquisition. Certainly the finding of Bates and MacWhinney that L2 processing strategies can reflect the structure of L1 for some individuals and not others would seem to support this position. That social factors may restrict language acquisition was interestingly detailed in Burling's personal account of learning Swedish. Also it is generally acknowledged that the negative attitudes of native speakers toward bilingual education, which is especially true in the United States, as Alatis and De

Marco, and Burling remark, can adversely influence the competency level that second-language learners may be able to achieve. Finally, there may be important differences between the language addressed to first-language learners and to second-language learners that might be investigated within the framework provided by Long.

No doubt social factors can affect the selection and utilization of acquisition strategies and, possibly, alter in significant ways the rule system that is constructed by the second-language learner. A distinguishing social pressure placed upon the adult language learner is the requirement of verbal production. Newly arrived immigrants must compete in the market-place and are often rushed into "crash" programs that demand production. The position taken by Asher, the Garys, and Winitz, in their presentations on language teaching, is that this strategy of training is in violation of a linguistic universal of child language that states that comprehension precedes production in language acquisition. This violation may cause language acquisition to be significantly retarded or, in some instances, may encourage the construction of underlying hypotheses that differ in signifi-cant ways from those formed by the native-language learner. Belasco, however, includes production experience as part of the early training of second-language learners, but his goal is essentially the same as that of Asher and the Garys. Whether production practice is to be included prior to significant training in understanding, is an issue that deserves consider-able attention in language teaching.

The comprehension-production issue is complex and continues to receive the attention of investigators. However, one reason for emphasizing comprehension in language training is that it permits the processes observed in child language acquisition to take place without being impeded or short-circuited. The individual is given the opportunity to listen to the input language and derive underlying regularity at his or her own pace without the need to satisfy the short-term goals of the classroom. Accord-ing to Winitz, regularization involves nonlinear processes that cannot be actualized easily through linear instructional programs. The process of restructuring knowledge in L1 acquisition was addressed by Bowerman and Bloom. Bowerman reported that young children often commit errors in the use of certain words that at a prior time were used correctly. These errors reflect an increased understanding and restructuring of the underlying grammatical system. Additionally, Bloom described how verbs enter into this process of continued development and refinement of the grammar.

In this conference, similarities and differences between native- and foreign-language acquisition were explored. No firm conclusions were made. However, there was a consensus among the participants that there are important parallels between L1 and L2 acquisition that merit continued attention. Of significance was the express belief that a comprehensive theory of human language learning should encompass comparative study of L1 and L2 acquisition in order to best understand universal acquisitional principles.

Index of Contributors

(Italicized page numbers refer to comments made in discussion.)